Christians in the Arab East

Christians in the Arab East

A Political Study

by

Robert Brenton Betts

JOHN KNOX PRESS
ATLANTA

Revised edition published simultaneously in the United States
by John Knox Press and in Great Britain by SPCK
and in Greece by Lycabettus Press.

Library of Congress Cataloging in Publication Data

Betts, Robert Brenton.
Christians in the Arab East.

Bibliography: p.
Includes index.
1. Christians in Arab countries. 2. Arab countries—Politics and government. I. Title.
BR1067.A7B47 1978 209'.17'4927 78-8674
ISBN 0-8042-0796-8

Printed in the United States of America
John Knox Press
Atlanta, Georgia

Contents

Maps

The Arab East

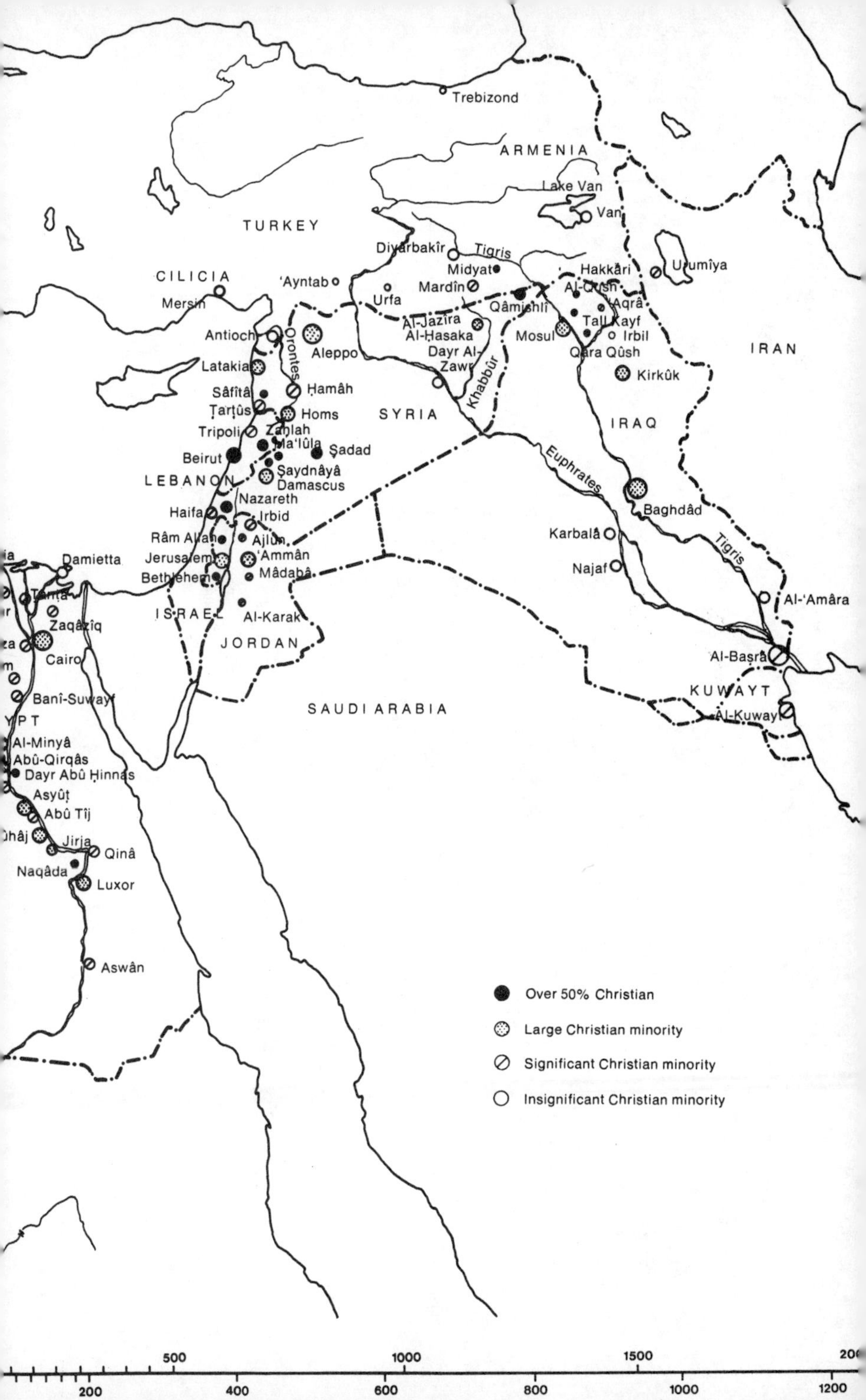

Trebizond
ARMENIA
Lake Van
Van
TURKEY
Diyarbakîr
Tigris
Midyat
Hakkâri
Urumîya
CILICIA
'Ayntab
Mardîn
Al-Qûsh
Urfa
Qâmishlî
Aqrâ
Mersin
Al-Jazîra
Tall Kayf
Al-Hasaka
Mosul
Irbil
Antioch
Orontes
Aleppo
Dayr Al-Zawr
Qara Qûsh
IRAN
Latakia
Khabbûr
Kirkûk
Sâfîtâ
Hamâh
Tartûs
Homs
SYRIA
Tripoli
Zahlah
IRAQ
Ma'lûla
Beirut
Sadad
Euphrates
Saydnâyâ
LEBANON
Damascus
Nazareth
Baghdâd
Haifa
Irbid
Karbalâ
Râm Allah
Ajlûn
Tigris
Jerusalem
'Ammân
Damietta
Najaf
Bethlehem
Mâdabâ
Tanta
Al-'Amâra
ISRAEL
Al-Karak
Zaqâzîq
JORDAN
Cairo
Al-Basra
Banî-Suwayf
KUWAYT
SAUDI ARABIA
Al-Kuwayt
Al-Minyâ
Abû-Qirqâs
Dayr Abû Hinnas
Asyût
Abû Tîj
Jirja
Qinâ
Naqâda
Luxor
Aswân
Over 50% Christian
Large Christian minority
Significant Christian minority
Insignificant Christian minority
500
1000
1500
200
400
600
800
1000
1200

Lebanon (1975)

To Homs
To Latakia
Qubayât
Halba
'Akkâr
To Homs
Burqâ'îl
TRIPOLI
Hirmal
Finaydiq
Al-Qâ'
Sîr
Zagharta
Indan
Ra's Ba'labakk
Ra's Al-Shakka
Amyûn
Bisharrî
Al-Kûra
Al-Batrûn
'Aynatâ
Laqlûq
'Aqûra
Al-Biqâ
Jubayl
Qurtaba
Afqa
Ba'labakk
Al-Kisrawân
Jûniyah
Bikfaya
Rayâq
Burj Hummûd
Antilyâs
Anti-Lebanon
BEIRUT
Ra's Al-Matn
Zahlah
Bihamdûn
B'abdâ
'Alayh
Shatûra
Shuwayfât
Kahhala
Sûq Al-Gharb
'Anjar
Dâmûr
Dayr Al-Qamar
To Damascus
Ba'aqlîn
Al-Masna'
Al-Shûf
Barjâ
Mukhtâra
Shihîm
SIDON
Saghbîn
Jûn
Jazzîn
Rûm
Râshayâ
'Ayn Siqî
Mashghara
SYRIA
Jibâ'
Hâsbayyâ
Nabatîya
Marj 'Uyûn
TYRE
Christian Lebanon
Principal Road
Christian town
Sunni town
Shî'a town
Druze town
Jabal 'Amil
Tibnîn
Nâqura
'Ayn Ibil
Bint Jubayl
Rumaysh
ISRAEL
20
40
60
80
100
120
140
20
40
60
80

Preface

A black man in the United States knows what it is like to live as a minority. Perhaps he alone, who has suffered sequestration because of race, can imagine what it is to belong to a religious minority in a state that makes but little distinction between God and government.

The merit of the study that follows is that it describes what few Western Christians can rightly conceive, the altogether different role that their co-religionists must play in the life of the Middle East where they are in proportion to the population less numerous than racial minorities in America.

A minority, sometimes welcome, sometimes not, is often wounded. It is drawn to its own community, where corporate strength is a precious resource. Survival requires special skill, special faith; the community is constantly winnowed by the loss of those without courage and those too selfish to persevere. So the little band is purged and matured, until it has a unique and precious contribution to make to the very society which is at the same time its scourge and its nourishment.

Such has been the role of Christians in the Moslem lands of the Middle East. Here is traced the history of their several communities in each country; complex, often tragic in the divisions among Christians themselves, but always exciting in the tracing of faith against adversity. How often it happens that special destiny is given not to the great and complacent majorities in the world, but to the little bands of people who never succeed so well as to be able to forget the Source of their strength and life.

God grant that the world may remember that! If it is to be so, then perhaps our Christian brethren of the East, whose life is here purveyed to us by Dr. Betts, will have borne a witness beyond their ken, for which we all must be more than grateful.

Francis B. Sayre, Jr.
Washington Cathedral
Washington, D.C.
June, 1974

Introduction

Twenty years ago, Dr. Charles Mâlik, prominent Arab statesman and then Lebanese Ambassador to the United Nations, asked rhetorically: "Is a Christian Arab possible? Is a Christian Arab culture possible?"[1] To many at the time this must have seemed a curious query coming as it did from an Arabic-speaking gentleman whose family's adherence to Orthodox Christianity in all probability pre-dates the Council of Nicaea by a century or two. That Christians indigenous to the lands of the Arab East exist today in large numbers is known to many in the West, not only to area specialists, and many of these Christians can legitimately lay claim to an Arab genealogy as pure as that of any *sayyid,* or direct descendant of the Prophet Muḥammad. Many more are Arabicized, rather than Arab, being the progeny of the indigenous Aramaic and Hamitic peoples who were gradually absorbed into an Arabic-speaking culture over the period of more than thirteen centuries of Islamic rule. But this is equally the case with the Muslim population of the Arab East outside the Arabian Peninsula.

The core of Dr. Mâlik's question revolves rather around the term "Arab" as it has come into use in this century, a term implying specific political and nationalist identity. Prior to the First World War, an Arab to most inhabitants of the Middle East was *badu* (Bedouin), an object in a modernizing world of undisguised contempt. For the early Arab Nationalists the term was used to cover all whose native tongue was Arabic. But during the interwar years, and particularly after 1945, a religious connotation came to be implied, so that in the past twenty-five years adherence to Islâm has been added as a usually unspoken but tacitly understood criterion for full membership in the Arab community. Dr. Mâlik posed his question at the very time when Arab Nationalism was beginning to take on its unmistakable Islamic overtones, in the very year in fact in which Jamâl 'Abd Al-Nâṣir first rose to power in Egypt. And Nasser, riding the wave of a nationalism which he hoped would carry him to the pinnacle of power as leader of a united Arab people, made much of Islam as an integral focus of Arab identity. Quite understandably, therefore, Christians in the Arab World have been forced to undertake a renewed search for their own identity during these past two decades, with an outcome not as yet totally clear, nor without its discouraging as well as optimistic conclusions.

It is the purpose of this study to look at the indigenous Christian of the Arab East today in the light of his fascinating past: his habitat, his social and religious institutions, and the role which he plays in all facets of the predominantly Islamic society that has been his environment since the first wave of Muslim invaders swept out of Arabia a third of the way through the 7th Christian century. His numbers today are probably in excess of five million and he is found throughout the historic Fertile Crescent and Egypt, in cities and hamlets stretching in an arc from Aswân in Upper Egypt to Al-Baṣra at the mouth of the Tigris and Euphrates. A majority in Lebanon only, he is nonetheless a visible presence in every major urban center of the region, and in many remote rural districts as well, involved in every conceivable occupation, found in every walk of life. Such a ubiquitous presence challenges the stereotyped observation of the Christian in a Muslim Arab environment as handed down to us through the first generations of Western missionaries, doctors, and educators who worked tirelessly in the last century to bridge the gulf separating Europe and the Levant since the Crusades. Traditional roles and patterns are nonetheless the heritage of present-day Middle-Eastern Christians, and, though beginning to show signs of change and even dissolution, they are for the rising generation still a frame of reference far more influential and personal than traditional Christian values are for its counterpart in the West.

In such an era of rapid social change both within the Christian communities themselves and in the larger framework of the Muslim Arab World, any study of a particular sub-group within the Middle-Eastern whole invites immediate dating. Yet with the death of Nasser an era has passed, an era of particular trial for the Christians of the Arab East in that it has been one of cultural revaluation and decision which will have lasting impact on generations of Middle-Eastern Christians to come. Nasser was no latter-day Al-Ḥâkim[2] casting down cathedrals and churches and imposing outward signs of persecution on minority peoples, as some conservative Christians in the Arab World would have the Westerner believe. But his concern for the indigenous Christian in Egypt and elsewhere was secondary to the cause of Arab Nationalism around which he built his political career, and a devotion to which he tried to instill in the predominantly Muslim masses. The most obvious channel of appeal to this basically parochial multitude was the universal Islam, and if by closely linking Muslim values and identity with Arab Nationalist goals he temporarily, or even permanently, denied the Christian minority full membership and participation this was in his own view a necessary, if vaguely regrettable, price. For Nasser the times demanded of Christians a commitment either to the Arab World and its problems or to the West and its essentially non-Arab values, a commitment which many Christians, accustomed to their self-styled, centuries-old role of "intermediaries between East and West," were reluctant to make. The impact of this challenge cannot be underestimated and has marked a turning point in the life of the indigenous Christian community as a whole, however reluctantly many individual members of this community have come to terms with it.

But it is only the most recent development in a long history of Muslim-Christian relationship in Egypt and the Fertile Crescent, and must be viewed in the context of these preceding centuries of hostility and cooperation, of finding the modus vivendi most acceptable to both parties. It is this whole structure to which this study is devoted, in the hope of contributing to a greater Western understanding of the present-day Middle East, the very land in which Western culture and values are so deeply rooted.

Robert Betts, Amida, 1974
Athens, 1977

I A History of Christianity among the Arabs and Arabicized Peoples of Egypt and the Fertile Crescent

The Pre-Islamic Era

The Koran (Al-Qur'ân) speaks of the years before the transmission of God's message to Muḥammad as those of "ignorance" *(jâhilîya)*, or more specifically as an age when Arabia and its inhabitants lived in ignorance of Allah, the one, true God. This is not to imply that the established religions of the day — Christianity and Zoroastrianism — were unknown. Even Judaism, in diaspora since the destruction of the Temple in 70 A.D., had significant numbers of native Arabian adherents. For the most part, however, the inhabitants of the "Arabian Island" *(Jazîrat Al-'Arab)*, cut off as they were from the mainstream of civilization in late antiquity by the twofold barrier of water and sandy wastes, remained faithful to their ancient cults and animistic deities. The non-settled population, constituting the vast majority of the population of the peninsula, was in particular oblivious to the sophisticated monotheism which prevailed to the north and west. A people on whom established religion has always sat lightly, the Bedouin in general scoffed at the attempts of Christian, Jewish, and in later years even Muslim, missionaries to convert them to a formal theological creed. Their adamant refusal to accept religious truth at the time of Muḥammad brought down upon them the eternal curse of Koranic judgment, the stern observation that "the desert Arabs are greatest in their unbelief, worthy but to remain in ignorance of God's command as revealed through his Apostle."[3] And if Islâm, tailored as it is to the life and needs of the Arab, met such steadfast resistance from those it set out to save, should it be surprising that Christianity failed after six centuries to gain a secure foothold?

On the other hand there is little evidence that any great effort was made in pre-Nicaean days to evangelize Arabia.

Though Arabic was one of the tongues vouchsafed to the disciples at Pentecost[4] there is no record of any one of them having penetrated the fastness of the peninsula to make use of this facility, unless Thomas touched land there briefly en route to India. By and large the early Church confined its missionary zeal to the civilized parts of the Roman Empire, and it was not until the reign of Constantine's son, the Emperor Constantius, that record of a Christian mission to the Arabs is found. And by this time Christianity had achieved virtual recognition as the state religion of the Roman Empire so that its expansion began more and more to coincide with imperial political aims. Thus the mission of the Arian priest Theophilus in 356, though it resulted in the raising of three churches in Arabia Felix (modern Al-Yaman), was directed primarily toward the establishment of a strong Roman presence at the southern end of the Red Sea so as to enable the imperial fleet to circumvent Persian control of the land route to India.

Such was the motive behind Justinian's support of the successful Ethiopian invasion of Al-Yaman in 525 to depose the pro-Persian Himyarite ruler of Jewish faith, dhû-Nuwâs, even though the ruler of Ethiopia was of the heretical Monophysite branch of Christianity. Any Christian presence, in Roman eyes, was preferable to Persian control of the strategic Straits of Mandab, particularly at a time when Justinian's government was attempting to bypass the Persian silk monopoly through direct naval contact with the southern coasts of the Indian subcontinent.[5]

Though small communities of Christians had existed in the Yaman, particularly at Najrân, for generations, the fifty-year Ethiopian occupation (525-575) gave official impetus to missionary efforts, and by the middle of the 6th century the great cathedral at Ṣan'â (present-day capital of the Republic of Yemen) was rivaling the Ka'ba in Mecca as the object of Arabian pilgrimage. And as large centers of Christianity sprang up throughout this populous southwest corner of the Peninsula, individual believers began inevitably to filter northward along the ancient frankincense route into the Ḥijâz and its cities of Mecca and Al-Madîna (then Yathrib). Even among the nomadic and semi-settled tribes on the southern frontiers of the Byzantine and Persian Empires Christianity had been gaining strength since the 5th century. The reign of the Emperor Justinian parallels that of the first great Arab Christian prince, Al-Ḥârith Al-A'raj (Hareth the Lame) of the tribe of Ghassân, who served the Byzantines as a valuable ally in the constant wars with Persia. Likewise the Ghassânids' hereditary enemies, the Lakhmid tribe of Al-Ḥîra on the edge of the Euphrates valley, served the Persian King of Kings in a similar capacity, and by the end of the 6th century had adopted Christianity along with their king, Al-Nu'mân III.[6]

What impeded further Christian expansion and in the end paved the way for the successful Islamic invasions was the overall lack of unity within the Church. Such a lamentable state was, of course, not a new development, having characterized Christianity even before its establishment as the official imperial religion. Even the apparent unity witnessed at Nicaea in 325 at the outset of this new era was in fact primarily an attempt to crush the Arian heresy which at the time enjoyed great strength throughout the Empire, and which in the ensuing decades nearly succeeded in supplanting Nicene Orthodoxy as the accepted Christian creed. No sooner had the disciples of Arius been dealt with, at least within the frontiers of the Empire,[7] than new Christological controversies plunged Christendom into theological confusion. By the middle of the 5th century two non-Orthodox schools, each with large numbers of dedicated adherents, stood in opposition to the Emperor and the Oecumenical Patriarch, and within a generation had virtually separated from the main body of Christianity as separate churches.

The first to break the outward unity of the Church were the Nestorians, followers of Nestorius, Patriarch of Constantinople (428-431), who in a manner reminiscent of the Arians, stressed the humanity of Christ and refused to recognize Mary as *theotokos*, or "Mother of God." The Council of Ephesus convoked in 431 at the insistence of Cyril, Patriarch of Alexandria (412-444), condemned Nestorius's views as heretical. The Patriarch himself was deposed at the same time, but his views gained wide acceptance in his home city of Antioch and further to the East in Mesopotamia where the native Christian community was encouraged by its Persian governors to adopt Nestorian views. Within the Persian Empire, in fact, Nestorian Christianity became virtually a second state religion (after Zoroastrianism), thus enabling the Sassanid Emperor's Christian subjects to preserve their faith without a compromising loyalty to Constantinople.

The Alexandrian reaction to the Nestorian heresy, successful as it was in preventing a rebirth of thinly-disguised Arianism within the Church, fed on itself and within a generation produced an equally extreme view which virtually denied Christ's humanity altogether. Led by Cyril's successor, Dioskorus (444-454), the adherents of this view, called Monophysitism ("one Nature"), prevailed upon the dying Emperor Theodosius II (408-450) to summon a second Ephesian Council, known to history as the "Robber Council of Ephesus" (449), where the assembled bishops were bribed and even physically forced into supporting the Monophysite cause. The Alexandrian victory was short-lived, however, and the new Emperor, Marcian (450-457), summoned a Council in 451 at Chalcedon on the Asian side of the Bosphorus immediately opposite the capital where he and his patriarch could exercise a restraining hand on the ecclesiastical proceedings. As a result, Dioskorus and Monophysitism were condemned by the Council, but once again dedicated followers of heresy refused to comply with the dictates of Orthodoxy, and within a very few years the Church in Egypt was securely in the hands of the Monophysite rebels.

Whereas Nestorianism had obliged the Emperor by confining itself largely to a Christian minority in a heathen Empire, the Monophysites were not so considerate. By far the dominant force in Egypt, the followers of Dioskorus spread throughout the Byzantine Empire and even to the capital itself where, until the eve of the Arab conquests, they threatened to dissolve the Empire in a disastrous civil conflict. During the reign of Justinian the Great, Monophysite strength was felt at the very pinnacle of power in the person of the Empress Theodora, whose public adherence to the heresy made doubly difficult the Emperor's attempts to re-establish Imperial authority in the staunchly Orthodox patriarchate of Rome, and the lost territories of the West in general. Though Orthodoxy in the end prevailed north of the Cilician Gates, the triumph of Monophysitism to the south was assured in 543 when the Emperor, at the request of his Bedouin phylarch Al-Ḥârith and at the insistence of Theodora, confirmed the appointment of the Monophysite monk Ya'qûb Al-Barda'î (Jacobus Baradaeus) as Bishop of Edessa. A Syriac-speaking native of Mesopotamia, Al-Barda'i worked tirelessly to spread the Monophysite doctrine throughout Syria, and with such success that his followers in the patriarchate of Antioch, among whom were the Arabs of Ghassân, came to be known as Jacobites (Ya'qûbîyîn), or followers of the Bishop Ya'qûb. A probable disciple (though in some sources described as a fallen-away Nestorian) was the celebrated monk Baḥîrâ (or Buḥayrâ) of Buṣrâ (Bostra in Syria) with whom the twelve-year old Prophet conversed while visiting the Ghassânid marches in the company of his uncle Abû-Ṭâlib, and who, according to legend, immediately recognized Muhammad's prophetic destiny. As related by a relatively recent theory, Râhib Al-Buḥayrâ may have been a wandering Syrian monk whom the Prophet met in maturity and from whom he obtained many of the Christian views and ideas (some of them curiously distorted) which appear in the Koran.

The Nestorian creed first reached the Arabs through the settled communities in Mesopotamia around the end of the 4th century, and from these converts, known as the *'Ibâd*, or servants of Christ, spread to the semi-settled Lakhmid nation of Al-Ḥira whose members had become fully Christianized by the beginning of the 7th century. The Christians of Najrân north of Al-Yaman, at first Monophysites under the influence of the Ethiopian occupation, turned to Nestorianism when they came within the Persian sphere in 575. Thus on the eve of the Islamic era, those Arabs who had been Christianized were almost to a man heretics, and for reasons more political than religious.

Undoubtedly the majority of Christians at this time took the issue of Christ's nature very seriously even though the theological hairsplitting that characterizes the so-called Christological controversies of the 5th century seems tedious if not ridiculous to most churchmen today. Yet the strong undercurrent of secular politics cannot be denied as a vitally active factor in the success of these centripetal movements within the Church. The intense rivalry of the four patriarchates — Antioch, Alexandria, Rome, and Constantinople — for dominance in the affairs of Christendom is recognized by scholar and theologian alike, and there are many who see in the Nestorian and Monophysite causes a nascent Semitic nationalism. [8] Resentment in Syria and Egypt on the part of the masses of Semitic faithful against the control of imperial and ecclesiastical offices by a Greek minority was intense. The readiness of the Aramaic and Hamitic inhabitants of Syria and Egypt to throw off Orthodoxy on the basis of theological definitions which few understood is indicative of an underlying malaise in these provinces which needed only the least excuse to manifest itself. By the eve of the Arab conquests, Syria and Egypt, though thoroughly Christianized, were inhabited by a populace in large part Monophysite. Only in the coastal towns and cities where Byzantine garrisons could enforce the imperial faith, and in scattered outposts in the interior, did Orthodoxy prevail, its adherents branded by their enemies as "Melkites," or "the Emperor's men" (from the Syriac *melk*, or king). In Egypt the anti-imperial feeling ran so high that Monophysites were referred to nationalistically as Copts, a vernacular term meaning "Egyptian," from the Greek word for Egypt, Αἴγυπτος. A native non-Greek inhabitant of Egypt in the 6th century was thus by definition a Monophysite, just as a Turk today is, by implication, a Muslim.

A final effort to reconcile the Monophysites to Orthodoxy was made by the Emperor Heraclius (610-641) during the dark days of the Persian occupation of Syria and Egypt in the second decade of the 7th century. The imperial gesture took the form of the so-called Monothelite doctrine which, while firmly attesting to the dual Nicene nature of Christ, credited Him with but one Will. While there appeared to be initial consent on the part of the Monophysites to accept the imperial proposal, the Church itself refused the Emperor's theological innovation and subsequently condemned Heraclius's compromise as heretical at the Council of Ephesus in 681, but not before a number of Syrians had embraced it, thus accounting for yet another schismatic group, the

Maronites, named after one Bishop Mârô (Mârûn), their alleged founder.[9] In Mesopotamia the Aramaic Nestorian population, though tolerated by the Persian authorities there, likewise felt the heavy hand of religious and racial discrimination by the imperial government of the Sassanids at Ctesiphon.

Thus when the armies of the Caliph (*Khalîfa*) 'Umar ibn-Al-Khaṭṭâb stormed out of the Arabian Desert into Palestine, Syria, and Mesopotamia, they encountered two empires, each exhausted by lengthy wars against the other, and populated on their southern flanks by non-Orthodox Christians — Copts, Jacobites, and Nestorians — all of whom were outside the prevailing ecclesiastical law and hostile to both Persian and Byzantine governments. For these Christians the invaders from the south, racial and linguistic cousins, were far preferable as rulers to the Greco-Roman Byzantines and the Aryan Persians. Not surprisingly, therefore, the Christians of Egypt, Syria, and Mesopotamia in many cases aided the invaders in defeating the imperial armies. And once removed from the political authority of Constantinople the Monophysites became, like the Nestorians, beyond all hope of reconciliation with Orthodoxy. The Arabs, like the Persians in Mesopotamia, found it expedient to perpetuate those divisions within Christianity which prevented the majority of their non-Muslim subjects from feeling a sense of loyalty, religious or political, to Constantinople. Thus both heresies, condemned by the Councils of Ephesus and Chalcedon, were permanently crystallized.

The Dark Millenium: from the Arab Conquest to the Napoleonic Invasion of Egypt (633-1798)

In less than a decade, from the year 633 to 641, all of Syria, Egypt, and Mesopotamia passed into the hands of the Muslim Arab conqueror. Yet these remarkable campaigns which brought an end to the Persian Empire and deprived Constantinople of its two fairest provinces, affected the local Christian population very little. According to covenants drawn up by the Caliph 'Umar at Damascus in 635 and Jerusalem in 637 the indigenous Christians who made up the vast majority of the population of Egypt and the Fertile Crescent at this time were permitted to keep their churches and their particular rites and beliefs in return for an individual head tax, the *jizya*, levied annually according to the individual's ability to pay.[10] The basis of this relationship was the Koranic revelation (sûra 9:29) which enjoined the faithful to "Make war upon those who believe not. . . even if they be People of the Book, until they have willingly agreed to pay the *jizya* in recognition of their submissive state." The "People of the Book" (*Ahl Al-Kitâb*) were those who possessed an earlier written revelation from God, specifically Christians and Jews. Muhammad in his own lifetime drafted the first of such covenants — with the Jews of Madîna in 623 and the Christians of Najrân and Ayla ('Aqaba) in 630 — upon which 'Umar drew when dealing with the larger communities of conquered Christians in the former Byzantine and Persian provinces.[11] In the legal terminology of Islam these groups of tolerated unbelievers were accorded *dhimmi* or "protected" status. Since only Muslims were permitted to bear arms, Jews and Christians paid a tax in return for which they were protected by the armed might of Islam. So long as the Muslim establishment carried out its end of the bargain — and it usually did — the exchange was a fair one. According to Muslim tradition (*ḥadîth*) the Prophet himself would stand in the Last Day as the personal accuser of believers who had violated the sacred compact between Islam and its protected subjects.

The status of the majority of the Christians who came under Islamic protection was far better than it had been under either Byzantine or Persian rule. Only the small minority of Orthodox Christians (Melkites) lost a position of privilege, and the vastly larger Monophysite and Nestorian communities gained for the first time a recognized legal status and freedom from overt governmental persecution. No attempt was made in the early decades of Islamic rule to convert Christians to the Way *(sharî'a)* of the Prophet, and throughout the era of the Orthodox *(Al-*

Râshidûn) caliphs (632-661) Muslims were not even allowed to settle in the newly conquered territories, being confined by law to the handful of military camp-cities erected at various strategic points within Egypt, Syria, and Mesopotamia. Even during the first twenty-five years of Umayyad rule Christians were hardly made aware of their secondary status. Indigenous Syrian Christians, chiefly Jacobites, predominated among the literary, artistic, and scientific circles that revolved around the Damascus court of Mu'âwiya, and some even rose to the ranks of personal advisors and provincial administrators. The favorite wife of the first Umayyad caliph was a Jacobite Christian, as had been the wife of the Orthodox Caliph 'Uthmân, and Mu'âwiya's son and successor, Yazîd, was raised in the Christian atmosphere of his mother's Christian Bedouin tribe, the Banû-Kalb.[12] His closest companion in youth was John of Damascus, an Orthodox Christian of native Syrian origins, later canonized by his Church for his theological contributions and recognized as one of the last great Fathers of Orthodoxy. His grandfather, Manşûr ibn-Sarjûn, had been one of the collaborators in a successful plot to betray Damascus to the armies of Khâlid Ibn Al-Walîd in 635, an indication that even among the Melkite Christians of Syria there was strong support for the Muslim invasion.

The relationship of mutual trust and even conviviality that characterized Christian and Muslim during the early Umayyad days began to change, however, during the reign of the Caliph 'Abd Al-Malik (685-705) and his four sons who succeeded him in turn. By this time the old restrictions concerning Muslim settlement in the new territories had long since been abolished, and successive waves of Muslim Arab immigrants from the Ḥijâz and the Yaman began irrevocably to alter the favored position which native Christians had at first enjoyed in the Islamic state. While positions of authority and prestige remained in practice open to Christians for the next hundred years or more, it was obvious that a far more secure route to political advancement lay in conversion to Islam. Many other Christians who found the cost of the *jizya* to be of more worth to them than their faith apostatized with increasing ease and in increasing numbers. Certain of the later Umayyad caliphs openly favored conversion from among the Christians, despite the loss of state revenue which inevitably resulted. The pious Caliph 'Umar II (717-720), when confronted with the declining *jizya* income by one of his financial advisors, replied fervently "as God lives I would hasten the day when all were believers, so that you and I would be obliged to till the soil with our very hands in order to earn a living."[13] Later Muslim jurists held that the purpose of the Prophet's covenant with the non-believers was to keep them among the Faithful so that they would be attracted to the beauties of Islam and willingly accept it.[14] And certainly more Christians embraced the faith of Muḥammad of their own will than were ever forcibly converted under threat of death.

By the middle of the 8th century the Christian communities and their leaders had come to recognize that the official Muslim toleration which had seemed so attractive a century earlier was in fact a rigid prison from which there was no escape other than apostasy or flight. And for all but the Melkites there was no place to flee. The *dhimmi* system, while allowing the Heterodox Christians to keep their religion, churches, and property, and to live according to the canon law of their particular sect, condemned them in effect to a slow but almost inevitable decline and death. They were not allowed to build new churches, and as succeeding caliphs became less tolerant, many of their old churches were appropriated by the state and made into mosques, the most famous example being the conversion of the Basilica of Saint John the Baptist in Damascus to the present-day Umayyad Mosque during the reign of Al-Walîd. All Christians were prevented from seeking new members from among even the non-Muslims of *Dâr Al-Islâm* (that territory under Muslim rulership), and apostasy from Islam was punishable by death. While the Nestorians of Iraq during the later years of the 'Abbâsid Caliphate managed to carry on extensive missionary activity beyond the frontiers of Islam (chiefly in China and Mongolia where they nearly succeeded in converting the Mongol race at the time of Genghis Khan), such energetic evangelization was unknown among the other Christian communities, and for that matter the Nestorians as well, during the greater part of the Arab and Ottoman eras.

By the time of the Crusades the Christian population of Syria and Egypt was less than half of the total, and Arabic was rapidly replacing Aramaic and Coptic as the first language of the indigenous inhabitants. On the other hand the pattern of Christian settlement never altered greatly from what it had been at the time of the Arab invasions: Monophysite Copts in Egypt, particularly in the Nile Valley south of Cairo; Orthodox Melkites in the coastal cities of both Egypt and Syria, from Alexandria to Antioch, where they were largely outnumbered by Muslim converts and immigrants; a Jacobite peasantry in the interior of Palestine and Syria with a nucleus of Maronites in Mount Lebanon; large numbers of Nestorians in both the towns and rural districts of Northern Mesopotamia. These Christian people were direct descendants of the Aramaic and Hamitic Christians who had been living there at the beginning of the Islamic age, completely unaffected by the successive waves of Muslim Arab immigration, since Christian men were forbidden to take Muslim wives (unless they embraced Islam) and since children of a Muslim man and a Christian woman were raised in the religion of their father.

This is not to say that the Christian "Arab" of today is simply an Arabicized Aramaean or Hamite with no Arabs in his ancestry. Quite the opposite is true, particularly in Syria, where many of the Christians at the time of the conquests were recently settled Bedouin tribesmen of the Ghassânid or other Christian nomadic nations. Of the numerous Christianized Arabs still actively following the *badu* life very few became immediate converts to Islam. Fewer still followed the example of Jabala Ibn Al-Ayham, *malik* of the Christian Arabs of Ghassân, who fled to the safety of Byzantine territory. Large numbers simply abandoned their nomadic way of life and during the ensuing decades settled among the indigenous Jacobite peasantry or the Melkite town-dwellers with whose families they inevitably intermarried. Others retained the Bedouin life and their Christianity for centuries (often refusing to pay the *jizya* as in the case of the Banû Taghlib and the Banû Kalb),[15] but these too inevitably settled among, and mixed with, the existing Christian population of Syria, or else converted to Islam. According to local tradition, the Christian town of Râm Allah in Palestine was settled in the

9th or 10th century by a Christian *badu* tribe from the East Bank of the Jordan whose *shaykh* had refused the hand of his daughter to a Muslim prince of that region and was accordingly forced to flee with his people.[16] In fact such tribes were still encountered by travelers in the 19th century, among them Charles Doughty,[17] and the last of these, sub-tribes within the Habashnâ and Majalî clans, have been settled in the vicinity of Al-Karak, Jordan, only in the past ten to twenty years.[18]

Major sources of Arab ancestry in the present-day Christians of Mesopotamia would have been the settled ʻIbad and semi-nomadic Lakhmids of the Lower Euphrates Valley, the nomadic Banû Tanûkh (members of which later migrated to Syria and became the nucleus of the present-day Durûz, or Druzes), and the large numbers of Christians living in the Arabian Peninsula at the time of the Prophet, among them the Nestorians of Najrân, who were forcibly resettled in Iraq by the Caliph ʻUmar I, and were soon absorbed by the indigenous Christians, mostly Nestorians, already there.

The native of Syria or Iraq who converted to Islam even more readily mixed his blood with that of Arabia through intermarriage with the large numbers of Muslim immigrants from the Peninsula, so that the Arabicized Muslims of mixed ancestry soon vastly outnumbered the purely Arab believer, to the extent that among Muslims in Syria and Mesopotamia today the undiluted Arab strain is found in very few (if any) of those who proudly call themselves Arabs.[19] It is highly possible in fact that the institution of slavery compromised the Arab ancestry of the Muslim to a much greater degree than was so in the case of the Christian population. It is certainly true that many native Christians intermarried with Europeans during the Crusades and have begun doing so again in recent years, but such mixing of Arab and non-Arab blood pales in comparison with the practice of Muslim men of means over the centuries who sired enormous numbers of half-breed children, by law Muslim like their father, from their inevitably non-Arab slaves and concubines. Only in Egypt where the pure Arab strain was introduced after the conquest does the native Christian stand racially apart from his Muslim countryman, and even here the native Hamitic element is largely predominant in the Muslim population as well. In Lebanon the Maronite community claims racial purity as the result of centuries of isolation in Mount Lebanon, but even here Arab blood of the purest order found its way into the finest Maronite families of today through the conversion of many Druzes during the 17th and 18th centuries.

The impact of the Crusades on the native Christian population is difficult to assess but it is probably greater than many historians and Middle Eastern scholars have been willing to admit. There has been a tendency to insist that the indigenous Christians of Syria loathed the Latin occupation as much as the Muslim population. Indeed after the shock of finding large numbers of Christian faithful in the very heartland of the Mohammedan heathen wore off, many Crusaders came to distrust the Eastern Christian with his non-Western dress and non-Latin religious rites. Many hapless Jacobites, Armenians, and even Greek Orthodox, suffered death at Crusader hands simply because they looked too much like Muslims when encountered in the heat of battle or the aftermath of pillage. And every time a new wave of Crusaders arrived from Europe to reinforce the old, the same problem of mistaken identity presented itself. On the other hand, most Christians (aside from the ever pro-Byzantine Melkites) generally preferred Latin rule to that of the Turks or even the Fatimid Egyptians whose treatment, despite the momentary excesses of Al-Hâkim, was just and tolerant. It was only after the last Crusader strongholds had fallen to the fanatic Mamlûk sultans of Cairo in the last years of the 13th century that the native Christians found it politically expedient to curse their erstwhile rulers from the West, and even then only because they had abandoned the Holy Land to the revengeful Muslim and not for any egregious persecution during their 200-year occupation. So long as there remained hope of support from Europe, the non-Latin Christians of Outremer were faithful subjects, again with the exception of the Melkites who went so far as to pray openly in Jerusalem for a Muslim victory at the moment the rest of the population was valiantly fighting to stave off Saladin's siege in 1187. Nor was the collapse of the Christian provinces even after the disaster of Ḥattîn a foregone conclusion. In the eyes of the great Arab historian of the Crusades,

Ibn Al-Athîr (d. 1233), had Frederick Barbarossa not died tragically almost within sight of Antioch after having led his vast army of German knighthood safely across hostile Anatolia, "men would today write that Syria and Egypt had once belonged to Islam."[20]

And while the Crusaders themselves were for the most part too busy with their own internal problems (when not at war with the Muslim powers which surrounded them) to attempt much serious proselytizing among the Heterodox Christian population of the Latin states,[21] they did succeed in promoting what William of Tyre terms "a wonderful change of heart" among the Maronite community, which led that entire nation of some 40,000 to accept a form of Latin Christianity in the year 1180 and to recognize the supreme spiritual authority of the Pope. The Maronites themselves claimed that they had been good Catholics all along and that their so-called heresy was simply a misunderstanding;[22] but however much they minimized the theological significance of their conversion, the long-term political effect was telling. The Roman Church was from the outset of the union exceedingly devoted to its newly-acquired community of indigenous faithful in the East, and allowed them the privilege of maintaining much of their ecclesiastical independence, their Syriac liturgy, and other religious customs and practices so long as they did not run contrary to the basic tenets of Latin Christianity. As the centuries passed and the Maronites maintained their faithful association with Rome despite terrible hardships suffered under Mamluk and Ottoman rule, the Church came to recognize the concept of rite as the best method for bringing about the reconciliation of the "schismatic and dissident" churches of the East.

The collapse of the Crusading states in the 13th century and the ensuing problems at home — the Babylonian Captivity and the Great Schism — prevented the Roman Church from immediately pursuing the goal of individual rites for each of the Eastern Churches. The Christians under Islamic rule were not forgotten, however, and in 1345 the Franciscan mission in Terra Sancta was re-established, and direct ties with the Maronites (many of whom had fled to Cyprus in the wake of the Mamluk conquest of the Latin States) and other Christian groups reforged. The fall of

Constantinople to the Ottoman forces in 1453 gave added impetus to Roman efforts in the East since Latin Christianity was no longer challenged by the existence of an Orthodox Christian empire, however tiny and weak, astride the Bosphorus. The immediate effect of Byzantium's fall on Eastern Christianity was that all churches and their adherents came under the single authority of the Orthodox Patriarch of Constantinople, Gennadius Scholarius. In the eyes of the conquering Turks, all Christians were regarded as forming a single nation or *millet* (from the Arabic *milla,* or nation), and no consideration was made for confessional, linguistic, or national differences. The Turks, who were as yet a numerical minority in the vast European and Asian territories that had become theirs since the early 14th century, preferred to leave all matters relating to the socially inferior Christians (contemptuously termed *rayah,* or flock, by the conquerors) in the hands of the most august Christian authority in the capital, whom they could easily control. Thus the patriarch came to inherit many of the privileges and prerogatives that had previously been the emperor's alone, and in his new mantle of authority exercised more power than any of his predecessors as "a kind of Christian caliph, responsible to the Sultan for all Christians."[23]

With the battle of Marj Dâbiq in 1516 and the consequent additions of Syria, Egypt, and Mesopotamia to the lands ruled by the Sultan (Arabic, *sulṭân,* he who exercises power), the geographical unity of the pre-Heraclian Byzantine Empire was restored. For the first time since the 7th century the Oecumenical Patriarchate exercised authority over the ancient patriarchates of Antioch and Alexandria and their diminishing, but still Heterodox, Christian populations. In his authority as *millet-baçi,* or head of the Orthodox nation, the patriarch was now in fact the regent of captive Christendom. And while recognition in 1461 of a separate Armenian *millet* by the Sultan lessened Constantinople's authority somewhat, the patriarch attempted to impose Byzantine ecclesiastical authority on Monophysite Copts and Jacobites, Nestorians, and Catholic Maronites. For the *millet* system of the Ottomans was scarcely different from the *dhimmi* establishment of Arab rule and placed in the hands of the Oecumenical Patriarch jurisdiction over all Christians, save the Armenians, who eventually came to act as intermediaries between the Porte and the Monophysite communities.

It is not surprising, therefore, that the non-Melkite communities in the newly acquired Arab territories of the Ottomans found this Orthodox re-ascendancy intolerable after centuries of autonomy, nor should it appear in the least unexpected that the Roman Church quickly assumed the role of protector with regard to its own Catholic congregations and offered its assistance to the schismatic churches in hopes of extending Catholic authority over these steadily declining, but not as yet insignificant, communities. Even before the Ottomans penetrated south of the Taurus, Catholic missionaries had been actively proselytizing among the Jacobites and Nestorians, and in 1551 succeeded in achieving the elevation of a pro-Roman bishop, Yuhannâ Sulâqâ, as Katholikos (patriarch) of the Nestorian Church. One of the first acts of the new patriarch was to visit Rome where early in 1553 he was consecrated by the Pope.[24] On his return, however, the unfortunate prelate was martyred at Diyârbâkîr in Eastern Anatolia by anti-Catholic partisans within his own community, and Rome, greatly weakened by the Reformation and ensuing religious wars in Europe, was not in a position to re-assert her tenuous ecclesiastical authority in distant Mesopotamia. By the beginning of the 17th century, however, her internal strength had somewhat revived and once again a considerable program was undertaken to bring about the incorporation of captive Christianity within the body of the Latin Church. In 1622 the Congregation for the Propagation of the Faith (usually referred to simply as the "Propaganda") was established in order to encourage and strengthen the rites and practices of the Oriental Churches, a step which French orientalist Pierre Rondot insists did not reflect momentary opportunism, as some Orthodox critics have charged, but rather a "deep respect for, and increasing appreciation of, these traditional liturgies, legacies of the Early Church."

> Rome accorded immense value to these ancient Eastern rites as vessels of spiritual treasure, finding in their Oriental splendor a symbolic fulfillment of the Psalmist's praise: "All

> thy garments smell of myrrh, aloes, and cassia; out of the ivory palaces, whereby they have made thee glad."[25]

Rome's oecumenical enthusiasm was not, needless to say, universally appreciated by the members of the separated churches, many of whom felt that the Catholic offer of rite — that is the privilege of retaining ecclesiastical autonomy and native liturgies, canon law, and individual religious customs intact in return for recognition of Petrine supremacy and the addition of the *filioque* clause to the Nicene Creed — was nothing more than a lure, and that union would inevitably result in Latinization.

By the middle of the 17th century it had become apparent to the "Propaganda" that a unison return like that of the Maronites in 1180 was not to be expected on the part of any of the other Eastern Churches, with the result that the Church adopted the policy of creating individual rites for each of the separate Christian communities around small nuclei of pro-Roman clergy and faithful. Thus it was hoped that these small, so-called "Uniate" churches actively supported by Rome would eventually attract the remainder of the parent ecclesiastical body. In 1672, more than a century after the failure of Patriarch Sulâqâ to initiate a unison Nestorian return, a separate Chaldaean rite was organized with its own Katholikos in direct and bitter rivalry with his Nestorian counterpart. Similar Uniate groups were established among the Orthodox in 1724, the non-Chalcedonian Armenians and Jacobites in 1742 and 1783 respectively, and finally in 1895 after many unsuccessful attempts a Uniate Coptic Church was established to minister to some few thousand pro-Roman native Egyptian Christians scattered throughout the Nile Valley. Without exception these new Uniate communities brought dissension and bitter hatreds to the fore within each of the ancient Churches of the East and failed in their effort to bring about acceptance of Roman primacy by more than a small minority of their brethren. And despite continued support by Rome in terms of money and manpower over the past three centuries, only one of the Uniate groups, the Chaldaean rite, has succeeded in eclipsing its parent church in membership and power. The remaining Catholic rites, though gradually increasing in strength over the centuries, remain today minorities within the total bodies of believers for whose conversion they have been striving since inception.

Their failure to achieve this goal is the product of many factors, chiefly political, which worked against the Roman missionary effort in the early, crucial years. The first barrier the pro-Uniate party in each Church had to contend with was the centuries-old suspicion that Rome was interested only in the eventual Latinization of the entire body of Christendom, a fear enforced by the general attitude of the Church during the later days of the Crusades and the actions of a minority of the Latin priests sent out by the "Propaganda" to help achieve union. Further fuel to the anti-Uniate fire was provided by Rome itself, which continued to support the Latin patriarchates of Antioch, Jerusalem, and Constantinople, whose titularies rivaled not only the patriarchs of the ancient Churches of the East, but the new Uniate Catholic patriarchs as well. These patriarchal sees, established during the Latin occupation of Jerusalem (1099-1187), Antioch (1098-1268), and Constantinople (1204-1261), served no ecclesiastical purpose since native Latin congregations were non-existent (except in Bethlehem and Jerusalem), and were regarded by Eastern Christians as ominous indications of what Rome eventually had in store for them.

The second political barrier to Roman success was the government of the Ottoman Empire itself which regarded the missionaries and their converts as the vanguard of a second effort by the West to re-Christianize the East. There was no doubt that European influence in the Empire, especially the capital itself, had been on the rise ever since the first commercial treaties (called "capitulations," from the Latin *capitula* as they were drawn up in chapters) were negotiated with the French and the English in the 16th century. The European powers, first the French, and later the Russians, came to view themselves as protectors of the native Christian communities and, as Ottoman power declined in the 17th and 18th centuries, advanced claims on their behalf. Unhappy with this trend, the Porte, supported by the hierarchies of the ancient Eastern Churches who likewise resented Catholic European designs on the unity of their flocks, began to take measures intended to curb the growth of the Uniate movement but in a manner which would not justify direct European intervention. The celebrated Turkish massacres of Eastern Christians were not undertaken until the last years of the 19th century, and in these earlier years persecution was usually carried out by the Orthodox and Heterodox authorities themselves against their own people who had left or threatened to leave the ancient fold. These intracommunal efforts were tacitly encouraged and fully supported by the Porte, which in the meantime had either granted *millet* status to the non-Chalcedonian Orthodox Churches, or at least pressured the Oecumenical Patriarch into permitting virtual autonomy. And as the Tsar of Russia began more and more to claim jurisdiction over the Orthodox peoples of the Ottoman Empire during the 18th century, the internal position of the ancient Eastern Churches became almost as untenable as that of the Uniate communities. Thus the picture of Christianity in the Arab East on the eve of its "rediscovery" by Europe in the 19th century was one of internal strife, growing weakness, and loss of members through the everpresent lure of full Ottoman citizenship in exchange for conversion to Islam, and corruption, to which the individual *millets* as integral parts of the Ottoman system were inevitably prone.

Revival (1798-1914)

When Napoleon landed in Egypt in 1798 at the beginning of his great Near Eastern adventure, the native Christian Copts were at the nadir of their long existence, a situation which was not immediately alleviated by the Corsican's declaration that he and his men were good Muslims. He nevertheless soon became aware of the administrative and linguistic skills which the Copts alone among the indigenous population possessed as the result of their long-standing roles of financiers (tax-collectors, village treasurers), merchants, and interpreters between Franks (Europeans) and the native Muslims.

But the leader destined to make most use of these Christian

skills and to restore the native communities to an honorable state in the 19th century Middle Eastern society was none other than the Albanian Muslim soldier of fortune, Muhammad 'Alî of Kavalla, who stepped into the power struggle between Ottoman and Mamluk leadership in the wake of the French departure, firmly establishing himself and his heirs as the undisputed rulers of Egypt, and, for a brief period, of Syria as well. Concerned only with the creation of a strong and modern Egyptian state, Muhammad Ali sought to make use of every resource at his disposal, finding in the indigenous Christian Copts a reservoir of talent heretofore untapped by his predecessors. During his long administration, Copts rose to positions of great authority both privately and within the government and in a relatively short period came to form the backbone of the Egyptian civil service. A number of Christian families were awarded the hereditary titles of "bey" and "pasha" during Muhammad Ali's reign, and all Christians were absolved from the medieval restrictions of dress, transportation, and conduct imposed by earlier Muslim rulers.

Much of this unprecedented tolerance was undoubtedly motivated by a genuine desire to bring Egypt into the 19th century socially and to facilitate a maximum utilization of Christian potential in achieving the manifold goals of modernization in a single generation; yet there is no doubt that the crafty grand pasha was intent on impressing the Western European powers with his devotion to the process of Westernization in hopes of securing their support in his long-range designs on the sultanate in Istanbul. The Ottoman administration, in continual decline since the 17th century, had failed conspicuously to institute any tangible Western-style reforms during the first twenty-five years of the 19th century and had in 1826 succeeded in destroying the reactionary Janissaries only at great cost to internal stability and external military strength. In 1824 the Sultan had been forced to request support from Muhammad Ali in putting down the Greek independence struggle, in return for which the latter was to be allowed to extend his pashalik to include Crete, the Peloponnesus, and Syria. The historic confrontation of Ottoman-Egyptian forces and the combined navies of Britian, France, and Russia at Navarino (Pylos) in 1827 brought to a disastrous end

Muhammad Ali's military campaign in Greece. He nevertheless felt justified in demanding territorial compensation for his substantial military contribution to the Ottoman war effort, and in 1832 seized Syria as far as the Taurus mountains, where his administration of eight short years brought irrevocable change to the large indigenous Christian population. The policy of tolerance and equality which had characterized his relations with the Copts in Egypt was extended to the various Christian communities in Syria. All religious distinctions were virtually abolished, and in 1837, for the first time since the Arab conquest, Christians were allowed to bear arms and encouraged to join the army. In all, some 7,000 Lebanese Christians were recruited by Ibrâhîm Pasha, son of Muhammad Ali, and deployed against the rebellious Druzes of Al-Ḥawrân in Syria who bitterly resented their new ruler's policy of universal military conscription.[26]

There is no question but that Muhammad Ali's social and religious policies were considered revolutionary by the population of Syria and viewed as a serious threat to the stabilility of the traditional Islamic state by the Muslim establishment, particularly in Damascus. On the other hand, toleration of religious differences had been a tradition in Syria since the days of the Umayyad caliphate and, of all the Arab provinces, it had been the most frequent meeting ground for Eastern Muslim and European Christian. The mountainous district of Lebanon in particular had, from the earliest years of Muslim hegemony in the area, stood apart as an island of religious minorities in a sea of Islam. Aside from a handful of small Muslim settlements along the coast (Tripoli, Beirut, Sidon, and Tyre) the Lebanon was inhabited by Christians, chiefly Maronites, Druzes, and a small community of the schismatic Shî'a. In general accustomed to political autonomy, the Lebanon had risen to considerable strength during the 17th century under the Al-Ma'n family, a native Druze aristocracy with strong Christian sympathies,[27] who were succeeded in the following century by the Al-Shihâb, a related clan which by the time of Muhammad Ali had for the most part adopted Maronite Christianity and reduced the Druze population to a minority in all but the mountainous area to the immediate south and east of Beirut. The seven-year occupation of Muhammad Ali gave tremendous additional impetus to the Maronite ascendancy so that by the time Ottoman authority was officially restored in 1840 the proud Druze remnant was in virtual bondage to the numerically dominant and economically powerful Maronite community.

Once extended, the freedoms which Muhammad Ali had granted Christians during his administration of Syria were extremely difficult to retract. Moreover, the pressure by Syrian Muslims in favor of a restoration of the traditional order was more than countered by insistent demands for modernization and Westernization with which the Porte had to contend or else lose European political support. Britain in particular, whose aid had been instrumental in restoring Syria to the Empire in 1839-1840, made it clear through her ambassador, Stratford Canning, that public opinion in England would not long countenance a status quo of traditionalism in the Ottoman East. Thus the Sultan Abdulmecid ('Abd Al-Majîd) upon his accession in 1839 inaugurated his reign with the dramatic program of Westernization known as the *Tanzimat* reforms. This program called for, among other things, the extension of citizenship to the Christian subjects of the Empire and complete freedom and equality for all non-Muslims. Though such a radical reversal of the traditional Islamic political system could not be successfully implemented even in the capital itself, Europeans took the moves at face value and credited the Porte with having at last come to terms with the Enlightenment. And for the Christians of Syria the Tanzimat prevented their Muslim countrymen from attempting a wholesale reversal of Muhammad Ali's liberal policies. The social tension remained acute, however, as Muslims began more and more to regard the Christians, with considerable justification, as pawns in the overall plans of the Christian European Powers to partition the Ottoman territories among each other. In Syria, the Druzes in particular were anxious to recover the position of power they had enjoyed in the Lebanon prior to the Egyptian occupation. Though the Ottoman restoration in 1840 had recognized the traditional Druze hegemony in the Lebanon south of the Beirut-Damascus road, the population over which the Druze *Qâ'im Maqâm* ruled was becoming increasingly Christian and difficult to administer. Druze-Maronite rivalry burst into open conflict in the summer of 1860, and despite the Christian numerical advantage which existed in nearly every *qaḍâ* of Mount Lebanon, the communal solidarity and warlike traditions of the Druzes enabled them to inflict heavy losses on the Maronites, who at this time were deeply involved in an internecine struggle which pitted the landowning aristocracy and religious hierarchy against the peasants and lower clergy. The conflict, remembered by the Christians today as *Ma<u>dh</u>abîḥ Al-Sittîn* (the massacres of '60), continued throughout the summer and cost an estimated 12,000 Christian lives in Dayr Al-Qamar, Jazzîn, Râ<u>sh</u>ayâ, Zaḥlah and Ḥâṣbayyâ. Not to be outdone, the Muslim population of Damascus rose in a body and, forcing open the gates to the historic Christian quarter at the eastern end of the city, set fire to the area and slaughtered some 10,000 of its inhabitants. The Christian leadership appealed to Europe, winning the support of the French Emperor, Napoleon III, who, anxious to reassert the historic presence of France in the lands of the Latin Kingdom, dispatched an emergency force of 7,000 French troops under General Beaufort d'Hautpoul, upon whose arrival in Beirut the massacres ceased.

Determined that such outbreaks should not be permitted to occur in the future, the Emperor persuaded the four other European Powers into pressuring the Porte to sign a *règlement organique* (9 June 1861) which created an automonous *mutaṣarrifîya* (governate) encompassing the entire Christian heartland of Syria stretching from Zaghartâ to Jazzîn, and from Zaḥlah to the suburbs of Beirut, exclusive of the latter city and the two other centers of Muslim settlement in Lebanon, Sidon and Tripoli. By the terms of the agreement, the governor of the region was to be a non-Lebanese subject of the Porte, Catholic Christian in faith, who would be directly responsible to Istanbul. Maronites were thus excluded from political control but because they constituted three-quarters of the quarter of a million inhabitants of the *mutaṣarrifîya* the governor was usually obliged to act on behalf of their wishes. Among the least heralded of Napoleon III's foreign ventures it was among his most successful, creating as it did an autonomous region in the strategic

Eastern Mediterranean whose Christian inhabitants — 90% of the population — were devotedly pro-French. The *reglèment* itself remained intact until the outbreak of the First World War during which period Lebanon enjoyed "exemplary order and prosperity"[28] and unprecedented freedom as well. Yet this half century of peace somewhat paradoxically witnessed the beginnings of an extensive and continuous Christian emigration.

Traditionally, the Mountain had been the homeland of the Maronite nation, and with the exception of their forced exile to Cyprus during the Mamluk period (14th and 15th centuries), members of the community rarely ventured beyond their mountain fastness. The establishment of the Maronite College in Rome (1584) had encouraged a small number of clergy to seek extended theological training in the shadow of Saint Peter's, but by and large these clerical scholars returned to their homeland and were in fact encouraged to do so by the Church itself. It is thus ironic that Maronites and other Christians in Syria and Lebanon began to emigrate at the very moment which saw the achievement of a new religious freedom unfettered by Islamic restriction and a political autonomy guaranteed by an historic ally, France, and the other European powers as well. Ottoman oppression cannot, therefore, be considered a prime and immediate cause for the exodus from the newly-created governate, as it can in the case of other parts of Syria and Mesopotamia where persecution and intolerance remained an ever-present threat despite the Tanzimat Reforms and the promulgation of Midhat Pasha's Constitution of 1876 — areas which contributed proportionately much less to the Christian diaspora than did free Lebanon. Perhaps the memory of the Massacres of 1860 were still too fresh and the fears they had instilled still too real to be assuaged by the promise of future security, however bright. But more probably, other factors such as rapid population growth in a country where agricultural potential is severely limited and the decline of certain important native industries were paramount in encouraging thousands of Christians from Mount Lebanon to leave their villages every year for the prospering cities of Egypt, and later for the rapidly-growing industrial centers of the United States and Latin America.

Such was the extent of the Christian, and especially Maronite, exodus that by 1913 on the eve of World War I the Maronite majority in the *mutaṣarrifîya* had shrunk from a substantial 75% in 1861 to a precarious 58%; and though the large Greek Orthodox and Greek Catholic communities swelled the total Christian majority to nearly 80%, the Muslims and Druzes who represented the remaining one-fifth of the total population had become an increasingly significant factor in the political life of Lebanon and a potential threat to the existence of the Mountain as an exclusively Christian enclave.[29] But despite increasing concern at the time for the future of Lebanon in the face of Christian emigration, there is no question that the period from 1861-1914 was among the most significant in shaping the political and intellectual context from which sprang many of the views and goals that have motivated and shaped the contemporary Arab World. In Lebanon itself, both the deeply-rooted French Catholic mission and its American Protestant rivals, active in the Levant only since the early 19th century, took advantage of the intellectual and political freedom which the *mutaṣarrifîya* brought to Lebanon by greatly expanding their already significant education programs. The French, whose Jesuit and Lazarist missionaries had been encouraged by both the Ma'nid and Shihâbi amirs, had actively pursued an education program aimed at serving the needs of the Maronite and other Eastern Catholic communities, culminating in the endowment of a series of secondary schools, notably 'Ayn Ṭûrâ (1734), 'Ayn Waraqa (1789), Ghazîr, and Zaghartâ in the Lebanon between Beirut and Tripoli, and the Lazarist School at Damascus (1775). The Protestants, though far more recent arrivals, quickly committed themselves to an emphasis on education in their approach to the indigenous Arab Levantine, Christian, Muslim, and Druze, and strengthened their program of school construction with stress on the use of Arabic as the medium of instruction, particularly at lower levels. Within a decade of the arrival of the first American Protestant missionary in Lebanon, an Arabic printing press was set up at the mission and devoted to the dissemination of secular as well as religious educational materials. The Catholics, who had long favored the use of French and to a lesser extent Syriac (the liturgical language of the Maronites, Jacobites, and Nestorians) were soon forced to meet this latest American challenge in the race for influence among the indigenous Arab speakers and in 1853, under Jesuit auspices, they established the still-flourishing *Imprimerie Catholique* whose publications in Arabic soon overshadowed its French and Syriac material. The organization of the Syrian Protestant College (now the American University of Beirut) in 1866 again forced the Catholics to extend the horizons of their education program so that within a decade the American Protestant university was rivaled by the French Catholic (Jesuit) Université Saint-Joseph. While the French were largely content, however, to confine their religious and political influence to Syria, the American Protestants branched far afield to nearly every corner of the Eastern Muslim World, establishing schools and medical care centers in Egypt (Asyûṭ College, The American University of Cairo), Asia Minor (Robert College in Istanbul, Anatolia College, and the American School for Girls at Smyrna), Persia, Mesopotamia, and even the Arab Gulf. And though essentially apolitical in their origins, the American schools in the Middle East soon became centers of indigenous political ideas and movements and contributed greatly over the years to the local political development.

Close behind the French in extending their political influence thoughout the Levant were the British who, like the Americans, by the end of the 19th century were established in nearly every corner of the Arab World, though in a far more political capacity. Nevertheless, the English Church was far from confined to looking after the needs of expatriate Anglicans and by the turn of the century was deeply involved with various indigenous Christian communities. In 1886 the Archbishop of Canterbury's Mission to the Assyrians confirmed British involvement in the affairs of the remnant Nestorian community in northern Mesopotamia and the mountains of Ottoman and Persian Kurdistan, while the Anglican bishopric in Jerusalem and St. George's and Bishop Gobat's schools for boys inevitably became the focus of a native Protestant community in Palestine.

In Egypt, however, where the English had been firmly established since the collapse of 'Arabi Pasha's revolt on the battlefield of Tall Al-Kabîr in 1882, British policy toward the indigenous Christian population showed itself to be fundamentally different in approach from that of the French. Whereas the latter openly favored the Arabic-speaking Christian (especially if he spoke French as well), the English tended to favor cooperation with the Muslim majority and its leadership as the best means of insuring a peaceful occupation. Thus Coptic power and indirect leadership which had reached a zenith under the independent Khedives of Muhammad Ali's line, began to diminish under the British protectorate. For while Muhammad Ali as a Muslim could appoint a Copt to the highest level in his government and be publicly applauded for his tolerance, a Christian British administrator left himself wide open to hostile charges of religious prejudice if he favored a Copt over a Muslim. The French were impervious to this kind of consideration and paid for it dearly; the British took the question very seriously, but can hardly be said to have profited from their alleged Muslim favoritism. The Copts themselves were in large part greatly disaffected by the British stance, and in 1911 convened a Congress despite official British attempts to prevent their doing so, and presented a prepared list of grievances. Many Christian Englishmen were openly chagrined at their government's failure to view the Copts in a more favorable light, among them Lady Duff-Gordon who noted, during the course of her residence in Egypt in the years preceding the British occupation, that "a curious instance of the affinity of the British mind for prejudice is the way in which every English man I have seen scorns the Eastern Christians."[30]

The Russians, though never in possession of territories in the Middle East south of the Caucasus, persisted in their self-appointed role as champions of all Orthodox Christians under Ottoman rule. Since 1774, when Catherine the Great's armies had forced the Porte to recognize Russian claims at Küçük Kainarca, the Tsar and the Russian Church had used the captive Orthodox communities as a direct instrument of Tsarist expansion in the Eastern Mediterranean. On many occasions this meant taking the side of the Greek patriarchs in the four ancient provinces of Christendom, such as in 1853 when Russian machinations on behalf of the Greek patriarch of Jerusalem led to the follies of the Crimea. In later years it meant siding with the Arabic-speaking faithful, who made up the great majority of the Orthodox communities in the patriarchates of Antioch and Jerusalem, against their self-perpetuating Greek hierarchy resident at the patriarchate in Istanbul. In 1899 the Russian-Syrian coalition succeeded in giving Antiochene Orthodoxy its first Arab patriarch in centuries, thus bringing to a close the Hellenic hegemony there which the Ottomans had restored in the early 16th century. Further attempts to end Greek domination of Orthodoxy in Jerusalem succeeded only in instigating a virtual war between clergy and laity which continues to this day, the tenacious hold of Christian Hellenism having been strengthened recently with the Israeli occupation of Arab Jerusalem. The Bolshevik Revolution of November, 1917, brought the activities of the Russian Church in the Middle East to a virtual standstill until 1945, and in the meantime the native congregations and their Russian-oriented (and frequently Russian-educated) higher clergy found themselves at the beginning of the Mandate period without the advantages which the Uniate communities enjoyed as wards of France. For the non-Catholic Christians of the East, therefore, including the Armenians and Jacobites who had likewise looked to Russian Orthodoxy for spiritual and political guidance, the alternatives were total isolation within the community, or a serious attempt to find common cause with the Muslim Arab majority — already the chosen route of many nationalist - minded Orthodox intellectuals.

The Prelude to Independence (1914-1946)

The First World War was for the Christians of Syria, Mesopotamia, and Anatolia a purgatory from which they emerged broken and decimated, a tragic chapter in their history of suffering which today, more than fifty years later, remains an omnipresent memory even to those born long afterward. Most Europeans and Americans are familiar with the terrible fate of the Armenians of Eastern Anatolia and Cilicia who were massacred by the hundreds of thousands in 1915 as the Ottoman armies retreated before the Russian advance on the Caucasian front. That these Christian peoples were potential or even active collaborators with the enemy has been used with some justification by Turkish apologists, but not even the pressures of war can begin to justify the wholesale slaughter that ensued, nor the forced overland march to Dayr Al-Zawr on the Euphrates southeast of Aleppo to which tens of thousands more were subjected and from the extreme trials of which most died horrible and often lingering deaths.

What is not so well known in the West is the extent to which many of the other ancient Christian communities suffered as well, notably the Jacobites, Nestorians, and Chaldaeans, neighbors of the Armenians in eastern and southern Anatolia, the Maronites in Mount Lebanon, and to a lesser extent all Eastern Christians subjected to the ruthless wartime administration of Jamâl Pasha. An estimated 100,000 Jacobites and Syrian Catholics are known to have perished from privation and massacre in their foothill strongholds of 'Urfa (Edessa) and Mardîn, while an equal number of Chaldaeans and Nestorians are estimated to have suffered a similar fate to the East in the mountains north of Mosul (Al-Mawṣil). The Chaldaean-Rite Catholic Church, which at the outset of the war counted slightly over 100,000 faithful, suffered the loss of six bishops, a score of priests, and untold thousands of its membership, as well as the total destruction of four dioceses, defunct to this day.[31] The Nestorian (Assyrian) community lost its patriarch, the greater part of its clergy and over half its numbers to Turkish and Kurdish massacre; thousands more succumbed to starvation, disease, and exposure during and after their flight through hostile Muslim territory to the safety of the British lines in southern Mesopotamia. In Lebanon, the *mutaṣarrifîya* was abolished shortly after the outbreak of Ottoman-British hostilities, and replaced by a repressive wartime government — the most disastrous administration in the history of the Mountain. During the next three years an estimated 100,000 Lebanese, virtually all of them Christian (largely Maronite), died of disease, starvation and execution — almost 25% of the total population of that populous region which had comprised the autonomous governate.[32]

The incalculable suffering which the Christians of Syria and Mesopotamia had endured at Turkish hands during the War caused many among them, heretofore sympathetic to the aims of nascent Arab Nationalism, to question their future under any Muslim administration, including the Arab Kingdom established by the Sharîf of Mecca's son, Prince Faysal, at Damascus immediately following the Ottoman collapse in 1918. Husayn himself had made considerable effort to assure his British allies that his future Christian subjects would enjoy religious freedom and civil liberty. In a letter to Sir Henry McMahon, British High Commissioner in Cairo, dated 6 November 1915, the Sharîf spoke eloquently of the common ties of Christian and Muslim in the Arab East.

> There is no difference between a Moslem and a Christian Arab: they are both descendants of one forefather. We Moslems will follow in the footsteps of the Commander of the Faithful 'Umar Ibn Al-Khattab, and other caliphs succeeding him, who ordained in the laws of the Moslem faith that Moslems should treat the Christians as they treat themselves.[33]

Faysal's embryonic government in Damascus took immediate steps to win Christian confidence "with the promise of putting religious separation out of sight,"[34] and in drawing up its boundaries which included Lebanon, recognized the pre-war autonomy of the *mutaṣarrifîya* to be in effect under Faysal's monarchy, but only insofar as the Christians refrained from foreign entanglements.[35] There were some Christians, predominantly Greek Orthodox and Protestant, who expressed guarded willingness to accept Sharifian authority, but the great majority of Christians and their religious and lay leaders looked to France and, to a lesser extent, Great Britain and the United States, to assist them in guaranteeing the autonomy of a Christian Lebanon and the security of all indigenous Christians elsewhere in the Fertile Crescent.

The American King-Crane Commission, dispatched to the Middle East by President Wilson to gauge popular political sentiment, found an almost universal desire among the Uniate communities for the establishment of a French mandate over Syria, and a fear among virtually every Christian Arab of immediate complete independence under an Arab government.[36] The Commission itself agreed with the Christians, asserting that protection of minorities would be impossible under an essentially weak Arab administration; and while recognizing that the Muslim Arab nationalists promised that their administration would be free of religious discrimination, it was necessary, in the view of the Commission, "to hold them to this view through mandatory control until they have established the method and practice of it."[37] Almost without exception the Christian communities found themselves in agreement with this recommendation. There was some opposition among the non-Catholics to the establishment of a French protectorate, but among the Uniate communities themselves there was no question as to their preference. Maronite Patriarch Ilyâs Buṭrus Al-Ḥuwayyik (1843-1932) told the Commission that while Lebanon desired full independence, if assistance were necessary, then only that of France would be acceptable.

In spite of an almost unanimous Christian opposition to the incorporation of Lebanon into Faysal's Arab Kingdom, Sharifian forces occupied Beirut on October 1918 and raised the Arab flag at B'abdâ, former seat of the *mutaṣarrifîya*. Within a week, however, these forces were driven out by a detachment of British and Franch forces led by General Allenby, and under the terms of the military occupation laid down following the successful entry into Beirut, all of Syria Maritime, from Ra's Al-Nâqûra in the south to the Cilician Gates in the north, passed under French control. Early in January of 1919, François Georges-Picot established himself in Beirut as French High-Commissioner in the Levant, and with him came those Lebanese nationalists such as Emille Idda (Eddé), predominantly Maronite, who had spent the war years in European exile having been sentenced to death in absentia by the Ottoman government. Idda and most of his fellow Maronites were intent on persuading France to establish an autonomous Lebanon under French mandate authority. Little persuasion was necessary. In August of 1919 the 76-year-old Maronite patriarch paid a state visit to Premier Clemençeau in Paris to request Lebanese independence and a restitution of the country's "historical and economic frontiers."[38] Al-Ḥuwayyik returned with assurances by Clemençeau that such measures would be carried out, and three months later Georges-Picot was replaced by General Henri Gouraud, "a devout Catholic whose very presence in Lebanon reassured the Christians."[39] The following summer Gouraud, succeeding where King Louis VII had failed nearly eight centuries before, occupied Damascus and effectively brought an end to Faysal's short-lived Arab Kingdom. Five weeks later (September 1920), the French announced the creation of an independent state of Greater Lebanon *(Grand-Liban)* within the Syrian mandate, nearly doubling the area of the former *mutaṣarrifîya* so as to include the coastal cities of Beirut, Tripoli, Sidon, and Tyre (Ṣûr), the rolling hills of the Jabal 'Amîl to the south, the strategic highlands of the 'Akkâr controlling the natural gate to the cities of inland Syria to the north, and the rich Biqâ' Valley to the East. For the Maronites, their rallying cry, "Truly France is our benevolent mother" *(Innâ Farânsâ Ummanâ Ḥanûna),* had proven to be more than a hopeful invocation. The benevolence of France had in fact never been more tangible.

The establishment of a Greater Lebanon had long been the goal of the aging Maronite patriarch, for the old governate without the granary of the Biqâ' and the ports of Beirut and Tripoli was an isolated island completely dependent upon the surrounding Muslim territory. The new areas included in the infant state, however, were predominantly non-Christian so that the 80% majority which Christians had enjoyed in the *mutaṣarrifîya* was reduced to barely more than half. Maronites themselves constituted less than one-third of the total Lebanese population, a far cry from the majority status they had previously enjoyed. Lebanese dependence upon France was thus increased, for without the French, Christians in Lebanon would have been hard pressed to maintain the country's autonomy in the face of Muslim pressure from within and without.

The Muslim population of the new state had been unanimously opposed to the establishment of a French mandate, and many, the King-Crane Commission reported, "were vehement and violent about it."[40] The creation of Grand-Liban intensified the Muslim resentment, especially among the Sunni communities in the coastal cities, and there was fear at the outset that any government which tried to achieve Christian and Muslim participation would be untenable. The Christians in contrast, with the exception of the Orthodox who were uneasy over the prospect of Maronite Catholic hegemony, could scarcely contain their enthusiasm for the French administration. Patriarch Al-Ḥuwayyik, in a proclamation of 8 December 1920, gave unrestrained expression of Maronite sentiment in terms which left no room for Christian commitment to the rising cause of Arabism.

> And now has the noble French nation given us in our poverty, misery, and affliction, a new and brilliant proof of her love for us and our welfare, and her concern for our affairs. Her righteous policy has triumphed in this land and confirmed the hopes to which we have tenaciously and affectionately adhered, and has offered to our cherished Lebanon her independence, extended her boundaries, and re-established for her people a living nation which, God willing, will stand with honor among the civilized nations. We are thus enjoined to render thanks to France and her people who have made great sacrifices on our behalf. And let us not forget that we are the sons of those yet more glorious who tasted great bitterness because of their love for, and devotion to France, which neither the tyranny of the unjust nor the oppression of the despot could dissuade.[41]

There is a temptation today to fault the patriarch and his people for such unbridled joy in their achievement, when a more sober appeal for cooperation to the suspicious Muslim population would have been more in order. But having snatched triumph from the jaws of suppression at a time when other Eastern Christians were facing extinction, and when the clouds of Zionism and stridently Islamic Arab Nationalism had yet to darken the horizon, the Maronites will surely be pardoned by history for giving vent to their innermost feelings — the capital indiscretion in Middle Eastern politics.

Nor were the Maronites of Lebanon alone among the Eastern Christians in their desire for autonomy guaranteed by Western strength. The Chaldaean patriarch appeared before the King-Crane Commission in August of 1919 calling for the creation of a European-protected autonomous state for Chaldaean, Nestorian, and Syrian-Jacobite peoples in Mesopotamia and the Syrian Jazîra (the land to the west of Mosul lying between the Tigris and Euphrates rivers), thousands of whom had only recently emigrated there, driven from their historic centers in the mountains and foothills of southern and eastern Anatolia by Turkish oppression. The Assyrian (Nestorian) community in particular was "allured by the ideas of autonomy and national unity"[42] and sought out every possible means of achieving it. The British, however, under whose aegis the majority of these people now fell following the Ottoman collapse, were far more interested in catering to the interests of Muslim leadership than in cooperating with Christian separatists, concessions to whom might easily edge the Islamic majority over the brink of rebellion. Thus while the Treaty of Sèvres envisioned an independent Kurdish state in which the rights of the Assyro-Chaldaean Christians were to be fully safeguarded, the British made no move to implement this provision in Iraq, and from the beginning attempted to discourage the young, British-educated Nestorian patriarch, Mâr Sham'ûn Ishay, and the forces behind him, in attempting to carry out their efforts to achieve political autonomy.

Though still denied self-governing status outside the tiny enclave of Lebanon, the Christians in the Arab East were for the most part satisfied with the protection afforded by the establishment of European authority under the mandate system, which by the end of 1920 had encompassed the entire Eastern Arab World excepting the greater part of the Arab Peninsula. Palestine and all of Iraq, despite Turkish claims to the Mosul district, had come under British control, already firmly established in Egypt, the Sudan, and the southern and eastern coast of the Arabian Peninsula, while the French had forcibly entrenched themselves in Syria. For the first time in seven centuries, and in some instances thirteen, the lands of the Fertile Crescent lay within the authority of a Christian power. The indigenous Christians, long denied equal status within the traditional Islamic system (save for Lebanon), were suddenly granted full civil liberties under constitutions drawn from European models, and permitted, even encouraged, to participate in the executive, legislative, and judicial exercise of national administration, hitherto exclusively within the control of the Sunni Muslim community. With their high standard of education, much of it in the European tradition, the Levantine Christians became a major source of manpower at the highest levels within the Mandate governmental structure.

The legal framework of the Mandates was particularly instrumental in raising the status of the Christians, having been borrowed, in many instances, directly from the liberal constitutional heritage of the Mandatory power itself. The Constitution of Iraq promulgated in 1924 under British supervision guaranteed "complete freedom to practice various forms of worship in conformity with accepted customs." It was further stated that "the electoral system shall guarantee equitable representation to racial, religious, and linguistic minorities," and an electoral law enacted in that same year created four Christian and four Jewish seats in the Chamber of Deputies. Moreover, missionary activity was officially permitted and any citizen over the age of twenty-one was given the legal right to register a change of religion; apostasy from Islam was no longer a capital crime.[43] Similar freedoms were guaranteed in the Lebanese Consitution of 23 May 1926, and the first Constitution of Syria (1930) reflected a like liberalization of religious outlook at the official level.[44]

Christians were not the only communities to benefit from the new legal structures. Early in 1926 a statute was passed in Lebanon granting the Shî 'a Muslim sect official recognition so that for the first time this community enjoyed jurisdiction in its own matters of personal status and civil law, thus directly altering the status of some 150,000 Lebanese Shî 'a who previously had fallen within the legal sphere of the Sunni *Sharî 'a* courts. The large Oriental Jewish communities in Baghdad, Cairo, Damascus, and Beirut likewise profited from these constitutionally guaranteed civil liberties to the extent that very few individual Jews showed any inclination to emigrate to Palestine until the tensions brought about by the creation of the state of Israel in 1948 forced most to break away from their ancient settlements.

In contrast to the outlook of Christians and other religious linguistic minorities, the Arab Muslim leadership and the masses for whom they spoke greatly resented the imposition of the Mandate system, and throughout the interwar years became increasingly active and uncompromising in their opposition to their European governments. Confronted with frequent riots and disruptive political activity, the French in Syria attempted to counter unrest by creating additional autonomous states centered around cohesive minority groups. Throughout much of the Mandate era Syria found itself carved up into four such separatist regions in addition to Lebanon: 1) the Jabal Al-Durûz district in the eastern Ḥawrân, 90% Druze in composition with Christians, chiefly Orthodox, forming the remainder; 2) the district of Latakia (Al-Lâdhiqîya), or "Alouites" as the French referred to it, to the north of Lebanon, whose population was made up largely of adherents of the 'Alawî or Nuṣayrî sect, with equally balanced minorities of Christians (again Orthodox) and Sunnis; 3) Alexandretta with its large Turkish and Kurdish minorities, as well as sizeable urban concentrations of Arab and Armenian Christians; and 4) the Jazîra plain to the east which, with the exception of unsettled *badu* tribes, was almost entirely non-Arab (Turk, Kurd, and Assyro-Armenian) in ethnic makeup and one-third Christian. The state of Syria proper was reduced to a narrow inland corridor of Sunni strength stretching from Aleppo southwards to Damascus and the Ḥawrân, though here again substantial minorities (predominantly Christian) accounting for over 20% of the population allowed the French administration to restrict severely Muslim political advancement.

By the eve of World War II France had become reconciled to eventual Syrian independence. Three of the five autonomous regions were re-incorporated in the parent state, but Lebanon, which had been proclaimed a republic in 1926, and Alexandretta, ceded to Turkey in 1939, were irretrievably lost to Syrian Arab administration. The Jazîra, moreover, had been placed under direct administration from Damascus in 1937 against the wishes of the overwhelmingly Christian urban population, and a massacre of Christians in that year at 'Amûda initiated a strong movement for local autonomy and even independence led by Cardinal Tappuni, then Syrian Catholic patriarch, which was abandoned only with the evacuation of French forces in 1946.

Anticipating the inevitable eclipse of French power in the Middle East as the result of the Second World War, Lebanese Christian nationalists reluctantly cut the political ties that had linked them with France since 1918, and in late 1943 came to terms with the Muslim population through an unwritten agreement known as the National Pact *(Al-Mîthâq Al-Waṭanî).* Negotiated between the leading political spokesmen for the Maronite and Sunni communities, Bis̲hâra Al-Khûri and Riyâḍ Al-Sûlḥ respectively, this covenant established Lebanon as an independent republic based on a rigid apportionment of political offices to the various religious groups on the strength of the Census of 1932 which had registered a narrow Christian majority. Christian hegemony at the political level was preserved, but only at the price of greater Muslim participation and the possibility of eventual Muslim domination should the Christian population fall below the 50% mark. Independence from France was declared by both Lebanon and Syria on 1 January 1944, and though French forces attempted to delay acceptance contingent upon concessions of military and naval bases, nationalist activity combined with British and United Nations' pressure forced the final evacuation of French troops during 1946.

Faced with similar resistance to Mandate administration in Iraq, the British had yielded to independence over a decade earlier, in 1932. At that time an independent monarchy under King Faysal (who had been installed in Baghdad by the British as a consolation for their failure to live up to an earlier commitment to the Arab Kingdom) was recognized, and Iraq became the first independent Arab state to join the League of Nations. Abdication of British authority, however, brought disaster to the Nestorian Christian community which had never ceased to agitate for autonomous status. Distrusted by the Arab Muslims for their separatist goals and the service they had rendered the British occupation as military mercenaries, the whole community became the object of nationalist reproach. In the summer of

1933 a wave of anti-Christian sentiment swept the country, culminating in the machine-gun massacre of several hundred Assyrian men, women, and children by the Iraqi Army at Simayl (north of Mosul), followed by further killings and looting throughout the month of August. The patriarch, "whose personal safety could no longer be assured, and was indeed hourly threatened,"[45] was removed to security in Cyprus by the RAF, while thousands of individual Nestorians, whose leadership had been pressing the League of Nations since 1931 for the creation of a national homeland somewhere outside the Middle East, took matters into their own hands and crossed into French Syria where they were resettled along the Khabbûr River in the Jazîra. In Iraq itself the government acted slowly but with conviction to guarantee the security of the remaining members of the dwindling Nestorian community there, and in 1938 assured the League that those still resident in Iraq, many of whom were by then re-established in villages "neither crowded nor unprosperous"[46] were secure in their status as citizens. The bulk of Christians in Iraq, chiefly Chaldaean Catholics, escaped the persecution to which the Nestorians were subjected by acquiescing quietly to nationalist administration in Baghdad, but to Christians throughout the Arab East the fate of the Nestorians augured ill for those contemplating their future under an independent Muslim-dominated government.[47]

In the remaining areas of British administration, Egypt, Palestine, and Transjordan, native Christians continued on the whole actively to support nationalist independence movements. In Egypt the Coptic Christian population, in large part disaffected by British failure to sustain them in the privileged position they had achieved during the reign of Muhammad Ali and his successors, joined with Muslim nationalists in supporting the *Wafd* Party in its efforts to force the evacuation of British presence, political and military. In 1922 independence was officially granted, but the continued presence of British political advisors, an English commander-in-chief of the Egyptian army, and thousands of British soldiers made it clear that ultimate authority still rested in London. Throughout the halcyon days of Egyptian nationalism in the 20's and 30's, Copts and Muslims cooperated under the banner of unity proclaimed by the Cross and Crescent movement. Christians rose to prominence in the *Wafd* and if anything were less corrupt than Muslim nationalists at the upper end of the political spectrum. The Constitution of 1930 and the Anglo-Egyptian Treaty of 1936 marked memorable nationalist advances at the expense of British hegemony, but it was not until the overthrow of King Farouk (Fârûq) in 1952 and the singular triumph of President Nasser four years later at Suez (Al-Suways) that Egypt could truly be regarded as independent, and by that time the Palestine conflict had intervened to discredit, however, unjustly, Christian commitment to the nationalist cause.

In Palestine itself the indigenous Christian population, between ten and fifteen percent of the Arab total, had provided much of the initial leadership in the early opposition to Zionist expansion, and earned for their communities — Orthodox, Catholic, and Protestant alike — an enviable record of unselfish dedication to the cause of Arab Palestine. As the mainstay of Palestine's commercial and educated class, the Christians were the first to recognize the immediate economic threat posed by the skilled Jewish immigrants from Europe, and were not long in foreseeing their ultimate destiny in the overall scheme of an independent Zionist state, thus accounting for the long list of active Christian participants in the Arab resistance movements that have come into being during the past fifty years.

The adjacent Mandate of Transjordan, originally created by the British in 1921 for the express purpose of finding a throne for Prince Faysal's younger brother Abdullah ('Abd-Allah), came to acquire special significance the following year when the Mandate for Palestine as approved by the League of Nations specifically excluded the territory east of the Jordan River from Jewish settlement. Having served the British and his people well during the interwar years, Abdullah was recognized as the sovereign of an independent Kingdom of Jordan in 1946 and fell heir four years later to the remnant of Arab Palestine, including the Old City of Jerusalem. The King's assassination there the following year evidenced the frustration of many Muslim Palestinians with Abdullah's failure to drive out the Zionists, but his record of religious tolerance encouraged many Christians from the Israeli occupied territories to the west to seek refuge in the economically weak and landlocked kingdom whose constitution and electoral laws guaranteed a place for non-Muslims in the national administration. In the new state of Israel, Christians formed nearly a quarter of the remaining Arab population of some 150,000, and in large part shared the all-too-familiar cup of second-class citizenship with their Muslim neighbors. Thus, of the nearly three million Christians in the Arab East at the outset of national independence, only those 600,000 in Lebanon enjoyed the security to which all had aspired in the wake of the Ottoman collapse. And even for the privileged one-fifth whose president was a fellow Christian, the challenges to their traditional outlook and accustomed way of life which the ensuing quarter century had in store were to be unparalleled in the Arab Christian's long history of constant change and adversity.

II The Religious Demography of Egypt and the Fertile Crescent

The pattern of Christian settlement in what is today the Arab East has changed very little from that encountered by the Muslim invaders in the 7th century and preserved through the *dhimmi* and later the *millet* systems of administration. The only differences in the pattern at the time of the Crusades were those brought about by the gradual numerical decline which had characterized all the Christian communities in the face of Arab immigration and a steady loss through conversion to Islam in every generation since the time of the first Umayyads. This trend continued as a matter of course following the fall of the Latin states, so that by the eve of Arab independence in this century there existed a number of gaps in the formerly unbroken chain of Christian settlements from Aswân to Basra where scarcely any Christians were to be found. The principal gaps were those in the Lower Delta region of Egypt from Rosetta (Rashîd) to Damietta (Dumyâṭ); the infamous "Bloody Triangle" (*Al-Muthâlath Al-Dam*) in the Judaean highlands of Palestine — so-called for the tripartite vendetta in which the Muslim families of Nâbulus, Janîn, and Ṭulkaram have been engaged for generations; in northern Syria from the Orontes east to the Euphrates (excepting the city of Aleppo); and in the Lower Mesopotamian Valley from Baghdad to Basra exclusive of those two cities. And even here Christians were simply uncommon but not unknown. Only in Eastern Anatolia had they all but disappeared, victims of the efficient methods of Enver Pasha and Atatürk in dealing with the thorny question of minorities.

Ecclesiastically the Christian pattern is infinitely more complex. Each community recognizes the leadership of its patriarch, with the exception of the Protestants, and as there are twelve Christian groups and only four patriarchates, rivalries obviously exist, many of them of fifteen centuries' standing. Alexandria has three patriarchal claimants — a Monophysite Copt, a Catholic Copt, and a Greek Orthodox, all of whom allege direct episcopal succession from Saint Mark, first Bishop of

Alexandria and founder of the Church in Egypt. The Patriarchate of Jerusalem, created in 451 by the Council of Chalcedon as the fifth ecclesiastical province of the ancient Church, has two principal pretenders, Greek Orthodox and Latin—in this particular case very much Byzantine and Roman—as well as an Armenian patriarch whose presence since the 14th century[48] has been largely political. Jerusalem also has been, since 1957, the seat of an Arab Anglican "Bishop in Jordan, Lebanon, and Syria." Prior to this (1841-1957) the incumbents were English.[49] To the north, Antioch is contested by no less than five patriarchs, three of them Catholic (Maronite, Greek Catholic, and Syrian Catholic), one Orthodox, and one Monophysite (Jacobite), each with his substantial numbers of faithful. The city of Antioch itself is now a small provincial city, Anṭâkiya, Turkish since 1939, with few Christian inhabitants (mostly Arabic-speaking Greek Orthodox) and without benefit of resident patriarchs since the Crusades.

To the east is Mesopotamia, modern Iraq, which never constituted a patriarchate since it was never politically a part of Christendom, having passed directly from the hands of Zoroastrian Persians to those of the Muslim Arabs. Nevertheless a large Christian population prospered here from the 2nd century onwards and, having adopted the Nestorian heresy in the 5th century, evolved its own patriarchal head, the Katholikos of the East, who rivaled Constantinople from Ctesiphon and later Baghdad. In the 17th century a Uniate Chaldaean Katholikos challenged the Nestorian titular and eventually triumphed. The Catholic Katholikos resides today in Baghdad; his Nestorian rival endured, until his recent assassination, a reverse Babylonian captivity in San Francisco. Finally, there are the Armenian Patriarchs of Sis (Cilicia or Lesser Armenia), Orthodox and Uniate Catholic, and the Gregorian Patriarch of Jerusalem. Jerusalem, as does Constantinople, falls under the patriarch in Soviet Armenia (Echtmiadzin). Sis is autocephalous. A situation as confused as this demands an attempt at clarification, sect by sect and country by country, before further analysis is undertaken.

Greek Orthodox. Heirs to the New Testament Church of Antioch, the Greek Orthodox communities in the Arab East are those which adhered steadfastly to the political authority of the Byzantine Emperor in Constantinople, and maintained a Greek liturgy though their ethnic stock and mother tongue was Aramaic or Hamitic, and later Arabic. Following the Christological controversies of the 5th century by which Orthodoxy lost the loyalties of most Christians to the south and east of the Cilician Gates, the few remaining faithful were contemptuously referred to by the heterodox masses as "Emperor's men," or Melkites, and survived only where the military arm of Constantinople was strong enough to protect them. So long as the New Rome held firm against first Arab then Turkish invaders, the Melkites of Egypt and Syria remained loyal to the Empire, but after 1453 they transferred their loyalties to the Ottoman Sultan through whom they achieved immense power and influence in the Porte's domains. When Turkish hegemony in the East began its decline, Orthodoxy looked once again to a sympathetic force, this time that of the Third Rome — Moscow — whose power at the Phanar (the former Greek quarter of Istanbul where the Oecumenical Patriarch still resides) became paramount in the 19th century, spreading its influence into Syria and Palestine as well. When Tsarist Russia collapsed in 1917, the Orthodox of the Arab East had no alternative but to begin forming cautious alliances with the rising Arab nationalist leadership, something the more adventuresome intellectuals of the community had been doing since mid-century. Thus, at the same time most Christians in the Fertile Crescent were casting their lot with the new European administrations whose days were already numbered, the Orthodox in Syria, Lebanon, and Palestine, both clergy and laity, fell in with the various Pan-Arab political movements — first the Sharifian Kingdom of Prince Fa̦ysal, followed by the secular Arab Nationalist parties and finally the radical Palestinian irredentist groups of today (see chapter IV).

Historically divided among the ancient patriarchates of Antioch, Jerusalem, and Alexandria, the indigenous Orthodox population of today is concentrated in the first two. The patriarch of Alexandria is a Greek who ministers to a predominantly Greek community of less than 50,000 in Egypt, an impotent remnant of the once flourishing Hellenic society that retained a strong presence in Cairo and Alexandria as late as 1956. The patriarch of Jerusalem, likewise a Greek, presides over the 75-100,000 indigenous Arabic-speaking Orthodox of Israel and Jordan. This archaic preserve of Hellenism in the Holy City has been a source of constant friction since the late 19th century. The British Mandate government and later that of Jordan forced the patriarch and his Confraternity of the Holy Sepulchre, a quasi-monastic order of some hundred, almost exclusively Greek, clerics, from which all bishops and the patriarch himself are chosen, to yield to increasing pressure from the Arab laity and lower clergy who wished a voice in the internal affairs of their Church. The seizure of Old Jerusalem by the Israelis in 1967 obviously has reduced the political pressure which the local Arabs were able to exert, and for the time being has confirmed Greek control of the Jerusalem patriarchate and the Orthodox Holy Places. Significant centers of Orthodox population in the patriarchate of Jerusalem are Amman (ʻAmmân), Kerak (Al-Karak), Al-Salṭ, ʻAjlûn, and Al-Ḥuṣn in Jordan, Jerusalem (Al-Quds), Bethlehem (Bayt Laḥam) inclusive of Bayt Jâlâ and Bayt Sâḥûr, Râm Allah and several surrounding villages on the occupied West Bank, Nazareth (Al-Nâṣira), Acre/Haïfa, and scattered Galilean villages in Israel.

The patriarch of Antioch, long resident in Damascus and an Arab since 1899, heads a prosperous community of Syrian and Lebanese Orthodox Christians whose numbers approach half a million, augmented by another 200,000 or more abroad. Assisted by numerous bishops assigned to both the local dioceses as well as those in North and South America to which large numbers of Antiochene Orthodox have emigrated since the late 19th century, the patriarchate has long been a political battleground between a leftist faction backed by the Soviets through the Russian Orthodox Church and a succession of left-wing Syrian governments, and a strong pro-Western element in Lebanon and abroad which for the moment is in the ascendancy despite the virulently anti-Western trend current in Arab politics. Principal Orthodox centers in Syria and Lebanon are Beirut, Damascus, Tripoli and the Al-Kûra district to the immediate south,

Latakia and the Wâdî Al-Naṣâra (Valley of the Christians) to the southeast, and the urban centers of the Orontes Valley.

Greek Catholic. Next to the Maronites the largest and most prosperous Uniate community in the Arab East, the Greek Catholics are those indigenous Orthodox Christians who have rallied around the Catholic Rite established by Rome in 1724. Known in the Middle East as Roman Catholics (Rûm Kâthûlîk), Rome in this case referring to Constantinople, whose Greek inhabitants continue to call themselves Romans (Ρωμαῖοι), and also as Melkites (Malkîyûn), a term which the Orthodox abandoned after 1453, the Greek Catholics are governed by a patriarch, likewise of Antioch resident at Damascus, and bishops representing both the Levant and the large expatriate communities in the Americas which number some 150,000 faithful. In Lebanon, Syria, Jordan, and Israel they total a quarter of a million strong, and are found wherever their Orthodox parent community is or was prevalent. The major Melkite communities are located in Beirut, Damascus, Aleppo, Haifa and the villages of Northern Galilee, southern Lebanon in and around Tyre and Sidon, and the northern Biqâ' Valley, principally the city of Zaḥlah (in majority Melkite) and surrounding villages. In Egypt, congregations totaling 7,500 members are found in the principal urban centers. The present patriarch is Egyptian-born Maximos V Ḥakîm, elected in November, 1967, to his seat in Damascus after having served the Melkites in Israel as Archbishop of Acre and Galilee for nearly twenty years. They are particularly noted for their high standards of education among both clergy and laity.

Syrian Orthodox (Jacobite). The Syrian Orthodox community of Lebanon, Syria, and Iraq today numbers barely 175,000, a tiny but vigorous remnant of the once-powerful Monophysite Church of Syria which even as late as the 13th century constituted a near majority of the rural population in the Antiochene patriarchate. A rapid decline set in, however, following the collapse of the Crusading Kingdoms, and by the 19th century they had been reduced to some 200,000 souls concentrated in the very north of Syria around their patriarchal seat of Dayr Za'farân (the Saffron Monastery) near the city of Mârdîn, since 1920 a part of Turkey. Once renowned for its contributions to the intellectual life of the 'Abbâsid caliphate as transmitters of classical Greek scholarship into Arabic, and as scientists and doctors, Jacobite society less than a century ago was characterized by illiteracy and isolation.[50] To some observers this isolation was in large part their strength. The American traveler, J.L. Porter, who journeyed through Syria in 1853, observed that the Jacobites of Homs "have not the cringing, subdued look of the other Christians, but are independent in spirit and bold and resolute in conduct."[51]

Decimated by massacre and starvation during the First World War, Jacobites who survived returned to their earlier stronghold in the Orontes Valley where the patriarchate was reestablished at Homs (Ḥimṣ), or else settled in the virgin lands of the Syrian Jazîra. Until recently a rural community, they have gradually become urbanized over the past five decades and have greatly elevated their previous economic and educational status.[52] In 1957 their newly-elected patriarch, Ignatius III Ya'qûb, moved his seat to Damascus and now commutes frequently to Beirut where increasing numbers of Jacobites have settled since the Second World War. Other major concentrations of Jacobites are found in Damascus, Homs, and the surrounding villages (a few of which, such as Ṣadad, have been Jacobite since the 6th century), Aleppo, the cities of the Jazîra (e.g. Qâmishlî and Al-Ḥasaka), Baghdad, and a handful of villages near Mosul, e.g. Barṭala. Outside the Arab countries the major centers are the United States, Canada, and Brazil (approximately 35,000 total), while a small community (about 4,000 families) struggles to survive in the shadow of Dayr Al-Za'farân, the ancient patriarchal see, in Turkey. Among the least Arabicized of the Christian communities at the beginning of this century, despite their medieval heritage, they are now virtually indistinguishable from the other Christian and Muslim Arabs with whom they reside, and refer to themselves as "Non-Chalcedonian Orthodox," rather than "Monophysites," the ancient theological terms implying a heresy forgotten by all but theologians on both sides.

Syrian Catholic. Organized as a separate Uniate rite in 1783 after nearly two centuries of unsuccessful attempts by Rome to effect a Jacobite "return" en masse, the early Syrian Catholics were primarily those remnant Jacobites of Western Syria and the Mosul Plain, attracted to the educational and political advantages of closer indentification with Rome. In the Jacobite heartland to the north, however, Rome's efforts met with less success, though it was at Mardîn that the Catholic patriarch resided, largely for political reasons, until the First World War. Like their parent community, the Syrian Catholics suffered at the hands of the Turks and from the general ravages of war during the holocaust of 1914-1918, and following the French withdrawal from Cilicia and Edessa (Urfa) in 1920 they and most other surviving Christians emigrated in large part to Syria, Iraq, and Lebanon. The patriarchate was re-established in Beirut following the exodus, and a permanent residence completed in 1932 at Fûrn Al-Shabbâk, a Christian suburb to the southeast of the city. Numbering between 80-90,000 in the Fertile Crescent today, Syrian Catholics are found principally in Beirut, Aleppo, Damascus, Cairo, Baghdad, the Syrian Jazîra, and the city of Mosul with its surrounding villages, chiefly Qâra Qûsh. Like the Jacobites, large numbers of Syrian Catholics have emigrated to the Americas in recent years where many still maintain their own churches and individual rite. The present patriarch, Ignatius Antonius II Ḥayyik, was elected in 1968 to succeed his notable predecessor Cardinal Tappuni, patriarch and prince of the Church for over three decades who, as an early leader in the oecumenical movement, almost single-handedly brought about the recovery of his community from the disasters of the First World War and, more than anyone else, is responsible for its present-day prosperity, vitality, and high standard of education.

Maronite. Unique among the Christian communities of the Near East are the Maronites, alone confined to one major geographical concentration, alone possessing absolute religious and political unity. Their origins are obscure, but most ecclesiastical historians credit them with having been disciples of a Monothelite heretic of the late 7th century, an association Maronites today deny. The first of the Eastern Churches to embrace Catholicism with their own liturgy and customs intact (1180), the Maronites were reaffirmed in their orthodoxy by the Council of Florence in 1439, and since that time, records Henri Lammens, "their beliefs have been absolutely irreproachable."[53] By the beginning of the 16th century any voice of dissent from within the Church with regard to the union with Rome had been effectively silenced and in 1515 Pope Leo X sent to the then Maronite patriarch, Sham'ûn Al-Ḥadathî, a bull confirming papal recognition of Maronite Orthodoxy and lauding those beleaguered Christians as examplary followers of the true faith who shone forth "in the midst of infidels and bastions of error, as roses among thorns" (...quod inter Ecclesias Orientales, quasi in medio infidelitatis et erroris campis, Altissimus servos suos fideles veluti rosas inter medias spinas...).[54] It was not until 1736, however, that the organizational structure of the Maronite rite as it stands today was established. In that year the convocation of the Synod at Luwayza (a monastery within sight of Beirut) corrected certain lingering irregularities in ecclesiastical practice.

Despite its early and continued association with Rome, the Maronite Church "was never subject to the same degree of Roman tutelage as [were] the other Eastern Christian Churches,"[55] and maintained an acute sense of communal pride in its rite and in the political autonomy it had preserved during many centuries of Islamic domination. Under the direct administration of their own patriarch of Antioch,[56] resident at Qannûbîn in the highest part of Mount Lebanon near the village of Bisharrî, the Maronites labored to preserve this communal identity and unity, keeping themselves apart not only from neighboring Muslims and Druzes, but from other Christian communities as well, particularly the Orthodox of the coastal towns and Syrian Plain.[57] "In times of danger," writes Salibi, "they came together and fought fiercely and effectively, keeping themselves so independent that Mamlûk officials complained of the total lack of correspondence between the Northern Lebanese districts and the chancery in Cairo."[58]

Historically centered in the very north of Lebanon, the Maronites of Bisharrî and Ihdan gradually extended their settlements southward during the reign of Fakhr Al-Dîn in the early 17th century, and later during the years of Shihâbî rule, so that by the mid-19th century Maronite villages stretched in an almost unbroken chain from Jazzîn in the south to the 'Akkâr in the north. The Mountain's heart — from Bisharrî to Kisrawân and the fringe of Beirut itself — was exclusively theirs. Only in the south and coastal regions was Maronite hegemony contested by substantial numbers of Druzes, Sunni and Shî 'a Muslims, Orthodox and other Eastern Christians. The establishment of the *mutaṣarrifîya* in 1861 was a triumph of Maronite national goals, expanded during the succeeding half-century to envision nothing less than complete Lebanese independence from the Ottoman Empire under French protection.

Maronites in the Arab East today number close to 750,000, centered almost exclusively in Lebanon. Elsewhere they are found in the urban environments of Cairo, Damascus, and Aleppo, and in several villages in the Wâdî Al-Naṣâra region of Syria, and within a few miles of the Lebanese border in Israel, altogether totaling some 40,000. An additional 250-300,000 Maronites live today in the Americas, Australia, and Europe where they maintain a close contact with their patriarch, Cardinal Paul Méouchy (Bûlus Ma'ûshî), who for a number of years served as a priest among the Maronite communities of California and the Midwest. His residence during most of the year is at Bikirka, overlooking the Bay of Jûniyah a few miles north of Beirut.

In contrast to the general rule among Levantine Christians, the great majority of Maronites are peasantry, inhabiting scores of small towns and villages on the western slope of the Mountain. Only in Beirut is there a sizeable urban concentration of Maronites who are, nonetheless, heavily outnumbered by both Sunni Muslims and Greek and Armenian Orthodox Christians. But, whether urban or rural, they share a conviction that Lebanon is their country, in effect their national homeland. This sentiment reaches greatest intensity among the leading Maronite families for whom an independent Lebanon under the political aegis of any but a Maronite hegemony is unimaginable. Solidly Lebanese nationalist in politics, exclusively Catholic in religion, decidedly pro-French in culture, prosperous, educated, dedicated to their community, acting as a majority when in fact they are not,[59] the Maronites of Lebanon are today very much what Charles Mâlik half-jokingly called them a few years ago: the Christian answer to Islâm.

Copt. The largest of the Christian groups of the Arab East, the Copts, comprising what is officially called the Coptic Orthodox Church, are found almost exclusively in the Nile Valley where they number at least 3 million, equally divided between urban and rural environment. The major concentrations are in Cairo and in Upper Egypt south of Al-Minyâ. Their patriarch, successor to Dioskorus, the Monophysite patriarch of Alexandria condemned along with his doctrine at Chalcedon in 451, has resided in Cairo since the 11th century. His hierarchy consists of roughly twenty-five bishops and several hundred monastics from whom the patriarch is traditionally chosen, as is the case in the Jacobite Church. The larger Ethiopian Coptic Church, for centuries within the ecclesiastical jurisdiction of Alexandria, has been autonomous since the mid-1950's, though strong fraternal ties remain. Copts have long viewed themselves as the "true Egyptians," the direct descendants of the Pharaonic race, but have sided for the most part with their Muslim countrymen in support of Arab, and particularly Egyptian Arab, nationalism. Nowhere a majority within the country (except for a few score villages scattered among larger and more frequent Muslim settlements in Upper Egypt), the Copts have largely avoided the communal isolation that has characterized some of the smaller, less socially integrated Christian communities.

Coptic Catholic. The most recent of the Uniate Rites formed by Rome, the Coptic Catholic Church, though tracing its origins back to Saint Francis of Assisi's famous confrontation with the Ayyûbid Sultan Al-Kâmil in 1219, has been officially in existence only since 1895. Their patriarch, Michael Cardinal Sidarrus, governs a community of some 100,000 converts[60] from the Monophysite parent church, centered primarily in Cairo, Alexandria, Minyâ, and Asyûṭ, many of whom, like the Protestant Copts, maintain close ties with the larger Monophysite community they have theoretically abandoned.

Nestorian. More often referred to today as "Assyrians," the Nestorian community of the Fertile Crescent is a pitiful remnant of what was once a great Christian body. The oldest of the surviving Christian heresies, Nestorianism flowered in Mesopotamia and Persia following the condemnations of its doctrine — a form of Arianism — at Ephesus in 431. Tolerated by the Sassanid Persian emperors as a politically expedient haven for their otherwise troublesome Christian minority in the Tigris and Euphrates Valley because its hierarchy was bitterly anti-Byzantine, Nestorian Christianity claimed the majority of the indigenous Mesopotamians at the time of the Arab conquests and a number of Arabian tribes, settled and nomadic, as well. During the five centuries of 'Abbâsid rule the Nestorians flourished throughout Eastern Islam and contributed some of the finest scholars, translators, scientists, and surgeons of the age. The Nestorian Katholikos presided from his seat in Baghdad itself over an immense and wealthy community stretching from the Orontes Valley to China. Though forbidden to proselytize within Dâr Al-Islâm, Nestorian missionaries from the 8th through the 14th centuries carried their Gospel eastward to the court of the Great Khan and nearly succeeded in converting the entire Mongol nation. Many individual conversions were made, however, to the extent that the wife of Hûlâgu Khan, whose armies destroyed Baghdad and what remained of 'Abbâsid power in 1258, prevailed upon her husband to spare the Nestorians of that great city.

Despite the decline of Mesopotamia in the wake of the Mongols, the Nestorian Church continued to flourish, reaching its zenith under the Katholikos Yahb-Allâha, a Mongolian monk from Peking (d. 1317). He came close to effecting the mass conversion of the Tartar and Turkic peoples who were to overrun the entire Eastern half of Islam and Christendom as well as few decades later. During his reign he sent an emissary on a state visit to Canterbury, Paris, and Rome, who was received with great pomp and honor, effected a temporary reunion with Rome, and in 1288 received the sacrament from the Pope himself at Mass.[61]

The failure of the Nestorians properly to evangelize Turkestan contributed greatly to their sudden collapse less than a century later. At the close of the 14th century a second wave of Asian invaders, this time led by the Mongol Timur Lang (Tamerlane), a Shi 'a Muslim with no particular love of Christians, slaughtered virtually the entire urban population of Persia and Mesopotamia, stacking skulls of Nestorians alongside those of Muslims without the slightest discrimination. By the time of his death the once great Nestorian Church lay in ruins. Its only survivors were those living in the remotest parts of Western Asia, specifically the Zagros Mountains of Kurdistan, who had been joined by the few surviving refugees from the valleys below. Eventually the latter returned to Mosul and Baghdad, but the leadership of the Church was now in the hands of those whose existence had been peripheral to it only a decade or two earlier. Unlike the great Nestorian community of Baghdad, the surviving tribesmen to the north were not the least Arabicized, speaking rather the ancient Syriac that their urbanized brethren had clung to only in their liturgy. By the 19th century barely 100,000 remained, nearly all of them poor, illiterate tribesmen of the Zagros, "totally pastoral, supported more by their goats and sheep than by agriculture."[62] A few had made their way back to civilization on the plain of Mosul and on the shores of Lake Urumîya in Persia, but by and large these exposed individuals soon fell under the influence of the Catholic Chaldaean Rite and the Roman priests whose funds and schools supported it.

Unique among the Eastern Christians, the Nestorians drew their patriarchs from one family whose authority passed in hereditary succession from uncle to nephew. During the 19th century the Nestorians came under the influence of the British, and in 1886 the Archbishop of Canterbury established his Mission to the Assyrians. As self-proclaimed allies of Great Britain in World War I, the Nestorians suffered greatly at the hands of the enemy Turks and Kurds. In 1918 the entire community fled the Zagros after their patriarch, the uncle of the present patriarch, was assassinated. Abandoning their ancestral homes and their patriarchal seat at Qudshanis (near Hakkâri in present-day Turkey) they made a desperate attempt to reach British lines.

Only about 50,000 succeeded, and many thousands of these died of exposure and disease at the camp set up for them at Ba'qûba to the east of Baghdad while it was being decided what should be done. Gradually they were allowed to settle in Iraq, many on the northern frontier in sight of their former homes, and during the Mandate period served the British as the famous "Assyrian Levies," performing "outstanding services. . . indeed [they] acquired and saved Southern Kurdistan."[63] But in doing so they earned the distrust of the general Muslim leadership in Baghdad, and their fate at the hands of General Bakr Sidqi in 1933 has already been mentioned. In 1939 the patriarch, after six years of exile in Cyprus and England, re-established his seat in Chicago along with 15,000 of his community. 35,000 live today in Iraq and in northeastern Persia, plus some 15,000 in Syria and Lebanon. The authority of the patriarch is daily challenged, while factionalism, feuds, and internecine rivalries have plagued the Church, threatening its future existence:[64] a sad twist to the optimism voiced a century ago at Urumîya by the American missionary Justin Perkins, who had prayed that "this ancient church, once so renowned for its missionary efforts, would again awake from the slumber of ages, and become as clear as the sun, fair as the moon, and terrible as an army with banners to achieve victories for Zion."[65]

Chaldaean Catholic. In direct contrast to the disorganized and slowly disintegrating Nestorian Church in the East is its larger, prospering Uniate branch. Though in origins the second oldest Uniate community, the Chaldaean Church has been an effective force only since 1834, but in that short time has grown from a nucleus of some 20,000 souls to a prosperous community ten times that size, while its parent body has shrunk to perhaps half the membership it enjoyed one hundred years ago.[66] Its Katholikos since 1834 has been drawn from the same family as his Nestorian counterpart and resides today in Baghdad, as does the majority of his flock, especially since the late 1950's when the Kurdish insurrection began driving many village Chaldaeans to the safety of the capital. Outside Baghdad sizeable communities exist in Mosul, the surrounding villages of the Mosul Plain (notably Tall Kayf and Al-Qûsh), Teheran, the Syrian Jazîra, Aleppo, Beirut, and the United States (particularly Detroit). Periodically augmented by disaffected Nestorian congregations, their priests, and even bishops, the Chaldaeans, with their 200,000 adherents, today form the largest Christian community in Iraq, and, because of the care of their clergy (though not always the faithful) in avoiding the deadly game of Iraqi politics, the most secure.[67] Smaller communities are found today in Iran (11,000), Syria (7,000), Lebanon (2,500), and the Americas (25,000).

Armenians. Having adopted Christianity shortly before the Council of Nicaea in the early 4th century, the Armenians proudly consider themselves to be the oldest Christian nation. An Indo-European people whose homeland in historical times has always been at the foot of the Zagros Mountains in Eastern Anatolia, Armenia was for centuries a buffer state between Persia and Rome, and later between the Muslim caliphate and Christian Byzantium. In the wake of the Saljûq victory over the Emperor Romanus Diogenes in 1071 at Manzikert (Malazgirt) near Lake Van, the heartland of Armenia, many Armenians fled southward where they flourished for a few centuries in present-day Cilicia (southern Turkey) in the vacuum of power created by the head-on collision of four great military powers — the Saljûqs of Rûm, the Zanjids of Mosul, the Orthodox Byzantines, and the Catholic Crusaders. Known as Lesser Armenia, this region housed a large Armenian population up until the massacres of the first decades of this century, and in the interim had become the seat of an Armenian patriarchate, Sis (Cilicia), second in importance only to the great patriarchate of Echtmiadzin in Armenia proper, today located in Soviet Armenia.

As the Copts and the Jacobites, the Armenians refused to adhere to the Council of Chalcedon in 451, though their association with the Monophysite doctrine was, in many respects, a historical accident. Theirs was a purely nationalist reaction against Byzantine political encroachment which was to manifest itself frequently during the ensuing centuries. Armenians were strong local supporters of the Latin Crusades, deeming Western rule far preferable to that of the Byzantine emperor or the Saljûq sultan. Following the Ottoman conquest of Constantinople, the Armenians became the first to achieve separate *millet* status (1461) from that single Christian nation established by the sultan in 1453 and dominated by the Greeks, having made it clear to Muhammad (Mehmet) the Conqueror that subjection to the Oecumenical Patriarch was an abomination which even the might of the Sultan's armies could not enforce. And as their mountainous homeland formed the Empire's strategic eastern frontier with Persia, the Porte deemed Armenian ecclesiastical independence a small price to pay for Armenian loyalty.

On this basis Armenians and Turks co-existed peacefully for four centuries, during which time Catholic and Protestant missionaries were able to make only slight inroads into the large body of Gregorian (non-Chalcedonian) faithful. A Catholic Armenian Rite was organized in 1742 but gained converts largely from among the scattered Armenian communities of northern Syria and Lebanon.[68] Likewise the Protestants were successful only in the towns and cities of Anatolia where their schools and hospitals were established during the last half of the 19th century. It was the growing nationalist sentiment of the Armenian people which precipitated the Ottoman brutalities of the two decades preceding the First World War, and it was the latter conflict which brought final disaster to Armenia and forced its surviving inhabitants to flee eastward into Russia and southward towards the protecting armies of Britain and France. By 1925 some 150,000 Armenians were found huddled and destitute on the outskirts of Beirut, crowded into their ancient but tiny quarters in Aleppo, Damascus, and Baghdad, and resolutely building makeshift shelters in what were then the open wastes of the Jazîra. Aided by the French Mandate government, by Armenian, European, and American charities, and in the final analysis by their unbroken will to survive, these homeless refugees were within one generation securely established in the Levant as a growing and thriving community, and an economic force to be reckoned with wherever they had sunk roots.

In Lebanon in particular their presence was becoming essential to the maintenance of Christian hegemony. Without the 35,000 Armenians counted in the Census of 1932, the total Christian population would have fallen 25,000 short of the combined Muslim-Druze total; instead, the narrow Christian majority registered forty years ago serves today as the only official basis for continued Christian rule. During this period the Armenian population has grown to an unofficial 200,000, swelled by a steady immigration from neighboring Syria where the capitalist economy on which the Armenian mercantile class thrives has given way to Arab Socialism. In Egypt, likewise, the Armenian community has declined substantially over the past two decades, from 40,000 to less than 15,000. Centered largely in Beirut where they outnumber all other Christian communities, the Armenians are still heavily Gregorian, with small minorities of Catholics (30,000) whose influence is admittedly greater than their numbers as the result of the political standing of the late Cardinal Gregory Agaganian, twice a leading contender for the papacy, and Protestants (10,000), again a vital force exercised primarily through Hagazian College, the only Armenian University in the Middle East. Though even today barely Arabicized, the Armenian community as a whole is becoming in each succeeding generation more and more a part of its Arab environment. A small minority have elected to emigrate to the Soviet Union, where Armenia as a political entity still exists. For this reason the Soviet influence at Anṭilyâs, the Beirut suburb where the patriarch of Sis has resided since the First World War, is weak. But tales of political and economic woe from behind the Iron Curtain have strengthened the resolve of the majority of Lebanese Armenians to remain where they are valued as a vital force in the continued effort of native Arab Christians to sustain the precarious communal balance that has characterized the life and politics of Lebanon since 1920.

Latin and Protestant. Poised on the fringe of Arab Christendom are the small communities of native adherents to the Catholic and Protestant rites of the West. Largely the product of 19th century French, English, and American missions, the present-day Protestants and Catholics of the Middle East are converts or the descendants of converts from previously Orthodox or Eastern Rite Catholic families. Only in Bethlehem had remnants of the medieval Latin community survived as "fils authentique des sujets locaux de cet ancien Royaume Franc de Jérusalem fondé par Godefroy de Bouillon."[69] For the 19th-century traveler, H.B. Tristram, the "wondrous beauty of the children, so fair and European like" gave clear testimony of the Christian population's Norman ancestry.[70]

The modern Latin Catholic community dates from more recent times, specifically 1847, when the Jerusalem patriarchate was revived under Franciscan hegemony, and during the succeeding century attracted a certain following, particularly in Palestine, from among the more educated and Europeanized element in Arab Christian society. The reasons for these conversions are not frequently elaborated upon by the Church, but many knowledgeable observers, including Catholics such as Donald Attwater, attribute it more to material and social motivation than to sincere religious conviction.

> In the eyes of some people, to belong to the Latin Rite stands for civilization and influence, for attractive ideas of progress, for prestige, education, commerce, pseudo-Parisian clothes; Eastern Rites are looked down upon as being for mere peasants. Too often Westerners accept rather than oppose such wrong views...Hence non-Catholic Easterners insist that Rome wants to turn them all into Latins.[71]

Increasing opposition to the Latin patriarchate by Eastern Rite patriarchs and prelates following the withdrawal of Western political authority, reflecting as it does an increased Arab or Eastern consciousness among the Christian community and their growing desire for unity, is only now having a decided effect. "The young Orthodox intellectual," wrote George Every, presently editor of the *Eastern Churches Review*, on a visit to the area in the mid-1950's, "who thirty years ago might well have become a Protestant at the American University or a Catholic at the French College, is now devoted to his own Church. . . ."[72]

Almost entirely urban, well-educated, and strongly Western oriented, the Arab Latin Rite Catholics number today about

110,000, with major centers in Jerusalem, Bethlehem, Beirut, Cairo, Aleppo, Haifa, and Nazareth. Roughly two to three times the Latins in number, the Arab Protestants with their tradition of liberal education represent "the most progressive and Westernized element"[73] in Arab society. Predominantly Presbyterian in Lebanon and Syria, owing to the American mission which sponsored the first native congregation in 1848, the Protestants of Palestine and Jordan are Anglican, reflecting the strong British influence which prevailed in and eventually dominated the region from the mid-19th to the mid-20th centuries. In Egypt and Iraq, both American and English missions have been active, and there, as in all the Arab countries, tiny congregations of the many other Protestant sects — Adventists, Quakers, Pentacostalists, Baptists, even Jehovah's Witnesses — are found. Of the 250,000 native Protestants found in the Arab Crescent today, close to 200,000 are Egyptians of Coptic ancestry with communities in Cairo, Alexandria, Asyûṭ, Al-Minyâ, and many of the more remote towns and villages of Upper Egypt.[74] Another 35,000 are centered in Beirut, Aleppo, Tripoli, and Damascus, with smaller congregations scattered throughout the Christian villages of Lebanon and Syria. Aside from perhaps 1,500 Protestants of various sects (largely of Armenian or Assyrian background) living in Iraq, the remaining indigenous congregations are found in Amman, Jerusalem, Haifa, and the Arab villages of Judaea and Galilee. Virtually all the native Protestant churches, including the Lebanese Evangelical Church and the Palestinian Anglican community, are headed by presbyters and bishops from their own native group.

Egypt. The Nile Valley, despite its present-day association with either Pharaoh or Nasser, is rich in Christian history. Traditionally a part of the Holy Land, it was here that the Holy Family fled to escape Herod's wrath following the birth of Jesus. It was here also that Saint Mark, as first bishop of Alexandria, spread the Gospel among the large Jewish community of that city and later to a native population which received the Christian message with enthusiasm. It was Egypt which bore the brunt of the massive wave of persecution launched by the Emperor Diocletian

(281-305) during the first year of his reign. According to local tradition an apocryphal 144,000 faithful were put to the sword, and it is with this event in this "Year of the Martyrs" that the Coptic Calendar begins. By the beginning of the reign of Constantine (324-337) Egypt was almost entirely Christianized, and in the ensuing century nurtured the beginnings of Christian monasticism.[75] Today Egypt is the home of some 3 to $3^1/_2$ million Christians, the vast majority of whom are still faithful to their ancient Monophysite heresy, the remainder consisting of foreigners — Europeans, Greeks, and Levantines — and those relatively few families from the indigenous community who have associated with the Uniate Coptic Catholic Church, and the various Protestant communities, products of the 19th century American and English missions. The official Census of 1960 — the first conducted since the Revolution of 1952 — counted 1,905, 182 Christians out of a total population of 26 million. In percentage terms, these results showed Christians as having dropped from 8.1% of the total in 1940 to 7.3%, a not unexpected decline in view of the exodus of tens of thousands of the foreign Christian community (and many of the wealthier Copts as well) during the first years of the Nasser regime. Of the estimated 250,000 non-Egyptian nationals of Christian faith resident in Egypt in 1940, fewer than one-third remained in 1960. The Census listed only 82,000 foreign Christians, of whom 46,500 were Greeks, 12,700 Italians, and only 5,400 Arab (chiefly Levantine); these numbers, moreover, have declined even further in the past decade. It is true that many of the non-Egyptian Arabs took out Egyptian nationality after the 1952 Revolution in the vain hope of escaping the new government's massive nationalization schemes which disenfranchized the wealthy, and unquestionably parasitic, foreign community, but by and large the great majority had by 1960 returned to Lebanon or else emigrated to Europe, Australia, and the Americas. The number of Copts who have opted out of the new nationalist society during its first decade and a half cannot be estimated, but emigration of native Christians is a phenomenon of post-Suez Egypt.

Nevertheless, in that all but a handful of the 1,823,448

Christian Egyptian nationals counted in 1960 were native Egyptians of either the Monophysite Coptic, Coptic Catholic, or Protestant communities, the indigenous Christian population still comprised the traditional 7% of the total population which the government had been quoting officially since the earliest Census. In fact the indigenous Christian percentage of the total population of Egypt has risen slightly (from 6.26% in 1900 to 7.06% in 1960) since the beginning of the century.[76] Yet the Copts themselves are not satisfied with this figure, and many foreign observers have supported their assertion that Copts are considerably more numerous than the government is willing to admit. While few accepted the exaggerated claims of some that Copts constituted one out of every four or five Egyptians, many felt the actual number of indigenous Christians to be as much as twice that of the official estimate. The figure most often heard in recent years has been four million, quoted by several reputable, though not necessarily unbiased sources.[77] These unofficial estimates are, even so, in all probability exaggerated, and based only on inflated Coptic head counting. Probably the leading Western authority on Coptic Egypt, Dr. Otto F.A. Meinardus, for twelve years on the faculty of the American University of Cairo, concludes that, "by the 14th century, the number of Copts in Egypt had decreased to one-tenth or even one-twelfth of the total population, a percentage which more or less has been maintained to this day."[78] This would put the Christian percentage between 8 and 10%, rather than at the 15% share asserted by the champions of the four million figure, and not far from the official estimate of 7%.

There are, nevertheless, reasons to suspect that the government quotation is somewhat low, given official desire to maintain the image of Egypt as the leader among the Muslim Arab states, and the resultant tendency to admit to as few non-Muslims as possible. One must consider as well the reluctance on the part of many Copts, particularly those in rural and or heavily Muslim areas where the government is viewed with suspicion, publicly to confess Christianity when asked their religion by the official government Census takers. Anyone who has read Cairo's principal daily, *Al-Ahrâm,* carefully over an extended period of time, cannot help but have noticed the large number of Copts whose passings are reported in the obituary column — often a majority of those deaths publicly noted. And while it is to be expected that the relatively affluent and socially conscious Christian community would be more inclined to make the effort to publicize the deaths of members within their community, it should be noted that by no means all of those Christian deceased whose names appear are from well-to-do families. Not infrequently such notices are accompanied by photographs of the faithful departed, clad in the *jalabîya* of the poorest *fallâḥ*. As a prominent Coptic author, now an American citizen, observed to the author in late 1968, perhaps only when an individual is beyond the threat of discrimination does the family feel that his Christian faith may now be publicly acknowledged. In all probability, therefore, the proportion cited by Meinardus is correct, the number of Egyptian Christians lying between 3 and 3½ millions, or roughly 10% of the total population.

As in 1940, slightly over half of Egypt's Christians (52%) were found by the 1960 Census to be living in the area of Upper Egypt stretching from Maghâgha southward to Luxor (Al-Uqṣur). The four provinces encompassing this Coptic heartland, Al-Minyâ, Asyûṭ, Al-Sûhâj (Sohag), and Qinâ, registered a total population of nearly six million, of which 943,000, or 16%, were Christian. In some districts, including Asyûṭ city itself, the Christian population reached as high as 35%, but this was still far from the majority to which Meinardus alludes when he states that, "Generally speaking, Upper Egypt, the region between Minyâ and Luxor, and especially Asyûṭ, has remained largely Christian. . . ."[79] Nonetheless the Christian, though a minority, does somehow seem to predominate here, and the landscape, dotted with seemingly as many churches as mosques, not to mention some three-score predominantly Christian towns and villages, gives the impression that it is the Muslim, not the Christian, who is the intruder.

The second major area of Coptic concentration is the urban environment of Cairo and Alexandria, whose rapidly expanding populations included in 1960 some 500,000 native Christians (378,000 and 116,000 respectively) side-by-side with the great

TABLE I

Egypt — Confessional distribution of the total population as reported by the official Census of 1960

Muḥâfaẓa	Population	Christian	Muslim
UPPER EGYPT			
Aswân	385,350	18,381	366,965
Qinâ	1,351,358	113,158	1,238,192
Sûhâj	1,578,858	239,946	1,338,905
Asyûṭ	1,329,588	283,147	1,046,435
Al-Minyâ	1,560,311	306,286	1,254,015
Banî Suwayf	859,732	51,352	808,379
Al-Fayyûm	839,163	37,630	801,526
Al-Jîza	1,336,437	45,141	1,291,097
Total Upper Egypt	*9,240,797*	*1,095,041*	*8,145,514*
LOWER EGYPT			
Al-Qalyûbîya	988,055	20,710	967,322
Al-Manûfîya	1,347,953	32,165	1,315,767
Al-Buḥayra	1,685,679	27,785	1,657,852
Kafar Shaykh	973,019	9,167	963,844
Al-Gharbîya	1,715,212	38,818	1,676,344
Al-Daqahalîya	2,014,883	30,576	1,984,223
Al-Sharqîya	1,819,798	30,941	1,788,840
Dumyâṭ	387,953	2,519	385,410
Total Lower Egypt	*10,932,552*	*192,681*	*10,739,602*
GOVERNATES			
Cairo	3,348,779	409,002	2,933,019
Alexandria	1,516,234	153.474	1,359,468
Port Sa'îd	245,318	18,775	226,499
Ismâ'îlîya	284,115	13,741	270,342
Al-Suways (Suez)	203,610	16,370	187,206
Baḥr Al-Aḥmar (Red Sea)	25,452	1,896	23,556
Al-Wâdî Al-Jadîd (New Valley)	33,932	307	33,625
Al-Sahrâ Al-Gharbîya	103,453	929	102,518
Al-Sinâ (Sinai)	49,769	2,966	46,803
Total Governates	*5,810,662*	*617,460*	*5,183,036*
TOTAI	*25,984,011*	*1,905,182*	*24,068,152*

Jew	Other	% Christian 1960	% Christian 1940	Number of Settlements	With Christian Majority	Exclusively Muslim	Mixed Christian/Muslim
1	3	4.7	3.4	88	0	33	55
3	5	8.4	8.5	209	2	28	179
5	2	15.2	16.0	273	9	14	250
3	3	21.3	21.7	260	28	28	204
9	1	19.6	17.9	352	25	15	312
—	1	6.0	5.5	221	1	31	189
6	1	4.5	4.7	166	0	26	140
53	146	3.4	2.8	186	1	17	168
80	*162*	*11.8*	*12.1*	*1,755*	*66*	*192*	*1,497*
6	17	2.1	2.1	156	1	34	121
11	10	2.4	2.6	305	4	113	188
10	32	1.7	1.6	436	0	170	266
3	5	0.9	—	199	1	74	124
31	19	2.3	1.3	344	0	171	173
25	59	1.5	2.0	439	7	257	175
10	7	1.7	2.0	441	2	180	259
11	13	0.7	1.4	64	0	31	33
107	*162*	*1.7*	*2.0*	2,384	*15*	1,030	1,339
5,587	1,171	12.2	15.7	207	4	7	196
2,760	532	10.1	18.2	117	0	1	116
6	38	7.7	—	—	—	—	—
1	31	6.7 { 4.8	— } 14.5	—	—	—	—
4	30	8.0	—	—	—	—	—
—	—	7.4	1.0	—	—	—	—
—	—	0.9	0.4	—	—	—	—
6	—	0.9	1.1	—	—	—	—
—	—	6.0	7.4	—	—	—	—
8,364	*1,802*			*324*	*4*	*8*	*312*
8,551	*2,126*	*7.33*	*8.09*	*4,463*	*85*	*1,230*	*3,148*

majority of Egypt's dwindling foreign Christian community (31,000 in Cairo, 37,000 in Alexandria). Only sixty years earlier, Copts had been a small minority (34,400) nearly lost amidst a total Christian community of 162,125, chiefly Greeks and expatriate Syrians and Lebanese. In Cairo itself, a handful of Copts (13,000) were still found clustered about their historic churches in what had once been the Roman fortress of Babylon, and a larger concentration (37,000) still clung to the historic old quarters of Al-Azbakîya and Qaṣr Al-Nîl, traditionally Coptic since medieval times, where Christians today constitute a large minority (40% and 26% respectively). But it is in the relatively new part of the city north of the walls where the majority of Christian Cairenes live, particularly the districts of Shubrâ, Rawḍ Al-Faraj, Al-Zâhir, and modern Heliopolis (Miṣr Al-Jadîda) which together held 60% of the city's Christians in concentrations ranging from 17% (in Al-Sâḥil) to 28% (in Heliopolis) of the total population. Of the remaining 400,000 Copts counted in 1960, half were scattered among the heavily Muslim towns and villages of the Delta, 150,000 were concentrated in the towns of the less-heavily Christian Upper Egyptian provinces of Al-Jîza (Gîza), Banî Suwayf, Al-Fayyûm, and Aswan, and another 50,000 in the three cities of the Suez Canal district, since 1967 relocated for the most part in Cairo.

Unlike the Muslim population, Egypt's Copts were prone to urban living. In 1960 nearly half (47%) were living in towns and cities with populations exceeding 35,000, as opposed to less than one-third of the Muslims (31%), and the general trend of rural migration to the cities has become even more pronounced among Christians in the last decade. Of the rural Christians, only some 160,000 (less than 20%) were found in 1960 to be living in the Christian environment of the 75 predominantly Coptic towns and villages. And fully one-third of these (61,000) were concentrated in the ten principal Christian settlements, among them Naqâda (7,700), Al-Kashah (6,500), Al-Bayadîya (6,400), Abû-Qirqâṣ (6,100), and Dayr Abû-Ḥinnis (6,000).[80] The remainder of the Christian population lived among Muslim majorities in some 2,800 villages of mixed religious composition that dot the Nile Valley. Only in the lower Delta region — the

27 *marâkiz* (subdistricts) stretching along the coast eastward from Alexandria (exclusive of the cities of Damanhûr, Maḥallat Al-Kubrâ, and Al-Manṣûra) — were Christians virtually unknown: less than 20,000 out of a total population of 3.5 million.[81]

The Christian birthrate pattern, as derived from the 1960 Census figures, reflects those trends found elsewhere in the Arab East. Though equal to Muslim productivity in rural areas, Christians in the urban districts of Cairo, Alexandria, and the Canal Zone fell considerably below Muslims in total number of live births. Of the 753,000 infants less than one year of age and possessing Egyptian nationality at the time of the Census, 50,600 or 6.7% were Christian, as opposed to the indigenous Christian percentage of the total population which stood at 7.06%. In Upper Egypt the Christian percentage of the total number of infants (11.8%) was exactly that of their share of the total population of that region, and in Lower Egypt it was only slightly less (1.61% as opposed to 1.73%). But in Cairo and Alexandria, and to a lesser extent the Suez Canal cities, the discrepancies were significant. Despite this confessional imbalance at birth, however, the generally higher standard of living enjoyed by Christian Egyptian, even among the peasantry, contributed to a higher rate of survival during the crucial years before maturity. In all but three provinces the Christian percentage in 1960 of those falling between the ages of five and twenty was higher than the Christian share of the total population including non-Egyptians: 7.6% as compared with 7.3%. Thus, despite a slightly lower birthrate, a tendency to marry later than Muslims (particularly in the urban areas where the percentage of married Christians under 20 was half that of the Muslims), not infrequent instances of conversion to Islam for reasons of political advancement or an easier divorce, and emigration on the part of young members of the wealthy, educated elite, it would appear that the Christian rate of growth in recent years has been very close to that of the Muslim population. And until such time as a less controversial tally of the Christian population is made by the government it will be fruitless to attempt to determine if the factors which at present threaten to inhibit Christian growth are in fact having a visible effect on the Copt-Muslim ratio, stable now for many centuries.

Palestine - Jordan. The Holy Land today, despite the predominance of Jews in the state of Israel and Muslims in the Kingdom of Jordan, is still home to a deeply-rooted Arab Christian population of nearly 200,000, almost entirely Greek Orthodox in origins. At the time of the Crusades there still existed large rural communities of Jacobites as well as smaller settlements of Nestorians and Armenians, but during the long period of Ottoman rule the ancient Melkite population gradually absorbed the Heterodox communities so that today only in Jerusalem and Bethlehem are non-Chalcedonian Orthodox to be found, centered around the churches of the Holy Sepulchre and the Nativity where both the Armenian and Jacobite Churches have resident rights. During the late 18th century, however, the Roman Catholic Church began seriously to encourage local Orthodox Christians to identify with the newly-created Greek Catholic Rite, and by the establishment of the British Mandate in 1920 had successfully recruited about 25% of Palestinian Orthodoxy, while another third had been lured away by the Latin Catholic and Protestant missions with their fine schools and dedicated clergy. The Orthodox Church in contrast was sadly divided over the question of ecclesiastical domination by the Greek patriarchate of Jerusalem, which cared little for the state of the relatively poor, Arabic-speaking community for which it was responsible. Thus governed by a Greek-speaking hierarchy that spoke no Arabic and included a poorly educated, generally corrupt lower clergy that had no authority, the indigenous Orthodox population was gradually drained of its most active and forward-looking element.

The official Census of 1931 registered 850,000 Arabs of Palestinian or other Arab nationality resident within the boundaries of the British Mandate (exclusive of Transjordan). Of these 80,500, or just under 10%, were Christian, half of them (38,100) Orthodox, the remainder being divided among Latin (18,000) and Melkite (12,500) Catholics, Protestants (5,500), Maronites (3,500), Armenians (3,000), and Jacobites (1,000). The latter two communities were exclusively urban and confined to the Holy precincts of Jerusalem and Bethlehem. The Latin population was likewise centered there, with smaller urban concentrations at Nazareth, Jaffa, and Haifa, and an occasional rural settlement such as Al-Zabâbida near Nablus. Maronites were found only in Haifa and in their two villages of Kafar Bir'im and Jish on the Lebanese frontier, while Protestants were scattered throughout all the towns and were a strong presence in such villages as Bi'r Zayt, Al-Zâbâbida, and Al-Râfidîya in Judaea, and in Kafar Yâsîf near Acre.

The Orthodox Palestinians were strong in Jerusalem, where the Arab population was equally divided among Christian and Muslim, in Bethlehem and its two equally Christian suburbs of Bayt Jâlâ and Bayt Sâḥûr, Râm Allah and a half-dozen Christian villages of Judaea such as Al-Ṭayyiba, Bi'r Zayt, Jifna, and 'Ayn Arîk, among larger Muslim communities in Jaffa, Ramla, Lydda, and Acre on the coastal plain, in half-Catholic Nazareth, and in several of the Christian hill-towns of Galilee, among them Al-Râma, I'billîn, and Kafar Yâsîf. Here also the Orthodox were prominent among the Christian minorities of the more numerous Muslim settlements. Melkites were particularly strong in Galilee, forming half the Christian population of Haifa, a large minority in Nazareth (20%), a large majority of the Christian halves of Shafâ 'Amru and Mughâr, and exclusive majorities in the Christian villages of Mi'ilyâ, Fasûṭa, Iqrît, Al-Baṣṣa, and 'Aylabûn.

To the east of the Jordan, Christians numbered between 25-30,000, with principal centers at Mâdabâ, Al-Karak, Al-Salṭ, 'Ajlûn, and Al-Ḥuṣn. Except in Mâdabâ the Orthodox were the predominant sect, with smaller minorities of Melkites and Latin Catholics.

The Palestine War of 1948-1949 and the crystallization of a large, permanent Zionist state west of the Jordan upset to a considerable degree the traditional demographic pattern of the area. In the wake of the retreating Arab armies an estimated 55-60,000 Arab Christians fled from their homes along the coast and from the Galilean highlands, as did probably half a million Muslims. Of the Christians, about half (29,000) settled in Jordan, either in the nearby West Bank districts clustered around traditional Christian centers such as Jerusalem, Bethlehem, and Râm

Allah (7,000, 4,500, and 5,500 respectively) or in 'Ammân and Mâdabâ to the east (9,000).[82] The remaining half of the dispossessed Christians, particularly those from Haifa and Galilee, fled to Lebanon where a sympathetic Christian government allowed them citizenship, often clandestinely, and always over the opposition of the Muslim population which resented the fact that few Muslim Palestinians were permitted this privilege. Undoubtedly President Bishâra Al-Khûrî was as eager as any of his Christian countrymen to take advantage of this opportunity to add more non-Muslims to the civil lists, particularly as recent vital statistics had shown the local Muslim birthrate to have soared beyond that of the native Christian communities since the end of the Second World War. On the other hand Christians from occupied Palestine enjoyed more practical advantages as well.

Under the best of circumstances the acquisition of Lebanese citizenship, like any bureaucratic exercise in the Middle East at the time, required a considerable financial outlay in the way of discreet bribes, and for the most part the Christian refugees were in a far better economic position to be able to do this. Moreover, there were few Palestinian Christian immigrants who could not point to a close relative, either direct or through marriage, who already enjoyed Lebanese nationality, and in a country which is always welcoming back former emigrés or sons of emigrés, proof of a Lebanese parent or grandparent was tantamount to a guarantee of citizenship. Few Muslim Palestinians had these family ties, and as a result they were generally confined to refugee camps while all but a small minority of the Christian refugees were absorbed within the economy of Lebanon after a year or two, or else emigrated to Europe, the Americas, or Australia. Several exclusively Christian refugee camps were maintained, however, such as Ḍubayya, northeast of Beirut, the first Palestinian camp to fall to the *Katâ'ib* forces in January 1976.

The areas of Palestine hardest hit by the Christian exodus were the coastal cities of Jaffa, Ramla, Lydda, and Haifa, along with the new city of Jerusalem, all of which passed under Israeli administration. The following table, showing the Arab and Christian population of these cities in 1931 and in 1961 clearly indicates the extent of the decline.

TABLE II [83]

City	Population 1931 Total Arabs	Population 1931 Christian	Population 1961 Total Arabs	Population 1961 Christian
New Jerusalem	19,223	11,526	2,313	1,403
Haifa	34,560	13,827	9,468	6,663
Jaffa	44,657	9,132	5,886	2,481
Ramla	10,345	2,184	2,166	1,302
Lydda	11,250	1,210	1,582	363

Only in Nazareth and Galilee did the Christian presence remain strong. Here both the natural reluctance of most Christians to leave their homes and the fact that the entire area was surrounded by Israeli forces at the time of the armistice in 1949 prevented a large-scale exodus. Of those remaining in Israel at the time of the cease-fire (about 30,000 Christians and 110,000 Muslims) the great majority have stayed, and despite a small, continuous emigration on the part of the young and educated Arabs who want no part of the second-class future that the Israeli state promises them, the Christian population had grown to nearly 60,000 by the time of the 1967 War. Likewise in Jordan the mixed community of native and immigrant Christians had grown — from 93,500 in 1951 to 115,000 ten years later. Thus by the outbreak of the celebrated Six-Day War, the Palestinian Christian community had once again reached the 175,000 figure at which it had stood before the initial hostilities began twenty years earlier. The official British estimate of the Christian population in 1944 was 135,500 in Palestine and 30,000 in Transjordan, a total of 165,550. The Israeli Census of 1961 counted 50,500 Christians, while the Jordanian Census of 1964 listed 115,500 (including 6,600 temporarily abroad) for a total of 166,000; today this figure is approaching 200,000 despite a second mass dislocation of Palestinian Arabs following the June War of 1967. An estimated 450,000 refugees previously living on the West Bank were reported to have fled to the East Bank, and from there another 150,000 emigrated to Kuwait and the other Gulf States. This time, however, very few of the refugees were Christians since hardly any settled Palestinians were uprooted, and by 1967 only a few thousand Christians remained in the United Nations refugee camps. In a few cases, Christian Arab leaders who objected vocally to the Israeli annexation of Old Jerusalem were forced to leave, among them Anṭûn 'Aṭallah, prominent Orthodox banker and former Jordanian Minister of Foreign Affairs (1963-1964), a post to which he was re-appointed following his exile. In all, probably no more than two or three thousand Christians were encouraged or forced to seek refuge in 'Ammân. According to figures published in the 1968 Israel Yearbook, the Christian population of Old Jerusalem and the West Bank stood at 12,000 and 30,000 respectively, roughly equal to the Jordanian Census figures of 1964 which counted 12,253 Christians in Jerusalem and its immediate suburbs (Jabal Al-Ṭûr, Bayt Ḥanîna, and Shu'fât) and 33,601 elsewhere on the Jordanian West Bank. Thus in 1970 the Christian population of what had been the Mandates of Palestine and Transjordan stood at approximately 190,000: some 75,000 within pre-June 1967 boundaries of Israel inclusive of the old city of Jerusalem, 30,000 in the West Bank districts, and roughly 85,000 in what remained of Husayn's Jordan.[84]

Within the same area, however, significant changes had taken place in the actual distribution of the population as compared with the demographic status quo of 1945. These changes were fourfold: 1) a major depopulation of traditional Christian centers along the coast (reference Table II); 2) a marked increase in the Christian population of Amman, from about 5,000 to more than 40,000 since 1948; 3) an increase in the already substantial urban concentration of the Christian population resulting in the loss of Christian majorities in several West Bank villages; and 4) the settlement of Muslim refugees in previously Christian towns and villages on both the West and East Banks following 1949 which erased or greatly reduced previous Christian majorities. This was true not only in Jordan but in Israel as well where a number of villages were demolished for security reasons (including three Christian Settlements; Al-Baṣṣâ, Iqrît, and Kafar Bir'im) and their populations resettled. The demise of Al-Baṣṣâ is particularly sad in light of its lengthy description by Tristram in 1865 as one of the most flourishing Christian Arab settlements in Galilee.[85]

In many cases, as Table III shows, the Christian decline had begun long before the Palestine War of 1948-1949; even in the brief period between the 1922 and 1931 Mandate Censuses, many villages had registered significant Christian losses. There were about ten exceptions to this rule, however — villages where the Christian percentage remained stable or even increased at the same time the total population was growing. In the two cases of significant Christian increase — Jish and Tarshîḥa — both the flight of the Muslim population in 1949 and the resettlement of Christians from the villages of Iqrît and Kafar Bir'im, destroyed by the Israeli military because of their close proximity to the Lebanese border, were the major factors contributing to this change.

On the East Bank of the Jordan the formerly Christian towns of 'Ajlûn, Mâdabâ, and Al-Karak (in 1964 respectively 37.5%, 32.0%, and 21.9% Christian) acquired large Muslim majorities as the result of the resettlement of refugees from the West. Thus the indigenous Christians who constituted majorities in 26 Palestinian villages and the Arab population of Jerusalem in 1922 were reduced to 15 such settlements in 1964, not including the cities of Haifa and New Jerusalem (that portion of the city west of the old walls) where the indigenous Christians accounted for a majority of the total Arab population. An additional 7 Christian settlements on the East Bank (notably Al-Ḥuṣn near Irbid with a population of 3,728, 55% Christian, and Fuḥayṣ near Al-Salṭ with 2,946 inhabitants, 81% Christian) raised the total number of predominantly Christian towns and villages to 22. Though encompassing a larger percentage of the native Christian population than in Egypt — 35% as opposed to 10% — these islands of predominantly Christian environment were for the most part surrounded by heavily Muslim districts, and in very few cases contiguous one with another, unlike Lebanon and the Wâdî Al-Naṣâra of Syria where Christian settlements were geographically linked in contiguous chains.

In addition to the four factors mentioned earlier as contributing to the recent changes in the pre-1948 patterns of Christian

TABLE III

Arab towns and villages in Palestine where the Christian percentage of the population declined substantially 1922-1972. Those villages in *italics* are located within the pre-1967 borders of Israel.

Town	Arab Population				Percentage Christian			
	1972	1961/64	1931	1922	1972	1961/64	1931	1922
Nazareth	33,837	25,045	8,815	7,371	45.2	51.6	61.4	65.8
Bethlehem	—	22,453	7,320	6,658	—	32.3	79.1	83.9
Râm Allah	—	14,759	4,286	3,104	—	56.0	87.9	95.8
Bayt Jâlâ	—	7,966	3,377	3,101	—	55.7	93.2	98.7
Shafâ 'Amru	11,616	7,216	2,823	2,228	39.2	44.7	49.6	55.2
Bayt Sâhûr	—	5,316	1,942	1,519	—	65.0	79.2	81.2
Sakhnîn	8,335	5,150	1,891	1,575	7.1	8.4	10.7	13.1
Kafar Kannâ (Cana)	5,244	3,546	1,378	1,175	20.5	25.9	35.0	42.1
Bi'r Zayt	—	3,253	1,233	926	—	43.8	70.6	83.9
Al-Râma	3,922	2,986	1,142	847	61.7	66.6	66.3	79.8
Kafar Yâsîf	3,808	2,975	1,057	870	60.0	58.7	72.1	76.4
Al-Rayna	4,126	2,861	1,015	787	26.2	29.7	38.3	55.1
Yâfât Al-Nâṣira	4,932	2,540	833	615	28.6	31.3	45.2	65.0
Ṭur'an	3,893	2,303	961	768	19.9	23.4	27.9	29.4
Dayr Ḥannâ	2,976	1,690	563	429	13.9	17.7	27.9	29.4
Al-Ṭayyiba	—	1,677	1,125	961	—	70.1	92.3	99.3
'Ayn Arîk	—	1,645	494	365	—	18.8	44.5	54.8
Abu Sinân	3,586	1,580	605	518	26.3	37.6	45.3	47.7
'Abûd	—	1,521	910	754	—	47.7	51.6	53.3
Al-Bi'na	2,302	1,496	651	518	16.5	23.3	32.3	40.0
Al-Makr	2,441	1,397	331	281	10.5	13.2	22.4	26.7
Al-Judayda	2,504	1,303	249	224	13.2	17.1	41.4	47.1
'Aylabûn	1,506	1,010	404	319	82.7	94.4	92.2	100.0
Râfidîya	—	923	355	418	—	39.1	80.9	73.3
Jifna	—	758	676	447	—	70.6	78.4	100.0
Nisf Jubayl	—	228	210	162	—	21.9	50.0	54.3

settlement must be added the undoubted higher Muslim birthrate and the Christian propensity for emigration. The Christian percentage of the total number of births in Jordan has always been lower than their percentage of the total population, at least since such records were first published. In 1951, at a time when Christians represented 7.5% of all Jordanians, they accounted for only 5.7% of the births for that year, and in 1964, the year of the Census which showed Christians as having slipped to

6.6% of the national total, their share of all births for that year had shrunk to 3.8%. The last complete figures published before the events of June 1967, those of the year 1966, give them only 3.7% of live births. Compounding this failure of Christians to reproduce at the same high rate as Jordanian Muslims was the high Christian death rate. In 1966, for instance, Christians registered 6.5% of all deaths, thus accounting for only 3.3% of the net national population growth for that year.[86]

In dealing with the raw birth figures, however, it should be pointed out that as elsewhere in the Middle East, Christian losses to infant mortality during the first year after birth were somewhat less than those of Muslims, so that the real birthrate of Christians — that based on the infants surviving their first year of life— was in fact slightly higher than the raw figures would indicate. Over the eight year period 1959-1966 Christians, according to official figures averaged 4.6% of Jordanian live births, but only 3.2% of infant deaths during the same period.[87] Moreover, in dealing with reported births and deaths among the Muslim population, one must take into consideration the practice common to the tens of thousands of Muslim refugees living in U.N. camps

TABLE IV

Arab towns and villages in Palestine where the Christian percentage of the population remained relatively stable or increased 1922-1972. The villages in *italics* are located within the pre-1967 borders of Israel.

	Arab Population				Percentage Christian			
Settlement	1972	1961/64	1931	1922	1972	1961/64	1931	1922
Fasûṭa	1,596	1,209	668	459	100.0	99.9	88.2	96.8
Mi'ilyâ	1,565	1,131	579	442	100.0	99.0	95.5	96.8
Jish	1,736	1,498	735	721	81.5	87.5	47.4	52.7
Tarshîḥa	1,823	1,340	2,522	1,880	63.8	75.5	18.4	19.0
Al-Zabâbida	—	1,474	632	524	—	73.1	85.6	79.8
I'billîn	3,674	2,407	1,116	817	59.1	62.2	59.4	64.6
Al-Buq'ay'a	2,253	1,491	747	589	33.4	29.0	33.0	38.2
Mughâr	6,477	4,005	1,733	1,377	29.1	32.5	31.7	31.7
'Isfîya	4,252	2,902	1,105	733	18.7	21.6	16.9	17.2
Kafar Summay'	906	576	213	171	19.9	21.2	16.0	14.0
Acre	8,202	7,074	7,660	6,342	16.0	19.2	19.8	21.2

to fabricate births and more often to fail to report deaths in order that the meagre family livelihood might be supplemented through means of the deceased or ficticious individual's ration card. In reality, therefore, the Muslim death rate is probably substantially higher both among infants and adults than that officially reported, and the real Christian birthrate somewhat greater than that derived from government statistics. In support of this hypothesis is the survey of the financial status of 2,924 Ammani household heads and their families conducted by the government in 1960, which showed the average size of the individual household or family interviewed to be slightly higher among Christians: 6.4 members as opposed to 6.0 among Muslims.[88]

Nevertheless, there is no question that the Christian birth rate in Jordan, even when adjusted, has been declining in recent years and that emigration has taken its toll here as elsewhere in the Levant. One definite indicator of this trend is the low percentage of Christian marriages. Between 1960 and 1966 the Christian percentage of marriages performed in Jordan was at no time higher than 3.8% (1960), and fell in 1965 to only 1.1%, rising again to 3.0% in 1966. Clearly a significant number of Christians of marriageable age had left Jordan to live, and presumably to marry, elsewhere. In support of this trend are the official government statistics which showed a net Christian growth of 35,000 from 1951 to 1964 (45,400 births versus 10,400 deaths); when added to the 1951 Census figure of 93,400 Christian residents in Jordan, this gives a figure of 128,800 when in fact the Census of 1964 counted only 108,800 resident Christians, a discrepancy of 20,000. The Census accounts for only 6,600 of these missing Jordanian Christians temporarily living abroad. The remaining 13,400 must be assumed to have emigrated.

In Israel the 1961 Census likewise registered a lower Christian Arab birthrate: 4.7 live births per Christian woman as opposed to 5.1 per Muslim woman. Significantly the same Census showed Christians under the age of 5 years to comprise only 13.9% of the total Arab population while registering 19.3% of the population as a whole. Unlike Jordan, Christians in Israel continued to marry in proportion to their national percentage

TABLE V[89]
Israel — Number of marriages in 1965 by religion, average age, sex.

Religion	Percentage of total non-Jewish population 1965	Number of marriages 1965	Percentage of total	Average Age Male	Average Age Female
Christian	19.3	415	18.2	28.0	22.4
Muslim	70.7	1,648	72.2	24.6	20.6
Druze	10.0	220	9.6	25.4	20.4

strength, but as late as 1965 were doing so at an appreciably older age than either the Muslims or Druzes.

By 1972 the Christian share of non-Jewish marriages had dropped to 16.0% vs. 73.2% and 10.8% for Muslims and Druzes respectively, figures roughly approximate to the total population distribution for the same year: Christians 79,600 (16.7%), Muslims 358,600 (75.2%), and Druzes 38,700 (8.1%).[90] As in neighboring Arab states, however, the impact of the higher Muslim live-birthrate was, in Israel, lessened somewhat by a rate of infant mortality that exceeded that of Christians. The 1961 Census reported the percentage of Muslim children who died before reaching the age of five years to be 20.1%, as compared with 14.5% for Christian Arab children. Significantly, the average size of the Christian Arab household as reported in the 1961 Census was only slightly smaller than that of the Muslim Arab: 5.0 as opposed to 5.4 members, indicating that in the end the higher Muslim birthrate was largely cancelled out by the lower rate of infant mortality and the greater longevity of the Christian.[91] Since 1961, however, the Christian rate of reproduction has declined substantially, to only 1.64 children per family as reported in the Census of 1972, compared with 2.38 in 1961. The figure is still slightly above the net Jewish rate of 1.47, but far below that of the Muslims (4.07) and Druzes (3.50) whose rates have declined only slightly, from 4.20 and 3.98 respectively, over the same period.[92]

Far more threatening to the future of the Israeli Christian Arab community than its lower rate of procreation was the propensity for emigration; for, as the best educated, most affluent, and urban of the Israeli Arabs, Christians were more prone to seek better compensation for their training and abilities in the Christian countries of the West, and as mentioned earlier, to avoid the second-class stigma inevitably attached to non-Jews in the Zionist Israeli state. No sectarian emigration figures are available for Israel (largely because the government does not wish to acknowledge publicly the large number of Jews, especially from the Sephardim, who are emigrating as well), but no less a personage than the Melkite Archbishop of Galilee, Georges Ḥakîm, spiritual leader of Israel's largest Christian community until his elevation to the patriarchate in 1967, has publicly acknowledged the trend among his flock and that of other Christian groups to leave their homes in Israel. "Still we are emigrating," he remarked several years ago, "slowly but steadily."[93] The population projection of the Israeli Central Bureau of Statistics up to 1993 estimates that while Christians in present-day Israel (that of the pre-1967 boundaries plus Jordanian Jerusalem) will number over 120,000 as opposed to 79,600 in 1972, this will represent only 11.5% of the total non-Jewish population, with the Druze declining to 7.7% and the Muslims increasing to 80.8%.[94] Barring major upheavals and unexpected changes, therefore, Christians in Israel can, by the year 2000, expect to account for only half the relative strength they enjoyed within the total Arab community in 1950.

Within the total Christian community of Israel and Jordan little change has taken place in the sectarian composition despite the alteration of demographic patterns. Of the 190,000 estimated to be living within the former boundaries of the Palestine-Transjordanian Mandates today, probably 85,000 are Orthodox, an equal number Catholic (45,000 Melkite and 40,000 Latin), 7,500 Protestant, 2,500 Maronite, and 10,000 other (Armenian, Jacobite, and Copt). Their geographic centers of strength are much the same as they were in 1949 with a few minor changes, and the resettlement of the predominantly Orthodox population of Jaffa, Ramla, and New Jerusalem in the East Bank, notably Amman.

Of the 160,000 Christians counted by the Israeli and Jordanian censuses of 1961 and 1964 respectively, only 22,000 or

13.5% were at the time living in settlements of less than 2,500 population, and well over half were concentrated in the major population centers of Amman, Zarqa, Jerusalem, Bethlehem, Haifa, and Nazareth. The Muslim population, by way of contrast, was about 75% rural in Israel, and less than half urbanized in Jordan.

Lebanon. The creation of Greater Lebanon in 1920 by the extension of the frontiers of the Ottoman *mutaṣarrifīya* was acknowledged at the time by Christians as having reduced their majority to only slightly more than half, but just how narrow their margin was did not stand revealed until the new Republic conducted its first Census in 1932. It was to prove to be the last. The results indicated a resident Christian population of 396,746 out of a total of 793,226 — an absolute Christian majority by 266 souls. The combined population of the Sunni and Shî'a Muslim communities and the Druze sect was only some 10,000 short of the Christian total, the remainder being made up of Jews, 'Alawîs, Bahais, and other diverse groups. Such a razor-thin margin would have made continued Christian hegemony impossible were it not for the presence of two highly significant factors: the existence of a large Christian emigré nation outside of Lebanon which had maintained its Lebanese citizenship though non-resident, and the sharp division of nationalist sentiment among the non-Christian population.

Of the nearly 200,000 Lebanese known to have left the Mountain during the half century prior to the creation of Grand-Liban, fully one-third, 67,403 individuals, opted for citizenship in Lebanon under the 1932 Census, and of these, 82% were Christian and over 50% Maronite. When added to the resident population, the emigré citizens boosted the Christians to a comfortable 54,000 lead over the Muslim-Druze total (see Table VI). To the Christians, the emigrant community was a vital contribution both numerically and economically to the nation. There was scarcely a village in Lebanon, and not a Christian family in the whole country, without representatives abroad; and the cultural impact of the many who had returned after years in the West and the enormous financial assistance rendered by the remunerations to relatives at home by those still abroad have proven to have been of great importance in shaping the lives of Lebanese Christians during this century. Many Lebanese towns and villages such as Zaḥlah have sent many times their population abroad and today enjoy new and modern schools, churches, and clinics which are gifts from their affluent sons and daughters overseas. President Bishâra Al-Khûrî termed them "la moitié perdu du Liban,"[95] and Lebanese Christians themselves speak of two Lebanons: *Lubnân Al-Muqîm* (Lebanon resident) and *Lubnân Al-Mughtarib* (Lebanon resident abroad).[96] Encouraged by the Christian-dominated government of Greater Lebanon, many thousands more of the emigré community chose to guard their native citizenship and to register themselves and their children on the village rolls. During the two year period, 1937-1939, thousands took final advantage of Article 34 of the Treaty of Lausanne permitting emigré option for citizenship status, more than doubling the figure of non-resident Lebanese to 159,571, 84% Christian, and nearly 60% Maronite.

For the Muslim communities this policy represented a direct threat to their security within the political structure of Lebanon and to their hopes of one day surpassing the Christian communities in total population. Before agreeing to an independent Lebanon, therefore, the Muslims insisted that non-resident Lebanese citizens were not to be calculated in figuring the confessional distribution of the Legislature, charging that the emigrés were responsible for "introducing to Lebanon foreign elements for the purpose of modifying the numerical importance of the religious communities to the detriment of the Muslims."[97] The Christian leadership agreed to this condition in 1943 prior to the drawing up of the National Pact. The emigré continued, nonetheless, to remain a significant factor in Lebanese politics, and as more and more Muslims, especially the Shî 'a, joined the annual stream of Christian emigrés, the latter's role in Lebanese national life, particularly in the economic sector, began to enjoy a wider appreciation. And while Muslims were able to prevent Lebanese residents abroad from figuring politically in the national life, any emigrant who returned from abroad — and there are many every year who come back having made their fortune — was immediately accorded resident citizenship privileges. And as many thousands of Muslim refugees from Palestine began to crowd into Lebanon after 1949, the Christians successfully resisted Muslim pressures to grant these new residents citizenship by insisting that such a move be accompanied by full citizenship for Lebanese abroad.

The other major factor operating to moderate open Christian-Muslim conflict was the lack of unity prevailing among the non-Christian communities. As indicated by the 1932 Census, the Orthodox or Sunni Muslim community, which was the most virulent in opposing the autonomy and independence of Lebanon, comprised less than half (45%) of the total non-Christian population, and by no means spoke for the other 55% in regard to nationalist sentiment. As heirs to some thirteen centuries of authority, they were anxious to identify with their brethren in neighboring Arab states who continued to exercise their heritage under newly-established national governments. But, as they constituted only one-fifth of the total population of Lebanon, they sought to include their more numerous Heterodox co-religionists in their Pan-Arab Nationalist aspirations in order to give greater strength to their cause. Their leaders spoke in terms of Islam and Muslim, rather than Sunni, Shî 'a, or Druze, and encouraged sectarian Muslims to do likewise.

Neither of the latter two groups, however, was particularly interested in political Pan-Arabism on the home front. The Shî 'a leadership had a considerable stake in the continued independence of Lebanon, and worked, despite momentary popular manifestations of Pan-Arab sentiment during the middle and late 1930's, to preserve the national existence and their own favored position in the internal power structure during the final days of the Mandate. Acutely aware of the importance of Shî 'a support for an independent Lebanon, the Christian leadership, especially that of the Maronites, sought to encourage them to play "a wider role in the government and to share in the responsibilities of the State as a means of bringing greater benefits to their community."[98] The statute of 1926, passed by Christian votes, which accorded the Shî 'a official recognition as a separate community, free from the social and legal restrictions of Sunni *sharî 'a* jurisdiction, did not fail to win community approval. The mass of Shî 'a, largely illiterate, entirely agrarian, and among the poorest segment of the Lebanese population, followed the leadership of its wealthy land-owning families (the As'ad, Bayḍûn, Ḥayḍar, and Ḥamâdî) in adhering to the idea of an independent Lebanese state. Strategically situated in the south along the Israeli frontier and in the northern Biqâ' next to Syria, the Shî 'a and their commitment to Lebanon have been "responsible more than anything else for establishing the Lebanese entity on a firm basis after the evacuation of the French."[99]

The Druzes were likewise hesitant to be submerged in the overwhelmingly Sunni society of the Arab East, and from the beginning cooperated with the Christian communities in securing the autonomy and later the independence of the Lebanon. Like the Maronites, they regarded Mount Lebanon (Jabal Lubnân), which for centuries had also been called *Jabal-al-Durûz* (Mountain of the Druzes), as their home. The difficulties which their coreligionists in southern Syria — residents of a second Jabal-Al-Durûz — encountered in maintaining their autonomy and social independence during the early years of Syrian independence contributed to an already strong Druze attachment to an independent Lebanon. The frequent massacres of the Druzes by the Ottomans and their persecution during the adminstration of Muhammad Ali of Egypt caused the Druzes to harbor an intense distrust of Sunni authority and an equal if not greater dislike of the Shî 'a, who for centuries had been gradually encroaching on traditionlly Druze territory from the south. To this day a Druze will go to great lengths to explain to a Westerner unfamiliar with the complex nature of Levantine sectarian divisions how he differs from a Muslim. In defense of this distinction Stephen Longrigg has observed: "In view of their communal and religious history, the claim of the Sunnis anxious to enlist their [the Druzes'] support and of the more Pan-Arab-minded among the Druzes themselves to be Muslim at all can, indeed, only with difficulty be accepted."[100] As the massacres of 1860 proved, the Druzes were not incapable of hostility toward Christians as well, but by the mid-20th century an alliance with Christians had become far preferable to one with Muslims. Existing as they do on the far periphery of Islam, the Druzes are well suited to their present pivotal role which the existing communal division has thrust upon them. Though accounting for only 6% of the total population of Lebanon, the Census of 1932 and later estimates have shown that Muslims approached the Christians in number only when the Druzes where included. Thus the Christians, anxious to preserve their own hegemony, were quick to foster nationalism of their own kind among the Druzes and to encourage an independent and separate Druze identity divorced from any form of Pan-Arabism. In this they have needed little encouragement.

Since the 18th century the Druzes have been concentrated almost exclusively in the mountain villages to the south and west of Beirut in the *qaḍâs* of 'Alayh, B'abda, and Al-Shûf (where 80% of the Lebanese Druzes lived in 1932). Stretching in an arc-like chain from suburban Beirut (Shuwayfât) to the edge of the Jazzin escarpment (Bâtir and Nîḥâ), the Druze settlements such as 'Alayh, Ba'qlîn, 'Amâṭûr, and Mukhtâra invariably included small Christian minorities, but rarely (except for the resort town 'Alayh) a Muslim family, a pattern followed throughout Druze villages in Syria and Palestine as well, and indicative of the present naure of Druze political alliances. A second Druze concentration was found in the shadow of Mount Hermon *(Jabal Al-Shaykh),* the Wâdî Al-Taym district which had been the earliest Druze stronghold. Today about 10% of Lebanon's Druzes live here, chiefly in Ḥâṣbayyâ and Râshayâ. The remainder are found in Beirut.

Despite the near equality in total numbers that characterized the Christian and Muslim sects in Lebanon, the Christians held an unquestioned strategic advantage in terms of their location and distribution. As the 1958 Crisis was clearly to demonstrate, Lebanese Christians were able to control all major highways and the railroads, to seal off all land exits, and to contain the non-Christian populations, particularly the Sunni, within their own enclaves. Christians controlled the coast from Diddah, just south of Tripoli, to 'Ayn Siqî, just below Sidon. The major Sunni Muslim concentrations in Beirut and Sidon were completely surrounded by Christian villages which controlled the heights above the two cities. Likewise, the dissident Sunni population of Tripoli was overshadowed by the large, militantly-Maronite population of Zaghartâ and its surrounding villages. The presence of large Christian (mixed Maronite and Orthodox) settlements in the 'Akkâr foothills (e.g. Qubayât, Raḥba, Burqâ 'îl, and 'Akkâr Al-'Atîqa) dominated the coastal road running north to Latakia, and the railroad and highway leading to Tall Kalakh and the interior of Syria. The strategic Beirut-Damascus highway and railroad passed through strongly Christian areas of the Mountain (with the exception of the Druze communities of 'Alayh and Ṣawfar) to the Biqâ' Valley, where the railroad diverged north past such exclusively Christian towns as Zaḥlah and Rayâq before entering Syria. The highway cut sharply south at Shatûra, passing through some Muslim villages such as Bar Ilyâs before reaching the Syrian frontier at Al-Maṣna'; but barely one kilometer from the latter border post was Ḥawsh Mûsâ (or 'Anjar), home to several thousand Armenian refugees of the 1915 massacres whose presence there since their resettlement in the early 1920's prevented any dissident Muslims from interfering with Christian control of traffic on the highway in times of emergency and, as in 1958, to act as a bulwark against potential Syrian infiltration.

The highway which ran through the strongly Shî 'a northern Biqâ' towards Homs in Syria was controlled at the frontier by the two large Greek Catholic villages of Al-Qâ' and Ra's Ba'labakk, while the southern entrance to the interior valley was guarded by the Orthodox town of Marj 'Uyûn (Merjayoun) and strategically located Christian villages such as Dayr Mîmâs and Qalî'a. And while the major artery through the southern Biqâ' traversed a region of predominantly Muslim and Druze villages, a parallel auxiliary road to the west linked Marj 'Uyûn and Zaḥlah through a succession of Christian towns and villages: Mashghara, Bâb Mâri', Ṣaghbîn, 'Ayn Zibda, 'Anâ, and 'Amîq. Finally, the southern frontier which overlooked northern Palestine was secured to the east by the Maronite villages of 'Ayn Ibil, Rumaysh, and Mârûn Al-Ra's, strategically placed amidst the strong Shî 'a hinterland around Bint Jubayl and Tibnîn, while the southern exit to the coastal highway and railroad to Palestine and Egypt was overlooked by the Greek Catholic border villages of Iskandarûna and Almâ Al-Sha'b. It should be noted also that the villages on the other side of the frontier were largely Christian (now interspersed with Jewish kibbutzim), chiefly Greek Catholic and Maronite.

Within the interior of Lebanon itself, the belt of Christian settlements stretching eastward from Sidon to Jazzîn and to Mashghara in the Biqâ', and from Jazzîn southward to Marj 'Uyûn and Dayr Mîmâs, served effectively to surround the Druze concentrations in the Shûf, B'abda, and 'Alayh districts, while at the same time acting as a buffer between the Shî 'a of the South and the Muslims of the Biqâ'. Thus while barely a majority in Greater Lebanon, the Christians had been careful to select frontiers over which they could exercise virtually complete control in time of emergency, while preserving the Mountain north of the Damascus highway to the heights of Bisharrî and Ihdan as an exclusive preserve in which they could always seek refuge should all else fail, as was the case in early 1976.

Despite Muslim demands in the early 1950's and continued pressure throughout the following decade, no official Census of Lebanon's population on the basis of religious community has been taken since the first and only such poll in 1932. In fact, no official estimate has been released since 1956, two years before the Crisis of 1958. Those figures, broken down by individual *qaḍâ* (see Table VII) showed the Christians as enjoying a clear majority of some 150,000 over the combined population of Muslims and Druzes — a direct contradiction of the Muslim charge that they now outnumbered the combined Christian community total. Muslims have for many years maintained that Christian emigration and a higher Muslim birthrate should have produced a non-Christian majority long ago. As there have been no official figures, however, relating to Lebanese vital statistics by religion since 1948 it is difficult to pass judgment on the Muslim allegation. In 1947 the official government figures showed Christians as accounting for a bare plurality of all births recorded (12,700 versus 12,525 for Muslims and 237 for others), while Muslims held a similar edge in total numbers of deaths (3,278 versus 3,266). In the following year the situation was reversed with Muslims outdistancing Christians in the number of births but accounting for fewer deaths. No more vital statistics have since been released. Statistics published in neighboring Arab states in recent years have shown that in at least two, Syria and Jordan, the native Muslim birthrate is notably higher than that of the indigenous Christian population, while in Egypt and Israel it was slightly higher. Only in Iraq were equal reproduction rates encountered as recently as 1957.

The only formal study of birthrates in Lebanon by religious community, that of David Yaukey (*Fertility Differences in a Modernizing Country,* Princeton, 1961), while only a survey of some 700 women, did produce some interesting statistics and conclusions. On the basis of the study, which measured the fertility patterns of 385 Muslim and 307 Christian women divided among village and city residence, one can conclude that at the village level there was little difference in the birthrate of the various Christian and Muslim groups.[101] In the urban environment of Beirut, however, the Muslim birthrate continued to approximate that of the rural level (6.53 live births per Muslim woman in town, 7.65 in the village) whereas among Christians it dropped by half (3.70 as compared with 7.18).[102] It should be noted also that the difference between urban Christian women and their rural counterparts was even greater among the younger generation. Significantly there was little difference, at least on the city level, between the various denominations within the larger religious groups. Thus the live birthrate for Maronites, other Eastern Catholics, and Orthodox in Beirut was 3.63, 3.81, and 3.65 per woman respectively, while among Sunni, Shî ‘a, and Druze women it was 6.45, 6.83, and 6.17 in that order. The reasons for the strikingly lower Christian birthrate among urban women was attributed by Dr. Yaukey to several factors, but primarily to the educated, Western-oriented outlook of the city-dwelling Christian population. As an example, the study showed that Christian women, even at the village level, employed contraceptive techniques more frequently than did Muslims.[103] Furthermore the tendency of Muslims to marry at an earlier age than Christians, especially in the city where the Christian girls were more apt to want to complete their education, has added to the higher rate of procreation among Muslims who would frequently marry as early as fifteen and thus have the benefit of their years of highest fertility in which to raise families.[104]

In figuring the total rate of procreation, however, consideration must again be taken of the higher incidence of infant mortality among Muslims. There have been no official government statistics on death by age and religion published since 1948, but two relatively recent studies, that of Yaukey and the *Report of Infant Mortality Survey of Rural Lebanon,* conducted by Salîm Khâmis of the American University in Beirut in 1955, include some significant, if limited statistics. The latter survey, while not broken down along confessional lines, does report by *muḥâfaẓa* (province) and here the rate of infant mortality is highest in those districts where Muslim concentration is the greatest. Thus in the province of Mount Lebanon where Christians constituted 72% of the population in 1956, the infant death rate per ten thousand live births was 112; in the province of South Lebanon, by way of contrast, where Christians are barely 30% of the total, the death rate for infants was 376, with similar relationships appearing in the other two provinces.[105] The Yaukey survey further supports the trend indicated by the above statistics. In breaking down the women interviewed by degree of literacy as well as religion on an urban-rural basis, Dr. Yaukey also included the number of siblings living at the time of each woman's marriage. Yaukey himself did not carry these figures beyond the raw stage, but if the total average of siblings alive at the time of marriage is figured on the basis of religion, the results are absolute confessional equality: an average of 4.53 siblings for both Christian and Muslim women interviewed.[106] A third, more recent study of social patterns of Maronite, Sunni Muslim, and Armenian lower-class families in Beirut likewise agreed with Yaukey's statistics, reporting the mean family size of those units interviewed to be equal: five members each for Maronite, Sunni, and Armenian alike.[107]

Thus while Muslim women marry younger than Christian women, and on average produce larger families, it is equally apparent that the death rate among Muslims between infancy and maturity in both urban and rural areas of Lebanon is such that the real birthrate of Christians and Muslims, counting only those offspring surviving infancy and childhood, is in effect identical. And though the figures compiled by the studies cited are by no means to be taken as reflecting a completely accurate and comprehensive picture of Lebanese fertility patterns, the trends to which they point are indeed significant and substantiated by other non-official, but informed, opinion. The *Area Handbook for Lebanon,* compiled from careful observation and reliable United States military and diplomatic information sources, states that "the higher death rate among the Moslem population may counteract their higher birthrate."[108] It would appear, therefore, that the purportedly higher Muslim birthrate may well be an insignificant factor at present in reducing the Christian majority once the equally higher level of Muslim deaths in infancy and adulthood is fully considered. Only when the advantages of modern sanitation and health facilities are extended to, and utilized by, the lower economic strata of Lebanese society in which the Muslim element predominates can the larger raw birthrate among Muslims be considered as the threat which most Christian Lebanese consider it to be to their continued political hegemony. And by the time this degree of progress has been attained, the economic and cultural level of the Muslim population will have been raised to one at which many of the sociological and cultural factors currently operating within the Muslim communities to prompt the rearing of larger families will have been negated.

One area in which Lebanese Muslims have already begun to emulate their Christian neighbors is in emigration. Traditionally the emigrés have been Christian, as indicated by the heavy Christian majority (80%) among those Lebanese abroad who by 1939 had formally confirmed their native citizenship. The great wave of Christian emigration — some 12-15,000 annually prior to the First World War — began to wane following the creation of Grand-Liban in 1920 at the same time that the Muslim communities began to appreciate the financial advantages which a large emigrant community offered those at home. During the 1930's the number of returning emigrés (1,600 per annum) almost equalled the number of those leaving Lebanon in search of economic opportunity abroad (1,850 annually).[109] Following the Second World War the growing pressures of over-population at home coupled with the lure of fortunes to be made in the oil fields of Kuwait, Saudi Arabia, and the Arabian Gulf, induced many Lebanese to seek residence abroad, the majority of them undoubtedly Muslim. The traditional goal of Christian Lebanese — the United States — had been virtually closed to permanent immigration since 1924, while the rigidly Muslim societies of the Arabian Gulf states and Saudi Arabia were bound to attract more Muslims from Lebanon than Christians. During the early 1950's nearly 4,000 Lebanese emigrated annually, at least half of them Muslim, if not more. The 1965 Census of Kuwait showed that only one quarter (26.8%) of its 21,000 resident Lebanese were Christian, while similar imbalances no doubt existed elsewhere in the oil-rich Arabian Peninsula. No official breakdown of its emigrants by religion has been made by Lebanon since independence, but according to Don Peretz, "during the 1950's Christians were emigrating at the rate of 100 a month."[110] If this is an accurate appraisal then only 43% (10,800) of the 25,660 Lebanese who emigrated during the years 1951-1959 would have been Christian. And certainly the obvious predominance of Muslims among the Lebanese emigrant communities of The Gulf and West Africa today, as well as the acknowledged dependence of many Muslim, particularly Shî 'a, villages (such as Jibâ' [Jbaa] in South Lebanon) on their emigrant citizens would tend to discount the Muslim allegation that Christian Lebanon today is suffering adversely from a steady loss through emigration. More likely it is the Muslims, who today have reached the economic stage at which Christians arrived more than half a century ago, and are sustaining a loss. No longer restricted by the rigid cultural patterns which previously prevented emigration, the Lebanese Muslim of today is just as capable of contemplating departure from his home village as his Christian neighbor. By the mid-1950's nearly every Muslim in Lebanon was able, according to Daniel Lerner's survey, to envision another country as a permanent residence.[111] And since it was the Muslim whose lower economic status would most profit from employment and even resettlement abroad it is doubtful that the previous Christian predominance among the hundreds of annual emigrants exists today.

On the basis of the real birthrates as estimated earlier in this chapter, and the rising percentage of Muslims among the small but constant flow of emigrés, it seems probable that the Christians in Lebanon today maintain an absolute majority of the total population, particularly when the factor of the many thousands of Palestinian and Syrian Christians who were able to acquire Lebanese citizenship during the 1950's is considered. There are no trends which would justify the gradual increase in the Christian population indicated in the 1944 and 1956 Estimates (see Tables VI-IX). The 1956 Estimate — the most recent official approximation of the confessional distribution in Lebanon — reported a total population of 1,416,520, of which nearly 55% (777,001) was Christian, and only 45% (625,669) Muslim and Druze, a considerable increase from the bare majority figure (50.01%) accorded Christians by the 1932 Census. The 1944 Estimate had already raised the Christian figure to 53% and on the basis of the Christian rate of growth postulated by these percentages, one could expect the Christian population by now to be approaching 60% of the total Lebanese citizenry — clearly the kind of redistribution of communal strength which the Christian-dominated government would like to see, but one which is hardly credible in the face of the studies cited earlier in this chapter. And in fact there are simply too many obvious discrepancies in the 1956 Estimate, such as the unrealistic changes in the confessional makeup of the 'Akkâr, Al-Shûf, Zaḫlah, Marj 'Uyûn, and Jabal 'Amîl (Tyre) districts, all in favor of the Christian population, and in particular the Maronite community. A continued even distribution of Christian and Muslim Lebanese, as first reported in 1932, is difficult enough to defend, but a Christian community growing at a faster rate than Muslims is improbable.

The only reliable figures with which to compare the 1932 Census results are those of the 1921 Census, likewise conducted under French Mandate auspices, which showed Christians to represent 51.12% of the total resident population, as opposed to 47.41% for Muslims and Druzes, with Jews and others making up the rest (1.47%). By 1932 the Christians had dropped to 50.5%, with Muslims and Druzes accounting for 48.7% and

Jews only 0.8%. Significantly, the major increase was recorded by the Shî 'a Muslims who grew by over 50% during the eleven-year period, compared with a growth of less than 30% on the part of the Maronites.[112]

As for the real population of the country, Lebanese Muslims have repeatedly pointed to the presence of some 250,000 (or more) Palestinian refugees in the country who would undoubtedly tip the scales in favor of the Muslims if granted citizenship as has been done in Jordan. Against these non-Lebanese Muslims, however, must be weighed the equal if not greater number of Christians who have been emigrating to Lebanon from Syria, Egypt, Jordan, and even Iraq since the mid-1950's who likewise do not enjoy Lebanese nationality. Nevertheless, the widely quoted ratio of 60-40 in favor of the Muslim population appears to be generally accepted by both sides in the absence of any official census along sectarian lines. The November 5th, 1975 issue

TABLE VI[113]

Religious distribution in Lebanon as reported by the Census of 1932 and the December 31, 1944 official government estimate of residents and non-residents.

Religious Community	Resident in Lebanon 1932	Resident in Lebanon 1944	Resident Abroad 1932	Resident Abroad 1944	Total 1932	Total 1944
CHRISTIAN	396,746	595,430	55,335	139,112	452,081	734,542
Maronite	227,800	327,846	33,243	91,276	261,043	419,122
Greek Orthodox	77,312	109,883	12,963	33,655	90,275	143,538
Greek Catholic	46,709	64,280	5,893	13,272	52,602	77,552
Armenian Orthodox	26,102	59,749	1,909	66	28,011	59,815
Other	18,823	33,672	1,327	843	20,150	34,515
MUSLIM	386,499	519,244	11,580	19,143	398,079	538,387
Sunni	178,130	235,595	4,712	4,913	182,842	240,508
Shî'a	155,035	209,338	3,390	9,367	158,425	218,705
Druze	53,334	74,311	3,478	4,863	56,812	79,174
OTHER (Jew, 'Alawi)	9,981	11,927	488	1,316	10,469	13,243
TOTAL	793,226	1,126,601	67,403	159,571	860,629	1,286,172

TABLE VII

Geographical distribution of religious communities in Lebanon by subdistricts (*qaḍâ*) as reported in the 1932 Census and the 1956 Estimate.[114]
The 1956 figures are listed below and parallel to the 1932 figures in each *qaḍâ*.

Subdistrict	Total Population	Christian % of Total Population	Maronite	Greek Orth.	Greek Cath.
NORTH LEBANON					
'Akkâr 1932)	49,844	*39.8*	16.6	21.1	1.2
1956)	72,828	*51.8*	21.1	26.4	1.6
Tripoli	59,575	*17.4*	5.3	9.7	0.4
	105,823	*21.5*	7.1	11.3	0.6
Kûra	18,241	*90.0*	26.8	62.8	0.2
	34,424	*88.7*	16.5	70.2	0.2
Zaghartâ/Batrûn/	48,876	*95.1*	86.0	8.0	0.9
Bisharrî	94,757	*95.3*	86.9	7.3	1.0
MOUNT LEBANON					
Jubayl/Kisrawân	56,062	*90.7*	84.7	1.9	1.0
	93,995	*92.3*	87.0	2.0	1.0
Al-Matn	39,626	*96.3*	59.2	14.9	8.8
	85,610	*96.7*	44.3	14.1	7.3
B'abda	42,268	*64.1*	50.8	8.7	3.3
	79,345	*65.3*	51.7	8.9	3.9
'Alayh	37,847	*51.1*	29.4	17.0	3.9
	67,579	*52.3*	32.2	15.8	3.8
Al-Shûf	53,025	*43.6*	34.6	0.5	8.5
	96,009	*47.2*	37.7	0.6	8.9
SOUTH LEBANON					
Sidon/Nabaṭîya	53,921	*17.9*	8.0	0.2	8.7
	93,829	*20.6*	9.6	0.4	9.7
Tyre/Bint Jubayl	49,301	*12.8*	6.1	0.3	5.9
	84,743	*17.2*	7.1	0.5	7.1
Jazzîn	16,744	*82.6*	65.3	0.2	17.0
	31,095	*83.6*	67.0	0.1	16.4
Marj Uyûn/Ḥâṣbayyâ	32,867	*25.2*	5.4	13.4	4.2
	55,051	*34.3*	7.8	18.0	5.7
AL-BIQÂ'					
Râshayâ	11,771	*32.4*	3.0	27.3	1.2
	18,914	*37.6*	4.3	30.2	2.3
Zaḥlah/Biqâ'	54,160	*59.7*	19.6	10.5	23.6
Al-Gharbîya	101,076	*65.3*	22.8	10.5	25.3
Ba'labakk/Hirmal	53,932	*21.9*	10.6	1.9	9.1
	83,302	*24.2*	11.9	1.6	10.3

Armen. Orth.	Other	Muslim % of Total Population	Sunni	Shî'a	Druze	Other (Jew, 'Alawî, etc.) % of Total Population
—	0.9	*56.2*	55.6	0.6	—	*4.0*
0.1	2.6	*45.2*	44.8	0.4	—	*3.0*
1.1	0.9	*78.8*	78.8	—	—	*3.8*
1.3	1.2	*74.7*	74.6	0.1	—	*3.8*
0.1	0.1	*9.9*	8.7	1.2	—	*0.1*
0.1	1.7	*11.3*	8.8	2.5	—	—
0.1	0.1	*4.9*	4.4	0.5	—	—
0.1	—	*4.7*	4.0	0.7	—	—
2.1	1.0	*9.1*	1.3	7.8	—	*0.2*
1.8	0.5	*7.7*	1.0	6.7	—	—
9.6	3.8	*2.8*	0.3	0.6	1.9	*0.9*
21.3	9.7	3.1	0.3	0.8	2.0	*0.2*
0.4	0.9	*35.7*	2.6	15.5	17.6	*0.2*
0.3	0.5	*34.7*	2.5	16.0	16.2	—
0.8	—	*48.7*	0.5	1.8	46.4	*0.2*
0.5	—	*47.7*	0.5	1.9	45.3	—
—	—	*56.4*	22.3	2.1	32.0	—
—	—	*52.8*	21.8	1.8	29.2	—
0.4	0.6	*81.4*	18.6	62.8	—	*0.7*
0.3	0.6	*78.2*	18.8	59.4	—	*1.2*
0.1	0.4	*87.1*	3.8	83.3	—	*0.1*
1.8	0.7	*82.6*	3.6	79.0	—	*0.2*
0.1	—	*17.4*	2.5	13.9	1.0	—
0.1	—	*16.4*	2.4	13.3	0.7	—
—	2.2	*74.6*	15.2	46.6	12.8	*0.2*
0.2	2.6	*65.7*	15.2	38.5	12.0	—
—	0.9	*67.6*	29.0	1.1	37.5	—
—	0.8	*62.4*	27.5	—	34.9	—
2.2	3.8	*40.0*	28.6	10.7	0.7	*0.3*
1.7	5.0	*34.4*	25.7	8.2	0.5	*0.3*
0.1	0.2	*78.0*	10.8	67.2	—	*0.1*
0.2	0.2	*75.5*	8.6	66.9	—	*0.1*

of *Al-Nahâr,* Beirut's largest and most prestigious daily, quoted unofficial population figures which estimated more than 2 million Muslims in Lebanon (970,000 Shî 'a; 690,000 Sunni; and 348,000 Druze), and approximately 1,250,000 resident Christians (496,000 Maronites; 260,000 Armenians; 230,000 Orthodox; and 213,000 non-Maronite Catholics) or a 62.5-37.5 split with Maronites, considerably less numerous than either Sunni or Shî 'a, and accounting for only 16% of the total. The reliability of these figures is debatable. Christians, moreover, particularly the Maronites, are unwilling to accept the political changes that such a ratio would predicate. In any event, the political situation within Lebanon, reflecting as it does a complex of alliances and ententes which criss-cross confessional lines in the interest of both private concerns and that of the state, would tend to reduce the significance of any purely demographic changes.

Unlike Palestine and Transjordan whose traditional demographic patterns were considerably altered by the political events of 1948-1949, there has been no visible change in the confessional makeup of Lebanon outside Beirut and its mushrooming suburbs. It is there that any transformation of the traditional confessional balance, as indicated by the above figures, has taken place. Beyond the Beirut metropolitan area, no major changes are to be seen. Sunnis are still concentrated in the cities of the coast, the 'Akkâr plain and foothills (such as the villages of Ṣîr, Finaydiq, and Mishmish), the central Biqâ' Valley, and in a coastal pocket of Al-Shûf between Beirut and Sidon encompassing the villages of Barjâ and Shiḥîm. The Shî 'a are restricted to the Jabal 'Amîl region east of Tyre, the northern Biqâ' Valley between Ba'labakk and Hirmal, the southern suburbs of Beirut (B'abdâ *qaḍâ*), and a few villages in Mount Lebanon to the east of Jubayl (Byblos), among them the popular ski resort of Laqlûq. The Greek Orthodox are urban like the Sunnis with a rural concentration in the Al-Kûra district south of Tripoli around Amyûn, several villages on the lower slopes of Mount Lebanon directly east of Beirut (e.g. Sûq Al-Gharb), and the town and satellite villages of Marj 'Uyûn in South Lebanon. Zaḥlah remains the principal Melkite stronghold while additional concentrations of Uniate Byzantines are found in the northern

TABLE VIII

Christian and Muslim-Druze percentages of the total population of Lebanon as reported in the 1932 Census and the official government estimates of 1944 and 1956 by *Muḥâfaẓa* (province).

	Percent Christian			Percent Muslim-Druze		
Muḥâfaẓa	1932	1944	1956	1932	1944	1956
Beirut	51.48	55.19	54.11	44.67	41.66	43.30
North Lebanon	52.69	55.93	58.85	44.93	41.93	39.09
Mount Lebanon	69.27	70.50	71.77	30.44	29.37	28.10
South Lebanon	24.88	26.31	29.77	74.81	73.37	69.73
Al-Biqâ'	40.02	43.64	46.91	59.90	56.25	52.87
Total Lebanon	50.01	52.85	54.84	48.71	46.09	44.17

TABLE IX

Confessional distribution of Lebanese population as reported in the Census of 1932 and the Estimates of 1944 and 1956.

Religious	Percent of Total Resident Population		
Community	1932	1944	1956
Maronite	28.72	29.10	29.91
Greek Orthodox	9.74	9.75	10.52
Greek Catholic	5.89	5.71	6.41
Armenian Orthodox	3.29	5.30	4.85
Armenian Catholic	0.74	0.93	1.03
Syrian Orthodox	0.34	0.33	0.34
Syrian Catholic	0.35	0.44	0.41
Chaldaean / Nestorian	0.09	0.12	0.10
Latin	—	0.28	0.31
Protestant	0.86	0.90	0.96
Total Christian	50.02	52.85	54.84
Sunni	22.45	20.91	20.22
Shi'a	19.53	18.58	17.70
Druze	6.73	6.60	6.25
Total Muslim / Druze	48.72	46.09	44.17
Other	1.26	1.06	0.99

Biqâ' and in the foothills to the east of Sidon. Aside from those villages already mentioned, the rest of the Mountain is Maronite, from Jazzîn through Dayr Al-Qamar north to Qubayât in the 'Akkâr, as is its coast from the northern suburbs of Sidon to the southern fringe of Tripoli, with major strongholds at Jûniyah, Batrûn, and the now devastated (Jan. 1976) Dâmûr, which is numbered among the more than 50 Christian settlements destroyed in the recent war.

In Beirut itself, a few of the old geographical patterns still hold, such as the Christian predominance in the eastern part of the city, particularly the Ashrafîya quarter, the Sunni concentration in Al-Baṣta, and the Armenian dominance in the Al-Mudawwur quarter and the suburb of Burj Ḥummûd immediately to the east. Elsewhere in Beirut and its suburbs, Christian and Muslim are completely intermingled, the official residents outnumbered at least 3:1 by Christian (particularly Armenian) immigrants from neighboring states (chiefly Syria), Muslim refugees from Palestine, and Lebanese from the Mountain and the Biqâ ' Valley where they still retain their official residence. Thus while the 1956 Estimate gave Beirut an official population of 221,000, in reality the figure should have been twice that number, and is today about three-quarters of a million. It is here that the old patterns are breaking down and the struggle for greater Muslim political power is being waged.

Syria. To the east and north of Lebanon, the Republic of Syria picks up again the traditional Levantine demographic pattern of Muslim cities with Orthodox (and Melkite) minorities along the coast and in the immediate interior, giving way to the presence of heterodox Jacobites, Nestorians, Armenians, and their Catholic counterparts from the Orontes eastward to the Jazîra and into Iraq. At the outbreak of the First World War the Christian population of what is today Syria was considerably less than it was on the eve of independence. The reason for this was of course the influx of large numbers of Christian refugees, particularly Armenians and Jacobites, fleeing Turkish persecution. The migration had begun even before the war but reached its climax from 1918 to 1920 in the wake of the French army withdrawal from Anatolia. While the Muslim population of Syria did not particularly favor this wave of destitute settlers, most of whom could not speak Arabic and had no interest in the native communities' desire for independence, the French Mandate authorities encouraged their resettlement in such Muslim nationalist strongholds as Aleppo, Homs, and Damascus, as well as in the strategic Jazîra hinterland where valuable petroleum deposits were rightly suspected. Between 1918 and 1939 some 100,000 Christians of the Armenian, Jacobite, and Nestorian confessions augmented the resident Christian population of 200,000, largely Orthodox and Melkite. Though most were refugees from Turkish Anatolia, the Nestorians — in number about 7,000 — entered Syria from neighboring Iraq where they had been victims of massacre at the hands of the newly-independent kingdom's military forces during the summer of 1933. In 1890 the Christian population of Aleppo had stood at 22,000. By 1925 that figure had risen to 59,000, while at the same time the Muslim population of 115,000 had not grown by more than 4,000. At the peak of their strength in 1955 the Christians of Aleppo numbered 136,000, of which two-thirds were Armenians and another ten per cent Jacobites, Syrian Catholics, and Chaldaeans.[115] Further south in Homs, where the Jacobite patriarch had taken up permanent residence in 1932, another 10,000 Anatolian refugees were resettled. In Damascus another large Armenian community emerged, while to the east in the Jazîra, 20-25,000 Jacobite and Armenian villagers settled along the Istanbul-Baghdad railway only a few miles from their former homes in Anatolia, where they were joined a few years later by the Nestorian refugees from Iraqi Kurdistan.

In Syria Maritime, the Orontes Valley, Damascus, and the Ḥawrân remained undisputed outposts of Byzantine Christianity. The province of Latakia (Alouites) from the border of Lebanon to that of Turkey contained an Orthodox minority nearly equal to that of the Sunni Muslim population, though both were small in comparison with the indigenous Nuṣayri (Alawite) community of the Jabal Anṣârîya. Both the port of Latakia and the smaller coastal towns of Bâniyâs and Ṭarṭûs (Tortosa) had sheltered substantial Orthodox populations since the earliest days of the Arab conquest, while in the coastal foothills to the east larger concentrations were found in the exclusively Orthodox town of Sâfîtâ and the numerous villages of the Wâdi Al-Naṣâra, the Valley of the Christians, along the upper reaches of the Nahr Al-Kabîr and in the shadow of the great Crusader castle of Krak des Chevaliers. Here also was the ancient Orthodox monastery of Saint George (Mâr Jirjis) with its venerable relics and icons dating from the Byzantine period. Further north towards the Jabal Akrâd other monuments of the Latin Kingdom (such as Saône and Margat) sheltered tiny settlements of Christians, some seven centuries after the last Crusader had departed from these imposing strongholds. Interspersed with the Orthodox of the Syrian coast were a few Maronite villages, scattered Melkite congregations, and an Armenian township at Kasab on the Turkish border within sight of Musa Dağ (Jabal Mûsâ), the celebrated site of heroic Armenian resistance during the World War I massacres. The province of Alexandretta to the north likewise had its Orthodox and Armenian minorities, especially at Antioch (Anṭâkiya), until its transfer to Turkey in 1939 when the majority of the Christian population resettled in Syria and Lebanon. Several thousand Orthodox families remain now with active parishes in Mersin, Antioch, and Seleucia (Samandağ), as well as an American community at Vakifli (pop. 218 in 1970). In the fertile lowlands of the Ghâb (Lower Orontes Valley) Orthodox communities of Byzantine origin flourished at Jisr Al-Shughûr, Al-Muḥarda, and at the conservative Muslim stronghold of Ḥamâh (ancient Epiphania), where Christian women went veiled into the streets well after the French occupation. Today an impressive new Greek Orthodox cathedral on the heights west of the Orontes is nearing completion, and Christians in general prosper as valued members of this flourishing Syrian market community.

In the south of Syria, equal numbers of Orthodox and Melkites populated villages on the Ḥawrân plain (e.g. Tissyâ, Baṣîr, Khabâb, and Jibbîn) and in the Jabal Al-Durûz to the east, while substantial minorities of both sects were found side-by-side with Muslim majorities in the towns of Dir'â, Izrâ', and Buṣrâ Al-Sham (Bostra). The capital city of Damascus sheltered the largest concentration of Orthodox and Melkite Christians (over 20,000 each on the eve of independence), crowded into their ancient quarter at the eastern end of the city (Bâb Al-Sharqî) into whose labyrinth of tiny alleys and covered streets lined with fortress-like homes protected by "securely padlocked iron doors…, zig-zag entrances… [and] barred windows… only the initiated would dare to venture."[116] North of the city, tucked away in the rocky folds of the Anti-Lebanon, were two remarkable relics of Syria's Christian past: Ṣaydnâyâ and Ma'lûla. The former, a thriving village of some 2,500 inhabitants, is celebrated today, as in antiquity, for its imposing convent, Notre Dame de Sednayë, which dominates the surrounding countryside from its acropolis-like vantage. Though securely in the hands of an Orthodox order of nuns, the convent has long been the object of bitter dispute between the township's equal numbers of Orthodox and Melkite citizens, who, like their counterparts in Damascus, are even today "fastes rivaux."[117] Ma'lûla's past is a little less stormy, its Melkite population of about 1,000 owing a certain fame to their survival as native speakers of Aramaic, the one-time lingua franca of Greater Syria, and no doubt the language of Christ and his disciples. Other, less colorful communities of Orthodox and Melkite Christians dot the Anti-Lebanon from Qaṭanâ in the south through Zabadânî and Al-Nabak to Yabrûd near the northern end of the chain.

At this point the strength of Byzantine Christianity begins to wane, first at Homs on the Orontes where large numbers of Jacobites were resettled with their patriarch in the 1920's and 30's, and finally at Ḥamâh, to the north and east of whose famed waterwheels the present-day heirs to the 5th century Christological controversies predominate. Only in Aleppo have Orthodox and Melkite settlements survived, numbering at the time of Syrian independence 10,000 and 12,500 respectively, or barely one-quarter of the city's Christian population. To the south and east of Homs were found the Jacobite villages of Ṣadad and Hafar "which the Moslem invasion seems to have left forgotten in the middle of the Syrian Desert."[118] Further yet to the east was Qaryatayn, predominantly Muslim but home to some 1,000 desert Monophysites and their Uniate brethren. Along the path of the railroad which from Aleppo to Qâmishlî forms the Syrian border with Turkey, occasional villages such as Jarâbulus, 'Ayn Al-'Arab, and Tall Abyaḍ interrupted the barren expanse of semi-arid plain, each with their several hundred Jacobite or Armenian inhabitants. At Al-Raqqa and Dayr Al-Zawr (Deir ez-Zor) on the Euphrates, a similar pattern was found among the small Christian populations there which today number about 600 and 1,500 respectively. To the northeast along the upper course of the Khabbûr River was the fertile Jazîra district with its score of Nestorian villages and prospering towns of Al-Ḥasaka, Ra's Al-'Ayn, 'Amûda, Dirbasîya, and Qâmishlî, heavily Christian, and chiefly Jacobite and Armenian with smaller numbers of Uniates. A century and a half ago the Jazîra was a windswept wasteland, described by G.P. Badger as being in "so dilapidated a condition... that the best lodging we could procure was an open recess."[119] The entire Christian population at the time totaled less than 1,000 individuals, composing some 20 Jacobite and 60 Chaldaean families.[120] By 1945 Christians numbered nearly 45,000, most of them recent settlers from Anatolia who had arrived with nothing, but in one generation had come to dominate the region economically as both merchants and landowners.

The official population estimate published by the Syrian government on the eve of independence (31 December 1943) showed a total settled population of 2,860,500, of which nearly 14% (403,000) were Christian (see Table X). The division between the native Christians of Byzantine origin (Greek Orthodox and Melkite) and those of the immigrant non-Chalcedonian communities (Jacobite, Armenian, Nestorian, and their Uniate branches) was roughly equal, as was the three-way sectarian split between Orthodox (137,000), Catholic (102,000), and Heterodox (151,000). The Muslim population was only slightly less divided. Though Sunnis officially constituted two-thirds of the population, a substantial number were non-Arabs of Turkish and Kurdish ethnic origins (and frequently speech as well). Equal to the Christians in number were the heterodox Muslims, chiefly Alawites (325,000) and Druzes (87,000) both of whose theologies and communal outlook removed them as far from Sunni orthodoxy as most Syrian Christians. The Alawites even included certain Christian practices in their religious ceremonies, and until very recently lived "leur existence solitaire, secrète et réprimé... sans communications désormais avec le monde exterieur."[121]

During the first ten years of national independence, the Christians of Syria flourished alongside the Muslim majority in both the political and economic spheres. Within the government itself Christians rose to positions of prominence including the office of Prime Minister, while in local commerce, foreign trade, and banking, both indigenous and immigrant Christians prospered. The impact of the Pan-Islamic nationalism of Nasser and the economic trend toward Socialism from the middle 1950's onward, however, greatly compromised both political and economic freedom in Syria, Christians being those most immediately affected. As a result, thousands of educated, politically-motivated, and prosperous Syrians began a quiet exodus to Lebanon and the Christian West which by 1960's had drained the country of more than half a million of its most valuable citizens, half of whom were Christians. Though official population estimates continued to show a steady population increase, the Census of 1960 revealed a resident population which was 560,000 less than the number registered on the official government lists. And of the 4,353,600 Syrians present at the time of the Census, only 361,000 were Christians, a net decrease of over 40,000 (and a percentage decline from 14% to 8%) while at the same time the official government estimated a Christian population of over 600,000 (see Tables X and XI).[122]

Significantly, the 1960 Census was not the only official source which lent credence to the long-suspected widespread emigration of Syrian Christians since the early 1950's. The official Vatican estimate of the various Catholic communities in Syria in 1963 showed numerous discrepancies when compared with the government projection for the same communities in that year (Table X). In view of the fact that official church sources have frequently been given to statistical inflation in the past, the extent of the Christian emigration from Syria gains even greater proportions. There were many irregularities in the pattern of exodus, but in general it affected the towns less than the countryside, largely because the urban Christian loss through emigration was temporarily compensated for by the natural movement of rural peoples, among them Christian villagers, to the cities. Thus Syria's Christian population which in 1943 was equally divided between urban and rural settlements was, according to the 1960 Census, nearly two-thirds (62%) urban: 224,000 city-dwellers as opposed to 137,000 provincials. A clear majority of resident Syrian Christians in 1960 were found in fact to be living in only six urban centers: Aleppo, Damascus, Qâmishlî, Latakia, and Al-Ḥasaka. The Muslim population of these same cities (1,028,000 compared with 181,500 Christians) was only 24.5% of their total strength, and in the nation as a whole Muslims were only 33% urbanized.

As may be seen from Table X, the greatest single instance of Christian depopulation occurred in the province of Aleppo (95% of whose Christians lived in the city itself) which in 1943 counted 123,000 Christians but which registered barely 88,000 seventeen years later. Here, however, the principal contributing factor was the Armenian community which accounted for two-thirds of Aleppine Christians in 1943 and which had since shown the greatest propensity to emigrate, either to Lebanon and the West, or to Soviet Armenia, encouraged both by the Soviet government and by the Gregorian Katholikos of Sîs during the late 1940's and early 1950's, Karekin Hovsepian. A United States diplomatic official in Syria confided to the author early in 1966 that an average of 2,300 Armenians from Aleppo and the Jazîra were emigrating annually to the Soviet Union and that many hundreds more were on the waiting list. And for every Armenian who left for Russia, there were probably two or three others who emigrated to Beirut, or to Canada and Australia. Further substantiating this Armenian exodus was the Aleppo telephone directory of 1961 which by the author's count contained twice as many identifiably Christian Arab listings as Armenian, both of which communities can be presumed to be of roughly equal economic levels on the overall community average (and thus equally apt to be able to afford the luxury of a telephone).[123]

In the Jabal Al-Durûz and Homs districts the local Christian population likewise lost from one-quarter to one-third of its

1943 strength, while Latakia and the Ḥawrân suffered net declines of 10-15%. The province of Damascus showed a stable Christian population of 70,000 throughout the 1940's and 50's (at the same time Muslims were increasing by nearly double), while Ḥamâh and the Jazîra alone among the provinces registered Christian growth (20% and 40% respectively). In both cases, however, the Muslim increase was far greater, and in the Jazîra only three of the urban centers—Qâmishlî, Dirbasîya, and Al-Mâlikîya—remained Christian in majority. The rural enclave of Nestorians along the Khabbûr likewise showed the effect of emigration, registering a slight net decline while at the same time the civil lists indicated a 75% increase since 1943. Significantly, the principal Nestorian village, Tall Tâmir, had shown no population change during the past quarter century in which the total population of the Jazîra had trebled.[124]

Other traditional Christian centers maintained majority strength in 1960, though often vastly reduced if not completely erased by substantially increased Muslim populations. In Syria Maritime, Christians still outnumbered Alawites in Kasab (2,700 to 1,000), Sâfîtâ (4,300 to 1,900) and the Wâdî Al-Naṣâra (19,400 to 2,800),[125] though in the Mashta Al-Ḥilû and Jabal Al-Ḥilû districts on the fringe of the Christian Valley proper Christian emigration and rapid Alawite growth had obliterated former Orthodox majorities (22,000 to 10,500). In the cities of Latakia, Homs, and Bâniyâs Christians remained at their 1943 strength in the face of 100% Muslim increases, while in Ṭarṭûs, the former Crusader stronghold on the coast north of Tripoli, the Christian population in 1960 (1,900) was little changed from thirty years earlier, while at the same time the Muslim population had quadrupled. To the south, the Jacobite/Syrian Catholic villages of Ṣadad and Hafar (population 3,500 and 1,050 respectively in 1960) retained their exclusive Christian character, but elsewhere to the south a rural Christian exodus was apparent. The Melkite village of Ma'lûla, for example, counted only 1,331 inhabitants in 1960, as opposed to 1,923 in 1936, 300 of whom were non-Aramaic speaking Muslim newcomers.[126] Nearby Ṣaydnâyâ, despite the protection afforded by its miraculous icon of the weeping Virgin, had also suffered a minor invasion of

Muslims from the valley below. Confiding in British author Colin Thubron in 1965, the mother superior of the Orthodox convent admitted that the village now housed 500 Muslims "where there had once been only three... No, certainly not converts: migration and heavy breeding..."[127]

The 1960 Census gave statistical support to the good Sister's casual observation. Of the Syrian population under five years of age at the time of the Census, only 6.6% was Christian, in contrast to the overall Christian proportion of 8.3%. As in Lebanon and elsewhere in the Arab Orient, however, the incidence of infant and childhood mortality is generally acknowledged to be higher among Muslims, thus lessening the impact of their greater rate of procreation. Emigration, therefore, remains by far the major cause of Christian depopulation, and until very recently loomed as a serious threat to the future of Christians in Syria. Present troubles in Lebanon, however, coupled with less restrictive financial controls and a generally improved economic situation since 1970 have resulted in the gradual return of many Christian Syrian exiles to their former homes, particularly in Aleppo and Damascus. Rural depopulation has tended also to subside in the past few years, though Christian villagers continue to seek seasonal employment in the larger cities. The alarming Christian exodus from Syria in the 1960's has for the most part ceased, and cautious optimism has replaced the gloom with which many Christian Syrians viewed their future only a few years earlier.

The present Christian population of Syria is the subject of widely differing estimates. The Christians of Syria themselves have never accepted the low figure of the 1960 Census, conducted during the brief period of union with Egypt, and speak today of one million or more resident Christians. *Newsweek* in its June 17, 1974 article on Syria, quoted the figure of 1,500,000 Christians out of a total of 6.9 million, or over 20% of the population.[128] Though probably inflated, these figures reflect an obvious Christian resurgence which the author has confirmed on his five visits to Syria between July 1974 and November 1976. Certainly a figure of 750,000 Christians in Syria today is not unrealistic.

TABLE X

Christian population of Syria as reported by the Government estimates of 1943, 1956, and 1963, and the Vatican figures for the latter year (Catholic communities only).

Christian Community	Government Population Estimates 1943	1956	1963	Vatican Estimate 1963[129]
Greek Orthodox	136,957	181,750	246,000	—
Greek Catholic	46,733	60,124	80,000	62,202
Armenian Orthodox	101,747	133,570	140,000	—
Armenian Catholic	16,790	20,637	24,000	18,000
Syrian Orthodox	40,135	55,343	72,000	—
Syrian Catholic	16,247	20,716	30,000	19,042
Nestorian	9,176	11,760	15,000	—
Chaldaean	4,719	5,723	7,000	6,000
Maronite	13,349	19,291	25,000	14,800
Latin	5,996	7,079	10,000	9,000
Protestant	11,187	12,525	11,000	—
Total	403,036	528,518	660,000	—
(Catholic)	(103,834)	(133,570)	(176,000)	(129,100)

TABLE XI

Christian percentage of the population of Syria by *Muḥâfaẓa* (province) as reported by the General Census of 1960 and the Government Estimate of the same year.

Muḥâfaẓa	Total Population Census	Estimate	Percent Christian Census	Estimate
Aleppo-Idlib	1,242,547	1,461,309	7.50	12.13
Damascus	985,359	1,022,081	7.05	10.44
Ḥamâh	313,101	369,929	7.76	10.85
Homs	380,471	480,444	16.30	24.00
Latakia	515,568	590,106	8.73	13.28
Ḥawrân	162,923	208,646	4.11	6.89
Jabal Al-Durûz (Suwaydâ)	92,011	144,557	5.54	9.95
Dayr Al-Zawr/Al-Raqqa	351,977	329,820	0.88	1.62
Al-Jazîra (Ḥasaka)	309,494	305,085	18.87	24.15
Total (exclusive of Bedouins)	4,353,451	4,911,977	8.29	12.84

Iraq. Ever since the final collapse of the great Nestorian Church of the East in the 15th Century, the Christian population of ancient Mesopotamia, today the Republic of Iraq, has been confined to three centers: the cities proper of Basra (Al-Baṣra) and Baghdad, and the Assyrian plain to the north. Until very recently this latter concentration, divided between the city of Mosul and several dozen villages to the north and east, was by far the largest. At the time of Iraqi independence in 1932, over two-thirds (70%) of the nation's Christian population of 111,000 was found here, as opposed to 24% in Baghdad and less than 4% in Basra. The remaining 3,500 Iraqi Christians were scattered throughout the country, principally in the oil-city of Kirkûk and the former refugee-camp town of Ba'qûba, a few miles east of Baghdad. In the populous lowlands stretching from Baghdad to Basra, some 500 Christians were submerged in a total population of 1.25 million, largely Shî 'a Muslims, with tiny communities of Sunnis (16,500), Jews (5,000), and Sabaeans (4,000), found principally, like the Christians, in the small river towns that served a vast rural hinterland. In comparison with their fellow Christians in the rest of the Arab Crescent, those of Iraq were therefore much less numerous (less than 4% of the total population), but like Syria and Lebanon owed much of what strength they had to the recent influx of Armenian, Jacobite, and Nestorian refugees from Anatolia.

Nearly 50,000 such refugees had passed through the camp at Ba'qûba between 1918-1921,[130] and though many continued their migration further westward, a substantial number stayed, nearly doubling the pre-World War I Iraqi Christian population. As late as 1957, 13,000 Christian Iraqis were listed by the Census of that year as having been born in what is now Turkey and Iran. Despite the exodus of nearly 10,000 Nestorians in the years immediately following the Massacres of 1933, and a political climate which is without doubt the most volatile and violent in the Arab East, the Christian population in the years since World War II has remained at a consistent level, registering 3.23% (149,700) of the total population at the time of the Census of 1947, and 3.25% ten years later (206,206). During this period, however, the former pattern of a majority Christian concentration in the region of Mosul began to change considerably. By 1947, the 70% figure of 1932 had shrunk to 57%, and ten years later to less than half (47%), even though the same Census (1957) showed that 59% of Iraq's Christians had been born in either the *liwa* (province) of Mosul or Irbîl (Arbela). The majority of these migrants had settled in Baghdad, whose Christian population grew 2½ times between 1932 and 1957, as did that of Basra, Kirkûk (a ten-fold growth during the same period), and the region surrounding the Ḥabbânîya Air Base west of Baghdad. Even the heavily Shî 'a provinces south of the capital showed a Christian increase from 500 to nearly 3,000 in the quarter century since independence. By 1957 over half (55%) of the Christian population was concentrated in the country's four principal cities (Baghdad, Mosul, Basra, and Kirkûk) as compared with less than 20% of the Muslim population.

The rural Christian population was centered principally in the seven heavily Christian townships of the Mosul plain (Tall Kayf, Tall Usquf, Bâṭnayâ, Al-Qûsh, Karamlays, Barṭala, and Qâra Qûsh — the first five Chaldaean Catholic, the latter two Jacobite and Syrian Catholic respectively),[131] the Chaldaean village of 'Ayn Kâwa just north of Irbîl, and Nestorian towns and villages such as Mankaysh, Sirsank, and Kânî Mâsî on the slopes of the Zagros mountains to the north. Substantial Christian minorities in predominantly Kurdish Muslim towns such as Zakhû, Dahûk, Bâṭâs, and Shaqlâwa, or among Yazidis in Ba'shîqa, Bahazânî, 'Ayn Sifnî, and Sinjâr, comprised the remainder. In many of these provincial towns the old Arab and Ottoman pattern of religious segregation by quarter remained prevalent, such as in 'Aqrâ, a predominantly Kurdish town of 6,000, which crowded most of its 400 Chaldaean Christians into an exclusive *Ḥayy Al-Naṣâra,* or Christian quarter. In the cities, however, Christians were found in virtually every quarter, and what segregation did exist was primarily economic. In Baghdad, for instance, half of the city's Christians (33,000) lived in the fashionable East Karrâda district in 1957, as opposed to only 15% (93,000) of the city's Muslims, a pattern common throughout the Arab Crescent where native Christians were on the average more affluent than Muslims. A large minority of Christians, 61,000 or 25% as reported by the Census of 1957, still spoke a form of Syriac as their native tongue; most, however, were villagers from Mosul (46,000) or Irbîl (5,000) provinces, and many of these spoke Arabic as well. In general such patterns of speech and dress that formerly differentiated Christians from the north from other Iraqis were dying out as more and more rural Christians migrated to Baghdad.

This population movement, already noticeable in the 1930's, has increased considerably since the last Census for a number of reasons, two of them, at least, political in nature. The Republican revolution of 1958 increased the political tension throughout the country, but particularly in the north where intercommunal hostilities have always been a political factor. These tensions were greatly exacerbated during the Kassem (Qâsim) administration by the open identification of many Mosul Christians with the Communist Party and the extreme left-wing element of the revolutionary government. The so-called "Mosul Massacres" of 1959-1960 in which conservative Muslim and anti-Kassem partisans were murdered at the hands of Communists following an abortive pro-Nasser uprising — events in which the Christians of Mosul and neighboring Tall Kayf were seriously implicated — raised religious hostilities to the breaking point. Following the Ba'th Party coup of 1963, many Christians from the north, fearful of Muslim reaction against Christian connections with the discredited Kassem government, fled to Baghdad. In addition, the Kurdish struggle for autonomy in which certain Christians were likewise known to be involved (see pp. 185-186) provided another political motivation for the Christian exodus. And even beyond the purely political considerations of the Kurdish War, the ravages of the conflict which destroyed many Christian villages in the Kurdish mountains forced thousands more to seek refuge among the burgeoning Christian community in Baghdad. The Auxiliary Bishop to the Chaldaean patriarch, Emmanuel Dillî (Dely), estimated the Christian population of Baghdad at the end of 1965 to be in excess of 150,000, more than double its size at the time of the Census eight years earlier.[132] At the same time it was estimated that the Christian population in Mosul had been halved, a startling demographic change confirmed to a great extent by official Vatican sources.

Between 1963 and 1966 the *Annuario Pontifico* reported the population of the Chaldaean diocese of Baghdad as having grown from 75,000 to 110,000 while that of Mosul declined from 34,000 to 14,560. The economic and social problems presented by these refugee villagers have been considerable, but at the same time the sudden influx of Christian immigrants has had a positive side effect in that Christians have suddenly become a significant political factor in the Iraqi capital and therefore the country itself, to an extent previously impossible due to their wide distribution in villages and towns throughout the north. With roughly one in seven Baghdadis now Christian, representing more than half the entire Christian population of the country, the potential for greater unity and influence has increased.

At the sectarian level, Iraq resembles Egypt in that a majority — probably two-thirds — of the Christian population is from a single confession, in this case the Chaldaean Catholic. Centered in Baghdad where their patriarch or katholikos, Bûlus Shaykhû (Paul Cheikho), resides, Chaldaeans are also the principal Christian community in Basra, Kirkûk, and Mosul, as well as exclusively comprising the six townships mentioned earlier. Another 10-15% of Iraqi Christians are Syrian Catholics, likewise centered in Baghdad — chiefly the Karrâda district where their imposing new cathedral is located, with smaller parishes in Mosul, Qâra Qûsh, and lesser villages of the north. Jacobites and Nestorians number each about 20-25,000, largely rural until the recent politically-motivated migration depopulated a number of their villages north of Mosul. The remainder of the Christian population is composed chiefly of Armenians (principally Gregorian Orthodox), found almost entirely in Baghdad.

Unlike the Christians of the Arab Levant, those in Iraq have not demonstrated a tendency to emigrate beyond their national frontiers in large numbers, an exception being found in the politically-insecure Nestorian minority. And though a higher percentage of Christians left than did Muslims, the actual numbers were small. The General Census of 1957 listed only 1,980 Christian Iraqi citizens living abroad, less than one percent of the total resident population. Jordan, by way of comparison, reported a proportion five times as great, and in Syria and Lebanon, the figure, though not officially established, has been shown to be even greater yet. In contrast to the Christian Lebanese who are more numerous abroad than at home, a very small number of Iraqi Christians have chosen to take up permanent residence abroad. There are a few small expatriate communities in the West such as New Telkaïf (Tall Kayf), a tiny area of Detroit populated by Chaldaean Catholics from the parent village north of Mosul, and a Nestorian community of some 10-15,000 in the vicinity of Chicago where their late patriarch was, until recently, based. Smaller settlements are found in New York, California, and Brazil, populated chiefly by expatriate Syrian Catholics and Nestorians, but on the whole they represent but a fraction of the Christian population still resident in Iraq. Moreover, many of those who do emigrate return if they prosper sufficiently or are able to find jobs in Iraq suitable to the training and education they have received in the West. Only among the Nestorians, many of whose roots in Iraq had been established only tenuously after World War I, was there a definite trend to stay abroad permanently.[133]

Also unlike their Levantine co-religionists, Iraqi Christians have tended to reproduce themselves as fast, if not faster, than the Muslim population, and this despite the fact that as elsewhere in the Arab World, Christians in Iraq marry later than Muslims.[134] The religious breakdown of the various age groups in the 1957 Census showed that while Iraqi Christians as a whole accounted for 3.3% of the combined Muslim-Christian population (exclusive of Yazidis, Sabaeans, and Jews), they formed 3.7% of the population under one year of age. Of those Iraqis, moreover, who had recently reached manhood having survived the high childhood and adolescent mortality rate, namely the 20-25 age group, 4.5% were Christian, indicating that the higher standards of health and sanitation enjoyed by Christians in the Levant generally also applies to Iraq.[135] Additional support for this trend was found in the greater prevalence of crippling diseases suffered at birth or in childhood among individuals of the Muslim community. Table XXXI of the 1957 Census revealed that 284 out of every 10,000 Muslim Iraqis were blind, one-eyed, deaf, crippled, lame, etc., as compared with 203 per 10,000 Iraqi

Christians, a rate 40% higher among Muslims than Christians. In conclusion it may be pointed out that the average size of the Christian Iraqi family, according to the Census, was all but equal to that of the Muslim Iraqi family: 5.41 as opposed to 5.48 members.[136] In view of these factors, Christians in Iraq can be assumed to form the same percentage of the population today that they did in 1957, or roughly 250,000 out of a total population in excess of eight million.[137]

Kuwait and the Arabian Gulf. Though home to no indigenous Christian Arab community since the Arab conquest in the 7th century, Kuwait (Al-Kuwayt — the diminutive form of *Kût,* the Arabic for "fort") and the principalities of the Arabian (Persian) Gulf have attracted foreign immigrants in large numbers — Arab Christians among them — as the result of the coincidence of the discovery of the region's phenomenal oil reserves and the Arab exodus from Palestine. Prior to 1948 there were only three Christian families of Kuwaiti nationality, and these of fairly recent Iraqi origin. True, there had been the presence of the American Dutch Reformed Church mission in Kuwait and other Gulf towns since the turn of the century, but this effort had been directed more towards the construction of schools and hospitals (e.g. 'Amâra, Basra, Kuwait, Buraymi, and Musqat) than to the establishment of native congregations.

During the 1950's, however, many thousands of Christians arrived from Lebanon, Syria, and the regions of Palestine recently incorporated into the new state of Israel, a few of whom were granted Kuwaiti nationality along with equally small numbers of foreign Muslims. The General Census of 1965 counted 134 Christians among those 220,059 residents possessing the greatly-coveted Kuwaiti citizenship, most of them originally of Palestinian or Iraqi nationality. Of the 247,000 non-Kuwaitis resident in 1965, 24,500 or one in ten were Christian. Of this figure, 13,400 were Arabs, chiefly Lebanese (5,600), Jordanian-Palestinian (3,000), and Syrian (2,500), the remainder being primarily Indian (5,900), British (2,700), and other European and American nationalities (1,400). The largest single Christian community is composed of the Catholics of various rites who share the recently-built cathedral near the old Jahra gate. Smaller numbers of Greek Orthodox, Copts, Jacobites, Assyrians, and Protestants also have active community organizations, both in Kuwait city and at the Kuwait Oil Company town of Aḥmadî. In the Lower Gulf (Qaṭar, Dubai, Abû-Ẓabî) the same pattern is found — significant numbers of Arab Levantine Christians and smaller communities of Indians and Europeans attracted by the wealth of recent oil discoveries, though no exact figures as to their numerical strength are available.

Turkey. Once home to large numbers of indigenous Eastern Christians, Turkey, by the time of Atatürk's declaration of the republic in 1923, had become almost exlusively Muslim. Virtually all of the Armenians in Anatolia were either massacred or deported during the First World War. Only those living in the relative security of Istanbul survived the war unscathed and remain today in numbers about 80,000. The few Armenians who survived the war in the provinces eventually emigrated or hid their religious and ethnic identity under a Turkish cover. Today, however, with the lessening of official Turkish animosity over the years, some tiny remnant communities have reemerged in such former centers as Diyârbâkîr, Mârdîn, Sivas, and Iskanderun (Alexandretta).

The Greek population of 1,600,000 was evicted from Anatolia following the collapse of the Asia Minor campaign of 1919-22 in exchange for some 500,000 Muslim Macedonians living in an area which had been occupied by Greece in the Balkan Wars of 1912-13. The Greek population around Istanbul and the islands of Imbros (Imroz) and Tenedos (Bozcada) at the mouth of the Dardanelles was permitted to remain. Numbering well over 100,000 as late as 1945, this community has been steadily emigrating to Greece, particularly since the troubles of the mid-1950's when the Cyprus issue produced anti-Greek demonstrations in Istanbul. Today no more than 25,000 Greeks remain in Turkey, though a number of Greeks now living in Athens keep their Turkish nationality along with homes in Istanbul and the Princes' Islands.

Of the 200,000 Jacobite and Syrian Catholic Christians

living in the Tur Abdîn region of southeastern Turkey at the outbreak of World I, many suffered the fate of the Armenians, and many others emigrated to Syria, Iraq, and Lebanon. Given a brief respite following the war by French occupation in 1919, the latter's withdrawal to the Aleppo-Baghdad rail line the following year left these beleaguered Christians once again exposed to a hostile Muslim environment. In 1924 the Jacobite patriarch abandoned his historic seat at Dayr Za'farân outside Mârdîn for the relative safety of French-occupied Syria (Homs) while his Uniate counterpart re-established his headquarters in the Catholic surroundings of suburban Beirut in 1932. Nevertheless, not all the Syrian Christians of what was to become Turkey felt forced to leave, and though subjected to many years of discrimination if not persecution, they have reemerged as a vital element in their historic homeland.

Some 45-50,000 Syrian Christians,[138] all Jacobites, save for a small minority of Syrian Catholics (3,000), live in Turkey today, augmented by an indeterminate number of Chaldaeans, probably in excess of 5,000, and Armenians scattered throughout Eastern Anatolia in isolated villages and in small urban concentrations.[139] Approximately 15,000 are now in Istanbul where they have emigrated since World War II in search of better jobs, a trend which continues at this writing. Another 5,000 are found outside the Tûr Abdîn proper, chiefly in the cities of Ankara, Adana, Mersin, Iskanderun, and the provincial towns of Gaziantep, Urfa, Diyârbâkîr, and Mârdîn. The remaining 30,000 are concentrated in and around what Freya Stark has termed "the double townlet, Muslim and Christian," of Midyat, in the center of the semi-arid Tûr Abdîn plateau.[140] The old town of Midyat remains today, a Christian stronghold of some 5,000 inhabitants, its steeple-dominated skyline broken by only one recently constructed minaret. The Muslim settlement two kilometers to the west is the Kurdish village of Estil whose inhabitants insisted on merging with Christian Midyat some years ago so that the honor of the provincial center should not fall to the despised Christian minority. In deference to local Muslim pressure, all government buildings, offices, and banks have been located in this Islamic appendage.

The 25,000 rurally-based Syrian Christians of the Tûr Abdîn are distributed among 30 surrounding villages and townships. Some are mixed Muslim (Kurd and Yazidi) and Christian, such as Arnas and Idil (Syr. Hazakh). Others are purely Christian, like Dereici (Syr. Kilith), a picturesque farming community of over 100 families nestled in a poplar grove along a branch of the Savur River whose aspect has changed relatively little since Badger visited here in 1850;[141] and Bakisian, a settlement of some 200 Christian families at the end of a rocky track some three miles beyond the town of Ḥâḫ (celebrated for its truly remarkable 5th-century church of the Virgin), who eke out a livelihood completely untouched by 20th-century technology.

Formerly the seat of both Jacobite and Syrian Catholic Christianity, Mârdîn today has but 1,000 Christians among its 35,000 inhabitants. Until 1969 it was the seat of a Jacobite bishopric, but following the death of its aged incumbent resident at Dayr Za'farân, it has come within the jurisdiction of the diocese of the Syrian Jazîra. A Syrian Catholic patriarchal vicar was in residence until 1973 when pressures from Turkish authorities forced him to seek refuge abroad as the result of his vocal criticism of government treatment of local Christians.

For many years the only Jacobite bishop remaining in Turkey was Ifrâm Bilgic, the 85-year-old-titular of Midyat, who has recently been succeeded by a younger replacement from Syria. Both the Jacobites and Syrian Catholics find it difficult to enlist the necessary qualified clergy since Turkish law requires that all Christian priests and bishops except those ministering to foreign congregations be Turkish born. Where the Jacobite church has been most successful is in reviving its monastic tradition. Many monasteries dot the landscape of Tûr Abdîn and half-a-dozen are still active, principally Mâr Gabriel (Dayr Al-'Umur) some 15 miles east of Midyat, and Dayr Za'farân, three miles east of Mârdîn. Both are well preserved and maintained by their small communities of monks and sisters who strive to nurture Syriac religious traditions and to educate the Christian children of the region in their ancient heritage.

Mâr Gabriel, dating from the late 4th century, is particularly well maintained by its 15 resident religious, and shows evidence of recent construction and expansion.

By and large the Syrian Christian population in Turkey, both urban and rural, is prosperous and relatively well educated. The villages in and around Midyat are locally famous for their vineyards and wines, and profit from modern agricultural methods acquired in recent years. Their coreligionist townsmen are chiefly gold and silversmiths — in Midyat and Mạrdîn as well as in the famous covered bazaar of Istanbul — though increasing numbers of the younger generation are entering such fields as engineering and international trade. Virtually all Syrian Christians in Turkey are bilingual and a great many are tri- or quadri-lingual. In Midyat the language at home is still Syriac, though for many in Mardîn and Diyârbâkîr and parts of the Tûr Abdîn such as Idil, it is Arabic. Turkish is learned at government schools, and many of the children now study English, particularly at the monastery schools. Two of the monks at Mâr Gabriel, for example, know English (one is in fact a graduate of New York University) as does the young schoolmaster, educated at the Syrian Orthodox monastery of Atshana in Lebanon.

Financially the Jacobite Church in Turkey is independent, though it does receive remittances from the faithful in wealthier dioceses such as Lebanon and the United States. The Syrian Orthodox Church in America with its headquarters at Hackensack, New Jersey, is particularly interested in helping to preserve the Jacobite tradition in the land of its birth, and has contributed towards the physical improvement of monasteries and churches, and has provided scholarships for clergy and laity wishing to study abroad. The Catholic Church likewise supports a modest charitable program, including orphanages, among the Syrian Catholic community.

The future of Syrian Christianity in Turkey is brighter now than at any time since the disaster of the First World War. Blessed with economic prosperity, large families, and unhampered by outright discrimination on the part of the Turkish government, the Church and its faithful will doubtless grow appreciably in the coming decades. It is probable that a certain number will continue the present drift to Istanbul and other larger cities, but it is unlikely that this will have a permanent effect on the fairly stable rural base of the Tûr Abdîn. The confrontations, moreover, between Christian emigrants from eastern Turkey and local working-class youths in Sweden (July, 1977) indicate that the promise of a better life in the industrial countries of northern Europe is not so bright as it once was. Both Sweden and Germany have tightened restrictions on Christians from Turkey and Iraq seeking asylum from alleged religious persecution at home (and thus gaining permanent residence status in their host countries), a factor that should lessen the emigration of young Syrian Christian families.

III Christians in the Present-day Social Structure of the Arab East

The physical and cultural isolation which Islamic society imposed upon its Christian population, particularly as the latter came gradually to be numerically inferior throughout most of the Arab East, was at once a protection and a barrier. There is no doubt that the survival of large Christian minority groups throughout the Arab East is due as much to the tolerance that has characterized traditional Islamic governments over the past thirteen centuries as to the tenacity and faith of the individual believers. Yet the same communal solidarity which the *dhimmi* and *millet* systems created within the individual minority groups was a strong barrier to the growth of modern nationalism since it precluded concern for, or even interest in, any people but those of one's own religious community. In an even larger sense it has created in this century a kind of dual conflict within each individual Christian in the Arab East, between the desire to identify with his own minority community and, on a wider scale, the Christian West and its cultural values, and a seemingly contradictory effort to establish his Arab identity as a justification for his presence in a predominantly Muslim society. Thus he might at once point with pride to the continuity of his descent from an ancient people antedating the Arab invasion — e.g. the Copts as the "true sons of Pharaoh," the Assyrians and Chaldaeans as the progeny of Sennacherib, the Melkites and Orthodox as heirs to the Byzantine Imperial establishment, and the Maronites as descendents of the Phoenicians — and at the same time trace his family back to the Christian Badu tribes of Ghassân and Al-Ḥîra, or to the Arab Christians of Najrân. As has been pointed out, there are historical justifications for both positions. The problem facing Christians as citizens of newly-independent Arab and, with the exceptions of Lebanon and Israel, Muslim states has arisen over the question of which of these two mainstreams in world society is to be emphasized in their own personal identity and outlook.

Christians in the Social Structure

The degree to which individual religious groups in the Middle East have guarded their peculiar customs and separate identity is difficult for a Westerner to comprehend. Despite having lived side by side for centuries, the individual *millets* had succeeded in avoiding meaningful contacts to the extent that few members of one group knew anything at all about the other. This was true not only of Muslim vis-à-vis his Christian neighbor, but of Christians from one communion with regard to those of another as well. The Rev. W.A. Wigram, writing of northern Mesopotamia during and immediately after World War I, tells the story of a Jacobite monk from Mârdîn who inquired of him if it were really true "that Nestorians wash their altar with asses' blood before they celebrate the Eucharist." According to Wigram, "the Nestorian Deacon who attended us and who heard this amazing aspersion, could hardly be restrained from falling on the inquirer there and then."[142] Even today most inhabitants of the Arab East know little or anything about the beliefs of those outside their own community other than what has been told to them by their fellow group members. Edward Atiya ('Aṭîya), a Lebanese Protestant of Orthodox origins, relates how, as he was growing up early in this century, he "developed, or rather inherited, a definite outlook common to all Syrian Christians of that time, a feeling of aversion for Moslems and Druzes (not to mention Catholic and Orthodox Christians), whom I learned to consider as our natural enemies. I felt that there was something alien and uncouth about them, that in some strange way they were not ordinary people like us."[143]

Whether he considered himself Arab, Assyrian, Phoenician, or Byzantine, the Christian of Egypt and the Fertile Crescent was irrevocably set apart from the mainstream of Muslim Arab society by the religious community into which he was born. And in a society where religion was the primary personal identity, a Christian could not escape association with it even if as a faith it meant nothing to him. For while most Christians were not branded with physical identity marks such as the crosses with which many Coptic villagers are tatooed on the inside of their wrists at an early age, the great majority were immediately identifiable as Christians by virtue of their name, the one means by which a person raised in the culture could, with rare exception, recognize the broad religious background of his neighbor. Discounting those first names of European, usually French or English, origin which only Christians bore — e.g. Charles, Joseph, Michel, Antoine, Georges, Pierre, etc. — certain family names were likewise irrevocably Christian owing to their meaning, such as Al-Muṭrân (archbishop, literally, "metropolitan"), Al-Khûrî (priest), Al-Shidyâq (deacon), and Al-Shammâs (sacristan) or to their New Testament association, like Bûlus (Paul), Buṭrus (Peter), Mattâ (Matthew), Sham'ûn (Simon), Sim'ân (Simeon), 'Azâr (Lazarus), Mikhâ'îl (Michael), and, from the Apocrypha, Rûfâ'îl (Raphael). Certain Old Testament names were more frequently employed by Christians than Muslims such as Dawûd (David), Ya'qûb (Jacob), and Ilyâs (Elias), while the names of certain early saints and martyrs — Istafân (Stephen), Mitrî (Dimitri), Anṭûn (Anthony), Taqlâ (Thecla), Mârûn (Maron), Sâbâ (Savas), and Niqûlâ (Nicholas), — have enjoyed continued popularity among Christians and are, of course, exclusively used by them.

A few names deriving from Church festivals were encountered, among them Bishâra (literally "Glad Tidings," the *'Id Al-Bishâra* being the Feast of the Annunciation) and Ghiṭâs ("baptism," or "Feast of the Epiphany"), as were names of Roman and Byzantine derivation such as Qusṭanṭîn (Constantine), Iskandar (Alexander), Kaysar (Caesar), Rûmî (Roman), and Bâṣil, and those deriving from Crusader influence: Al-Faranjîya (Frankish), Duryân (D'Orient), Duwayḥî (de Douhai), Bardawîl (Baldwin), Tarabayh (Torbey), Ashqar (blond, fair-complexioned), and Ṣalîbî (Crusader), chiefly among Maronites and Greek Orthodox. And while most family names beginning with *'Abd* ("slave of," e.g. 'Abd Al-Nâṣir — Nasser) had strong Muslim associations, there were Christian examples as well, e.g. 'Abd Al-Masîḥ ("slave of the Messiah") and 'Abd Al-Nûr (slave or servant of the Light).

Surnames such as Ḥaddâd (smith), Najjâr (carpenter), Khayyâṭ (tailor), Ṣâ'igh (goldsmith), Ḥallâq (barber), Ḥaffâr (engraver), Ḥajjâr (stonemason),[144] and Khâzin (treasurer), denoted trades, or in the case of the last-mentioned, positions of community responsibility, in which Christians had traditionally been prominent, Islamic society having reserved the tasks performed by artisans, craftsmen, and handlers of money for members of religious minority communities — Christians and Jews especially.[145] Other family names such as 'Arîḍa, 'Aṭîya, 'Aṭallah, Dibbâs, Ghanîma, Sursûq, Tâbit, and Ṭirâd, carried no specific religious meaning, yet nevertheless were almost invariably borne by Christians, frequently of one particular sect. In formal situations one's religious preference can be known by the title with which one's name is prefaced, Muslims being traditionally addressed as *sayyid* (literally, a descendant of the Prophet Mohammad) and Christians as *khawâjah* (sir).

First names, such as those already mentioned, and others like Ramses and additional Pharaonic derivatives in Egypt, as well as those such as Isaac and Benjamin which were almost invariably borne by Jews but employed as well by Assyrian Christians, were, when combined with an obvious or even potentially Christian family name, as telling of the individual's religious background as a cross about the neck. For this reason many Christian families, especially in recent years, have often preferred to give their children those names of Arab origin devoid of Islamic connotation yet employed not infrequently by Muslims. Common examples would include 'Afîf (righteous), Amîn (faithful), Fâ'iz (victor), Fâris (knight and Persian), Ḥabîb (beloved), Kamâl (perfection), Khalîl (belovèd friend), Na'îm (felicity), Najîb (noble), Wadî' (gentle-hearted), and Samîr (companion). To this list must be added as well Jesus, Mary, and Joseph ('Îsâ, Maryam, Yûsuf), indicating by their popularity among Muslims as well as Christians the high place which the Christian Lord and His parents occupied in Islamic hagiology. To a lesser extent, names usually associated with Muslims, such as Fu'âd (heart), Ibrâhîm (Abraham), Ismâ'îl (Ishmael), Sulaymân (Solomon), Manṣûr (victorious), Tawfîq and Muwaffaq (success), and even 'Umar and Muṣṭafâ have been given to Christian children, primarily as a means of emphasizing their Arab rather than Christian identity. Instances of Muslims bearing names generally associated with Christians were far rarer, though the Alawites not infrequently used certain Christian first names (hence their derisive nickname "Nuṣayrî" or "Little Christians"), while among the Druzes both first and family names of generally Christian association were encountered.

From the earliest days of the Muslim conquest of Syria, Egypt, and Mesopotamia, native Christians, in particular, those of educated backgrounds, sought to escape the narrow confines of their communities by acting as intermediaries between the Christian and Muslim cultures. The history of the Umayyad and 'Abbâsid caliphates is studded with individual Christians of the Orthodox, Jacobite, and Nestorian communities who served the Muslim society in which they lived as translators, scientists, physicians, poets, and ministers of state. John of Damascus, one of the "Fathers" of the Orthodox Church, grew to manhood during the early years of the Umayyad caliphate as one of the boon companions of the young Caliph Yazîd I, in whose company he was seen at the increasingly frequent drinking bouts which scandalized the more pious among Damascene Muslims.[146] Though a Melkite by religion, Saint John was of purely Syrian origins and served the caliphate as financial administrator of Damascus, a position which his father and grandfather[147] had held before him. Later removed from office on a false charge of collaboration with the Byzantine Emperor, John retired to the monastery of Mâr Sâbâ (Saint Savas) near Bethlehem where he devoted his life to the struggle against the iconoclastic movement which the Emperor Leo the Isaurian (717-741) had championed after 728, and also to the careful preparation of arguments which his co-religionists in Dâr Al-Islâm could offer Muslims in defense of their Orthodox Christian faith. During the 'Abbâsid period, Nestorians such as Jirjis Ibn-Bakhtîshû (d. ca. 771) and Ḥunayn Ibn-Isḥâq (d. 873) served the caliphate as court physicians and translators of the great scientific and medical works of antiquity, while an equally laudable company of Jacobites, among them Yaḥya Ibn-'Adi (d. 974) and Al-Muṭrân (metropolitan) Abu 'Alî 'Îsâ Ibn-Zur'a (d. 1008), "busied themselves with the revision of existing editions of Aristotelian works or the preparation of fresh translations thereof and were... the chief influence in introducing Neo-Platonic speculations and mysticism into the Arabic world."[148]

The Crusades forced many indigenous Christians to make a choice for the first time in centuries between their Christian faith and their Islamic environment. And while few supported the Franks to the extent of the Maronites who provided Raymond of Toulouse "with guides and a limited number of recruits" in his successful campaign through Palestine and the siege of Jerusalem (1099),[149] all suffered from the taint of collaboration with the enemy once the Crusaders were finally driven from Syria in 1291. Nestorian and Jacobite scholars flourished under the patronage of the early Mongol Il-Khans (e.g. the Jacobite Katholikos Abû-Al-Faraj Ibn-Al-'Ibri, 1226-1286, the "Barhebraeus" of medieval European scholars), but once the seventh of these Mongol princes, Ghâzân Maḥmûd (1295-1304), abandoned his predecessors' long flirtation with Christianity and adopted Islam, Christian influence began to wane rapidly. Both the later Mongol rulers and the Mamlûk counterparts in Egypt came to depend less and less on their Christian subjects in those areas where they had previously served the princes of Islâm, and not infrequently imposed severe restrictions on all non-Muslims, thus driving them into a more rigidly self-contained society which no longer interacted productively with that of the Muslim majority. Many Christians during this time apostasized, while others, particularly the intellectual element, sought refuge in safer havens such as the recently re-Christianized, but still oriental, Sicily. During the reigns of the Norman kings Roger II (1130-1154) — to his critics the "half-heathen king" — and his grandson William II (1166-1189) Muslim and Christian lived together in a tolerant society all the more remarkable for the intolerance which surrounded it, attracting many Christian refugees from Muslim persecution in the Levant. One such figure was Roger's greatest admiral, Jirjis of Antioch, while one of the highest personages in the magnificent Palermo court of Frederick II Hohenstaufen, king of Sicily (1215-1250) and Jerusalem (1229-1244), was the Jacobite astrologer and translator Thâdhûrî (Theodore), likewise of Antioch.

The small, but steady migration of Christians from the Arab East to Europe was augmented in 1584 with the establishment in Rome of the Maronite College by Pope Gregory XIII for the training of Maronite students for the priesthood. Most returned eventually to Lebanon, but others remained in Europe where a revived interest in the East created a demand for native scholars to occupy chairs of Oriental languages and history at the University of Paris and other seats of Western learning.

With the destruction of the decadent and oppressive Mamluk power at Marj Dâbiq (near Aleppo) in 1516, and the subsequent extension of Ottoman authority over Syria, Egypt, and eventually Mesopotamia, the lot of indigenous Christians improved appreciably, particularly that of the Orthodox. But with the decline which set in only a century later, Christians throughout Ottoman dominions began to look increasingly to the West for assistance against the oppressive rule of independent and rapacious governors who were beyond the control of Istanbul, and gradually during the course of the 17th and 18th centuries, the European powers, particularly the French, established unofficial protectorates over Levantine Christian minorities such as the Maronites and other Uniate groups. Throughout the 19th century this relationship became firmer and by the eve of World War I most Christians of the Arab East looked to Europe both for protection and cultural inspiration. Edward Atiya recalls how in his youth "European morals, habits, ways of living, dress and general behaviour were idealized as belonging to a superior race."[150] In his own mind the Christian Arab thought of himself as the chosen intermediary between East and West. Just as his ancestors had salvaged that which was great in Byzantine and Roman culture, translated it into Arabic, and preserved it while Europe slumbered, he now felt it time to complete the cycle, to reintroduce the great ideas of antiquity as revived and enlarged during the Renaissance and Enlightenment to his uneducated and benighted Muslim countrymen who labored under a yoke of a decadent medievalism in a world which demanded rapid change and Westernization. Not surprisingly most Muslims resented this role which the Arab Christian had carved for himself, and continued to regard the various Christian groups as second class citizens who were unworthy of respect as either political or social equals.

There was no doubt, however, that by the beginning of this century the average Christian in the Arab East was far superior to his Muslim neighbor in terms of education and material well-being. While education for most Muslims consisted of rote memorization of the Koran, and this only for the men, Christians in the 17th century had begun in earnest to revive their long tradition and high standards of learning under the influence of Catholic, and later Protestant, missionaries. Though the motives of their European and American benefactors were not always those of pure education, the Arab Christian profited enormously from the efforts of the various missions to promote their theological messages by means of Western instruction methods. And as the political power of Europe was extended into the Middle East in the late 19th century, the already existing educational establishments which missionary rivalry had fathered were institutionalized and in the ensuing decades secularized to a great extent, particularly in the case of the Protestant schools which by the eve of World War II stretched in a long chain from Luxor (Al-Uqṣur) to Basra. Catholic institutions as well were divested, particularly outside Lebanon, of their heavily religious curriculum and broadened in their scope so as to attract non-Catholics and even non-Christians whose own religious beliefs were scrupulously respected. The bigotry with which many missionaries and educators viewed the ancient Christian communities of the East, among them no less a figure than the Rev. Daniel Bliss, founder of the American University of Beirut,[151] was replaced in the early part of this century by a deep respect for these venerable bodies whose survival greatly enriched present-day Christianity by preserving a heritage of religious practices which could be traced directly to the earliest New Testament churches.

The great contribution of the mission schools was of course to focus attention on the need for universal education, prompting Muslims to abandon their previous complacency and likewise strive toward raising their own people from the illiteracy, or near-illiteracy, that characterized all but a tiny minority. In the meantime, however, these schools gave native Christians an initial educational advantage, which they still possess today.

Though most Arab states now have extensive public education systems which are compulsory from the ages of seven through twelve, it will be at least a generation, and perhaps two, before the level of Muslim literacy approaches that of the Christian Arab. Even in progressive Lebanon enrollment in public schools has only recently come to equal that of private and religious institutions and there are still an estimated 100,000 school-age children, almost entirely Muslim, who are not today receiving the education to which by law they are entitled. Thirty years ago, on the eve of Lebanese independence, only 15% of the country's students were enrolled in public schools, in view of which the present-day achievement should not be minimized; nevertheless there still exists a disparity in Lebanon and in every other state of the Arab East between the percentage of literate Christians and those Christians currently receiving an education, and the Muslim population within the same categories. In 1942, over two-thirds (70%) of the school enrollment in Lebanon was Christian, while at the same time the total Christian population was officially acknowledged to be slightly over half.[152] A survey of literacy rates among the various Lebanese communities taken two decades later still showed a Muslim illiteracy rate half as high again as that of Christians in the rural areas.[153] And in urban areas such as Beirut and Tripoli where Christian literacy was virtually universal the disparity was probably greater.

The 1960 Census of Egypt registered a 41.4% rate of literacy among native Christians (54% among men) as opposed to 23.8% for Muslims.[154] The Syrian Census of the same year showed an equal discrepancy in Christian and Muslim educational background, with over half of the Christian population of the legal marriageable age (53.1%) being judged as literate, while less than one-third (29.2%) of the Muslim population of the same age was so designated.[155] In Iraq the difference was even more marked: 53% of all Iraqi Christians over the age of five years (64% of the men) were literate as compared with only 16% of the Muslim community, as indicated by the 1957 Census.[156] Of Israeli Arabs of Christian background, 76% were literate in 1961 as compared with 38% of their Muslim countrymen.[157] The Social Survey of Amman conducted in the early 1960's showed that over 80% of the Christian household heads in that city had completed basic elementary studies (through age 12) as compared with barely half of their Muslim counterparts (54%), a pattern which is encountered throughout the Kingdom of Jordan.[158]

At the university level, Christians until very recently far surpassed Muslims in terms of percentage attendance within their own communities. In Lebanon the two oldest universities, Saint-Joseph and the American University of Beirut, have traditionally maintained Christian majorities (roughly 85% and 55% respectively) in their total student bodies, as have the smaller Western-oriented universities such as the Beirut University College, the Hagazian College (Armenian Protestant), and the Middle East College (Seventh-Day Adventist), respectively 56%, 79%, and 87% Christian in their enrollment in 1968. The more-recently organized Arab University, a branch of the University of Alexandria, and the public University of Lebanon, have attracted heavy Muslim enrollment in recent years[159] but their impact on the traditionally Christian university-educated class in Lebanon will not be felt for some time, particularly in that the general level of instruction and calibre of student is undeniably inferior to that of the older institutions.

Elsewhere in the Middle East, Christians constituted a percentage of university graduates disproportionate to their actual numbers. In both Egypt and Syria, the censuses of 1960 showed 20% of their respective university-educated citizens to be Christian (at the same time finding that Christians numbered only 7-8% of the total population), while in Iraq, Christians, who counted only 3.25% of the total population in 1957, comprised 21% of all Iraqis possessing secondary school diplomas, and 43% of those having university degrees.[160] This latter imbalance was due largely to the fact that the only first-rate secondary school in Iraq at that time was Baghdad College, founded by American Jesuits from Boston in the early 1930's, whose enrollment was from half to two-thirds Christian (the actual Muslim percentage varied from year to year depending on the internal political situation), and whose graduates were in the forefront of those Iraqi secondary graduates accepted for university training abroad. The Jesuit program was extended in 1958 to include a four-year university, Al-Ḥikma, which together with Baghdad College continued to provide the finest higher education available in the country until the Fathers were forcibly evicted in 1968 by the radical Ba'thist government then in power, for the most shortsighted of political motivations.

In all states of the Arab East, the Christian percentage of public as well as private school faculty far surpassed the Christian share of the total population. Christian faculty members in the Arab schools of Israel, to take an extreme example, actually outnumbered Muslims as late as 1955 even though the Muslim enrollment was 65% of the total.[161] At the administrative level, Christian leadership in the offices of high-school principal, university president, and even Minister of Education, was far greater than their purely numerical strength at large would indicate. The first President of the heavily Muslim University of Baghdad in 1956 was a Jacobite Christian, Mattâ Al-'Aqrâwî (Metti Akrawi), the beginning of the decade having witnessed the appointment of a Greek Orthodox Christian, Qusṭanṭîn Zurayq, now one of the leading professors of the American University of Beirut, as the first president of the University of Damascus. Their faculties, like their student bodies, were likewise disproportionately Christian, while in the private and foreign institutions of higher learning, where political pressures were less demanding of a majority Muslim presence, the Christian ratio among the faculty was even greater. In Lebanon, where the numerical strength of Christians and their considerable tradition of learning made Christian presence in all areas of education dominant, the post of Minister of Education has been traditionally held by either a Maronite or a Greek Orthodox (e.g. Orthodox publisher Ghassân Tuwayni in the first cabinet of President Sulaymân Faranjîya, September 1970); another Lebanese Christian educator, Khalîl Bustânî, continued in the tradition of Baghdad and Damascus as first president of the recently-organized public University of Lebanon. Outside the Middle East, those Arab historians, economists, and political-scientists best known to the Western reader were, until very recently, almost exclusively Christian, for example Philip Hitti, Charles

Issawi, Majid Khadduri, and Kamal Salibi.

In other related areas such as journalism and the arts, Christians have played a significant, and sometimes dominant, role in all countries of the Arab East. The best-known Arabic language daily in the Middle East, *Al-Ahrâm* of Cairo, was originally founded in the late 19th century by Lebanese Christian emigrants and still today has a strong Christian, chiefly Coptic, representation on its staff. The new chairman and chief editor of *Al-Akhbâr,* the daily with the largest circulation in the Arab World, is a Copt, Mûsâ Ṣabrî. Probably the most objective and widely read Lebanese daily, *Al-Nahâr,* is published by former Minister of Education Ghassân Tuwayni, while the great majority of Beirut's many competing journals, both in Arabic and in European languages, are headed by Christian editors. In Syria, Jordan, and Iraq as well Christians have served as editors of newspapers covering the whole spectrum of political orientation (e.g. Emille Shuwayri and Luṭfî Ghantûf for Damascus' *Al-Ba'th,* Rûfâ'îl Bûṭî and Dawûd Ṣâ'igh for Baghdad journals, now defunct, representing respectively moderate Socialist and outright Communist viewpoints). In the fields of Western music, art, and literature, the Christians of the Arab East, particularly Armenians, still hold unchallenged hegemony; the more traditional oriental music world likewise has its Christian luminaries such as singers Fayrûz, Ṣabâḥ (respectively Nuhâd Ḥaddâd and Jeanette Faghâlî) and Wadî' Al-Sâfî, as well as classical lutenists Munîr and Jamîl Bashîr. In the world of Arab cinema individual Christians are well established, some, such as Omar Sharif (born Michel Shalḥûb) having achieved international recognition. In the field of literature, many Christians have made significant contributions to the body of contemporary Arabic language works, and a few, notably Khalîl Jibrân, a native of the Maronite mountain stronghold of Bisharrî in North Lebanon, who emigrated to the United States and died there in 1931, are world renowned.

For many of these prominent figures, Jibrân among them[162] the religion into which they were born had ceased to be of any personal importance, but for the majority of Christians of the Arab East, their religious identity and their practices continued to exact a strong, if sometimes grudging, loyalty. To the Western observer, many of these practices, ranging from the role and training of the clergy to the actual liturgies themselves, seemed far removed from Christianity as practiced in the West. With the exception of the Latin-Rite and Protestant churches whose congregations follow the liturgical customs prescribed by their parent bodies in the West, Middle Eastern Christians adhered to rites and customs as foreign to those of Rome, Geneva, and Canterbury as can be imagined. Conducted in Greek, Syriac, Coptic, Armenian, and Arabic the liturgies of the churches of Syria, Egypt, and Mesopotamia invariably incorporated many of the ancient forms of Christian worship which had long since disappeared from Western religious observance.[163] Jules Leroy, who visited the Chaldaean Monastery of Our Lady of the Seedtime near Mosul in the early 1950's, remarked that "it is a curious sight to see monks carrying out actions which I had always associated with Moslems, though in fact they are in the oldest Christian tradition."[164] Here he was specifically referring to the practice of praying standing up in regular rows, often separated according to sex, a custom observed in one form or another in all Eastern Churches including the Uniate Catholic Rites. Only among the Maronites has it become acceptable to kneel in the Western manner, and, generally speaking, for women only. For many of the more primitive congregations, particularly among the Copts, Jacobites, and Nestorians, it is still common for a supplicant to assume the ancient upright pose, arms half-extended with palms held upward before addressing his creator.

With further reference to Chaldaean ritual, Mr. Leroy, despite his otherwise favorable approach to Eastern Christians and their customs, could not resist describing the daily religious office of the Chaldaean church, which is composed of readings, psalms, and hymns sung by two antiphonal choirs entirely from memory, "as absolute cacophony," an effect which was heightened by the use of drums and cymbals at such sacred moments as the Consecration, likewise encountered in Coptic rituals. A similar reaction was recorded a few years later by a young English exchange professor attending a weekday mass at the Chaldaean Cathedral in Tall Kayf who, according to his author companion, remarked as they left the church that "I now see what primitive Christianity must have been, and why the Romans disliked it so!" He was, nonetheless, deeply impressed — as are nearly all Western Christians — with the obvious intensity of the worshippers' faith as expressed through these ancient rituals.

> Even at three o'clock on a Tuesday afternoon it [the Chaldaean Cathedral at Tall Kayf] is packed, seething with a strange, weird life of its own. If the dirtiest church ever seen, it is also the most fervent... the singing has a wild ululant force, a plainsong that cannot throw off its Arabian influence; it rises suddenly to a climax, then resolves again into a continuous flat howl. It is very fervid. It seems the kind of prayer apt for those who feel surrounded. Perhaps they wailed like this in Constantinople as the Turkish armies closed round the city: the more fanatical, the more hardpressed...[165]

Yet such intensity of religious expression is not confined to the isolated outposts of Christianity as Tall Kayf. The author has experienced it many times in the relative security of Aleppo, Jerusalem, Haifa, and Cairo, and even in the complacent atmosphere of Christian Lebanon itself. Christianity in the Arab East still believes in miracles, apparitions, and visitations. All of Lebanon rejoiced when Pope Paul VI, in 1965, beatified the 19th century religious hermit and Maronite mystic, Shirbal Makhlûf, to whom thousands of miraculous cures had been attributed since his death on Christmas Day in 1898. Church bells in Lebanon rang throughout the day on Sunday, 5 December, at the same time as the Beatification ceremonies were being held in Rome in the presence of the Maronite Patriarch, 550 clergy from all the Christian communities of Lebanon, and an official delegation of Lebanese notables, headed by Speaker of the Parliament, Ṣabrî Ḥamâdî (a Shî 'a Muslim), and including several other Muslims and Druzes. Hilltops and rooftops were brightly lit as thousands gathered in their homes to watch live television coverage of the consecratory mass, celebrated by Patriarch Méouchy at the high altar of Saint Peter's in the presence of nine Lebanese bishops, eighteen Cardinals, and "a host of foreign bishops."[166] At the monastery of Mâr Mârûn at 'Anâyâ, near Byblos, where Father Shirbal had lived most of his religious life in quiet and anonymous meditation, thousands flocked to continuous masses celebrated from dawn to midnight.

Such manifestations were far from uncommon. Only a few months later, in April of 1966, some 4,000 faithful gathered to the village of 'Ayn Al-Dalb near Sidon on Good Friday to keep the Easter Vigil with a fourteen-year-old schoolgirl, Warda Jirjis Manṣûr, who in the previous week had received two visions of the Virgin Mary. The story of her confrontation, reminiscent of the visitation at Fatima a half-century earlier, dominated the front pages of the Lebanese newspapers for a week.[167] Two years later, another celebrated apparition appeared in Cairo over the Church of the Virgin in suburban Zaytûn. First reported on 2 April 1968, the vision was witnessed by thousands of worshippers on the Coptic Easter, 21 April. Accompanied by miraculous cures, the apparition was verified by the Coptic Patriarch, Kyrillos VI, on 4 May, "with full confidence and great joy,"[168] sending thousands of pilgrims, Egyptian and foreign, to the site of the miracle in the weeks that ensued, a fitting prelude to the dedication of the new Coptic Cathedral of Saint Mark at 'Abbâsîya in June (1968), at which time historic relics of that saint — the patron of Egyptian Christianity — were returned by the Roman Catholic Church in a significant gesture of oecumenism.[169] The most recent documented miracle occurred in the summer of 1970, when the Virgin, appearing to thousands of Lebanese witnesses, hovered over the dome of the Jacobite church in the Musayṭba quarter of Beirut for three consecutive nights in August.[170] A miraculous tale which was widely circulated in Beirut in the midst of the September 1975 outbreak of Christian-Muslim hostilities in Lebanon, and given considerable credence among the faithful at the time, told of a Maronite taxi-driver who picked up a heavily cloaked female passenger one evening during a lull in the fighting. She asked to be taken to a point in the center of the shooting, and when the driver hesitated, she proffered a 100-pound note ($45); during the course of the journey he raised the subject of the current hostilities and expressed a pessimistic forecast. The soft-spoken lady in the back seat quietly assured him that by Christmas the forces of Christ would triumph and that everything would be as it had been before. A moment later when the driver looked around, the lady had vanished though the taxi had at no time slowed its rapid pace nor had the driver heard a door open or close. Word of an apparition of the Virgin quickly spread, but alas, Christmas 1975 came and went with some of the heaviest inter-communal strife to date and prospects of a settlement seemed as bleak as ever.

The clergy and hierarchy of the Eastern Churches continued to play a far more personal and influential role in the life of their communities than was found in the Christian West. All of the Christian communions of the Arab East, Orthodox, Catholic, and Heterodox, permitted marriage of the clergy, requiring celibacy only of their bishops and patriarchs who were usually drawn from the ranks of monastics. The parishes and even dioceses were usually small so that the priest and bishop were well known to virtually every member of the local community. Very often the priest would have an additional vocation, particularly in the Orthodox and Jacobite churches, either as a tradesman or farmer, assuming his religious duties only on Sunday or whenever else they were required. Thus the separation of clergy and laity that has become such an issue in Western Christendom, has never been a problem in the East. Many Roman Catholics find the existence of married priests in their Eastern Rites somewhat bizarre, since their own Church in the West is fighting strongly to retain the rule of celibacy which it adopted in the 11th century; but for Eastern Catholics it is an accepted social phenomenon to the extent that an unmarried priest, particularly in the villages and rural areas, is exceedingly rare.

In the economic sphere, Christians, with their long-standing Western ties, freedom from religious restrictions relating to usury, and desire to compensate for their political insecurity under Islamic rule through the amassing of private fortune, had succeeded, by the eve of national independence, in widening the gap separating them from their Muslim counterparts in terms of income level. The Christian prosperity cut across confessional lines, but most often in Syria and Lebanon it was the urban Orthodox families, as a rule on closer terms with the ruling Muslim establishment than other Christians, who most frequently achieved great wealth. With the coming of the European Mandates, greater numbers of Christians of all sects prospered as the demand for bi- or multi-lingual personnel increased, not only in the government administration, but in all areas — education, health, commerce, services, and tourism. Christians, with their tradition of learning, commercial enterprise, and above all their acceptance, or at least awareness, of Western values and their frequent connections with Europe and its institutions, became the natural inheritors of the growing prosperity that was fostered during the relatively stable period of the Mandate era through foreign investment, government grants, technical assistance programs, etc., and in the post-World War II years of unprecedented oil-based prosperity.

As the Middle East embarked on an independent national course in the years following World War II, the Christians in the various Arab states formed a dominant force in the commercial and financial establishment of the Arab East and, on the average, were considerably more prosperous than the Muslims, the vast majority of whom were then still largely illiterate, unskilled, and in rural areas afflicted with crushing poverty and disease. In Beirut, the Christians, as observed by Pierre Rondot in the early 1950's, "with the greater part of commercial operations, control banking, industry, small manufacturing and the greater part of the white-collar professions."[171] In Aleppo and Damascus, the large Arab as well as Armenian Christian population prospered as the money-changers, brokers, and finally the principal money-lenders, positions which made of this numerical minority a predominant force on the financial scene.[172] In Baghdad and throughout Iraq, virtually all private services from hotels and restaurants to riverboat transportation were in the hands of Christians, notably Chaldaeans from Mosul. In Lebanon, more than a quarter-century after independence, Christians still supplied the vast majority of government revenues, controlled industry, the tourist trade, commerce, and above all, banking. "It is a fact," observed Charles Issawi during the mid 1960's, "that most businessmen — and therefore most of the rich — are Christians."[173] The governor of the Central Bank of Lebanon is always a Christian (for years President Ilyâs Sarkîs) as are virtually all the top men in the nation's numerous banking institutions. Moreover, the executive elite of all major foreign companies with Lebanese offices and of all financial institutions operating directly in or through subsidiaries in Lebanon are, with few exceptions, Christian.

The Intra Bank crisis of late 1966, which severely damaged Lebanon's economy through loss of foreign confidence and capital (chiefly Saudi and Kuwaiti Arab), was nothing more than an in-group struggle between various Christian factions in the Lebanese banking world. The motivating factors behind the crisis were as much political as personal; but the religious factor was also significant insofar as Pierre Idda (Eddé), former Minister of Finance and later President of the Lebanese Bankers' Association, was held chiefly responsible for his bank's failure by the late, flamboyant Intra Bank President, Yûsuf Baydas (Beidas). As scion of one of the great Maronite Catholic families in Lebanon, Idda was bound to resent the phenomenal success of Baydas, a Palestinian-born Greek Orthodox whose English, Protestant education (Saint George's Anglican School, Jerusalem) prevented his ever being accepted by Idda. As were nearly all the prominent figures in Lebanon's financial establishment, Idda was trained in the old French Catholic tradition. Significantly, Baydas was replaced by Lucien Daḥdâḥ, scion of an old *shaykhli* Maronite family.[174] This undercurrent of conflict among Catholic and non-Catholic Christian (virtually all of Baydas's close associates were either Orthodox or Anglican, with a scattering of Druzes and Muslims) was of considerable concern to fellow Lebanese, for not only do Christians as a whole, being the controlling factor in Lebanon's Banking and Commerce, have the most to lose in an economic crisis, but there is little doubt that if the Lebanese banking structure were to collapse the whole economy would crumble with it. And if current prosperity, however shaky, were to vanish as it surely would in the event of a total banking collapse, the old political rivalries and hostilities, once cushioned by the fat of plenty, would again be exposed. The government has, therefore, belatedly but wisely taken steps to prevent the repetition of such a crisis, and to all appearances has succeeded,[175] but only at the price of having to solicit international banking interests on a heavy investment basis in order to keep the many Lebanese banking institutions afloat. Nearly all Lebanese banks are in fact now Lebanese in name only, controlling interest having been acquired by American, British, and French houses.

Despite Christian dominance at all significant control points in Lebanon's economy,[176] Muslims nevertheless participate in, and prosper from, the current system. And though a majority of the wealthy are still Christian, a growing percentage of Muslims are earning their place among the economic elite through the Lebanese financial system itself or by means of emigration to Kuwait, West Africa, Libya, Australia, the Gulf, or wherever economic opportunity beckons. Unquestionably the economic level of Muslims in Lebanon is appreciably higher than that of their brethren in Syria, Jordan, Iraq, and Egypt, and obviously it is in the Christian interest to maintain the current level of prosperity and to see that everyone shares in it.

In Syria, Christians, traditionally the country's economic elite, have greatly weakened their former financial, commercial, and professional strength through emigration. Despite a considerable numerical decline since the mid 1950's, however, Christians are still more frequently encountered in the fields of business, trade, education, medicine, law, engineering, and other professions, than their numbers would indicate. As in Lebanon and Jordan, the governor of the Central Bank, Dr. Karâm Tûmâ, is a Christian. The only official confirmation of the Christians' higher economic level was the Census of 1960 which showed a higher percentage of Christians to be classified as "employers" than Muslims. In all but two provinces the percentage of the Christian work force so classified was considerably higher than their proportion of the total population, and in these two (Homs and Ḥawrân) was equal to it. The overall national percentage of

Christians among Syrian employers was half again as high (12.5%) as their share of the total population (8%), and in Aleppo where the Christian population was only 19% of the total, they constituted nearly one-third (29.2%) of the employers, presumably businessmen and professionals.

A survey of the telephone directories of Aleppo and the Jazîra for the year of the Census showed a higher percentage of Christians to be in a position to afford the luxury of telephone service at their home or private business establishment than did Muslims. Thus in Aleppo, only 19% Christian in 1960, identifiably Christian names were found to constitute one-third (32%) of the telephone listings. In the Jazîran cities of Al-Ḥasaka and Qâmishlî (43% and 58% Christian respectively in 1960), the percentage of identifiably Christian listings was likewise considerably higher (63% and 69% respectively).[177] In Aleppo more than half the doctors and a high proportion of the lawyers and engineers officially listed in the directory were Christian, while in the cities of the Jazîra a large majority of the representatives of these three professions were either Arab or Armenian Christian. In Jordan, Christians prospered at a level considerably higher than that of the Muslims. As in neighboring Syria and Lebanon they constitute a higher percentage of the professional and commercial element, and further exert a control over the large and lucrative pilgrimage traffic to the Holy Sites in Jerusalem, Bethlehem, and other localities now occupied by Israel, as well as in Nazareth, Israeli since 1948. At a higher level, the governor of the Central Bank since 1963 has been Dr. Khalîl Sâlim, a Greek Orthodox Christian from the Christian village of Al-Ḥuṣn on the East Bank near Irbid, and Minister of National Economy before appointment to his present office. Veteran Minister of Foreign Affairs, Anṭûn 'Aṭallah, one of Jordan's most prominent Christian officials, is by profession a banker, as is Sulayman Ṣaqr, the Greek Catholic General Manager of the Jordan National Bank and former mayor of Amman in the early 1950's. A sociological survey of Amman published by the Jordanian government in 1960 on matters relating to the social, economic, and educational status and patterns of the inhabitants of the Jordanian capital (40,000 of them Christian), showed, when broken down by religious affiliation (2,476 Muslim and 448 Christian households were surveyed), that the average monthly income of the employed Christians interviewed was double that of the employed Muslims: 38.2 Jordanian Dinars ($107) as opposed to 19.3 Dinars ($54). One out of every six employed Christians was, moreover, earning over 50 Dinars ($140) per month as compared with only one out of every sixteen employed Muslims; and of those 28 Ammanis surveyed who earned over 200 Dinars monthly ($560), nearly half (13) were Christians. At the other end of the spectrum, the percentage of Muslims who earned less than 5 Dinars ($14) monthly was three times as high as the proportion among Christians (13.3% vs. 4.7%).[178] Not surprisingly the average Christian household unit expenditure per month was on the average twice that of the Muslim family surveyed. Of additional interest was the fact that 15.5% of the Christians employed were women, compared with only 7.1% of the Muslim work force, indicating that Christian women enjoyed considerably more freedom and opportunity to escape the traditional family role as mother and housekeeper than did their Muslim sisters. In neighboring Israel, the predominantly urban, universally literate, and often college-educated Christian was likewise on an economically far higher plane than that of the Arab Muslim, and even the Oriental Jewish immigrant.[179]

Iraqi Christians were to all appearances significantly more prosperous, some three and a half decades after independence, than their Muslim neighbors, despite a large, generally poor, rural population. As in all the other states of the Arab East, Christians had served their government in the highest financial positions, including that of Minister of Finance, held three times during the 1930's and 40's by the late Yûsuf Ghanîma. No current figures are available which indicate Christian as opposed to Muslim average income, but the 1957 General Census showed that in the area of housing, the Christian advantage was considerable. At that time more than one-third (35%) of Iraqi Muslim families were found to be living in lean-to shanties or tents, as opposed to only a few Christian families (1.5% of the Christian total), while another quarter (28%) lived in only slightly better mud and reed dwellings, compared with half that percentage (14.5%) of Christian families. At the other end of the housing spectrum, 21% of Christian families enjoyed the luxury of four or more rooms of living space as compared to only 8.4% of Iraqi Muslims, and at the highest level — those Iraqis living in private homes or villas — over 12% were Christian, four times their percentage of the total population.

In Egypt, a large number of rural Copts in Upper Egypt shared a poverty almost as abject as that of the Muslim *fallaḥîn* — in fact some of their villages seemed even poorer and certainly dirtier because of the large herds of pigs which only Christians were allowed to tend. In the towns and cities, however, Christian Egyptians were in general better off economically than the Muslim population, being particularly strong in the professions, civil service, and private business, where their presence was roughly 20% of the total, a figure which corresponds to the Christian percentage of those Egyptians possessing university degrees in 1960.

The combined advantages of affluence, education, higher health standards, and a strong sense of community worked to create an enviable social image for Christians throughout the Middle East. In the sphere of family life the barriers which both Orthodox and Catholic canon law placed before members seeking divorce, for instance, resulted in an outward stability which Muslims with their easy access to divorce through traditional Islamic law did not possess. Official statistics in all the states of the Arab East supported this commonly accepted condition. The Egyptian Census of 1960 counted only 0.29% of the resident divorced nationals as being Christian, and in Iraq a similar count three years earlier had shown the Muslim divorce rate there to be six times that of Iraqi Christians. In the Kingdom of Jordan during the years 1960-1967 Christian ecclesiastical courts granted only one divorce while in the same time the Muslim *sharî 'a* courts dissolved some 30,000 marriages. An additional 47 Christian women were granted divorces through the Muslim courts, either from Muslim husbands or from Christian husbands who converted to Islam specifically in order to obtain the divorce, but this still amounted to less than 2% of the total number of Christians married during these same years, compared with a figure of 30% for Muslims. Lebanon has not published any vital statistics by religion since 1948, but in that year Christians, though officially accounting for 53% of the population, registered only 15.5% of the divorces.[180] And while ecclesiastical laws prohibiting divorce in most cases was the major deterrent to a higher Christian rate, it is significant that in such countries as Egypt and Iraq where civil marriages and divorces are easily obtainable the Christian divorce rate was scarcely different from countries like Lebanon and Jordan where individual church courts still passed judgment in the civil cases involving their members.

In addition to the inhibiting factor of church law was the average age of Christians at the time of marriage, which seemed universally to be higher by several years, than that of Muslims throughout the Middle East; and in almost any society greater maturity on the part of those to be married can be regarded as a factor contributing to the stability and permanency of their union. Beyond these considerations, however, was the more intangible spirit of community which in most areas of the Middle East virtually dictated to minority Christians a life characterized by strong family-unit solidarity as one of the best defenses against weakness from within in the face of persecution from without. The same spirit extended to private life as well so that almost invariably Christians were conspicuously absent from the world of criminal activity, particularly when it involved the violent (e.g. murder and vendetta) or the sordid (e.g. prostitution of both women and young men). From a purely economic standpoint this is not surprising in that these were generally the crimes of the lower economic and social classes to which relatively few Christians belonged. Those who did were in general barely noticeable except in times of crisis such as the mid-1960's in Iraq when the troubles in the north stemming from the Kurdish insurrection and the anti-Kassem purges sent many already poor village Christians fleeing homeless and penniless to Baghdad. Thus visitors to that city in 1965 and 1966 were for a brief period more apt to be confronted by beggars clad in the colorful and unmistakable garb of the Christian villages of the Mosul plain rather than the usual supplicant wrapped in the black Muslim

ʻabaya. But more than the economic factor, it was a generally higher standard of moral conduct among Christian families buttressed by a fear of creating unfavorable notice that kept them from the world of street crime.

In the area of non-violent crime involving money, the Levantine Christian was not infrequently encountered, and often at relatively high levels. A most celebrated case was that involving the Maronite Bishop of Kisrawân, H.E. ʻAbd-Allah Nujaym, who was arrested in 1966 on charges of having counterfeited $193,000; similar, though usually not such spectacular, cases involving embezzlement or mismanagement of funds tended to crop up in Lebanon several times a year which directly implicated Christians.[181] Also the illicit traffic in hashish was another highly lucrative racket which was known to involve certain Lebanese Christians, particularly at the highest levels of the smuggling organization, though in general it was Shî ʻa Muslims from Baʻlabakk and Hirmal who actually grew the weed and served as the contact men in personal transactions. Moreover, the general spirit of corruption which infected Levantine business methods, the *bakshîsh* factor extending from the lowliest peddler to the Ministries of Finance themselves, as a matter of course involved a great number of Christians, who after all formed the heart of the business community in many towns and cities throughout the Levant. Yet this method of carrying on business was virtually an institution of its own and had generated over many years a kind of separate morality with unwritten codes which, when transgressed resulted in the swift implementation of commonly accepted punitive measures. In this sense, therefore, Christians were no more guilty than Muslims of a breach of ethics, and if accused of such would immediately dismiss it with an eyes-to-heaven shrug and an oblique reference to "render unto Caesar."

The other area of Christian society in the Levant which tended to stand out from the Islamic norm was the already-alluded-to status of women. In the sphere of social progress, it was the Christians who most conspicuously adopted the Western development of the emancipation of women, and later, female suffrage. The restricted status of Muslim women in traditional

Islamic society had changed relatively little as late as World War II in the major urban areas, and remains unchanged today in the vast rural districts. Only in the large cities with substantial Christian Arab and European concentrations and influence have Muslim women begun to share in the progress enjoyed by their Christian sisters. In the traditional society the latter had suffered many of the restrictions and prejudices that characterized the Eastern view of a woman's place in society, but never to the degree endured by Muslim women. The Christian woman in the Arab and later the Turkish Empires always enjoyed greater personal freedom, and, as a result of the Christian insistence on monogamy, a stronger, more secure place in the family and community. Official Christian abhorrence of divorce further strengthened her importance, in contrast to the Muslim view which threatened the wife with perpetual marital insecurity.

The Western missions in the 18th and 19th centuries, especially those of the Protestants, stressed the independence and opportunities which Western Christianity promised women in the East, and, along with the somewhat more traditional Catholics, introduced on a large scale the education of girls — an innovation extended to Muslim women on a similar level only within the last two decades. The "desperate bondage" of Muslim women has from the time of the Napoleonic adventure in Egypt elicited strong protest from lady visitors from Europe and America, and as late as 1956 could provide English novelist Rose Macaulay with a plot base for her fanciful *Towers of Trebizond*. By the mid-20th century, literacy among Christian women in the Arab World, though not as high as that of Christian men, was many times that of Muslim women whose rate of literacy even in Lebanon rested between five and ten per cent in most areas, and often higher than that of Muslim men. In Iraq in 1957, the level of literacy among Christian women stood at 42%, as compared with 25% for Muslim men, and only 5% for Muslim women. Similar disparities existed in Egypt where, in 1960, 29.3% of Christian women were literate, compared with 10.5% of Muslim women and 38.6% of Muslim men, and in Israel where female Christian literacy was a healthy 66% as opposed to 14% for that of Muslim women. A slight improvement was noted there among the 14-29 age group, 25% of which was literate in the case of Muslim women, and 84% of Christians. Conversely, less than 2% of Muslim women in Israel over the age of 65 could read, in striking contrast to 41% of the Christian women.

Most of the more restrictive influences of Islamic traditionalism, vestiges of an imposition of Muslim values over the centuries, had been shed by Christian Arab women by the beginning of this century. Only in a few areas, largely rural, did Christian women adhere to the outward Muslim forms of submission. Most notable of these exceptions was the city of Ḥamâh in central Syria, until very recently one of the "few places outside the Holy Cities of Arabia where the Faith has remained so aggressive and fanatic... [that] even the Syrian Christians adopt a protective mimicry, veiling their women and assuming a Muslim pose whenever they can, while the Sisters of the Sacré Coeur are obliged to tuck their crucifixes out of sight whenever they go abroad."[182] The reaction of such traditional Muslims to the recent election of a Lebanese Christian model, Georgina Rizq, as "Miss Universe" at Miami Beach, Florida, in July of 1971 after having paraded publicly in a see-through evening-gown before a panel of male judges can only be imagined.

In all other cities and large towns of Syria, Egypt, Palestine, Iraq, and throughout Lebanon, Christian women enjoyed a freedom which, while failing sometimes to approach the European and American standard, particularly in the areas of career, marriage, and sexual independence, greatly surpassed the all-too-frequently cloistered existence of their Muslim sisters. In 1953 Lebanon, with its Christian-dominated government, became the first country in the Middle East to grant universal suffrage, thus extending the privileges which a woman could enjoy, especially if she were Christian, unhampered by the strong traditional values which Muslim society still imposed, however subtly, on her daily life. Daniel Lerner, writing of the Near East in the mid-1950's, quoted a Christian co-ed at the University of Damascus as saying, "I hate it here; I'd rather be in Beirut... a woman is so restricted here... nothing is changed by this new politics."[183] Such impatience was indicative of the level of independence and free expression which Christian women had attained by the outset of national independence, and while few have yet made their mark on the Arab political scene — with the exception of such individualists as Rose ("Red Rose") Khaddûri in the Iraqi Communist Party during the late 1950's — it seems only a matter of time until Christian women will begin challenging those final barriers to the achievement of complete equality in their own smaller communities and in the greater context of the Muslim Arab World as well.

IV Politics and Christianity in the Arab East

The Christian in the Middle East makes his presence felt in national politics through two divergent avenues: that of the ecclesiastical hierarchy whose interests are primarily those of the church establishment, and that of individual politicians from the various Christian communities whose activities are frequently unrelated to the policies of their churches and may or may not be in the specific interests of the Christian community at large.

The political involvement of religious leadership is a tradition of long standing in the Middle East and was until very recently the only channel through which the minority communities could take political action in a system dominated by Muslims. From the time of the Arab conquests up until the fall of the Ottoman Empire, the various Christian patriarchs of the East exercised enormous political authority both as unchallenged leaders within the individual communities themselves and as the representatives of these communities before the supreme political authority of the caliph or sultan. Lesser members of the clerical hierarchy likewise exercised considerable influence: not only bishops but priests and itinerant monastics, despite their general lack of formal education and training, particularly in the non-Catholic churches, were looked to for leadership by their flocks in all matters involving political action, not merely those requiring spiritual counsel.

When national independence came to the Middle East in the wake of Ottoman collapse and the Mandate era, the traditional political role of the clergy was carried over into the secular government of the new states, and in some cases actually enhanced. Endowed with legislative, judicial, executive, coercive, doctrinal, administrative, and legislative powers, the patriarch, as "père et chef de son église... en tient, dans le cadre du patriarcat, le gouvernement suprême et l'administration générale, "[184] with authority to define and apply ecclesiastical canons, execute their prescribed sentences, punish offenders, pass judgment on the legality of the actions of his bishops and clergy, and in the case of the Uniate churches, to put into practice the papal directives and prescriptions for his patriarchate.[185] In every instance this internal authority was recognized by the newly independent states and made of the patriarch a figure of considerable political importance, depending of course on the numerical strength and economic power of his community. In the case of the Maronite patriarch, both Al-Ḥuwayyik (d. 1932) and Anṭûn 'Arîḍa (1932-1954) "wielded an incalculable influence over the political life of the country [Lebanon]" in its early formative years, which the present incumbent, Paul Méouchy continues to exercise. The Syrian Catholic patriarch, Cardinal Tappuni (d. 1968), was likewise known to involve himself directly in secular politics, particularly in 1930, as advocate before the League of Nations and the foreign ministries of the Mandate powers, of the cause of political autonomy for the Jazîra district of Syria with its then overwhelmingly non-Arab and considerable Christian population. The present Melkite patriarch, Maximos V Ḥakîm, is a living example of the political influence which a lesser ecclesiastical figure can acquire, when as Archbishop of Galilee from 1946-1967 he emerged as an effective spokesman for the rights of all Arabs living under Israeli jurisdiction. Only when Christian leaders sought to exercise temporal authority in the face of secular legislation did they run afoul of direct governmental restrictions such as those imposed on the Nestorian patriarch shortly after Iraqi independence in 1932.[186]

As the very visible head of his community the patriarch is supremely conscious of his own political role and sensitive to any action taken by the secular state, and in the case of the Uniate churches, by the Vatican, which might tend to lower his status in the eyes of his community and the public in general. Thus when Maronite Patriarch 'Arîḍa, then spiritual head of some 275,000 Catholic Maronite Christians in Lebanon, learned in 1937 that Ignatius Tappuni, patriarch of the Syrian Catholic church only recently established in Beirut, and leader of only 3,500 Lebanese faithful, had been elevated to the rank of Cardinal, thus achieving the status of first-ranking Catholic prelate in Lebanon, he ('Arîḍa) flew into a violent rage that lasted several days. More recently in 1961 the official journal of Damascene Orthodoxy, *Al-Ḥaraka,* complained that the seating arrangement at a reception for President Nasser had been such as to offend the person and office of the Greek Orthodox patriarch of Antioch, Theodosius VI Abû-Rijayla.[187] Such incidents of seemingly trivial importance, involving only a matter of protocol, were nonetheless of real significance to Middle Eastern Christians who see in any official slight, however small and unintentional, a possible indication of a change in government policy which may have direct effect on their precarious minority status.

Within the individual communities themselves, the struggle for ecclesiastical power was as unrelenting as it had been in the days of Byzantine ascendancy. In the Uniate churches the situation was tempered somewhat by the authority of the Vatican which could, and did, step in to settle internal political battles when they threatened to disrupt the internal cohesion of church organization and communal unity. As recently as 1954 the Vatican felt obliged to "retire" Patriarch 'Arîḍa whose aggressively pro-Lebanon policies of the past (to the extent of publicly sympathizing with Israel as an anti-Muslim force) and advancing senility were a source of considerable political embarrassment to Rome. And, fearing that a synod of Maronite bishops would have elected an equally intransigent successor, it took the drastic precaution of directly appointing the then archbishop of Tyre, Paul Méouchy, to the patriarchate in 1955 over the opposition of his less moderate fellow bishops. Following Méouchy's death on January 19, 1975, the synod of Maronite bishops, fearing that similar steps would be taken if it failed to elect a suitable successor promptly, took only two weeks in closed council at the patriarchal church in Bikirka to choose Anṭûn Khuraysh, Archbishop of Sidon, as Méouchy's successor on February 3.[188] The autonomy of the Orthodox and Heterodox communities, however, gave ample opportunity for the clergy and laity to give full vent to their natural Levantine inclination towards bitter and prolonged political struggles. The Orthodox patriarchate of Antioch was particularly prone to the kind of internecine power struggles that gave the term "Byzantine" its pejorative connotation. On the whole Orthodoxy in Syria and Lebanon was in far better shape as it entered the sixth decade of this century than it had been in living memory. "Our Church," stated Patriarch Theodosius in 1963, "is healthier today than it has been for the last thousand years,"[189] a sentiment echoed three years later by leading Orthodox layman, Qusṭanṭîn Zurayq who saw in the laying of the cornerstone of an impressive new Orthodox Theological Academy, now completed, beside the Monastery of Balamand (Belmont) near Tripoli, a witness to "the spiritual renaissance of the Orthodox Community of Antioch."[190] But despite physical prosperity, greatly enhanced by generous contributions from the large emigrant Antiochene community abroad, and an active youth movement organized in the late 1940's with an aim of revitalizing the spiritual life of the community, the internal political struggles within the patriarchate continued unabated. The century had in fact begun with a bitter struggle against the Hellenic hegemony of the Oecumenical Patriarchate which resulted in the election of the first indigenous Arabic-speaking Syrian patriarch in over two centuries in 1899. The victory had been achieved, however, with considerable assistance from Russia, and despite the Bolshevik Revolution of 1917 the Russian Orthodox Church has to this day remained a vital and disruptive force in the internal politics of the patriarchate.

Even during the Mandate years the Russian faction was operative, and in 1932 succeeded after a three-year struggle in electing as patriarch Russian-educated (Kiev Seminary) Alexandros III Ṭaḥḥân who presided over his Church for a quarter of a century and was largely instrumental in renewing the close ties of Antioch with Moscow. In 1945, newly-elected Patriarch Alexei of Moscow visited Antioch and Jerusalem pledging in the course of his voyage "de resserrer de plus en plus les liens de l'Eglise orthodoxe russe avec les Eglises orthodoxes de l'Orient."[191] He was followed in succeeding years by an increasing number of Soviet prelates and clergymen. In the meantime, Alexandros returned Moscow's state visit in 1947, joining with Russian Orthodox clergy in unanimously censuring the Catholic and Protestant missions. In the same year he issued a statement in which he expressed the opinion that the Russian Church was not under Communist influence, and in the following year sent a mission to Moscow to seek closer cooperation with the Russian patriarchate. Three years later, in 1951, he again visited Moscow and was quoted by TASS as supporting Soviet policies of world peace and as denouncing American efforts to gain world domination.[192] He likewise denounced the Oecumenical Patriarch of Constantinople, Athenagoras — formerly Greek Orthodox Archbishop of North and South America — as an agent of the United States, and called upon Arab Orthodox faithful in America to dissociate themselves from imperialist policies. As the result of these attacks, many congregations of the Syrian Antiochean Orthodox Church in America (the Greek Orthodox congregations whose members traced their ancestry to the patriarchates of Antioch and Jerusalem) which in 1965 numbered some 115,000 in the United States, and over 200,000 in Latin America, publicly disavowed his authority.

Despite such reaction, Alexandros continued his pro-Soviet policies and pronouncements, and in 1952 sent the metropolitans of Homs, Ḥamâh, and the Jabal Al-Durûz to Moscow on the occasion of the Jubilee of Patriarch Alexei. Alexandros, in the later years of his reign, freely accepted financial support from the Soviet legations in Damascus and Beirut, and surrounded himself with openly pro-Communist prelates and archimandrites. There were those who maintained that Alexandros's close ties with the Soviets were pragmatically motivated — chiefly for monetary gain — and that political association was in truth minimal. The Antiochean Orthodox Bishop of New York, visiting Damascus in 1954 on the occasion of a patriarchal Jubilee, stated to the Syrian Press that "les rélations que nous gardons avec l'Eglise russe sont purement réligieuses et fraternelles et ne se rapportent nullement au gouvernement communiste qui est anti-religieux."[193]

Nevertheless, the patriarch's continued and growing contacts with Russian Orthodoxy were the cause of increasing tension within the community, and upon Alexandros's death in 1958 at the age of 89, open contention was prevented only through the election of a compromise candidate, Theodosius VI Abû-Rijayla, a native of Beirut, educated at Balamand

(Belmont, Lebanon), Athens, and Istanbul, and less tied to the policy of open political attachment to Moscow than had been his predecessors. Already in his late seventies at the time of his elevation, Theodosius was expected to play an interim rôle, and as his death became imminent, the Russian Orthodox Church, with the inevitable contest of his succession in mind, established a small but permanent delegation at Beirut in July of 1968 under the direct authority of the patriarch of Moscow. It was, however, too late to stem a pro-Western trend which had been growing within the Antiochene patriarchate, particularly as Lebanon replaced Syria, with its pro-Soviet government, as the residence of the majority of the Church membership following the post-1950's migration of Syrian Christians.

The crucial test had occurred in 1966 when the Soviet faction, sensing a trend to the right, attempted, at Homs, with tacit approval of the Syrian *Ba'th* government, to consecrate a bishop of their own choosing to the vacant see of Latakia without the required approval of all bishops of the patriarchate in synod. As pro-Western churchmen in Latakia itself literally laid siege to the bishop's residence in order to prevent the hastily consecrated prelate from assuming his seat, a directive from Patriarch Theodosius ordered the dissident bishop, Anṭûn Shadrâwî, back to his diocese of Mount Lebanon where he had previously served as archimandrite. Fearing intervention by the Syrian government, the patriarch, on 28 July 1966, convened the Holy Synod of the patriarchate in Lebanon at the convent of Mâr Ilyâs Shuwâyâ near Dhûr Shuwayr in the heart of the Christian mountain. At the convocation it became immediately apparent that the right-wing, Western-oriented faction of the episcopate enjoyed a bare absolute majority of seven of the thirteen participating bishops (the patriarch himself has no vote). On 6 August, the seven pro-Western metropolitans (Beirut, Tripoli, Aleppo, Ḥamâh, Mount Lebanon, Rio de Janeiro, and Buenos Aires) elected conservative clerics to the vacant sees of Latakia and New York, increasing the anti-Soviet bloc within the synod to nine of the fifteen episcopal and archepiscopal sees (the pro-Soviet sees at this time included Homs, Jabal Al-Durûz, Zaḥlah, 'Akkâr, and Marj 'Uyûn, with Toledo,

Ohio, assuming a neutral stance). The death of the dissident Metropolitan Nifon Sâbâ of Zaḫlah one month later (10 September 1966) increased their majority to ten. Following a second internal rupture in 1969, the Lebanese pro-western faction within the Church Synod emerged even stronger, thus enabling the election of one of its own to the patriarchate the following year as Ilyâs IV Mu'awwaḍ, successor to the late Theodosius VI.

Throughout the rest of the Arab East the dual spectre of internal discord and Soviet interference continued to haunt the non-Catholic Christian bodies, in particular the Armenians, Nestorians, and Copts. Soviet influence in the Gregorian (Orthodox) Armenian Church has already been cited, due largely to the attraction of the Soviet Armenian Republic for Armenians in the diaspora. In general the Hunchak (Communist) faction within the total Armenian community remained small in comparison with the anti-Soviet Tashnak party. But regardless of an individual Armenian's political affiliation within his own community, the influence of the Soviet Union loomed large as the result of family ties with, or simply sentimental affection for, the Armenian homeland, a remnant of which had been Soviet since 1920. A most recent example of Communist infiltration of Armenians in the West is the case of Sarkîs Paskalian, a 36-year-old Lebanese-Armenian jeweler. A resident of New York, he was arrested there in July 1975 and later sentenced to 22 years in prison for obtaining and transmitting U.S. and NATO defense documents to the Soviets.

For the Nestorians, association with the Communist party in Iraq had great appeal as one area of political activity in their country which was not divided along confessional lines. Since the very earliest years of Iraqi independence Nestorians had been active in the Communist movement, often at the very core of leadership. The celebrated Communist Yûsuf Salmân (better known by his code name "*Fahd*," or "panther"), who was executed by the Nûrî Al-Sa'îd government in 1949, was a Christian, and during the Kassem regime a number of Nestorian (and other Christian) Communists achieved prominence as the government acquired an ever stronger leftist bent up until the Ba'thist coup of 1963. In the anti-Kassem reprisals that followed, many Nestorians were arrested and tried as Communists, and the popular association of this community with extreme leftist movements in Iraq has made their position in recent years almost untenable.

Communist activity among the Copts of Egypt has been less of a factor, due in large part to the strict watch which Nasser kept throughout his administration on the growth of illegal leftist as well as rightist (e.g. Muslim Brethren) political activity. Nevertheless, Soviet and Russian Orthodox influence in the ecclesiastical ranks of the Coptic Church has grown in recent years, commensurate with the Russian ascendancy in Egypt since 1956 and especially since 1967. Significantly, the gold altar of the recently-dedicated Coptic Cathedral of Saint Mark in Cairo was a gift of the Russian Orthodox Church. Internally the Coptic Monophysite Church has had its share of political struggles, though not to the desultory extent of the Nestorians, whose communal structure had been greatly weakened in the chaotic years since the exile of their patriarch from Iraq in 1933. For the Copts, internecine struggles were reserved for the question of patriarchal succession, an event occurring once every 15 or 20 years. The greatest crisis of this century developed during the early 1950's over the failure of then Patriarch Anbâ Yusab II, elected in 1946, to cope with political problems facing all Christians in Egypt as the result of the Republican revolution of 1952. The issue came to a head in September of 1955 when the Church Synod, endorsed by the Community Council of Laity, relieved the patriarch of his power and banished him to the monastery of Dayr Al-Muḥarraq in Upper Egypt. A triumvirate of bishops was elected to administer the Church until Yusab's death a year later. After a three-year period of bitter internal bickering which gave the government an excuse to interfere directly in the electoral process, a successor was finally chosen by lot from among the leading candidates on 19 April 1959. The new patriarch, Kyrillos VI, gave from the beginning every indication of becoming the strongest Coptic religious leader in modern times and prompted Dr. Meinardus, leading Western authority on the Coptic Church, to observe at the time that "a new age of spirituality, enlightenment and oecumenical cooperation [within the ancient Church of Saint Mark] has commenced."[194]

And indeed the twelve-year reign of the late patriarch, who died unexpectedly in February, 1971, was one of far-reaching change and reform, though the recent issue of succession has again brought to the fore the many internal factions whose various views and political leanings were reflected in four out of five of the principal rivals for the vacant see. This time, however, the issues were less bitterly contested, and within eight months of Kyrillos' s death a successor was chosen by the "hand of God" (a blind-folded six-year-old boy drawing lots from a silver chest in the presence of a large congregation) from among three leading candidates chosen by the 700-man electoral college of the Church. On 14 November 1971, the former Bishop Shanûda became Shanûda III, 117th Coptic Patriarch of Alexandria, and, in the eyes of most knowledgeable observers, the best possible successor to the late Kyrillos, one who would continue the work of reorganization and spiritual revival within the ancient church.[195] A committed disciple of the Oecumenical movement, Patriarch Shanûda journeyed to Rome in May of 1973 on the 1600th anniversary of the death of his historic predecessor Athanasius (Patriarch of Alexandria 328-373) and in an emotional meeting with Pope Paul VI called for closer ties between the two ancient patriarchates, long divided by schism. The patriarch has likewise sustained Coptic participation in the World Council of Churches. At its most recent convocation in Nairobi (late fall, 1975), Coptic Orthodox delegates played a vocal role, though obviously to the discomfort of Western church leaders who resented Coptic leadership in the move to condemn Zionism as a racist and atheistic movement in obvious emulation of the United Nations declaration of November in the same vein.

Within the Uniate Churches the quiet but effective political authority of the Vatican prevented the same internal free-for-alls from developing. If there did appear to be a serious threat of internal discord over the question of patriarchal succession, the Church would step in effectively, as it did in the Maronite succession issue of 1955, and appoint its own candidate. Such action undeniably worked to the greater good of internal unity within the various Eastern Catholic Churches, but was regarded by the non-Catholic communities as an example of the kind of restrictions which a 'return' to Rome would entail.

The fear of "Latinization" had long been an undisguised factor in the refusal of the Greek Orthodox, Jacobite, Gregorian, Nestorian, and Coptic Churches to yield to Roman pressures and accept Uniate status. The greater part of Catholic conversions had been made in the 18th and 19th centuries, and by the mid-20th century the lines between the Uniate groups and their parent Orthodox and Heterodox bodies were clearly drawn and more or less crystallized, with only the Chaldaean Church continuing to attract a small but steady stream of converts from the other side. Several of the Catholic patriarchs, including Cardinals Tappuni (Syrian Catholic) and Maximos VI Ṣâ'igh (Melkite) repeatedly offered to relinquish their offices in favor of their rivals if the latter and their Churches would accept reunion. Despite a warming of relations between Catholic and non-Catholic clergy in the Middle East since World War II, no such spectacular conversions were achieved during the long tenure of either of these two Uniate patriarchs (d. 1967 and 1968 respectively). But in an age of increasing oecumenism no one on either side was ruling out the possibility of eventual unity. Unity, in fact, has been the acknowledged goal of all Christian groups in the Middle East in recent years, particularly since the convocation of the first Vatican Oecumenical Council in the fall of 1962 by Pope John XXIII, and the historic meeting between his successor, Paul VI, and the late Athenagoras, Patriarch of Constantinople, in Jerusalem a year later (January, 1964). Marking as it did the first meeting between the patriarchs of Rome and New Rome since 1439, and the first since the schism of 1054 on terms of absolute equality, the response among Middle Eastern Christians as well as those throughout the Catholic and Orthodox world was one of great enthusiasm. The Patriarch of Jerusalem, Benediktos, expressed the belief that "la racontre de Paul VI et d'Athénagoras I constitue le premier pas sur la voie qui doit amener le rapprochement des Eglises."[196] For Ignatius Ḥâzim, then superior of the Greek Orthodox seminary at Balamand and later Metropolitan of Latakia, the meeting "has proven that union between the churches emanates from the very depth of Christian faith throughout the world and is necessary for its survival."[197] "This pilgrimage," concluded the Beirut daily *Al-Safâ'* (owned by the Ma'lûf family, a prominent Lebanese Orthodox clan), "will bring to fruition the initial steps taken by the Oecumenical Council to realize Christian unity."[198]

Clearly this sentiment was the express belief of both Paul and Athenagoras. "From now on," stated the Patriarch after his meeting with the Pope, "we mean business."[199] And events since the meeting have confirmed his initial prophecy. The following June another historic meeting took place — one of the greatest significance for Christians in the East — when Melkite Patriarch Maximos Ṣâ'igh visited Athenagoras at the latter's residence in Istanbul. In April of 1965, Cardinal Bea visited the Oecumenical Patriarchate, assisted at daily offices in the patriarchal church and attended Divine Liturgy celebrated by Athenagoras himself. In October of the same year, the Vatican, as a gesture of good will, returned the relics of Saint Savas to their original resting place at the Orthodox monastery founded by that Saint in the 6th century near Bethlehem, from whence they had been taken to Venice in the 12th century by the Latin Crusaders, a gesture repeated in June of 1968 when relics of Saint Mark were returned to Egypt on the occasion of the dedication of the new Coptic Cathedral in Cairo. Barely one month after Savas had been returned to his original resting place, Paul and Athenagoras issued a joint declaration (7 December 1965) nullifying the mutual exchange of excommunications pronounced over 900 years earlier which had resulted in the breach now separating Rome and Constantinople. The declaration, read in Saint Peter's in the presence of Orthodox prelates representing Athenagoras, and in Istanbul before a special Vatican delegation, stated that the two leaders "regret the offensive words, the reproaches without foundation and the reprehensible gestures which, on both sides, have marked or accompanied the sad events of this period... and likewise regret and remove both from memory and from the midst of the Church the sentences of excommunication which followed."[200] Less than one year later, Athenagoras predicted flatly that "la réunion de l'Eglise orthodoxe et de l'Eglise Catholique Romaine n'est pas très éloignée... peut-être pas de mon vivant car je suis un homme très âgé, mais certainement de votre vivant." [201]

More than a decade has elapsed since the patriarch, who died in July, 1972 and was succeeded by the self-effacing Dimitrios I of Imbros, issued this prophetic statement; and although no dramatic progress has been made towards the unification of the two great bodies of Christendom, what was accomplished by the historic joint declaration has not been forgotten. On December 14, 1976, the tenth anniversary of the lifting of the 11th-century anathemas was celebrated both at Saint Peter's in Rome and at the patriarchal church of Saint George in the Phanar (Fener) district of Istanbul.

At the celebration in Rome, metropolitan Meliton of Chalcedon, head of the Orthodox delegation and acknowledged power behind the new patriarch, declared that in this "acte de souvenir — le souvenir de l'oubli du passé" could be found "le sens d'un nouveau movement oecuménique, fondé cette fois-ci sur une base ecclésiologique." At the conclusion of the service, Pope Paul, in an unannounced and unprecedented gesture of reconciliation, set aside his miter and, unaccompanied approached Meliton, knelt and kissed his feet. Following the celebration at the Phanar, the Catholic delegation made a pilgrimage to Nicaea (Iznik), site of the first (325 A.D.) and last (787 A.D.) oecumenical councils of the Church when the Orthodox East and Catholic West were still one, with representatives of the patriarchate. Amid the ruins of the ancient church of Aghia Sophia where the councils were held, the two groups recited together in Greek and Latin the Nicene Creed, the basic affirmation of faith in both liturgies (and, significantly, an important subject of unresolved theological division which arose in the 9th century with the Western addition of the *filioque* clause, which Orthodoxy still does not accept).

Finally, to commemorate the occasion and to lay the groundwork for future, more concrete progress, an interorthodox commission composed of representatives from the patriarchates and autocephalus churches of the Orthodox World was appointed to prepare for a theological dialogue with a corresponding Catholic commission. Such gestures of unity constitute strong evidence that the desire on both sides to pursue all possible avenues leading towards a closer communion of the two churches remains strong.[202]

At the parish level a considerable groundswell of oecumenism has built up during the past decade and a half which has gone a long way toward reversing the isolation and distrust which has characterized inter-sectarian relationships among Middle Eastern Christians. In all but the extremely fragmented Nestorian community, leadership in the Eastern Churches has encouraged this trend and there is no question but that the long-held communal rivalries are beginning to disappear. Yet old fears of unity remain, held not only by the non-Catholic churches in the Middle East but by Uniate Catholics themselves who have long felt that they were due more independence than Rome has in the past been willing to grant them. Despite Vatican assurances to the contrary[203] there has always been an undercurrent of paternalism in the attitudes of Rome towards her carefully-guarded Uniate Churches which has made Eastern Catholics feel, as Cardinal Ṣâ'igh once observed, that they were looked upon by their Latin cousins more as anthropological curiosities than as living witnesses to the faith. There has always been the concern that when Latins spoke of rite they were referring only to liturgical texts and ceremonies rather than to the whole institutional and cultural complex which is peculiar to each of the several non-Latin Catholic churches.

Efforts by Eastern Catholic leaders, Cardinal Ṣâ'igh in particular, in recent years to abolish vestiges of the previously dominant Latin establishment in the East, have given Rome the opportunity to prove her sincerity by according full equality to her Eastern branches. The suppression, therefore, in 1963 of the titular Latin patriarchates of Antioch, Alexandria, and Constantinople, served to remove "the thorn in the side of the Eastern Church," often complained of by Ṣâ'igh and others, and "to bring joy to the spirits and hearts" of Eastern Christians.[204] Action of this kind by Rome was applauded with equal enthusiasm by the Orthodox who had long feared that the cherished autonomy of their patriarchates and autocephalous churches would disappear if union with Rome were to become a reality. And indeed there was good reason for their concern. Rome's historical emphasis on ecclesiastical centralization has from the beginning overshadowed the oecumenical mission of the Uniate churches and at the present time continues to arouse concern despite oecumenical progress. Maurice Villain, writing in the *Eastern Churches Quarterly* in 1961, charged that "the very notion of a patriarchate implies an autonomy which they [the Uniate Churches] are simply not in a position to exercise, bound up as they are in the general system of Roman centralization, which is inexorably, if unconsciously, paring away the rights and privileges of the 'united patriarchates,' so that these latter become less and less capable of being set forth before the Orthodox as models of what Orthodox patriarchates would become if they themselves were to consent to union."[205] Five years later, Cardinal Ṣâ'igh echoed this concern, calling on the Roman Church to rediscover, in the interests of oecumenism, "the true value of the patriarchal office and to allow the oriental patriarchs to regain their status as ranking counsels in the government of the Universal Church."[206]

In this area the Vatican has done much in the last ten years to atone for past injustice. By the close of the final session of the Oecumenical Council in December of 1965, four of the six Uniate patriarchs had been raised to the Cardinalate (Syrian Catholic, Melkite, Maronite, and Coptic Catholic) while the Armenian Catholics were represented by their noted former patriarch, the late Gregory Agaganian;[207] only the Chaldaeans remained unrepresented among the princes of the Church. In recognition of the equality in which the legal institutions and governing authority of the Eastern Churches were held by the Vatican, three of the five Uniate patriarchs — Ṣâ'igh (Melkite), Méouchy (Maronite), and Sidarrus (Coptic Catholic) — were named on 12 November 1965 to the Pontifical Commission for the Revision of Canon Law. In that the purpose of the Commission was to revise the Canon Law of the entire Church in the light of the Vatican Council's historic decisions, the Eastern Churches were thus assured a voice in the continuing drama of reform and reorganization of the Church during the important post-Oecumenical Council years. During the Council sessions themselves the Uniate prelates, particularly Ṣâ'igh and other Melkite delegates, were outspoken in the cause of unity and reform, and antagonized many of the more conservative bishops from the West by pointedly advocating a more liberal approach to socialism and atheism[208] as well as a more realistic approach to the question of divorce and complete abandonment of the system of indulgences. As regards the ever-sensitive issue of clerical marriages the Eastern position was, needless to say, whole-heartedly in favor of abandoning the rule of celibacy.[209] In one of many public assurances of Vatican support for the continued independence of the Eastern Rite Churches, Pope Paul VI recently lauded these communities for steadfastly adhering to their traditions at a time of "unbridled craving for freedom and novelty."[210]

The leadership of the eastern patriarchs within their own churches was balanced by an equally active involvement in the political life of those Middle Eastern countries where their faithful lived. Earlier examples of ecclesiastical involvement in domestic Arab politics have already been cited, and to these should be added more recent instances such as the public opposition of Cardinal Ṣâ'igh in 1950 and 1954 to the inclusion of a provision naming Islam as the official religion of Syria in the Constitutions of those years, and more significantly the role played by newly-elected Maronite Patriarch Méouchy in the Lebanese political crises of 1958, in which he found himself among the opposition resisting Maronite President Camille Chamoun (Sham'ûn) in his attempt to seek a second term. The political question which involved all Arab Christian prelates simultaneously, however, was the celebrated decision of the Vatican Council in 1963 to re-examine the historical position of the Catholic Church in regard to the role of the Jews in the trial and crucifixion of Christ. Almost from the moment the decision was announced, the Christian Arab leadership, lay and clerical, Catholic and Orthodox, came under heavy Muslim pressure to thwart the Vatican move. From a theological point of view, the question of whether or not the Jews should bear the responsibility for the death of Christ was of no concern to Islam, which teaches that the whole drama of the Passion culminating in the crucifixion is a Christian fabrication, and that Christ, as is stated in the Koran, was rather "raised up by God unto Himself."[211]

Obviously, therefore, the real concern on the part of Arab Muslims was completely political in its basis, reflecting a fear shared by many Arab Christians as well that the Vatican Council's decision was but a prelude to a softening of past Papal policy regarding the state of Israel, and, in the words of a spokesman for the Coptic Catholic patriarchate, a move which "would provide the Jews with a moral weapon which they would exploit for their own ends against Arab countries." [212]

During the two years that elapsed before a final declaration on the subject was made, certain changes in the original wording were made so as to minimize the political implications of the document. Frequent reassurances from the Vatican, moreover, were released unofficially to spokesmen in the East confirming that in no way was the Council's decision to be linked with a change in Rome's policy of non-recognition towards Israel. Private sources in the Vatican in fact made it clear to the Eastern prelates and their flocks that the measure was being enacted largely to stabilize the Jewish communities outside Israel, especially those in Catholic countries (e.g. France and Latin America), in an attempt to insure that they would never again be driven by some new Christian persecution to mass emigration to the Zionist state.[213] The final declaration ruled simply that responsibility for the death of Christ "cannot be attributed to all Jews," and was approved on 15 October 1965 by a lopsided vote of 1,875 to 188; the text went on to deplore anti-Semitism and overt discrimination and stated that "although the Church is the New People of God, the Jews should not be presented as rejected by God or accursed, as if this follows from Holy Scriptures." An earlier passage, much more specific in its content and particularly odious to the Eastern Christians which stated that the Jews should not be considered guilty of deicide (God-killing), was omitted in the final draft. Likewise the term "Jews" was replaced with "the Jewish religion" in deference to the Arab position that the Zionists are not religious Jews at all.

While the final document was considerably more general in its wording of the absolution, the reaction was predictably unfavorable throughout the Middle East. Christians demonstrated in large numbers in Aleppo and Jerusalem, and the

Orthodox Patriarchate of Antioch condemned the action. The patriarch, Theodosius VI, in a public statement, asserted that the cry of the Jews before Pilate — "His blood be upon us and upon our children!" — related in the Gospel of Saint Matthew, implicated all unconverted Jews, living and dead, in the responsibility for "this odious crime."[214] The Jacobite patriarch, Ya'qûb III, charged that "the freeing of the Jews of the blood of Christ is the greatest of sins,"[215] and was joined by Theodosius who, in a final appraisal of the move, charged that the Council's decision "undermines the basic principles of Christianity."[216] His counterpart in Jerusalem, Benediktos, stated simply that the document was "inconsistent with Holy Scriptures."[217] On the political scene, Cairo's *Al-Ahrâm* voiced the fear that the Zionists would "speedily exploit the decision to their own ends,"[218] while the Lebanese Foreign Minister, Dr. Georges Ḥakîm, an Orthodox Christian, stated cautiously that "it would have been better if the Oecumenical Council had not approved the declaration," but acknowledged that the final draft was an improvement over the original document.[219]

Most Catholic Church leaders in the Arab countries remained conspicuously silent following the adoption of the controversial resolution, deferring to apologiae emanating from the Vatican and Papal nuncios in the Middle East. Msgr. Nihma Sim'ân, Latin Patriarchal Vicar of 'Ammân, asserted somewhat lamely that the declaration of the Council "deprived the Jews of the weapon they had used to return to Palestine — namely that they were God's chosen People" — pointing out that the Council had referred to Christians as the "New People of God."[220] He also reminded the faithful that the efforts of the Eastern patriarchs and bishops had been largely responsible for the amended, less offensive, text of the Declaration. In this connection, the then Melkite patriarch Ṣâ'igh, in a declaration published in *L'Orient* of 24 October 1965, called attention to Israeli dissatisfaction with the new Declaration as evidence of its acceptability to the Arabs. Condemning the original text as one in which "le Sionisme usurpateur" had prevailed, he wrote that "the Episcopate in the Arab countries has rallied to the new text, knowing that the Zionist press has considered it as a retreat by the Catholic Church in the face of pressures exerted by the Eastern patriarchs and their clergy."[221] Only two months later, however, Ṣâ'igh felt moved to strengthen his possibly tarnished anti-Zionist image by parroting the hardline Arab view on Israel in the Christmas issue of the Syrian military journal, *Al-Jundi,* stating that "the Arab countries are struggling against International Zionism... which imposes a Jewish state in the heartland of the Arabs and drives out its people... and the schemes of Imperialism... Truly we are obedient soldiers in the service of God and country."[222]

The Eastern Christian establishment, particularly that of the Uniate Catholics, was visibly assisted in its face-saving defense by the Papacy itself. The council in the preface to the Declaration stated that it was "moved not by political reasons but by the Gospel's spiritual love," while on the day before the vote the Pope assured Father Ibrâhîm 'Ayyâd, a Latin priest from Beirut known for his ardent commitment to Palestinian nationalism (to the extent that he was exiled from Jordan on suspicion of having collaborated in the successful plot to assassinate King 'Abd Allah in 1951) that the council "would not allow its decision to be exploited by the Israelis," and that the decision would not adversely effect "the legitimate rights of the Palestinian people."[223] 'Ayyâd further acknowledged that considerable pressure had been exerted by Arab diplomats and politicians, including Lebanese Catholics — notably President Charles Ḥilû (a former ambassador to the Vatican), and the late Fu'âd 'Ammûn, former Foreign Minister and then a member of the International Court of Justice at the Hague, both of whom urged that the Declaration be postponed or at least amended — to weaken the impact of the Council's move.[224]

In an effort calculated to ease Muslim-Christian relations recently strained by the controversy, the Council, at the urging of the Pope, concluded the Declaration with an article concerning universal brotherhood in which the delegates "reproved as foreign to the mind of Christ, any discrimination against men, or harrassment of them because of their race, color, condition in life or religion." The aim of the declaration was to close forever the era of the Christian Crusades against Islam.

In this connection the Synod observed that "in the course of centuries quarrels and hostilities have arisen between Christians and Muslims. This Synod urges all to forget the past."[225] The following Sunday the Pope preached on the common origin of Muslims and Christians and Jews alike, and told more than 30,000 worshippers in Saint Peter's Square that he was praying for the followers of non-Christian religions, especially the Jews and Muslims, and pointed out that Christians have closer ties with Muslims than any other religion, citing the respect with which Jesus and the Virgin are revered in the Koran.[226] One year earlier, in June of 1964, the Pope had quietly announced the creation of a secretariat designed to intensify relations with the non-Christian World, with a special section for Islamo-Christian relations. Activities of the Secretariat were crowned with an encouraging reward in 1970 when Lebanese Muslims responded favorably to a papal message calling on Christians all over the world to join in the Muslim festivities on the occasion of the Feast of Al-Aḍḥâ in February of that year. Commenting on the message, Shaykh Hasan Khaṭîb, Chief Justice of the Sunni Muslim High Court in Beirut, gratefully acknowledged the Pope's gesture, and promised in return that Lebanese Muslims would join with their Christian countrymen in observing Christmas.

Thus the efforts by the Vatican appear to have achieved their desired effect. The firm diplomatic ties maintained by the Papacy with the Arab states have survived the Council's Declaration on Jews, and in fact were augmented in June of 1968 with the addition of Kuwait to those states maintaining ambassadors at the Holy See. On the individual level, however, the Decree reinforced the traditional suspicion with which the Muslim masses have long regarded Arab Christians — Eastern and Western, Catholic and Orthodox, particularly those who would link all Christians with the creation and preservation of Israel. Isolated incidents at the time of the Declaration, such as in Aleppo where the city's Grand Mufti railed for three hours against the Council's decision in the presence of the Syrian Catholic bishop and other clergy, were undoubtedly reflections of this sentiment; but there is every indication that the most bitter hostility engendered by the Declaration had been relieved by the following year.

More serious, perhaps, were the reactions of the Orthodox and Heterodox communities to the Declaration. How much opposition may have resulted from the desire to appease the Muslim political establishment or from the opportunism of those who felt that progress toward unity had been made far too quickly in the preceding few years, will never be known, but it can be assumed that resentment against what were felt to be the political implications of the Vatican action as regards Israel were indeed deeply sincere. The current situation indicates that the incident has not seriously impeded the recent progress in improving Orthodox-Catholic relations, but as in all instances involving politics — whether secular or ecclesiastical — in the Middle East, one can never be sure when a past incident, seemingly forgotten, may suddenly be revived to complicate present issues. Many old wounds remain unhealed, notably the continued existence of a Roman Catholic patriarch of Jerusalem, and until the Vatican is willing to abandon this vestige of the First Crusade, further implementation of the rapprochement begun in the early 1960's will be impossible.[227] Likewise the change in patriarchal leadership within the Antiochene Orthodox and Melkite communities has temporarily delayed progress on the road to unity until such time as both of the patriarchs feel sufficiently secure on their home ground to embark on new oecumenical programs. What has not changed is the continued political importance of the patriarchal office in its traditional role of representing the needs and wishes of the Christian population in the Arab East before the Muslim establishment and the secular state. This is not to minimize the growing participation of Christians in the political life of the countries in which they live, outside of any direct link with the ecclesiastical organization of their respective communities; but to ignore the direct influence of the various churches through their patriarchs and clergy in the politics of the Arab East would constitute a failure in fully understanding how Christians, regardless of their personal religious beliefs, continue to function productively in a Muslim society.

Participation by Christians in the Secular Political Life of the Arab East

The involvement of individual Arab Christians in the internal politics of Egypt, Jordan, Lebanon, Syria, Iraq, and even Israel, both within and outside the accepted governmental framework, has been a feature of the Arab East since independence, and this involvement can be traced back over a century to the first stirrings of Arab Nationalism, the original exponents of which were in fact Levantine Christians. At that time, many among the emerging ranks of Christian intellectuals came to reject the Ottoman society, with its political-religious structure and Pan-Islamic outlook, in favor of a wholly Arab culture based primarily on the Arabic language, the greatest single tie linking Christian and Muslim in the Levant. Arab culture, unlike that of the Ottoman Turks, had Christian as well as Muslim origins, and it was felt that renewal of its glory accompanied by the religious tolerance that marked the early structure of its political embodiment — the Caliphate — would benefit all Arabs, regardless of their religion. As early as 1847 young Christian students in Beirut had begun to organize themselves into learned societies whose purpose was to initiate a renaissance of Arab learning, culture, and society. The earliest of these organizations, the Arab Society of Arts and Sciences, founded by Nasîf Al-Yazîjî and Buṭrus Al-Bustânî with the aid of the American missionaries in Beirut, was followed three years later in 1850 by the Jesuit-backed Oriental Society. These early groups were entirely Christian in character, their affiliations with the Protestant and Catholic missions precluding any participation by potential Muslim sympathizers. But as the success of any Arab movement was wholly dependent upon substantial cooperation on the part of the intellectual elite from among the Muslims, efforts were made at an early stage to enlist their support. The Syrian Scientific Society founded in 1857 was the first such organization to boast both Christians and Muslims in its membership; and while the hostilities of 1860 temporarily halted any joint nationalist effort, the society was resumed in 1865 under official Ottoman recognition. "It was probably the first group," states Don Peretz, "that truly manifested an 'Arab' consciousness in modern times and the first group in which non-Muslims were truly on a level equal to the followers of the Prophet."[228] Yet despite such isolated examples of interfaith cooperation on the threshold of Arab political development, few if any Muslims of the time questioned their allegiance to the sole political embodiment of Orthodox Islam, the Ottoman Empire, their grievances being more often those born of national jealousies and a desire for a greater Arab role in an Islamic Empire than those reflecting secessionist intent.

The Christian-sponsored nationalist movement which was not encumbered by any such restraints, continued to attract a strong following, particularly among the Orthodox and Protestant Arabs, and in 1875 a small group of Syrian Protestant College alumni organized a secret society aimed at spreading the ideals of Arab Nationalism, and dedicated to the expulsion of the Ottomans from Syria.[229] The Society collapsed after less than a decade, however, having been unable once again to attract the necessary Muslim support. In the words of Fâris Nimr, co-founder of an early Cairo newspaper, *Al-Muqaṭṭam,* and a contemporary of the event, the Society "became convinced that between Christians and Muslims no understanding or agreement could be reached on the expulsion of the Turks from Lebanon and therefore no unified action was possible."[230]

During the remaining years of the 19th century, Arab Christians continued to advocate an Arab revival, and gradually began to attract a vital Muslim following. The oppressive rule of Sultan Abdulhamid, and the rapid decline of the Ottoman Empire, coupled with the spread of Western learning among a small but important group of Muslims studying in Europe, encouraged many to invest their loyalty in the cause of Arab nationhood. The Young Turk revolt of 1908 and the deposition of the Sultan acted as a catalyst, freeing the Arabs of the strong religious ties that had previously bound them to the government in Istanbul. Conservative Muslims, deploring the secular bias of the 1908 insurgents, began to look toward Mecca and its sharîf for leadership in an Imperial Arab revival. And following a brief period af Ottoman-Arab good will, the growing Arab intelligentsia became seriously disillusioned with Young Turk motives and, as a consequence, began banding together in numerous secret nationalist groups throughout the empire. In contrast to the earlier nationalist groups these organizations were overwhelmingly Muslim in membership; and though each group had Christian representation, and in two cases Christians among its founders,[231] the new nationalist movement came to bear a markedly Islamic stamp. A large number of the Christian intellectuals continued, nonetheless, to identify themselves with this movement to which they and their predecessors had been so deeply committed for over half-a-century, and in whose success they had a great stake and greater hope. To the Christian, the rise of nationalism offered for the first time the opportunity to act directly in and for the state.

> . . . as pioneers they could free themselves from prejudice and suspicion by demonstrating that they were in, and were working for, the nation... and without clearly examining the favorable results this line of conduct might yield them, they spontaneously and generously put at the service of the nascent Arab nation their qualities of innovators and mediators, their knowledge and understanding of Western values, and their penchant for enterprise and adventure.[232]

The first Arab Conference, held in 1913, witnessed many expressions of Christian-Muslim cooperation and solidarity in the cause of the nationalist movement; indeed half the delegates, mainly Syrians and Lebanese, were themselves Christian.[233] Aḥmad Ṭabbâra, a Muslim delegate from Beirut, defined the term "Arab" in an address before the conference as "...all Arabic-speaking peoples without distinction between Muslim and non-Muslim," and delegate Nadhra Muṭrân, a Christian, cited historical proofs that "the Arab's pride of race takes precedence over religion."[234] For a large segment of the Christian population, however, the Arab Nationalist movement held little promise; and for the ardent Lebanese Christian, separatist nationalists, it posed a direct threat to the cherished Christian autonomy enjoyed in the Mountain since 1861. As has already been seen, most Levantine Christians favored the imposition of European Mandates following the First World War, rather than the Arab Kingdom of Prince Faysal. The chief exceptions to this rule were the Orthodox Christians, particularly in Palestine and Syria. A number of prominent Orthodox laymen opted for commitment to the sharifian cause,[235] and throughout the Mandate years a very large and vocal element from within the community zealously supported nationalist causes, lay and clergy alike. Sir Anton Bertram, writing of the Greek Orthodox community in Palestine during the early 1920's, observed that "the dearest thought of every young local Orthodox Christian is that he is an Arab, and his most cherished aspirations are those of Arab nationalism, which he shares with his Moslem fellow countrymen."[236] Albert Hourani, writing 25 years later, noted this widespread tendency among the Levantine Greek Orthodox to identify with the Arab Nationalist cause:

> It is not simply isolated individuals who feel sympathy with the national movement. Sympathy is widespread among the Greek Orthodox who are altogether Arab in culture and feeling. This is true of the clergy as well as the laity, and of the higher clergy as well as the lower.... The younger generation, brought up under the influence of nationalistic ideas in school and out of it, tend to be as wholly devoted to the Arab cause as their Moslem contemporaries.[237]

Not surprisingly, some of the leading Arab Nationalist leaders of the interwar years were Orthodox Christians, and two in particular stand out as founders of important political parties and movements still extant today — something of a record in the highly transitory world of Arab politics. These two movements, the *Al-Ba'th* (Renaissance) and *Al-Ḥizb Al-Qawmi* (Nationalist Party), are in many respects divergent in their aims, reflecting as they do the particular ideologies of their founders, Michel 'Aflaq, scion of a prosperous Damascene Orthodox family, and Anṭûn Sa'âda, a repatriate Lebanese of South American birth. The latter was more narrowly nationalistic in his view, espousing a Syrian rather than the Pan-Arab Nationalism of 'Aflaq. But like so many nationalists of Christian birth, both men removed religion altogether from the realm of national action and based their social philosophies on a completely secular society,[238] forgetting that most Muslims were not willing to cast off Islam so casually. For these Christian nationalists and intellectuals, Muḥammad became a purely political figure, one to whom all Arabs owed primary allegiance as the founder of a united Arab nation. Thus while it may seem curious to the Westerner to read of Christians in the Arab East advocating "with even more vehemence and eloquence than the Muslims that the relationship between Islam and Arab Nationalism is intimate and that Islam should be the special object of veneration for all nationalists, no matter what their actual religion,"[239] it is a fact that they pointed out this relationship earlier and more frequently than Muslims. Dr. Qusṭanṭîn Zurayq, a Damascene Orthodox like 'Aflaq, made this point in 1938, 'Aflaq alluded to it in 1943, and the late Nabîh Fâris concurred in 1947 when he stated that "the birthday of the Prophet is the birthday of Arabism."[240] The ambiguity of this position for Christians was best illustrated by Makram 'Ubayd, leading Coptic figure in the nationalist *Wafd* party in Egypt during the interwar years, who once stated, "I am Christian by religion but Muslim by nationality."[241] Even in contemporary Lebanon where Christians have not felt so obliged to identify with Muslim Arab nationalist values, the Greek Orthodox community continues to contribute leaders who advocate secularization of the political system and identification with the mainstream of Arab politics, among them Nasserist Deputy for Beirut, Najâḥ Wakîm, elected in 1971 in his late 20's as the youngest and most politically radical Lebanese parliamentarian, who has played a prominent role in the leftist leadership during the recent civil strife. For the majority of Christians, however, some kind of commitment by Muslims to a purely secular nationalism was necessary before they would abandon themselves wholly to the Arab cause. This view was clearly set forth twenty years ago by Dr. Charles Mâlik, who, while acknowledging that "for the Christian of the Near East, Moslem culture... is in a deep sense their culture," and that "they cannot be too deeply interested in the development of their common heritage," felt strongly that there was a need for reciprocity on the part of the Muslim as well, for whom Christianity was an important part of this cultural heritage. Writing in 1952, Dr. Mâlik indicated the minimal extent to which he felt such efforts had been made.

> There is an amazing ignorance of Christian literature, doctrine and life, despite the fact that Christ and his Mother are deeply revered by Islam. There isn't a single Moslem scholar in all history, so far as I know, who has written an authentic essay on Christianity; whereas Christian scholars, both Arab and non-Arab have written authoritative works on Islam, and other religions too.... There will always be fear, uncertainty, embarrassment, uneasiness, lack of joy, lack of freedom, and a pre-disposition to self-defense, until this intellectual and spiritual imbalance is redressed.[242]

The situation pointed out by Dr. Mâlik is clearly indicative of the superiority with which Muslims had held their own religion and culture in comparison with other faiths — an outlook not lost on Christians who had lived under Islâm for centuries. Thus while some of them could identify with a nationalism based on the "culture" of Islam, and rationalize away the religious context of both Islamic and Christian ideology, there was little indication that many Muslims were willing to do the same. Many Christians could accept Michel 'Aflaq's reference to Islam as "a response to Arab needs at the time of Muhammad..." and "not explicitly a divine revelation,"[243] but few indeed were the Muslims who would publicly agree, despite the extent of their education or degree of Westernization. For this reason, the majority of Christians on the eve of national independence sought secure legal and constitutional guarantees of their political and communal rights, continuing to participate in the political life of the independent states as they had during the Mandate years, as Christians first, and nationalists second.

Egypt. Constitutional provisions in all the newly-independent Arab states of the Levant guaranteed, at least officially, complete freedom of religion and the equality of all citizens before the Law. The first to so provide was Egypt's Constitution of 1922, and in the ensuing three decades of monarchical rule, Copts participated actively in national political life. Prior to the achievement of independence, native Egyptian Christians had struggled with the Muslim majority for self-rule, and under the aegis of the *Wafd* — the principal nationalist party whose first leader, Zaghlûl Pasha, was the focus of the independence movement — a number of Copts rose to national prominence. Chief among the political leaders of Christian background was William Makram 'Ubayd (Obeid), "thin-lipped and sharp-minded with a passion for rooting out corruption,"[244] who figured prominently in the interwar cabinets, last serving his country as Finance Minister from 1944-1946. He died in 1961. Given his abilities and popular support it would appear that only his Christian identity prevented his attaining the highest post of Prime Minister; only once in modern Egyptian history had a Copt reached this level of political authority — Buṭrus Ghâlî Pasha in the first decade of this century — and the widespread opposition to his appointment on the part of the Muslim masses led to a series of violent outbreaks culminating in the ill-fated Prime Minister's assassination in 1910.

The Christian contribution to the crucible of post-World War II politics in Egypt has been by any standard far below the earlier performance of the interwar years when the "Cross and Crescent" movement of the initial struggle for independence was still a vital force.[245] Since 'Ubayd's departure from active political life in 1946 no Copt has risen to national prominence, save perhaps the notorious figure of Ilyâs Indrâwus (Elias Andraos), corrupt financial advisor to King Fârûq during the last years of his reign. During the 18-year administration of Nasser, Coptic participation in the government was confined to the extreme periphery of power. Though inevitably accorded one representative at the ministerial level, Copts have had to settle for portofolios of minimal political influence. In recent years, Coptic ministers have been Dr. Kamâl Ramzî Istînû (Stino), Deputy

Prime Minister for Supply and Internal Trade, and Jamîl Henry Bâdir, Minister of Communications appointed in 1966,[246] both competent administrators but lacking in the decisive political leadership that 'Ubayd had given the Coptic community in earlier years. Currently Egypt's Copts are represented in Sadat's administration by Undersecretary of State, William Shanûda, whose responsibilities include the operation of the Aswân High Dam.

In the legislative branch of the Egyptian government, Coptic presence has been notable for its insignificance. The parliamentary elections of 1964 returned only one Copt, Halîm Jirjis Bishay of Sidfâ (Asyûṭ province), out of 360 deputies elected. To redress the obvious imbalance, President Nasser, who by constitutional provision was permitted to appoint an additional ten members to the parliament, selected eight Copts. The total number of nine, however, still fell far below the Christian proportion of the total population, which even according to the official government figure of 7% would have allotted Christians a minimum of 25 seats. Clearly the abolition of guaranteed confessional representation in the legislature in 1955 (along with other remnants of the Ottoman *millet* system which had maintained separate civil courts for Christians) had worked to the temporary disadvantage of the Coptic population in the political life of their country.

In the military, Christians are likewise less frequently encountered at higher levels than their numbers would warrant. Meinardus cites the figure of "one to thirty" as the ratio of Copts to Muslims among the officers of the Egyptian Armed Forces,[247] or roughly half the Christian strength in the population as a whole. Nonetheless, Christian generals are not unknown, and one, General Ra'ûf Maḥfûẓ, received citations for personal heroism in the Battle of Sharm Al-Shaykh during the Suez War of 1956. During the recent hostilities of October 1973, Christian officers (among them Gen. 'Azîz Ghâlî, commander of the Second Egyptian Army, which was in the forefront of the successful assault) and enlisted men fought with valor, and in a meaningful gesture of respect for the holy month of Ramaḍân which coincided with the war, observed the ritual fasting side by side with their Muslim comrades.

What the future holds for Copts under the Sadât government is a question to which all Egyptian Christians are anxiously awaiting an answer, but from some initial trends it would appear that the coming years may once again witness more positive Christian participation in the political life of Egypt. The Russian presence, albeit reduced, has tended to discourage such a change since the majority of politically-minded Copts are decidedly pro-Western in their outlook, and for this reason any Christian resurgence may well have double significance both in terms of discernible change at home and in the nation's international political orientation.

At the social level, ancient tensions are still present despite the general pattern of Muslim-Christian cooperation in this century, as witnessed by the outbreak of anti-Coptic feeling by the Muslims of Al-Khanka, a Cairo suburb whose Christian population numbered only 615 out of 21,631 in 1960, in mid-November of 1972.[248] Both President Sadât, who is a product of Christian schooling and the first Egyptian head of State to have made an official visit to the Vatican (April 8, 1976) and Patriarch Shanûda acted immediately to condemn the hostilities which resulted in the burning of a Coptic church and several Christian-owned businesses, and to prevent further troubles. But such incidents serve to illustrate the inability of any Arab government, however liberal or concerned for its international image, to prevent old hatreds and rivalries of past centuries from surfacing at unexpected times and places.

Jordan. The British Mandate of Transjordan was granted full independence in May of 1946 and in its first electoral law promulgated a year later (5 April 1947) Christians were guaranteed four seats in the 18-man Council of Representatives, the kingdom's single elected representative body. The members of the senate were appointed directly by the monarch and usually included a generous sampling of Christian dignitaries. Following the annexation of the Arab remnant of Palestine in 1949, twenty more seats were added to the Council, three of them Christian, bringing the total to seven Christian representatives (one each from the districts of Amman, Al-Salṭ, Irbid, Karak,[249] Jerusalem,

Bethlehem, and Râm Allah) from among an elected body of 38 members, a percentage nearly twice that of the Christian share of the population as a whole.[250] The Constitution of 1952 guaranteed freedom of religion and perpetuated the *millet* system of civil law, placing all Christians under the jurisdiction of their own religious communities, just as Muslims came under the authority of the Sharî 'a courts.[251]

The political administration of the nation has from the very beginning remained securely in the hands of the East Bank Muslim establishment, though inclusions of West Bank Palestinians and even some refugees from Israel have been made in the interests of political expediency from time to time. Recognition of the interests of the Christian population has been made since 1949, as J.C. Hurewitz has pointed out, by the appointment of at least one Christian, usually a Greek Orthodox, to every cabinet, even to such an important post as Minister of Foreign Affairs, held by an Orthodox Christian, Anṭûn 'Aṭallah, in 1963-1964 and again in 1970 during the crucial period of the late summer conferences of King Husayn and President Nasser in Cairo over the Commando crises. On 29 August 1970 it was announced that 'Aṭallah would head the Jordanian delegation to the United Nations General Assembly (convened 15 September), it being speculated at the time that his presence would open the way for the elevation of Arab-Israeli peace talks from the ambassadorial to the ministerial level. The last cabinet formed before the June War, that of Sa'd Jum'â on 22 April 1967, included a Christian, Sim'ân Dawûd, as Minister of Justice, and this tradition has been continued to the present despite the loss of nearly half of the Christian population along with the West Bank territories.

In other areas of the Jordanian power structure Christians were also well represented. In the Foreign Service a sizeable number have reached the highest levels over the past quarter-century, among them Anasṭas Ḥannânîya (appointed Ambassador to Great Britain in 1959) and Anṭûn Nâbir (posted to Washington as First Secretary in 1963). In the elective Council of Representatives Christians continue to be allotted a disproportionate number of seats — ten out of sixty in the four-year parliament elected 15 April 1967. As of the spring of that year there were to the author's knowledge no less than six Christians among Jordan's top military personnel, including three Greek Orthodox brothers from Al-Ḥuṣn, Colonel Ibrâhîm Ya'qûb Ayyûb (Director of Military Intelligence of the Army General Staff), Brigadier General Najîb Ya'qûb Ayyûb (Chief of the Royal Signals), and Major Tawfîq Ya'qûb Ayyûb. The other three included Major Fu'âd Salâma Ḥaddâdîn (Commander of the Jordanian Coast Guard), Colonel Buṭrus Hamârna (Provost Marshal, Army General Staff), and Colonel Salîm Sulaymân Kanda (Royal Military Academy Commandant). Like the Ayyûb brothers the other Christians mentioned were natives of East Bank towns — Ma'an, Mâdabâ, and Irbid respectively — an indication that governmental preference for Trans-Jordanians in positions of authority over Palestinians transcended religious lines.

Except for Lebanon, the Kingdom of Jordan has to date offered its Christian population the greatest opportunity for economic and political self-fulfillment and for this reason the great majority of Jordanian Christians have shown themselves to be extremely loyal to the monarchy. Only among the Palestinians have the anti-Husayn forces found Christian recruits, but here again Christian leadership has been very significant (see "Christian Arabs and the Palestine Conflict" at the end of this chapter).

Israel. The role of Christians in the political life of Israel is unique in the Near East, molded as it is by the rigid restrictions which the Zionist administration has imposed on all Arab participation in the national political scene, but characterized by the degree to which these restrictions have been surmounted — in sharp contrast to the manner in which the more numerous Muslim Arabs have met the similar challenge. Predominantly urban, universally literate, often college-educated, and economically on a far higher plane than the average Arab Muslim, Israel's Christians, particularly the Greek Catholics among them, have carved for themselves a significant place in Israeli society on both the political and economic level. The Muslims, largely rural and considerably less literate on the average, have been easily controlled by the Israeli government through their shaykhs and *ulamâ'*, isolated, except for radio contact with Beirut, Cairo, and other Arab capitals, from the surrounding Arab World. The Christians, in contrast, have kept regularly in close contact with the neighboring states by means of the unique privilege of being able, prior to 1967, to cross into Jordan twice annually at Easter and Christmas for purposes of religious pilgrimage to Christian shrines in Old Jerusalem, Jericho, and Bethlehem. Thus, unlike the Muslims, they were able to visit with relatives and friends from Jordan, Syria, and Lebanon, and keep informed on events and happenings outside the Israeli enclave. Between 5,000 and 10,000 Israeli Christians took advantage of this opportunity each holiday occasion.[252] Others, moreover, met, and still meet, relatives and friends in Cyprus, the common close meeting ground available to both Arabs in Israel and elsewhere, or in Europe — an advantage which is again the result of the higher financial status enjoyed by Christians among the Israeli Arab population.

In addition, the Arab Christian clergy in Israel has been relatively free to visit the neighboring Arab states and to maintain regular contact with Europe and America. The Catholic prelates in particular have been in continual close touch with their Arab World brethren and the general body of world clergy as the result of the Oecumenical Council in Rome (1962-1965). For the small Israeli Arab Anglican community, regular contact was maintained with Arab Anglicans elsewhere from 1950-1967 through the offices of the Rt. Rev. Campbell McInnes, archbishop in Jerusalem (Jordan), who prior to the June War commuted often between his seat in the Arab sector of Jerusalem and the churches in Haifa and Galilee. The Arab Bishop of Lebanon, Syria, and Jordan, Najîb Cubain, travelled frequently to Beirut from Jerusalem, via the Ra's Al-Nâqûra checkpoint, otherwise closed to traffic since 1948. Well aware that pressure from Europe and America restrains the Israeli government from taking any action which might be viewed in the West as prejudicial to Christians, Arab Catholic leaders, especially Georges Ḥakîm, Melkite Archbishop of Galilee for two decades prior to his elevation to the patriarchate in November of 1968, have led the struggle in acquiring the same civil and property rights for Arabs which are granted to Jewish citizens, and have successfully forced the government to return large portions (though by no means all) of the ecclesiastical and private lands confiscated during and after the 1948 War.

Such united Arab efforts, even when aided by the support of international opinion and diplomatic pressure, do not, however, always succeed. The most recent example of Arab Christian failure to regain lost property is the concerted attempt of dispossessed villagers of Iqrît and Kafar Bir'im to re-occupy their homes and churches through a series of strikes, sit-ins, and protests in July and August of 1972. In 1948 these two villages, the first predominantly Greek Catholic, the second exclusively Maronite, were occupied and forcibly evacuated by Israeli troops owing to their proximity to a hostile Lebanese frontier. Though promised resettlement or new lands, these several hundred families received neither and finally, backed by the new Melkite Archbishop of Galilee, Joseph Raya, they returned without permission to claim what was left of their homes and their lands, much of which had been given in the intervening years to Jewish immigrants.

Though supported by international Church groups, Arab leadership in Israel, and even prominent Jewish leaders including Golda Meier's special adviser on Arab and Druze Affairs, the Prime Minister repeatedly refused to permit resettlement. Christian churches throughout Israel closed in protest, and Archbishop Raya publicly criticized the Prime Minister's refusal as an act of "persecution and crucifixion of my people." Though once again dormant, the issue is by no means settled and will continue to exacerbate already deteriorating Christian-Jewish relations at official levels in Israel until some agreement, satisfactory to the dispossessed villagers who now number some 4,500 in Israel, is reached.

The major sphere of secular Christian political activity in Israel has been, rather ironically, the tiny, but vocal, Israeli Communist Party. In 1961, for instance, Nazareth, which is wholly Arab and in majority Christian, gave 46.3% of its vote in the

Knesset elections of that year to the Communists,[253] indicating that Christians were beginning to take advantage of the Party as yet another opportunity of identifying with an organization maintaining external ties, and as a highly visible, yet legal, means of venting their dissatisfaction with Zionist administration. Suddenly made aware of their potential role in the fragmentary Israeli Communist Party (M.A.K.I.) in the early 1960's, the Arab faction challenged the Jewish leadership in 1965 and formed a splinter group (R.A.K.A.H.) under the leadership of a Christian Arab triumvirate, Tawfîq Tûbâ, Emile Ḥabîbî, and Emile Ṭûmâ. Leaders of the two rival factions were summoned to Moscow in the same year in an attempt to heal their differences, but these conciliatory moves were so unsuccessful that both groups had to be invited to the 23rd Congress of the C.P.S.U. Later, in 1965, R.A.K.A.H. polled twice the vote of M.A.K.I. in the Knesset elections of that year (27,000 votes versus 13,000), most of it from Nazareth and other Christian Arab centers in Galilee.[254] Of the twelve members of the Nazareth city council in 1966, six were Communist as was the mayor, himself a Christian. On the national level, the Christians, prior to June 1967, occupied three of the seven Arab seats in the Knesset (one would have been sufficient to represent their numerical strength in the total Israeli Arab community), and two of the three were in 1966 Communist, as opposed to only one of the four Muslim delegates. The Soviets, however, refused for long to tolerate an ethnic split in their already tiny representation in Israel, and late in 1966 a third group, the New Communist Party, was formed, uniting Jew and Arab, so that by 1969 this new party had succeeded in electing three members to the Knesset, two of them Arab (one each Muslim and Christian) though the party leader, Meir Wilner, was a Jew. At the present time the Communist strength among the Christian Arabs is still growing, having secured the official blessing of the Melkite Archbishop of Galilee, Joseph Raya (Hakîm's successor), who announced in November of 1969 that he intended to vote Communist in the next election because the Communists alone were expressing concern for the poor and dispossessed Arabs.

Communist prestige rose substantially following the victories of the Russian-backed Arab armies in the October War of

1973. Moreover, the recent government plan for the Israeli economic development of the predominantly Arab area of Northern Galilee, announced in November 1975, strengthened the power of the Arab-dominated R.A.K.A.H. to the extent that it was able to gain an absolute majority on the Nazareth city council (11 of 17 seats) and elect its mayoral candidate, Muslim parliamentarian Tawfîq Zayyâd, in special elections held on December 10. The fear that this project represented nothing more than an attempt by Israel to Judaize the area by forced confiscation of Arab lands and resettlement of Jewish immigrants no doubt contributed greatly to the Communist victory, and has led no less a figure than 'Aṭallah Manṣûr, well-known Melkite Arab commentator for the Hebrew daily *Ha'aretz* and normally a moderate in his views regarding Israel and the ultimate Palestine solution, to voice the deep-seated fear of all Arabs — Christian, Muslim, and Druze — that the Israelis' final aim is to transfer all Arab lands to the government land authority or the Jewish National Fund, leaving the non-Jewish population totally dispossessed.[255] There exists manifold precedent for this fear. Christians have only to point to the destruction of three of their villages in the North (and subsequent confiscation of the lands of Kafar Bir'im, Iqrît, and Al-Baṣṣâ), and more recently to the 1973 seizure of 350 acres of valuable vineyards on the southern edge of Bethlehem, ostensibly for "security" reasons, but clearly for purposes of re-establishing four Jewish settlements destroyed in the 1948-49 fighting. The city's Christian mayor, Ilyâs Firayj (Freij), has protested loudly and long, but — as usual — to no avail.[256]

The success of the Communist movement among Israel's Arabs has left the government with only two loyalist Arab groupings — the Druze and the Bedouins, whose numerical strength (40,000 and 25,000 respectively) account for only 15% of the non-Jewish population.[257]

Not surprisingly, Christian-Muslim relations in Israel are stronger than anywhere else in the Middle East, due not only to the two communities' equal status as minorities, but as the result of the leadership Christians of both the laity and clergy have exercised in opposing the efforts of Israel to win Arab obedience and to incorporate these 350,000 non-Jewish citizens, resident remnants of the Palestinian nation, into the overall Zionist framework. The small community of Druzes, in contrast, is generally mistrusted by the other Arabs for its cooperation with the government, to the extent of voluntarily serving in the army. An incident in early 1966 in which a Druze border patrol fired on and killed several Christian Arab Israelis attempting to flee into Lebanon raised tensions between Druzes and their Christian and Muslim brethren to a dangerously high point, affecting, at least for a short time, the security of the larger Druze communities in Lebanon and Syria. In Lebanon, for instance, the Druzes have found it expedient to give lip service to the Commando movement, to the extent that in November of 1968 the Druze Community Council formally rejected any peaceful solution of the Palestine question and urged the continuation of an armed struggle as the only means of liberating Israeli-occupied territory. Druze deputy Kamâl Junbalâṭ, speaking at the Community Council meeting in Beirut, urged the formation of popular fronts in all Arab countries to aid Commando efforts, and stated that "Arab commando activities should not be hindered on the southern Lebanese borders."[258] Such a militant attitude can hardly be said to jibe with earler actions of the Druze population in Israel itself. Since the 1967 War, however, there has been evidence that the Druzes in Israel have begun to alter their position, as witnessed by arrests of a 48-man Druze spy ring in May, 1973, and further arrests in March, 1974, of additional Druzes, all of whom were accused of working on behalf of Syria in the Golan area. Also the fact that following the successful commando raid on Qiryat Shimonah near the Lebanese border, Israeli Druze border guards were attacked by the grieving populace for allegedly assisting the three guerillas in their mission would indicate that Druze loyalty to the state of Israel is no longer taken for granted.

Though economic pressure incurred by the socialist Israeli economy, coupled with political and social discrimination, have encouraged a small but steady emigration among young Christians especially, the future of the greater community in Israel is brighter than might have been expected in the aftermath of the

1948 War. Many of those who emigrate plan to return, if for no other reason than out of a sense of duty to maintain a strong Arab presence in Palestine until some political solution is achieved, and undoubtedly they will be demanding a large role in Israeli political life, now that the de facto Arab population of Israel inclusive of the territories occupied in June 1967, is 40% of the total. "Time is on our side," remarked then-Archbishop Ḥakîm some years ago, "it is only a matter of time." [259]

Syria. In Syria the electoral laws enacted in 1946, the year in which French troops were finally evacuated (two years after independence had been proclaimed), conformed with Article 37 of the 1930 Constitution which stated that such a law would provide for confessional minorities *(minorités religieuses)*. Some controversy developed over the application of this provision, particularly in regard to whether each sect deserved individual representation or whether the parliamentarian's adherence to the Christian faith, regardless of his particular confession, was sufficient.[260] The former interpretation received governmental sanction, and the Syrian Chamber of Deputies elected 7 July 1947 was divided along strict sectarian lines: 116 Muslims (100 Sunni, 12 Alawites, 3 Druzes, and 1 Ismâ'îlî), 18 Christians (7 Greek Orthodox, 2 Gregorian Armenians, 2 Jacobites, 2 Melkites, and one each from the Syrian Catholics, the Armenian Catholics, and the Maronites, with two other seats for the remaining Christian groups), and one Jew, appointed accordingly from among the Syrian *muḥâfaẓât*. Nevertheless, the distribution with the greater Christian community was far from proportional since the Greek Orthodox were given a greater share than they merited numerically, while the Armenians were drastically under-represented. The Syrian Constituent Assembly elected 15 November 1949, the last before the Constitutional Crisis of 1950, was likewise divided along confessional lines with 14 Christian deputies and 100 Muslims of the various sects. Unlike the situation prevailing in neighboring Lebanon, the Syrian ministries were not apportioned on a sectarian basis; nevertheless Christians were invariably included in each new cabinet as they had been during the Mandate, most often as Ministers of Finance, Education,

Agriculture, or Health, the more politically sensitive Ministries such as Defense, Interior, and Foreign Affairs being traditionally reserved for members of the majority Sunni Muslim community.

The Constitution of 1950, promulgated in the immediate aftermath of the Arab defeat in Palestine, reflected an increasing Islamic tenor in the Arab Nationalism of the day, and resulted in the provision of Islamic Law as the basis of the national legal system, and restricted the office of President of the Republic to Muslims. An attempt to make Islam the official religion of the state was temporarily blocked by a concerted effort of Christian leadership, lay and clerical, and such secularist movements as the Ba'th.[261] Four years later the same coalition was unable to prevent this provision from being included in a revision of the 1950 document. Partly in an effort to appease Christian opinion, the Muslim political establishment in that same year raised the leading Christian nationalist figure, Fâris Al-Khûrî, a Greek-Orthodox Damascene who had played a major role in the Syrian independence movement throughout the Mandate era, to the second-highest position of Prime Minister. Nevertheless, for most Christians the increasing Islamic fervor of Arab Nationalist sentiment in Syria, coupled with rising political confusion and economic decline, gave impetus to a steadily growing Christian emigration.

As was pointed out in Chapter II, probably half of the half million or more Syrians estimated to have left in the past decade in search of new jobs and homes in Lebanon or abroad were Christians, representing a very high percentage of the professional and commercial classes of the nation. And while the governmental policies of extreme socialism and nationalization, plus the incidence of natural disasters such as a near decade of drought in the Jazîra contributed greatly to the exodus, there lay beyond these purely economic factors the feeling of insecurity shared by all Christians which had been augmenting steadily since the first Constitutional crisis of 1950. Msgr. R. Etteldorf observed of Syria in the late 1950's that "there has been evident... a trend so to emphasize adherence to Islam as a condition of citizenship that Christians are to be driven out on grounds that they are not citizens."[262] Though a Western Catholic clergyman would almost inevitably present a biased view on Middle Eastern politics where it involved Christians versus Muslims, many isolated incidents can in fact be cited to support the existence of such a trend. In 1955, for example, a popular *imâm* (prayer leader) of the Umayyad Mosque in Damascus declared that as far as he was concerned an Indonesian Muslim was closer to him than the Syrian Christian Prime Minister of his own country (Fâris Al-Khûrî).[263] Since that time, no Christian has served in such a high political capacity (Al-Khûrî died in 1962) as administration has replaced administration in a chain of increasingly nationalistic, anti-Western, even pro-Communist governments in which most Christians came to feel they had little or no voice.

The extent to which the feeling of political isolation was felt by Christians as early as a decade ago was voiced in an editorial published in 1961 in the journal of Damascene Orthodoxy, *Al-Ḥaraka,* in which the author or authors complained that "la situation reservée aux Chrétiens, en Syrie... s'agit à se sentir étrangers dans leur pays...,"[264] essentially a reiteration of the fear expressed seven years earlier by the then Patriarch Ṣâ'igh in his Easter sermon delivered in the midst of the second Constitutional Crisis (1954) — namely that the inclusion of official references to the religion of Islam in the Constitution would make of Christians "refugees in their own country."

The 1958-1961 union with Egypt resulted in the abolition of the communal system in the political structure of Syria, at least on the previous carefully divided sectarian basis, religious distinction during this period being made only on the level of Christian, Muslim (including Druze and Alawite), and Jew. Legislative power remained nominally vested in a unicameral legislature in which Christians were granted minimal representation, but following the Ba'thist coup of 1963, all previous guarantees were swept aside. The Provisional Constitution promulgated on 25 April 1964, a little more than a year after the Ba'thist rise to power, specified, as in earlier documents, Islam as a qualification for the presidency, and Islamic jurisprudence as the major source of legislation, but made no mention of the special rights and electoral representation previously accorded Christians and non-Sunni Muslim religious groups. The National Revolutionary Council set up in 1965 served as the unicameral legislature with membership chosen on an occupational basis. This is not to say that Christians were unrepresented, for the Ba'th party had attracted substantial Christian membership since its beginnings in 1940 under the co-leadership of Michel 'Aflaq, still the movement's leading ideologue, largely due to its absolutely secularist approach to nationalism. Other minorities were likewise attracted, notably members of the Alawite and Druze communities whose adherents had long formed a strong if not dominant element in the higher ranks of the Syrian military. The coup of February 1966 was in fact engineered by an Alawite General, Salâḥ Al-Jadîd, in close collusion with another of his own sect, General Ḥâfiẓ Al-As'ad, and Major Salîm Haṭûm, a Druze from Suwayḍâ.[265] Christians, too, had been found in high places in the military since the Mandate era, notable among them was Colonel Gabriel Bîṭâr, a Greek Orthodox from Latakia who, after 1965, had served as Chief of Staff for the Southwestern Front Command, a position of great responsibility in view of the area's contiguity with Israel, and, it should be added, its subsequent loss to the Zionist state in 1967.

On the national political level, Christians continued to figure peripherally in the formation of cabinets; that of President Nûr Al-Dîn Al-Atâsî, announced in February of 1966, included As 'ad Taqlâ, Minister of Industry, Petroleum, and Electricity, and Samîḥ 'Atîyâ, Communications Minister, and one of two Communists included in this the most left-wing of modern Syrian cabinets.[266] In the cabinet formed eight months later on 16 October 1966 only 'Atîyâ of the Christian ministers was retained, and the cabinet of 30 October 1968 included only one Christian, General Louis Dakar, along with one Druze, one Ismâ' îlî, and three Alawites, the remaining members of Al-Atâsî's 26-man government being Sunnis.

In November 1970, Al-Asad, then Commander of the Air Force, seized power from Atâsî and Jadîd in an inter-party struggle arising over Syrian policy towards Jordan following King Husayn's "Black September" crackdown on Palestine commando activity in his own country. Al-Asad opposed the armed intervention proposed by Atâsî favoring instead a Nasser-type policy that would not support the Palestinians to the extent of provoking Israeli counterattacks — an approach that Al-Asad has obviously continued to implement in the present Lebanon crisis. Though the majority of present Syrian leadership remains firmly in the hands of Alawis, President Al-Asad has maintained very cordial relations with the Syrian Christian communities and included individual Christians in his government, though not at the highest level.

In the diplomatic corps, Syrian Christians have long held prominent positions, and on at least one occasion since independence have served as their country's principal envoys to such major posts as Washington, Moscow, London, Paris, and Athens. Syria's most prominent Christian diplomat has been Georges Ṭu'ma (Tomeh), for over a decade his nation's ambassador to the United Nations, and internationally recognized as an articulate spokesman for the many regimes he has represented since his appointment. As a Christian, Tu'ma has attested to the ability of non-Muslim minorities to rise to prominence in a state where Islam predominates.[267] The absence of any legal or judicial guarantees for Christians and other minorities, however, has revived old fears and apprehensions, and prompted many politically-motivated Christians either to emigrate or to accept secondary positions within the existing system in hopes that current secular trends will ultimately work in their favor.

Iraq. The first Constitution of Iraq (1924) provided in Article 13 for "complete freedom of conscience and freedom to practice the various forms of worship in conformity with accepted customs" with respect to all inhabitants of the country. This constitution likewise provided (Section 2 of Article 4) that "the electoral system shall guarantee equitable representation to racial, religious, and linguistic minorities in Iraq." In accordance with the latter provision the various communities were given representation in the royally-appointed Senate (one Christian and one Jew), and by the Electoral Law of the same year which allotted a fixed number of seats in the elective parliament —

four each in the case of Christians and Jews.[268] An electoral law dated 27 May 1946 augmented this number to six for both communities, the Jewish representation being reduced to one after the general exodus of Iraqi Jews to Israel in 1949-1950.

On the ministerial level, Christians were represented in the first Iraqi cabinet of 1920,[269] and in several cabinets since then, though not as frequently as in the neighboring Arab states where the Christian proportion of the total population was considerably higher. To the author's knowledge, only two Christian Iraqis achieved the rank of minister during the quarter-century of independence under the monarch — Yusuf Ghanîma (thrice Minister of Finance) and Rûfâ'îl Buṭî (Minister of State in two successive cabinets in 1953 and 1954). The Republican revolution of 1958 abolished the parliament in favor of rule by a succession of military and revolutionary councils with no provision for confessional representation. It was deemed highly significant, therefore, that the cabinet formed on 9 August 1966 by Prime Minister Najî Ṭâlib, the first Shî 'a premier in many years, included for the first time in over a decade a Christian minister, Dawûd Farhân Sarsam, as Minister of Municipalities and Public Works. Granted it was one of the lesser ministerial posts to which he had been appointed, and as a Jacobite he was a member of the smallest, and most pro-Arab nationalist of the four principal Christian sects in Iraq, as had been Rûfâ'îl Buṭî before him. But for all Iraqi Christians his appointment spelled out a trend in the direction of an implementation of the principles of religious freedom and equality by the revolutionary Ba'thist government, and was viewed as particularly welcome coming as it did in the aftermath of increased Muslim-Christian hostility in the north generated by overt Christian connections with Communism during the earlier Kassem régime. Of added significance, especially for Iraqi Catholics (representing three-quarters of the country's Christian population) was the announcement, issued the same day as Sarsam's appointment, of the new Iraqi government's intention to establish diplomatic relations with the Vatican at the ambassadorial level. Still only 8 out of 117 Iraqi government leaders during the years 1963-1968 were either Christian or unidentifiable as to their religious background.[270]

Inequalities of representation remained in some areas of the government and military, particularly at high levels, but few Christians actually discussed it openly. There were two reasons for this silence: first, a fear that any complaint would jeopardize progress made already in improving recently-strained relations with the vast Muslim majority, and secondly, isolated instances of Christians being appointed to positions of authority in areas of national life previously closed to them. During the Kassem régime, for instance, a Christian, Najîb Ṣâ'igh, was named Ambassador of Iraq to Lebanon, the first time that an ambassadorial post had ever been entrusted to a Christian in the history of the Iraqi diplomatic service. Two prominent Iraqi Christians had represented their government at the San Francisco Conference in 1945 (Majîd Khadduri and Fâris Ma'lûf) which brought into being the United Nations, but prior to Ṣâ'igh's appointment their role in the national diplomatic corps had been decidedly secondary.

The Christian laity and particularly the clergy with whom the author conversed in the fall of 1965 in Baghdad and on several occasions outside Iraq since that time, were hesitant to discuss at any length the political situation in respect to the Christian communities. Some refused even to touch upon it at all. "Al-Siyâsa? Abadan!" "Politics? Never!" was the answer received from an otherwise cordial and loquacious Syrian Catholic priest in Baghdad in response to a question touching upon the degree of Christian involvement in Communist activity during the Kassem régime. In all probability only a very small percentage of Iraqi Christians was at any time actively Communist oriented, primarily dissatisfied rural Christians from the Mosul district, and a handful of vocal intellectuals, journalists, and occasionally priests from Baghdad. Christians and other minorities, particularly Kurds, had nevertheless been linked for many years with the Communist party throughout the Middle East, and Iraq was no exception. One of the founders of the Iraqi party was an Assyrian, the already-mentioned Yûsuf Salmân, and at the time of the Kassem administration, both the officially-recognized Communist party and a splinter faction were led by Christian chairmen, Dawûd Ṣâ'igh and Zâkî Kharî Sa'îd, respectively. Two Iraqi Jacobite priests attended the Communist-dominated Congress of the Partisans of Peace at Stockholm in July 1959, and were summarily excommunicated by their patriarch. On the other hand, several prominent Christians took stands against Communism at the time when, in view of the official position of the Kassem government, it was impolitic to do so. Notable among them was the aging Chaldaean archbishop of Basra, Joseph Gogué, who spoke out from the pulpit of his cathedral church in 1959 only to be placed under house arrest several hours later. Likewise his patriarch, Bûlus Shaykhû, speaking for the clergy of all the Christian communities in Iraq, denounced in his Christmas sermon of 1960 "the bloody acts of Communism and other philosophies that deny the existence of God and insult the dignity of human liberty."[271]

There was no question, however, that numerous Christians had taken part in Communist activity in the north during 1959-1960 aimed at preventing a Nasserist overthrow emanating from the conservative Muslim establishment in Mosul. Not surprisingly, a 1962 Egyptian publication damned the so-called "Mosul Massacres" and at one point demanded judgment against the "Criminals of Tall Kayf," Christian villagers who reportedly participated in a Communist rally chanting, "The religion of Muhammad is null and void!" and later assisted Communists and government forces in carrying out a small-scale pogrom against conservative Muslim and pro-Nasser elements in the city of Mosul itself.[272] Muslim reaction following the overthrow of Kassem in 1963 forced a large percentage of the Christians from Mosul, Tall Kayf, and surrounding villages — an estimated 30,000 by 1965 — to flee their homes for safety in Baghdad,[273] and it was generally feared by all Christians, the majority of whom had no contact whatsoever with Communism, that they would also be forced to withstand increased hostility from an angry and suspicious Muslim majority.

The Christian community in Iraq has, as a result, been exceedingly careful to avoid further complications, and their leaders consistently refrain from any public reference to religious inequalities for fear that it might simply precipitate increased Muslim reaction. Their position, however, has been compromised by factors other than simply the Communist connections of the Kassem era; for it is well known that Christian support for the Kurdish drive for autonomy is strong in some quarters, and that a considerable number of Christians living in the mountainous Kurdish districts north of Mosul — chiefly Nestorians with smaller numbers of Chaldaean Catholics — have joined the Kurdish insurgents in the fight against the government regulars. In his 1964 account of the Kurdish struggle in Iraq, Dana Adams Schmidt reported:

> Since the Iraqi government dissolved the Assyrian Levies, who were as good at fighting in the mountains as the Kurds, the Assyrians have identified themselves with the Kurdish population, so that in one unit of 200 Kurds there were, as I recall, about 30 Christians.[274]

The leader of the Kurdish separatist forces, Mullâ Muṣṭafâ Al-Barazânî, is himself reputedly of old Nestorian stock, his family (from which sprang twelve bishops of the Church) having converted to Islâm only a century ago. Schmidt further recounted how one of the most famous figures in the fighting was a young Chaldaean Catholic girl, Margaret George (Jiwârjis), who at one time commanded a troop unit in the area of 'Aqrâ and was famed for her courage. Still active in 1970 when Dr. Meinardus visited the area (though according to him a Nestorian), she had achieved virtual sainthood among the Christians of Reza'iya (Urumîya) in neighboring Iranian Kurdistan. The Nestorians of the district refer to her as *Shamîram* or (Semiramis), and with her "following of 14-20 officers and 5,000-7,000 men, she is a formidable threat to the Arabs of Iraq."[275] The recent flare-up of Kurdish-Iraqi hostilities has not been without visible signs of Christian sympathy in Iraq itself, such as a public statement by the Assyrian Bishop of Zakhû in March, 1974 pledging his and his flock's cooperation with the Kurdish insurgents. Further evidence of Christian collaboration with the Kurdish movement can be seen in the activities of Chaldaean Bishop, Paul Bedari, at one time a member of the Supreme Command Councîl of the Kurdish Revolution, who tried unsuccessfully to persuade Mulla

Muṣṭafâ to agree to the establishment of an autonomous Assyro-Christian district with the Kurdish-occupied territory, indicating that the post-World War II movement among Christians in Iraq to create their own homeland was far from dead.

Such instances of open Christian contribution to and sympathy for the Kurdish cause could not help but reflect ill on all Christians, the majority of whom professed complete loyalty to the government in Baghdad. For despite frequent declarations of a patriotic nature by lay and religious leaders, the active participation of individual Christians in anti-Iraqi and anti-Arab nationalist causes such as the Kurdish rebellion and the Communist movement continued to evoke considerable suspicion in the minds of many Muslims, suspicions which were further confirmed in August of 1966 when an Iraqi Christian pilot, Colonel Munîr Rufa'a, fled with his Soviet MIG-21 to Israel in an incident of major international significance. The pilot, a Catholic from the North, stated to the world that he had sought asylum in Israel in order to escape the religious intolerance to which he as a Christian was subjected in Muslim Iraq, and in protest over having had to participate in the "immoral war" against innocent, unarmed Kurdish villagers.[276] There was no official Iraqi reply to the pilot's charges, but the incident reportedly, and not surprisingly, increased Muslim-Christian tension, particularly in Mosul, the home of the defecting pilot. Among Iraqi Christians the defection was noted with great regret, linking as it did all Christians inescapably with Israel at a time when Arab-Zionist hostilities were on the upswing, and, moreover, compromising without question the position of those Christians who, despite difficulties, had overcome the handicap of their religion — with credit due both to themselves and the Muslim establishment — to win promising careers as officers in the armed forces,[277] heretofore the most exclusive preserve of Muslims in all Arab states, excluding Lebanon.

There were many who saw in the inclusion of a significant proportion of Christians among those Iraqis hanged for supposed collaboration with Israel and the CIA in 1969 evidence of a Muslim reaction to this internationally publicized defection. Of the 14 Iraqis publicly executed in the first wave of hangings in late January 1969, nine were Jews, three Muslims, and two Christians;[278] of the second group of eight hanged a month later, at least one, 'Imâd Ḥannûsh Jiwârjis, a student leader as reported by government information, was a Christian.[279] These hangings, according to the president of the court which condemned the accused to their deaths, were not prescribed on any religious basis,[280] but there were many who were not so sure.

It is probably too soon, in terms of the slow-moving Middle Eastern concept of time and history, to evaluate the actual extent of the reaction among Muslims to the Rufa'a incident, or the activities of Margaret Jiwârjis and her Christian partisans, but such activities certainly render any prediction of the future of Christians in the political, economic, and military levels of Iraqi national life virtually impossible. On the basis of overt Christian connections with the Communist movement, the Kurdish rebellion, and most recently Israel, the Iraqi government may well consider itself justifiably discouraged from extending further trust and responsibility to the Christian population in the face of popular mistrust currently running at a level higher than normal among the Muslim masses. Whether or not the previous trend of greater tolerance will in the long run be seriously impeded or even reversed remains to be seen, but there is no reason for looking to the very near future with a great deal of optimism.

Lebanon. An analysis of the Christian political role in Lebanon at the time of this writing (Christmas 1976) is virtually impossible in the wake of the recent civil war (April 1975 - December 1976), which has seriously challenged the traditional political establishment, and the military occupation of the country by the Syrian Army (in the guise of a pan-Arab peace-keeping force) which has given rise to grave questions concerning the future existence of Lebanon as an independent political entity. After twenty months of bitter inter-communal hostilities, the country is effectively partitioned into spheres of influence of the several warring factions, and it remains to be seen what, if anything, can be done to restore the previous precarious unity of Lebanon's multi-confessional population. All that can be done is to consider the system as it existed until April 1975 and to examine prospects for its survival and the roles that the various Christian groups can reasonably be expected to play.

In the Republic of Lebanon since independence (1944) the principle of confessional representation has been applied to every conceivable level and branch of the public sphere. The Muslim-Christian agreement embodied in the unwritten National Pact *(Al-Mîthâq Al-Waṭanî)* of 1943 recognized a parliamentary ratio of six Christians to five Muslims (including Druzes) in all succeeding constituent assemblies, whose total numbers have always been some multiple of eleven, ranging since 1944 from 44 to 99 members. Parliamentary seats have been thus apportioned to the various religious communites according to their official numerical strength in the total population, so that a typical Lebanese Chamber of Deputies would be broken down as follows: total seats, 99; Christians, 54 seats (Maronites 30, Greek Orthodox 11, Melkite 6, Armenian Orthodox 4, Armenian Catholic, Protestant, and other Christian 1 each), Muslims, 39 seats (Sunnis 20, Shî 'a 19), and Druzes, 6 seats.

A similar apportioning of other governmental posts was effected on the basis of Article 95 of the Constitution of 23 May 1926 as amended on 9 November 1943, which provided "as a provisional measure and for the sake of justice and amity, the sects — religious communities — shall be equitably represented in public employment and in the composition of the Ministry." By unwritten agreement, the President of the Republic since independence has been a Maronite Christian, the Prime Minister a Sunni Muslim, with the remainder of the parliamentary offices and cabinet posts distributed so as to provide representation for the six major religious communities (Speaker of the House a Shî 'a, Vice-Speaker a Greek Orthodox, etc.). Of the Ministries, Justice, Education, and Foreign Affairs have become traditionally Christian posts, whereas Defense has tended to rest either with a Druze or Maronite. That of the Interior normally falls to a Sunni, Agriculture to a Shî 'a or Druze, while Finance and Health have come to be shared equally by Christian and Sunni Muslim ministers.[281] Matters of civil jurisdiction are kept strictly within the sphere of the religious communities, so that for legal purposes every Lebanese is forced to adhere to one or another religious faith whether he is in fact a believer or not. And while some reforms of personal status laws were carried out during the Mandate years — a commission was established in 1923 by the French to reform the civil legal structure — and some systematization introduced and inconsistencies eliminated in 1930, the contracting and dissolving of marriages, guardianship and legitimization of children, religious endowments, inheritance and wills, still remain today purely the prerogative of the ecclesiastical authorities of the individual sects.[282]

To change one's religious affiliation, even in the tolerant atmosphere of Lebanon, involves difficulties. In most of the neighboring Arab states with Christian minorities it is an easy enough thing for Christians to adopt Islam (as a small number do every year for purpose of political, social, or economic advancement, or simply to obtain an easy divorce), but for Muslims to do the reverse it remains virtually impossible. The right of Christian churches (and occasionally foreign missions) to evangelize the Muslim population, though tacitly sanctioned, is invariably curtailed on the strength of the additions to every Arab constitutional article of religious freedom, prohibiting any activity which conflicts "with the maintenance of public order and morals." [283] As Stanley Morrison pointed out in the late 1940's, "nothing excites the fanaticism of the Muslim masses more than the word *tabshîr,* 'the preaching of the Gospel,' or rumors that a Muslim has been baptized."[284] In the debate on Human Rights before the third session of the United Nations' General Assembly, Pakistan was the only Muslim state which stood out uncompromisingly for full freedom of Christian missionary work as would have been provided for by the inclusion of the phrase "freedom to change religion or belief."[285] The delegate from Egypt, supported by the representatives of all other Arab states, except Lebanon, sought to delete that phrase. And while in Lebanon alone, the sole nation in the Arab World in which Islamic Law was not accorded constitutional recognition as "a major," or "the major source" of the national legal framework, could a Muslim, as Pierre Rondot indicates, "abandon Islam and turn to another faith... without risk or scandal,"[286] conversion to Christianity from Islam was rare indeed (one notable instance being that of scholar Mâjid Fakhrî, scion of a prominent Shî 'a family from Sidon)[287] and officially discouraged owing to the violent reaction such instances provoked among the Muslim population.

The delicate balance on which Lebanon's divided government rests has been threatened almost continually, ever since the National Pact was promulgated nearly three decades ago, by the Muslim population supported by Arab nationalists outside the country. They were determined that Lebanon should recognize its Arab heritage and that the narrowly-Christian nationalist view held by Maronites such as Emile Idda, who felt that Lebanon belonged to the Mediterranean World of which France was a part, "rather than as part of the Arab World which he is said to have associated with desert," [288] should not prevail. The greatest cause of Muslim dissatisfaction with the status quo post-1943 in Lebanon was not the system itself, however, but rather their contention that the system had not been fairly administered, and that they, not the Christians, now constituted a majority. Official statistics published at irregular intervals since the Census of 1932 have failed, as has already been seen, to admit this change, and have in fact showed the narrow Christian majority as having increased to a suspicious 150,000 by 1956 (the year of the last government "estimate"). In 1953 an anonymous English-language pamphlet entitled *Moslem Lebanon Today* was circulated throughout Beirut, in which Muslim grievances were openly aired. Among the remedies called for were citizenship for Palestinian refugees, deprivation of citizenship held by the largely Christian emigrés abroad, abandonment of the National Pact, and a new Census. Christians reacted predictably with protests and a judicial proceeding against the pamphlet's suspected perpetrators, and one year later with elaborate celebrations in honor of the centenary of the adoption of the dogma of the Immaculate Conception by the Roman Catholic Church, which culminated in a huge procession from downtown Beirut to the shrine of the Virgin at Ḥarîṣâ, some ten miles north of the capital, overlooking the Bay of Jûniya. The Muslims, accordingly, felt moved to demonstrate their rival strength and unity a month later by celebrating Muḥammad's birthday with a resplendent torchlight procession in downtown Beirut. Because of inattention to safety details, however, fire broke out and in the ensuing panic some twenty-one persons were trampled to death and several hundred more seriously injured, "not without some malicious satisfaction on the part of. . . Lebanese Christians." [289]

During the next four years Lebanese Muslim opinion, like that of Arab Muslims elsewhere in the Middle East, began to rally ever more strongly around the nationalist banner of Nasser. The refusal of President Camille Chamoun (Sham'ûn) to break off diplomatic relations with France and Great Britain following the two European powers' joint attack on Suez in October of 1956 (an action justified by the government as having been dictated by consideration for the interests of Lebanese living in British and French territories abroad) greatly increased Muslim hostility since Chamoun was of course a Christian, and the interests for which his government was so concerned were largely those of fellow Christians. In March of 1957 when Chamoun and his pro-Western Minister of Foreign Affairs, Dr. Charles Mâlik, accepted the controversial Eisenhower Doctrine, Sunni opposition was pushed to the danger point, as all Arab Muslims viewed this latest move as a distinct breach of the National Pact, in that it implied that the Christians were calling upon the United States to replace France as their traditional benefactor and protector, and to intervene on Christian behalf.

What actually precipitated the Lebanese political crisis of 1958 was a combination of earlier political developments, notably the decision of President Chamoun to seek an unprecedented second term (and, when the Muslim members of his government resigned in protest, his staging of undoubtedly rigged elections which returned a parliament overwhelmingly favorable to his course of action), as well as the union of Syria with Nasser's Egypt which threatened to engulf Lebanon in a tidal wave of Pan-Arabism. The actual events of the Crisis itself are not the specific concern of this study, except insofar as the interplay of individuals and political factions did represent a departure from the purely religious alignments of past internal struggles. The sporadic fighting was not without incidents bearing ugly religious overtones. As an example, on 12 May 1958, less than a week after the assassination of Maronite editor Najîb Al-Matnî of the left-leaning — some would say Communist — journal, *Al-Tilighrâf*, which began the crisis, a band of 200 armed men crossed into Lebanon from Syria at the border post of Al-Maṣna‘ on the Beirut-Damascus highway, and attacked the military garrison there which consisted of five Christians and one Muslim. The Muslim they took with them; the Christians were castrated and disembowled.[290] On the other hand, the anti-Chamoun forces within Lebanon itself included a number of Christians, prominent Maronites among them (e.g. ex-president Bishâra Al-Khûrî and the president's own patriarch, Paul Meouchy). On the side of Chamoun were a small number of Sunnis from the old Beirut establishment, including Sâmî Al-Sûlḥ, kin of Riyâḍ Al-Sûlḥ, co-author of the National Pact, and Prime Minister under Chamoun. For his highly unpopular stand, Al-Sûlḥ earned the epithet "Mârûn" from his Muslim constituents in the Basta quarter of Beirut, while equally unhappy Maronites referred not so privately to their patriarch as "Muhammad" Méouchy. The Druze population was likewise split, those loyal to Shaykh Majîd Arslân of ‘Alayh supporting Chamoun, and those partisans of deputy Kamâl Junbalâṭ, the President's long-time rival from his home district of Al-Shûf southeast of Beirut, opting for the opposition.

There is no doubt, however, that this criss-crossing of traditional loyalties in fact saved Lebanon from total civil war, and enabled a third force to emerge, headed by General Fu'âd Shihâb, which forced Chamoun to resign thus permitting the peaceful formation of a new government. Shihâb, a Maronite whose family still included a Muslim branch from the days when its members ruled Lebanon as princes under the Ottoman Empire, was the logical choice for presidential successor to Chamoun, and with his election all factions were temporarily reconciled, and the situation returned to that which had existed prior to the Crisis.

At the time of the death of President Nasser of Egypt twelve years later (October 1970), the political structure of Lebanon stood little changed from that which emerged from the compromise accord reached during the 1958 Crisis. The regime of Fu'âd Shihâb (1958-1964) had been characterized by prosperity, good will among the various communities and, despite the abortive "Rosewater Coup" of 1961,[291] political stability. The peaceful succession to the nation's highest political office by Charles Helou (Ḥilû) in 1964 reaffirmed the willingness of the Muslim leaders to stand behind the original agreement in the National Pact of 1943 whereby it was accepted that the President of the Republic should always be a Maronite: a tradition once again confirmed six years later with the peaceful election of present President Sulaymân Faranjîya. The opposition Muslim leaders of the 1958 troubles were quickly reinstated in the national political scene, and indeed two of the most prominent — Rashîd Karâmî of Tripoli and 'Abd-Allah Al-Yâfî of Beirut — have served as Prime Ministers in numerous post-1958 governments. The small loyalist Muslim faction has likewise regained its place in Lebanese political life. Sâmî Al-Sûlḥ, who had been virtually ostracized from his own Sunni community as the result of his pro-Chamoun position in 1958, was in 1964 re-elected to the Chamber of Deputies from his former constituency in Beirut and publicly honored by both Muslim and Christian on his death four years later at the age of 78. Ṣâ'ib Al-Salâm (Saeb Salam) was fully reconciled in 1970 with his appointment by President Faranjîya to his first Prime Ministership since the 1958 Crisis. The Christian forces of the opposition were again reunited with the more conservative element, while the leaders of the third force, Shihâb and Helou, pre-empted Maronite leadership for the next twelve years.

On the surface nothing had changed. The pre-1958 confessional distribution of parliament and the ministries operated as before. Christians enjoyed their traditional 6:5 edge over Muslims and Druzes among the elected representatives and continued to share cabinet posts equally with the non-Christian communities. The weak and hydra-headed party system, consisting of a dozen or more groupings of one or another religious group centered around a single strong leader, continued to operate according to a kind of political logic indigenous to Lebanon alone. Only the right-wing, paramilitary *Phalanges*

Libanaises (Al-Katâ 'ib) representing the most intransigent anti-Muslim Christian element, chiefly Maronites, and its antithesis, the *Najâda* party made up of strongly pro-Nasser Pan-Arab Sunni Muslims, commanded any popular base or exerted tangible strength.[292] In the parliament itself, the return to the multi-seat, long-list constituency system[293] after 1958 insured that the more moderate element in both the Christian and non-Christian power groups would prevail and, moreover, acted to preserve the continued hegemony of the closed clique of politicians — members of the most prominent Lebanese families, Muslim and Christian alike — who had governed Lebanon since 1958 in the same manner as had their fathers, uncles, and cousins before them.

The long domination of the Chamber of Deputies by a handful of well-entrenched politicians was confirmed several years ago in a study of the first seven Lebanese parliaments (1943-1964) which showed that one-third of the available seats had been occupied during that period by 14% of the deputies elected.[294] On the basis of age-distribution and new-member data of these seven parliaments, Dr. Ralph Crow proposed that one "would be tempted to conclude that the recruitment process is not only stable but oligarchic... if anything the age data suggests the existence of a parliamentary oligarchy since the mean age has risen from 46 in 1943 to 50 in 1964."[295] One progressive development, however, to which the author points was the percentage decline in recent years of feudal landlords and lawyers — the traditional Lebanese political establishment — in the makeup of the Lebanese parliament. Whereas the two groups comprised about 80% of the 1943 Chamber, they barely dominated the body in 1964, businessmen and professionals having climbed to a position of near equality in terms of numerical strength.[296] On closer examination, however, this encouraging trend appears to be less extensive than it would seem at first glance. For in many cases the outward professional change has been only a matter of the son or nephew of a former M.P. who had been either a lawyer or landlord, having chosen a profession other than that of his elder, but still entering parliament on the same family connections. Since the above study was made, the trend towards a more diversified parliament and cabinet has continued, with the addition of many younger, and thus less traditional, members to the government as a whole. The administration of President Faranjîya has been noted for its youth, including as it has a number of cabinet members and parliamentarians in their early 30's, and represents a positive step towards re-attracting the nation's politically conscious and rebellious student population who in recent years have protested loudly over their exclusion from the old system of government.

The traditional distribution of the ministries among the various religious commuities has continued to follow the general pattern set at the beginning of independence. Ralph Crow, in his study of the first 26 governments of the Lebanese Republic (1943-1961), found the Minister of Foreign Affairs and Education to have been virtually always Christians (as is the case in the cabinets appointed by President Faranjîya after his election in August of 1970), the Minister of Defense, frequently a Druze (though since 1967 a Maronite or Melkite Christian), the Ministers of Agriculture and the Interior predominantly Muslim, while those of Finance, Justice, and Health were as often one as the other. Of the 208 ministers appointed to serve during the first 26 administrations, 106 were Christian, and 102 Muslim or Druze, an even apportionment not, however, necessarily reflected in the distribution of the posts within the sub-groups of those two major religious divisions themselves.[297] And when these established patterns of religious confessionalism in the ministries are compared with the sectarian makeup of one of the last peacetime cabinets (that of Prime Minister Tâqî Al-Dîn Al-Sûlḥ formed 7 August 1973), no major deviation from the norm is to be found.[298] The 22 ministerial appointments were, as usual, equally divided among Christians and non-Christians; of interest, however, is that for the first time the major sectarian groups — Maronite Christian and Sunni Muslim — who theoretically, at least, make up 50% of the population, were with only four ministers each, considerably outnumbered by the four other principal communities, Shî 'a Muslim, Druze, Greek Catholic, and Greek Orthodox. For the smaller Christian communities who together represented less than 10% of the total Lebanese population, ministerial representation was rare, though in recent years it has not been uncommon to include an Armenian Orthodox deputy in the cabinet, i.e. Khatchig Babikyân, *Katâ'ib* deputy from Beirut who was appointed Minster of Health in the cabinet of Rashîd Karâmî of 16 January 1969, and Surân Khân Amerian, the Minister of Tourism (1973-1974). At the provincial level the same balance was maintained, though as a rule, governors of the various *muḥâfaẓât* were not from the same community which predominated in their respective governates (e.g. a Sunni Muslim for Mount Lebanon and an Orthodox Christian for the Biqâ').

In only one area of the Lebanese government, the diplomatic service, did a noticeable confessional imbalance exist. The Crow study showed that since 1955, Christians have held over 60% of Lebanese diplomatic posts, due primarily to the virtual exclusion of Shî 'a Muslims from this area of administration. For while Sunnis held 27% of all foreign diplomatic posts, a higher proportion than their share of the total population warranted, and the Druzes with 7.2% were likewise more than fairly represented, the Shî 'a were given less than 4% of diplomatic appointments.[299] Christian predominance in the diplomatic field is, however, not surprising in view of their higher level of education, their noted facility for foreign languages, as well as the fact that the Lebanese diplomat in probably the majority of posts must maintain close contact with large numbers of emigrant Lebanese resident there, and their descendants, the great majority of whom are Christian.

Despite the generally even distribution of power among Christian and Muslim at the official level in Lebanon, there has never been any doubt that final decisions rest with the Christian establishment. Not surprisingly, therefore, Muslims have continued to press for a new Census which they feel will show them to be a numerical majority deserving of more power than that accorded them by the National Pact of 1943. The more extreme Muslim nationalists such as the leaders of the Pan-Arab *Najâda* party have openly proposed radical changes in the structure of the Lebanese government as it was originally established. Asserting that the National Pact was "an unholy bargain among unprincipled politicians,"[300] *Najâda* chairman 'Adnân Ḥakîm insisted in the years following the 1958 Crisis that the present political system be changed to include a rotating presidency, alternating between a popularly-elected Muslim and Christian, and a Vice-Presidency to be occupied by a member of the opposite confession. Conferring to this end with President Shihâb in 1960, Ḥakîm likewise counseled that Lebanon should evolve toward a closer association with other Arab states and eventually become part of a larger political Arab unity.[301] When *Al-'Amal,* the *Katâ'ib* party daily, challenged his proposals with the charge that "there is no single Arab nation and Arab people or Arab nationalism, but diverse Arab peoples and nations," Ḥakîm replied through his own party journal, *Ṣawt Al-'Urûba* ("The Voice of Araby") on 10 February 1961, predicting that "history will vanquish you [the *Katâ'ib*] and... whether you like it or not, there will be a great, noble Arab Union some day."[302] Active throughout the 1960's, Ḥakîm presented himself to the Chamber of Deputies in 1970 as a Muslim candidate, albeit a notably unsuccessful one, for President, in order to dramatize his complaint against the present system which reserves the office exclusively for a Maronite Christian.

Controversy of this kind, however, was by no means new to Lebanon, and in comparison with some earlier Christian-Muslim embroglios, only a weak echo. Ḥakîm's proposed changes, not illogical in theory, were in fact advocated by no significant group other than his own, until the present crisis brought the continued existence of Lebanese governmental structure into question; for among the Muslim community as a whole the prevailing sentiment was one of quiet moderation. Like all Lebanese the Muslims shared in the post-World War II economic boom that raised Lebanon's standard of living far above that of her neighbors. According to the I.R.F.E.D. Mission Report of 1962, exactly half of the Lebanese population was classified as middle-class or higher, and less than one in ten Lebanese (8.8%) were counted as "wretchedly poor." The per capita income for that year — U.S. $350 per annum — was twice that of any other Middle Eastern country with the exception of Israel and the oil-rich shaykdoms of the Persian Gulf.[303]

Thus while poverty is known to half of the nation's inhabitants, it is of quite a different order from that prevailing elsewhere in the area, as seen by the average "poor" family's income of 2,000 Lebanese Pounds a year, or nearly U.S. $700, with a purchasing power approximately four times that figure.[304] In such a relatively prosperous and outwardly religious society as Lebanon, therefore, it is not surprising that the Communist Party has been traditionally weak. It is, nevertheless, allowed legal status and is, from time to time, active. As in the rest of the Arab East, Christian intellectuals have been leading contributors to the Communist movement, though in Lebanon where it is the Muslims who, if any, are the disaffected element, Sunni, Shî 'a, and even Druze participation has been a feature. Thus while the current secretary-general of the Lebanese party is a Christian (Niqûlâ Shawwî), the editor of the party journal, *Al-Nidâ* (closed indefinitely by the Syrian peace-keeping force in December 1976) is a Muslim, Suhayl Yammût.

In addition to the prosperity at home, moreover, the concurrent difficulties encountered by the late President Nasser in trying to meet the almost impossible economic needs of his nation, and the decline in every sector of the economy of neighboring Syria since 1958, had lessened to a great extent the fervent enthusiasm for Arab Nationalism and union so prevalent among the great majority of Lebanese Muslims, especially Sunnis, a decade earlier. A new generation — considerably more secular in its outlook that its predecessor (a characteristic also true of young Lebanese Christians) — was rising to prominence. Fewer and fewer were those, as Kamal Salibi observed, who could remember the Ottoman days when one could travel from Beirut to Damascus without crossing a frontier and without having to show a Lebanese identity card.[305] The intransigent, uncompromising Pan-Arabism that characterized the Sunnis of the Mandate and early independence years appeared to be yielding to a modest but unmistakable Lebanese patriotism.

Among the Shî 'a and Druzes, loyalty to Lebanon remained even higher than it had been at the outset of independence. Thus there was little base in Lebanon for any activity or movement whose goals would in any way greatly alter the status quo. Most Muslims felt that while inequalities existed in the present structure, any attempts radically to change the system, economically or politically, would affect them as adversely as their Christian countrymen, among whom loyalty to the independence of Lebanon was now virtually universal. One could thus agree with Albert Hourani's assessment of the Lebanese political situation as he saw it in 1958:

> While the existence of Lebanon, and the moral ascendancy of the Christians in Lebanon may seem therefore to be precarious... both, however, are far more stable than they seem. First of all, most citizens of Lebanon now want it to exist as an independent state. If they do not believe in it in principle, they derive advantages from it — prosperity and individual freedom — and there is a general feeling that it can only exist on the basis of some such compromise as the National Pact.[306]

And while acknowledging that most Sunni Muslims at the time of the 1958 Crisis, "except those with a vested interest in the independence of the country, would at least acquiesce in the incorporation of Lebanon in Syria," Hourani affirms that "most of the Druzes would probably oppose it," while the Shî 'a would be loath to relinquish the "advantages as a community it derives from the independence of Lebanon such as it would not have in a mainly Sunni state."[307] The pro-Lebanon sentiment among the Shî 'a has in fact been proven time and time again, most recently during the political crises brought about by Palestinian commando activity in Southern Lebanon. Though the Shî 'a districts were those most affected by Israeli counterattacks on Lebanese soil, and despite criticism of the Lebanese Army for its failure to protect the southern districts under attack, the president of the Lebanese Shî 'a community, Imâm Mûsâ Al-Ṣadr, was nevertheless speaking for his people when in July of 1969 he reaffirmed his faith in an independent Lebanon:

Les Chiites sont attachés a leur patrie, le Liban, de toutes leurs possibilités. Ils considèrent que l'indépendence du Liban, sa souveraineté et la sécurité de son territoire les concernent en propre et que sans ces trois critères susmentionnés il n'y a point de dignité pour eux. [308]

This is not to say that the Shî 'a have failed to complain about the ways in which they have been frequently by-passed in the political life of the country. In February of 1974, for example, Imâm Ṣadr spoke out against the general failure of the government to devote enough attention to South Lebanon in general and the Shî 'a in particular, calling for more high-ranking non-Christians in the Civil Service. Soon after, some significant appointments of both Sunni and Shî 'a administrators were made, in spite of bitter opposition on the part of rightist Christian leaders Camille Chamoun and Pierre Jumayyil.

The crucial factor, however, even more significant than the political advantages enjoyed by the Shî 'a and Druzes in Lebanon which they would forfeit under the aegis of Arab unity, remained that of economic prosperity. For this reason there was considerable fear in Lebanon and abroad that the economic and financial decline initiated by the failure of Intra Bank in Ocotber of 1966, and greatly exacerbated by the sudden collapse of the tourist trade after the June War of 1967, would lead to a political crisis that could destroy the fragile communal alliance of 1943. Not without justification, therefore, the upsurge of popular Muslim support for the Palestinian commando movement in 1968-1969 seemed at the time to be the very issue which could bring traditional Lebanon to the point of collapse.

By the fall of 1968 the Muslim and Christian power blocs had reached an impasse over the question of Palestinian commando activity in South Lebanon, resulting in the resignation of the cabinet on 9 October, followed ten days later by the threatened resignation of President Helou himself. Faced with the prospect of absolute chaos, the conservative forces from both sides rallied behind the president who, 18 hours after his announced resignation, rescinded, and on 21 October appointed an emergency cabinet consisting of only four ministers: Dr. 'Abd

Allah Al-Yâfî, Prime Minister for the ninth time since 1958, the late Ḥusayn 'Uwayni, Foreign Minister, Pierre Jumayyil (Gemayel), leader of the *Katâ 'ib* party, as Minister of Interior, and Raymond Idda, son of the early Lebanese nationalist Emille Idda and leader of the right-wing National Bloc Party, as Minister of Planning. Al-Yâfî and 'Uwaynî were Sunni Muslims (though educated in French Catholic schools), Jumayyil and Idda Maronites, a clear illustration of the basic political reality in Lebanon — that stability ultimately rests on cooperation between these two major religious groups, a fact which is usually clouded by communal representation at the cabinet level for all six principal Lebanese sects, but which in time of crisis is rendered absolutely unmistakable.

The basic issue of the moment, however, remained the commando activity inside Lebanese territory which threatened peace at home and elicited counter-attacks from Israel, the most celebrated being that of the raid on Beirut Airport on 28 December 1968 which served to bring about the downfall of this short-lived government *à quatre*. A more representative cabinet of 16 ministers was formed by veteran Prime Minister Rashîd Karâmî on 16 January 1969. This government, too, floundered, and until stability was restored a few weeks later, the insecurity which had been building up ever since the Intra crisis two years earlier was such as to unleash a capital exodus of over $125,000,000 from Lebanon in the first two weeks of the new year.

Faced with the prospect of Israel taking advantage of the commando raids from inside Lebanese territory to justify the annexation of Lebanon south of the Litani River (referred to by the Israelis as "Northern Galilee"), the largely Christian-led armed forces of Lebanon began to crack down on Palestinian activity, despite local, particularly Muslim, resistance. A crisis point was reached in March 1970, when open warfare broke out between Arab guerillas and Christian mountaineers at the village of Kaḥḥâla (on the Beirut-Damascus highway below 'Alayh) and between the Lebanese Army and another detachment of guerillas at a Palestinian refugee camp near Beirut Airport. Almost simultaneous with these events was the kidnapping of

Bashîr Jumayyil, son of *Katâ'ib* party chairman and Minister of Transport and Public Works, Pierre Jumayyil. The response was immediate. Hundreds of the *Katâ'ib* militia rushed from their headquarters and laid siege to the Palestinian refugee camps, strongholds of guerilla units, engaging them in a series of bloody gun battles until the government was able to secure a promise from the commandos that Bashîr would be released. Not long afterwards, Danny Sham'ûn, son of former president Camille Chamoun, was likewise kidnapped, to be released only after being held hostage at the Intercontinental Hotel in Amman, then virtually in the hands of *Al-Fatiḥ,* and for an undisclosed settlement with his wealthy and influential father.

Reaction in Lebanon to commando activity directed against Arabs instead of Israelis was focused on the forthcoming presidential elections. Former President Fu'âd Shihâb, a long-time favorite, suddenly found his moderate position less attractive than before. Faced with strong opposition from the right, Shihâb dramatically withdrew in favor of his own hand-picked candidate Ilyâs Sarkîs, governor of the Central Bank of Lebanon. An initial favorite, Sarkîs was in the end victim of the strong Christian opposition to the guerilla movement, and on 17 August 1970, the 99-member Lebanese parliament elected Minister of the economy, Sulaymân Faranjîya, as successor to Charles Helou by a single-vote majority (50-49). A known ally of former President Chamoun and Phalangist leader Jumayyil, Faranjîya had publicly declared his opposition to Palestinian commando activity from Lebanese territory, and, as a native of the Maronite district of Zaghartâ, famous for its vendettas and frequent resorts to arms in settling disputes, was not to be taken in the same pacific vein as his predecessor.

As in all other areas of the Lebanese power structure, the small but vital military establishment has traditionally reflected the accepted confessional proportions of the total population, particularly among enlisted men and lower-ranking officers. In the upper echelons, however, Christians have always exercised firm control.

The commanding general of the Lebanese Army since independence has been, until very recently, like the president, a Maronite. And like the president he is a prime political target. The incumbent throughout the 1960's, Emile Georges Bustânî, was cashiered in 1969 for alleged misconduct in the French missile scandal of that year; of his successors, Jean Nujaym died July 26, 1971 in a helicopter crash only two years after his appointment, and Major General Iskandar Al-Ghânim was dismissed September 10, 1975 in favor of the Brig. Gen. Ḥannâ Sa'îd, a moderate who was deemed acceptable to leftist factions. Christian officers, largely Maronite, also serve as commander of the air force, commander of the gendarmerie, and the deputy chief of staff. The only high-ranking non-Christian throughout the period since the 1958 crisis has been a Druze, Col. Yûsuf Shumayt, army chief of staff since 1959, recently retired as a general. His position as the ranking non-Christian officer was taken by another Druze, Sa'îd Naṣrallah, who on February 19, 1975 was promoted to brigadier general ('Amîd Awwal), a position in the chain of command second only to General Ḥannâ Sa'id himself.[309] Sunni and Shi'a Muslim officers served as commanders of various infantry batallions, but even at this level they were out numbered by Christians. The facts that Maronites have jealously garnered both the positions of defense minister and commanding general to themselves and that Christians in general have excluded Muslims from high-ranking positions in the military have been in large part responsible for the current outbreak of Muslim-Christian hostilities. With the escalation of the civil war in 1976, virtually all Muslims dropped out of the army, either to support their own paramilitary groups or simply to sit out the conflict. On his inauguration as president, Ilyâs Sarkîs appointed Col. Aḥmad Al-Hajj, a Sunni Muslim, as commander of the armed forces, and a Greek Orthodox Shihabist, Fu'âd Buṭrus, as minister of defense. Though seemingly a radical departure from past appointments, these are for the moment meaningless since the Syrian Army, which backs the Maronite establishment, is in full control.

It is impossible to pinpoint the exact beginning of the recently-ended disorder in Lebanon, as it had in fact been building up since the aftermath of the 1967 Arab war with Israel. Like the 1958 crisis, however, the actual fighting can be traced back to the assassination of a leftist political figure. In 1958 it was a Christian, Najîb Al-Matnî, editor of the left-wing daily *Al-Tilighraf;* in 1975 it was the killing of former deputy Ma'rûf Sa'd of Sidon, a Sunni Muslim, in early March as he attempted to calm demonstrators there (who were protesting a government decision on fishing rights) in their confrontation with the predominantly Christian army called in to restore order. The fighting quickly spread to Beirut and Tripoli setting the stage for the April incident which touched off the country-wide strife. The gunning down of a busload of Palestinian Muslims by Maronite *Katâ'ib* (Phalangist) militiamen at 'Ayn Al-Rumâna, a Christian suburb southeast of Beirut, on April 13th, brought the whole simmering Lebanese and Palestinian, Christian and Muslim issues to a head.

Many Christians believed that the *Katâ'ib* had over-reacted to a Palestinian confrontation outside the church where their leader, Pierre Jumayyil, was attending Sunday morning mass; but they were likewise fearful of allowing the Palestinians to take full advantage of the situation and thus increase their already formidable strength in and around the capital. The ensuing bloodshed brought down the government of Prime Minister Rashîd Al-Sûlḥ on May 15th, but not before the latter had placed full responsibility for the crisis squarely on the *Katâ'ib* party. In his resignation address before a nearly full parliament (*Katâ'ib* deputies were absent), Al-Sûlḥ called for an equal role for Muslim officers in the army and citizenship for long-time Muslim residents of Lebanon, i.e. Palestinians.

Maronite president, Sulaymân Al-Faranjîya, reacted by attempting to impose military rule with the appointment of an unknown Sunni Muslim retired army officer, Nûr Al-Dîn Al-Rifâ'î, as prime minister and giving all but one ministerial post to other Christian and Muslim officers in accordance with the traditional sectarian formula, ordained by the 1943 National Pact. The Muslim population and leadership — Lebanese and Palestinian — refused to acquiesce in this ploy, and within a matter of hours Faranjîya was forced to accept the resignation of his military cabinet and to call upon his personal enemy and veteran prime minister, Rashîd Karâmî, to form a new government on May 28th. After weeks of negotiations with both Christian and Muslim factions, the Palestinian and other leftist leadership, Karâmî put together the so-called National Salvation cabinet at the end of June, composed of five veteran politicians (six including Karâmî) representing the major sectarian groupings (excluding the Armenians); Karâmî for the Sunnis, former president Camille Chamoun for the Maronites, journalist Ghassân Tuwaynî and veteran minister Philippe Taqlâ representing the Greek Orthodox and Melkites, and 'Adil 'Usayrân and *Amîr* Majîd Arslân, the Shî'a and Druze respectively. Throughout July and much of August the situation remained relatively quiet as the cabinet worked to resolve the crisis in traditional fashion; their failure resulted in a return of civil disorder on a wide scale at the end of August which continued until the present, leaving Beirut a ruined, depopulated shell, and the government and army powerless to intervene, despite mediation attempts on the part of Syria, France, the Vatican, and finally all the Arab states in concert.

The struggle has been punctuated by provocative acts on both sides, from bombings of churches to public burnings of the Qur'ân,[310] thousands of sectarian-motivated killings, as well as bloody clashes within the larger religious groups themselves (e.g. Maronite *Katâ'ib* against Orthodox P.P.S. forces in Al-Kûra, and rival Muslim factions — Karâmî vs. Muqaddam in Tripoli at the outset, and, as Syrian forces moved in, Chamounist paramilitary forces vs. the *Katâ'ib* and PLO against Syrian-backed *Sâ'iqa* commandos in bitter and bloody exchanges).

The fighting which raged unchecked throughout most of 1976 witnessed excesses on both sides, notably the Muslim massacre of thousands of Maronite Christians at Dâmûr and Al-Jiyya along the coast of Al-Shûf in late January, and the brutal Christian seizure of Tall Al-Za'tar refugee camp in mid-August which resulted in an equal number of Muslim dead and dispossessed. The election of a new president in May to succeed outgoing incumbent Sulaymân Faranjîya brought to the forefront the latter's previous election rival, the Shihâbist banker Ilyâs Sarkîs, but not before the small moderate Maronite faction headed by unsuccessful candidate Raymond Idda was virtually ostracized from the already weakened parent community. Neither Sarkîs' election, which had been carried out against the wishes of the opposition forces in Parliament led by Kamâl Junbalâṭ as well as the Palestinian leadership, nor his installation in September at Shatûra in the Biqâ' Valley under Syrian military protection, did anything to halt the fighting, and it has taken wholesale Syrian intervention and occupation of the entire country to impose an effective cease-fire so as to enable the new president to form his first cabinet, announced on December 9, 1976, under the premiership of Sunni Muslim, Salîm Al-Ḥaṣṣ.

To date no major change in the governmental structure has taken place other than a general agreement on all sides that the composition of a new parliament should be equally divided among Christians and Muslims instead of being allocated to the various sects according to the previous 6:5 ratio that favored the Christians, and that confessional distribution of civil service jobs be abolished.[311] On the other hand, parliament has not sat since the Syrian occupation, and on December 24, a majority of the members, individually approached, approved a measure submitted to them by premier Al-Ḥaṣṣ at the obvious request of presidents Sarkîs and Ḥâfiẓ Al-Asad of Syria, allowing the president and his cabinet to rule by decree for six months under the state of emergency provision set forth in a 1953 law. In effect, therefore, nothing has changed on the surface. Lebanon is ruled by a Maronite president and a Sunni Muslim prime minister. The newly-appointed eight-man cabinet is a careful composite of the traditional sects in the same ratio as before (two Maronites, two Sunnis, one each Greek Orthodox, Greek Catholic, Druze and Shî'a). The difference is that Syria is in firm control and unwilling to tolerate any opposition (as is seen in the closure of the leading independent daily, *Al-Nahâr*, on december 19 along with other journals of the center and left opposed to Syrian occupation and continued Maronite hegemony) until a new modus vivendi is established, possibly in the context of some far-reaching Middle East settlement.

The exodus of Lebanese, particularly Christians (chiefly Orthodox, Melkites and Armenians) has ebbed, and many have already returned with their families. Life in Beirut is rapidly being restored to some semblance of normalcy. Yet it appears unlikely that any kind of permanent stability can be established until the outstanding issues, such as the future of Palestinian presence on Lebanese soil — both military and civilian, the general secularization of the state organization, and some official recognition of the major changes in confessional population distribution that most sources believe to have taken place, are in some way resolved. This must surely be the primary task confronting both the Sarkîs government and its Syrian protectors. Thus for the time being at least, the Christian (and especially the Maronite) position is secure. World public opinion seemed startled when predominantly Muslim Syria intervened on behalf of the beleaguered Christian side in the recent struggle, but it had become obvious to President Al-Asad and his ruling *Ba'th* party that a conservative Christian government in Lebanon was more in the interests of Syria than a radical, Palestinian-dominated Muslim state, which could easily have dragged Syria into an unwanted war with Israel. Also, it should not be forgotten that President Al-Asad, like his top army command, is a member of the Alawite community which traditionally has distrusted the Sunni Muslim establishment of Syria and maintained friendly relations with Maronites and other Christians in the district of Al-Lâdhiqîya where they live side by side.

There are those Christians who maintain that the recent conflict was not religious at all, but political in its origins, pointing to, among other things, the strong Christian presence in the Palestinian command, and the number of non-Maronite Christians, both Lebanese and Palestinians, who openly sided with the Left. Many Christian groups, in fact, did not actively participate in the fighting, notably the Orthodox, Melkites, and Armenians, though there is little doubt which side the great majority of all Christians in Lebanon — the non-Palestinians at least — supported. Likewise the majority of Lebanese Muslims including the Druze (with the prominent exception of their outspoken leader, Kamâl Junbalâṭ) refrained from more than sporadic participation throughout much of the war, leaving the bulk of the fighting to be suffered by the Palestinians who have borne the greater part of the war's awesome casualties. The Maronites by their dogged persistence in resisting political change which would have driven them from power have temporarily at least retained their position of strength, however precariously.

The problem still lies in the fact that the Maronites no longer occupy the position which enabled them with French assistance to dictate the National Pact of 1943, but they are unwilling to yield any of their prerogatives either to the Muslims or to other Christian groups. For it is not only the Sunni Muslims who want to elect a president. The Orthodox as well, not to mention the smaller Christian sects, would like the opportunity of full upward mobility within the government and the military. The late Kamâl Junbalâṭ did not disguise his own presidential ambitions in the past, and the Shî'a Muslims, who claim to be the largest of the sectarian groupings, are not without their own designs to national leadership.

On June 22, 1975, the Maronite League issued a communiqué on behalf of Patriarch Khuraysh which stated that no change in the National Pact would be tolerated, that all aliens must be controlled, and that Lebanese sovereignty be imposed.[312]

For the majority of Lebanese, however the 1943 National Pact is a relic of the past. The most extreme position is that of the Sunni Muslims, for whom the 1943 agreement no longer exists. "What National Pact?" was the retort of Lebanese mufti, Shaykh Ḥassân Khâlid when queried about the covenant's role in the current situation.[313] For all other groups, the National Pact is simply outdated and must be revised to include greater participation from non-Maronite Lebanese. The spokesman for the Shî'a Muslims, Imâm Mûsâ Al-Ṣadr, has repeatedly expressed his preference for maintaining the tradition of a Christian president, but not necessarily a Maronite.[314] The Greek Orthodox have likewise called for a secularization of the government, while Kamâl Junbalâṭ for the Druzes demanded the abolition of sectarianism in all state posts and in the makeup of the government. Like Ṣadr, however, he supported the idea of a Christian president, at least in public. "We hope that the presidency will remain in the hands of the Christians," he was quoted as saying in June 1975 (and here he certainly speaks for the majority of Lebanese Durûz who distrust both Sunni and Shi'a leadership), "but not in the hands of one Christian sect to the exclusion of another."[315] Hand in hand with this basic problem of religious sectarianism is that of social welfare and a more equitable distribution of national wealth. But the latter cannot be attained until the former is solved. The Maronites led by the *Katâ'ib* and the even more intransigent Chamounists, have until now been unwilling to accept anything less than the 1943 Pact, unless it be partition, something which no one else in Lebanon wants.

Continued Maronite hegemony is unrealistic, however, particularly in that Syria appears adamantly opposed to any partition scheme. The Maronites are also discredited for having openly solicited Israeli support, not only in the south along the frontier which is dotted with Maronite villages, but in their acquisition of military supplies with which to fight the Palestinian forces in the north. What appears inevitable, therefore, is some major revision of the 1943 National Pact, with the Maronites as the long-run losers, and the various other Christian groups and the larger Lebanese Muslim communities who sat out much of the war as those who stand to gain the most. A Lebanon without a strongly Maronite-dominated government is not likely to lose its Christian character regardless of what political changes are made. Christians of all communities are determined to play a continuing strategic role in the political and economic life of the country. The reorganization under emergency rule in the first half of 1977 should help to clarify the course of political reform in Lebanon for the next several years, as well as the manner in which the relative position of the various religious communities will be affected.

Kuwait. Though this wealthy shaykhdom's Christian citizenry numbers less than 200 souls, they are in no way precluded from positions of importance in the government. The present ambassador to France (and former ambassador to Moscow), Sa'îd Shammâs, and the commander of the internal security forces, Yûsuf Shuhaybar, are examples of the tolerance which the Amîr and his government extends to all Kuwaiti nationals regardless of their religion.

Christian Arabs and the Palestine Conflict

The unsuccessful outcome of the two-year struggle between Arab and Zionist in Palestine (1948-1949) had great social and political repercussions throughout the Arab East, not least among the indigenous Christians who, as a non-Muslim Arab community, were targets of increased hostility engendered by ardent Muslim nationalists who began to imply that the Christians had somehow aided the Western "imperialist" powers in establishing the state of Israel, and had contributed to the defeat of the Arab armies. With very few exceptions these charges were without basis. During the Palestine Mandate local Christians had worked zealously with Muslims in combatting the expansion of Zionism. Both Catholic and Orthodox participated in many of the anti-Zionist, Arab nationalist organizations, among them Alfred Rûkk (Roch), a Latin Catholic lawyer from Jerusalem of mixed Arab and European ancestry, appointed first vice president of Grand Mufti Al-Husayni's Palestine Arab Party *(Ḥizb Al-'Arabî)* in 1935; and Orthodox laymen Khalîl Sakâkînî — first secretary of the executive committee of the Arab Congress of Palestine during the 1920's; Ya'qûb Faraj — one of the nine members of the Arab higher executive committee set up in 1936 under the Mufti's chairmanship; George Anṭûnyûs (Antonius) — prominent nationalist, scholar, and government administrator who resigned his post with the Mandate in protest over British pro-Zionist policies; and 'Isâ Al-'Isâ — editor of the Jaffa newspaper, *Filasṭîn* ("Palestine"), and member of the Al-Nashâshibî faction of the Palestinian nationalist movement, the National Defense Party (*Ḥizb Al-Difâ '*).[316] Earlier, in 1928, an attempt to unite the two Arab Nationalist factions in Palestine — the parties of Al-Nashashîbî and Al-Ḥusayni — at an Arab Congress in Jerusalem, had resulted in the election of a 48-member executive which included 12 Christians — or one out of every four —[317] whose purpose was to speak for the entire Arab community on the Jewish immigration question. Other nationalist parties during this period also included Christians in their leadership, chief among them the National Bloc Party *(Ḥizb Al-Kutla Al-Watanîya)* which, under the guidance of its secretary-general, Fu'âd Busṭânî, now a Beirut lawyer, sought to find a common ground between the two major nationalist factions. Nor was nationalist activity limited to Christian laymen alone; Hourani cites as an example the two Arab clergymen who gave evidence against Zionist partition proposals before the Royal Commission deliberating the Palestine problem in 1937.[318]

Despite the fact that an estimated 55,000 Christian refugees fled that part of Palestine which fell to the Zionists during the 1948-1949 conflict and, during the immediate aftermath, shared all the misery and suffering endured by Muslim Palestinian refugees, they represented only about 60% of the Christians living in what was to become Israel after the Armistice, the remaining 40% having opted to remain behind, as compared with only 20% of the Muslims.[319] There were many reasons for this imbalance, the most prominent, according to one Haifa-born refugee clergyman, being the nature of the military activity in Galilee during the last weeks of the war and the sudden collapse of Arab resistance at Nazareth which trapped the great majority of the Galilean Highland Arabs — nearly half of them Christian — behind Israeli lines with no chance of escape.[320] In those areas from which they had time to flee (e.g. Haifa, Jaffa, and Ramla), Christians showed no more desire to remain under Jewish sovereignty than their Muslim countrymen. Undoubtedly there were those who stayed behind because of considerations of property and family, or because — like the Druzes — they felt that as a minority they would fare better than the Muslims who in the Jewish mind were identified with the violently anti-Zionist activities of Grand Mufti Al-Ḥusayni. It is, moreover, an open secret that the more extreme Lebanese Christian nationalists gained satisfaction from the humiliating defeat of the overwhelmingly Muslim Arab armies, while the Maronite patriarch, Anṭûn 'Arîḍa, is said to have welcomed the addition of another non-Muslim state in the Middle East. Significantly, nearly the entire Maronite community included in the new state of Israel chose to remain.

In the years following the Armistice, Christians inside Israel and those refugees outside gradually began to fare better than their Muslim counterparts. The reasons for this disparity were many, among them a willingness to adjust and to meet the necessary changes dictated by circumstances, a higher level of education and training which fitted them for specialized employment, and the assistance of Western church-affiliated organizations which set up refugee resettlement programs, largely for Christian expatriates. Many Christian Palestinians, moreover, escaped the oblivion of refugee status through contacts in Lebanon where many of them eventually resettled. This was especially true of the Melkite refugees, 10,000 of whom had established themselves in an around Beirut by 1951, in contrast to Jordan where only 2,500 of them chose to resettle, and Syria and Egypt both of which absorbed only a few hundred each. Owing to their lack of family ties in Lebanon and their lower economic level which prevented them from being able to buy a Lebanese or other Arab passport, very few Muslim refugees, as has already been mentioned, were able to pursue those channels open to Christian Palestinians, thus giving rise to subsequent Muslim charges of preferential treatment of Christians by the Bis͟hâra Al-Khûrî government.

All the major Christian communities, indigenous as well as foreign, set up private relief agencies for refugees, Christian and Muslim, unable to find immediate employment and resettlement; Christians, however, tended to overcome all the social and economic handicaps inherent in their refugee status much more quickly than did Muslim Palestinians. The U.N.R.W.A. statistics for Syria in 1951, for instance, showed that nearly one-third (31%) of the Christian Palestinian refugees resident there were no longer dependent upon some form of United Nations' aid, as opposed to only 6% of the Muslim refugee population.[321] One of the most active and influential religious organizations aiding Palestinian refugees was the Roman Catholic

Pontifical Mission for Palestine *(Al-Bî'tha Al-Babâwîya lî'l-Filastîn)*, established in 1949 under American Jesuit auspices, and which, during the ten years following the partition, administered some $34,000,000 in aid to refugees through 270 social welfare centers distributing food, clothing, and medicine; during the same period nearly 33,000 refugee children received free education at Mission schools.[322]

It should be pointed out that such relief organizations shared their facilities as much as possible with Muslims once the needs of those from their own religious community had been adequately met,[323] but there was, nevertheless, an undercurrent of resentment among Muslims at the rapid recovery made by Christian Palestinians, manifested in hostile rumors and charges that this economic rebound must somehow have its roots in a previous cooperation with Zionism and the Western powers that supported Israel. The Rt. Rev. Najîb Cubain, reflecting on what he and many other Arab prelates and laymen had experienced, admitted that "Christians have suffered because of Israel;"[324] and there can be no doubt that this is indeed so.

Such a situation is, however, ironic in view of the fact that the Christian refugees from Palestine have shown themselves to be often even more bitter, if this is possible, than their Muslim counterparts. The intensity with which the question is viewed by Christians may be seen in the fact that the Arab Anglicans — almost exclusively Palestinian and probably the best educated and most highly Westernized Arab community — have exorcised most references to Israel in their translation of the Book of Common Prayer. Among Arab political leaders, Christians have often been the most uncompromising in terms of any agreement with Israel. Fâris Al-Khûrî, Christian Prime Minister of Syria in 1954, criticized those Arab leaders who intimated that peace with Israel might be achieved if the original United Nations' resolutions were adhered to and refugees allowed to return. In a broadcast over Radio Damascus on 3 November 1954, monitored in Israel, Al-Khûrî stated:

> Certain Arab leaders say that there can be no peace with Israel before the implementation of the U.N. resolutions of 1947.... They link peace with Israel with these terms. I denounce such a statement and say that there is no connection between peace with Israel and the return of the refugees and the U.N. resolution.... Whether they return the refugees or not, peace must not be concluded with Israel in any form. I do not believe that the Arabs would approve such a peace so long as the Jews remain settled in that spot — the heart of the Arab states — threatening all those around them, and spreading corruption and evil.... How could we find it possible to make peace with them while they remain there? This was the first round and, unfortunately, it was not successful. The Arabs — we included — should prepare for a second round and do their utmost.... [325]

In view of the Arab passion for poetic expression and inflammatory rhetoric, there is a tendency to dismiss statements such as the above as meaningless, or at best intended primarily for Muslim ears in an effort to over-compensate for the basic Christian insecurity. But such a view would in this case be an unfair generalization and an underestimation of the genuineness of Palestinian Christian sentiment. There can be no doubt that all Palestinians, and most Christian Arabs elsewhere, have always deplored the idea and existence of Israel, despite which they have still had to bear the additional cross of suspicion on the part of their Muslim countrymen as well as that of the loss of their homeland.

Christian commitment to the liberation of Palestine has very recently manifested itself in the post-1967 commando activity. In the largest of the new guerilla organizations, *Al-Fatiḥ* (Al-Fatah), a number of the leaders and commandos themselves are Christians, chiefly Orthodox, notable among them the late Chief of Information, Kamâl Nâṣir, a native of Bi'r Zayt. A graduate of the American University of Beirut and internationally respected, Nâṣir was long regarded as the leading spokesman for the Palestinian cause, and has achieved certain immortality in its hagiology by his martyrdom in April of 1973 at the hands of Israeli assassins. On 21 November 1974 the Israelis expelled five prominent West Bank Arab residents of Râm Allah for alleged membership in the P.L.O., and imposed rigid economic restrictions on this predominantly Christian town. Of the five, three were Christian, among them Dr. Ḥannâ Nâṣir, president of Bi'r Zayt College (Arab Anglican secondary), and cousin of the late Kamâl Nâṣir (see above). Bâṣil 'Aql, the PLO representative, with whom three U.S. Senators met in Cairo in November 1976 to discuss possible solutions of the Middle East question acceptable to Palestinians, is a Christian. Leonard Wolf, in his recent narrative *The Passion of Israel* (Boston, 1970), records a revealing interview with a Christian Palestinian guerilla awaiting trial for murder, William Nassar, while it was another young Christian Palestinian, Sirḥân Bishâra Sirḥân from Al-Ṭayyiba, Jordan, who shocked the world with his assassination of Robert F. Kennedy in June 1968, allegedly in reaction to the latter's pro-Israeli statements made a few days earlier during his campaign for president.

It is, however, the most radical of the Palestine Nationalist groups, the Popular Front for the Liberation of Palestine, in which Christian presence is strongest. Internationally known for its spectacular highjacking successes in 1968, 1969, and 1970, the P.F.L.P.'s leader, Dr. George Habash, a native of Ramla, and second in command, Dr. Wadî ' Ḥaddâd, are both Orthodox Christians. Sufficient numbers of actual commandos were Greek Orthodox in 1970 as to warrant a chaplain, Ḥannâ Sakkab.[326] On the extreme left of the Palestinian nationalist movement is the Popular Democratic Front for the Liberation of Palestine (PDFLP) led by former Habash disciple turned Maoist, Nâyif Ḥawâṭima, of Christian birth like his erstwhile mentor (whom he now belittles as a fascist demagogue). Christians recently acquired their own counterparts to the daring Muslim lady commando, Layla Al-Khâlid, with the highjacking of a Sabena Boeing-707 on May 8, 1972, by Therèse Halasa and Rîmâ 'Isâ Ṭannûs, both from well-established Palestinian Christian families. The following summer (July, 1973) a P.F.L.P. highjack of a Japan Airlines 747 ended in failure after a three-day tour of

Arab airports primarily because the group leader, a Christian Iraqi woman identified as Katherine George Thomas, was killed when a grenade concealed on her person exploded at the very outset of the takeover. Acknowledged as Layla Khâlid's successor for P.F.L.P. operations in Europe, Miss Thomas had been privately briefed for the operation by Dr. Ḥaddâd, and had not passed these instructions on to any of her associates. Such active participation in the various commando groups bears witness to the ubiquitous presence of Christians in every area of Arab political life, and give lie to the all-too-frequent view of Arab Christians as passive partners in the Arab political power structure, or as reactionary obstructors of the natural political and economic evolution in the Arab East.

The participation of Greek Orthodox clergy in the Arab nationalist movement, and more recently in the Palestine Liberation effort, has been consistent with the long-standing association of lay members of the community in such political activity. Clergy from other communities have more recently joined the Orthodox in their identification with the Palestine cause, notably the Rev. Ilyâs Al-Khûrî, an Israeli Anglican priest who was arrested by the authorities in 1969 for commando-related activities, and expelled to Jordan where he was asked to join the Executive Committee of the Palestine Liberation Organization (P.L.O.) in which capacity he now serves; and likewise the Very Rev. Hilarion Capucci (Kapudji), the Aleppo-born Melkite Archbishop of Jerusalem who was arrested in August of 1974 by the Israeli security forces for having illegally transported a substantial amount of weaponry through the Ra's Al-Nâqûra checkpoint destined for Palestinian commandos active on the Israeli-occupied West Bank, thus bringing the Vatican, which does not recognize Israel, into direct confrontation with the Zionist state, to the obvious discomfort of both. But while officials in Rome have expressed regret over the situation, the Melkite episcopal synod in Beirut roundly condemned the arrest in an obvious expression of Arab Catholic solidarity with the Palestine cause. More recently the Vatican has shown visible distress over Israel's failure to respond to discreet diplomatic pressures aimed at implementing Pope Paul's original plea for clemency. In early November 1975 the Pope sent the imprisoned archibishop what was described as a "warm, personal letter" which conferred upon him "a very special apostolic benediction"[327] A month later the Pope abandoned indirect methods and appealed openly to the Israelis for recognition of the rights and legitimate aspirations of the Palestinian people, "which like them [the Jews] has suffered long."[328] Christians dedicated to the Palestine cause could hardly have asked for a stronger commitment from the Christian world's most powerful and influential authority.

V Evaluation and Future Assessment

In the years since World War II a relaxation of the once rigid communal distinctions in the Arab East has unmistakably occurred, not only among the previously segregated and frequently hostile individual Christian sects, but in regard to Muslims as well. The spread of education and increased contact with the West have undoubtedly been major factors in the change, but of equal significance in recent years has been the immediate impact of political and religious leaders, Christian and Muslim, who in the past two decades have begun, in the words of Lebanese Muslim author and statesman, Ḥasan Sa'b, "to stress the common,"[329] not only in polemic — Abraham as opposed to Christ and Muḥammad — but in society and culture as well — the recognition of the Arabic language[330] and other secular values and cultural features shared by both Christian and Muslim as uniting force. The oecumenical trend within the Christian Churches, Orthodox and Catholic alike, in the past fifteen years has had a great effect in broadening the Christian outlook, while the recent Vatican attempts to reach an agreement and rapprochement with Islam has forced Eastern Christians, particularly Catholics, to regard their Muslim neighbors in a less hostile light.

There has been a very deep and significant revaluation by clergy and laity as to the nature and present role of the Christian Arab in a predominantly Arab Muslim society. Twenty years ago, Dr. Fâ'iz Al-Ṣâ'igh (Fayez Sayegh), priest's son, Palestinian refugee, and recently special advisor on foreign affairs to the government of Kuwait, lamented the "hopelessly negative and essentially un-Christian defensive... attitude which... characterizes their [Arab Christians'] position — a sad mixture of feelings of superiority and fear."[331] Only a decade later, a Melkite bishop, Neophytos Edelby, was striking at the very heart of this traditional Christian outlook in a proposal to his fellow Eastern Christians that they abandon what he termed "une psychose de minoritaires," and choose rather a vocation which promises "total immersion in the life of each of our individual countries... that you place yourself at the service of your country and work for its advancement." Observing how in the past Christians have been generous to a fault in providing for the educational and charitable institutions of their own communities, Bishop Edelby challenged all Arabs to involve themselves financially and intellectually in the economic and social expansion of their nation, without consideration of religion.

> Confidence in the nation, total immersion in its destiny, fidelity and generosity in its service, frank and complete collaboration with our non-Christian citizens, adherence to an exemplary Christian life; this is the witness which we must render to Christ in the world of Islam; this is our first and most important mission. [332]

"The Christian Arabs," wrote Joseph Hajjâr a few years ago, "have the opportunity of rediscovering, under the aegis of independence, the privilege of acting as unequalled intermediaries between the ascendant Muslim East and the nominally Christian West, retreating from its traditional position maintained by overt force"[333] for nearly a century in the Arab World. The question remained, however, whether or not the Muslim majority in the seventh decade of the 20th century was ready to accept the "total immersion" into the life of the Arab states by Arab Christians, and their self-appointed role as "unequalled mediators" in helping their particular countries confront the problems of the technological, ideological, and social revolutions affecting every part of the world.

Contrary to what would have been the response even twenty years ago, there are strong indications that among Muslims — the rapidly-growing intellectual elite in particular— is to be found a deepening awareness of the contribution which Arab Christians were willing to make, and were uniquely capable of making in every area of national life in the Arab states where they live in significant numbers. The new outlook among Christians which has evolved particularly since the Lebanese Crisis of 1958 has been generally received by Muslims as a grudging repudiation of much of the old minority complex, and particularly the inherent factors of isolation and dependence on the West which comprised it. The strong position assumed by Maronite Patriarch Méouchy throughout the conflict in favor of closer Lebanese identification with the Arab East was regarded by the Muslim establishment as indicative of a tangible change in the political outlook of Christian Arab leadership. The fact that Méouchy's commitment contributed in large part to the collapse of the Chamoun regime's attempts to perpetuate itself, this particular administration having represented for Muslims all that they had come to distrust in the traditional Christian outlook, was of significance in that it demonstrated the strength which this new Christian leadership was able to mobilize in support of its ideas.

Chamoun was accompanied in his fall by many of the philosophical reinforcements of the old establishment — the "Phoenicianism" of Emille Idda and the "Mediterranean Culture" of Charles Mâlik. Likewise on the decline were the purely secular nationalist schemes of the *Ba'th* and the Partie Populaire Syrienne. By 1966, Michel 'Aflaq, himself outside the mainstream of the party he had co-founded, was "at a semantical impasse... He recognized his form of Arab Nationalism as having failed, but refused to acknowledge it since it means the death of his party."[334] The earlier systems, though committed in theory to the Arab and his culture, had consciously ignored the religious heritage of both Islam and Christianity — an omission which has proven itself unacceptable to Arabs of either faith.[335]

To the Muslim, Islam continues to figure as an integral part of his Arab character, and to the nationalist as a built-in factor to be exploited in the cause of Arab unity. The Christian Arab, in recent years increasingly aware of his unique heritage of Christianity in its earliest Apostolic form, has resisted the intellectual forces operating either to deny his faith a proper role in the modern world or to neutralize its Eastern character through the adoption of Roman Catholic and Protestant traditions. In identifying with Eastern forms of his faith, the Arab Christian has affirmed his intention to remain in the Arab World and to become a more integral part of its every level of national life. The sermons of Eastern Catholic prelates urging their brethren to abandon their minority psychosis and commit themselves totally to their national community, the efforts of Patriarch Sâ'îgh and others to strengthen the role of the Uniate Christians in the World Catholic community, to purge Eastern Christendom of Latin forms and institutions, and to initiate oecumenical confrontation among Eastern Christians independent of Roman direction; the convocation of multi-national synods such as the Pan-Orthodox conferences at Rhodes and the conferences of the Non-Chalcedonian Orthodox Churches at Addis Ababa and Cairo in 1965 and 1966; the revival of dying artistic and literary traditions unique to individual communities (e.g. Syriac calligraphy among the Chaldaeans, Byzantine hymnody and iconography among the Melkites, decorative religious tapestry weaving in the ancient Coptic style among Egyptian villagers;[336] the resurgence of the missionary spirit, particularly among the Coptic and Greek Orthodox patriarchates of Alexandria, both of which have met with success in winning many thousands of converts from the body of non-Christian peoples in sub-Saharan Africa; and finally the commitment of many Christians to the Palestinian cause — all are new manifestations of an internal reawakening and a new-found independence which are rapidly changing the narrow traditionalism that once marked the Arab Christian communities.

The Roman Catholic Church in response to this recent and dynamic revival has wisely chosen in the main to encourage her Uniate branches in asserting their independence. And it is precisely this emergence from within the shadow of Western protection and identification that has permitted Arab Christians to re-analyze their relations to Islam and its nationalist manifestations. "It is our role," states Bishop Edelby, "to understand the legitimate reactions of Islam [to the modern world] and to understand its aspirations and to act so that its rights may be recognized. I do not ignore the fact," he continues, "that the Arab awakening is and has been accompanied at the beginning by a religious xenophobia. We will simply have to await the clarification of concepts without ever refusing our affection and cooperation."[337]

Such frank commitments to the cause of the Arab nation have met with favorable response from prominent Muslim Arab leaders. To be sure, much of the old anti-Christian prejudice survives, particularly among rural and uneducated Muslims, while on the political level identification of Arab Nationalism with Islam remains strong. In 1966, for instance, King Faysal of Saudi Arabia, during a visit to Jordan for purposes of promoting his "Islamic Pact," referred to Islam as "the heavenly message and the basis of our Arab Nationalism;"[338] such invocations, however, were generally not aimed at Christians, but at least in Faysal's case toward the "atheistic ideologies and contradictory values," that is, Communism.[339] From 1958 up until the time of his death, President Nasser in particular sought to regain the support of Arab Christians, whom he had earlier alienated, especially the Copts of his own nation, through a revival of the "Cross and Crescent" movement which once united Christian and Muslim in the cause of Egyptian independence. Professor Elie Sâlim of the American University of Beirut, a Lebanese of Greek Orthodox origin, on a visit to Cairo in September of 1959 made some random recordings of slogans chanted by nationalist demonstrators; while nearly every one had an Islamic connotation, several were pointedly aimed at encouraging Christian participation and support. "Allahu Akbar," the demonstrators shouted, "Muḥammad wa 'Isâ rasûlayn Allah!" "God is omnipotent! Muḥammad and Jesus are the two prophets of the one true God;" and, "Injîlîya Qur'ânîya qawmîyatûnâ Al-'Arabîya" "Our Arab Nationalism is from the Gospel and the Koran."[340] During the summer of 1965, Nasser, in his first appearance at a Christian ceremony since his rise to power in 1953, spoke on the occasion at which he and Patriarch Kyrillos laid the cornerstone of the new Cathedral of Saint Mark of Cairo (dedicated three years later, likewise in Nasser's presence). "We are all Egyptians," affirmed the President. "Islam recognizes Christians as brothers in religion and brothers in God... God calls for love, and we will not tolerate any more fanatics who create obstacles and problems for the people in their revolution,"[341] a none-too-veiled challenge to the reactionary Muslim Brethren (Ikhwân Al-Muslimûn) which since its inception has advocated a strict implementation of the traditionalist *dhimmi* status for non-Muslims in Islamic countries.

In direct opposition to this old view, the prominent Muslim scholar and highly-respected nationalist theoretician, Sâṭiʿ Al-Ḥuṣrî, affirmed a place for the Christian in Arab Nationalism in his classic study, *The Evolution of Nationalist Thought* (see footnote 234). In direct answer to Charles Mâlik's query, "Is a Christian Arab possible?" Ḥuṣrî observes:

> historically the development of the Arab nation is closely bound up with Islam, if its citizens ceased to be Muslims they would still be Arabs. Thus, the Arabic-speaking Christians are Arabs in precisely the same sense as Muslims and they can be Arabs without having to give up anything in their own religious tradition or being required to accept that of Islam. Indeed, it is precisely by way of their own religious tradition that they have become aware of their Arab nationality; their nationalism began with the struggle of the Arab Orthodox to throw off Greek control of the patriarchate of Antioch, and that of Eastern Uniates to prevent the encroachment of Latin customs, rites, and ways of thought.[342]

This enlightened view is a far cry indeed from the pessimistic appraisal of Muslim religious tolerance voiced by Albert Hourani 25 years ago when he stated that "the tolerance which the present-day Moslem professes for Christians... is too often not that of a humble believer for those whom he recognizes as serious seekers of the same truth, but contemptuous toleration of the strong for the weak."[343] Yet Al-Ḥuṣrî was by no means alone in his liberal approach. Dr. Hâzim Nusayba (Nuseibeh), Princeton-educated former Prime Minister of Jordan, in his *Ideas of Arab Nationalism,* applies the ideals of Ḥuṣrî's nationalism to the actual role of Christians in the national life of the Arab states. For Dr. Nusayba it is essential that Christians "be persuaded to participate actively and whole-heartedly in the nation-forming process." Such a commitment, he asserts, must, however, be encouraged by the removal of politics from integral association with Islam.

> It is not merely a question of tolerating non-Muslims, as the literature of the Muslim Brotherhood seems to indicate. The principle of tolerance has always been recognized, and there is no reason to assume or fear that it will not be even more meticulously observed in the future. What is involved is whether or not the non-Muslims are to participate as full citizens and without any disabilities on account of their creeds in the conduct of national life. This they cannot do if religion is the axis around which public life revolves.[344]

Dr. Nusayba's challenge to his fellow Muslims reflects a revolutionary departure from the traditional Islamic attitude towards the Christian *dhimmi,* and embodies in a very few sentences the goals toward which Arab Christians have been striving for centuries. And yet it is basically the most elementary example of common sense. For a country to deny full participation in its national life to any segment of its population on the basis of religious distinction — particularly when that segment comprises a very high percentage of that country's educated, prosperous, multi-lingual, financially talented, and politically dedicated citizenry — is in this tolerant age the most destructive of follies. It serves not only to frustrate the minority community by preventing its members from utilizing their abilities to the fullest, but deprives the nation of some of its finest human resources.

Nusayba's call for religious equality, however, is not without its challenge to the Christians themselves. For when he advocates the abolition of religion as "the axis around which public life revolves," he is surely not referring only to those Arab nations in which one's adherence to Islam is a necessary qualification for advancement in the political, military, and economic sectors, for without doubt Lebanon is the most apparent example of the survival of religion in national life. And until Christians are willing to relax the strict confessional restrictions governing the political life of that country, Muslims will remain suspicious of Christian dedication to the Arab nation.

The time is now at hand when Lebanon and its Christian population in particular must weigh its own system in the balance with the modern political institutions operative elsewhere. The coming decade will undoubtedly witness closer contact, and hopefully, closer cooperation between Muslims and Christians throughout the world; for this reason, if for none other, Lebanon's unique status as the only state where adherents of the two greatest world faiths live in balanced numbers and share the responsibility of government should be preserved as a guide to future sharing on a world-wide basis.

The Vatican in its recent efforts to widen contact with the Islamic World has openly designated Lebanon as "un pays-pilote pour le développement des rélations islamo-chrétien,"[345] reaffirming an earlier assessment by Pope Pius XII who saw in Lebanon "un précieux trait d'union entre monde d'occident et celui d'Orient." From the Muslim side, Dr. Ḥasan Sa'b called for a dialogue between Islam on the one hand, and Christianity and modern civilization on the other. This exchange, observes Dr. Sa'ab, "is a necessity of even deeper import in Lebanon where Islam is in permanent confrontation. . . with both."[346]

With the events of the recent Lebanese civil struggle in mind it is difficult to assess the future in a country where "permanent confrontation" between Christianity and Islam has resulted in two prolonged periods of strife in the past twenty years. The present civil unrest in Lebanon has illustrated the lengths to which the Christian element, the Maronites in particular, is willing to go in order to prevent submersion in the Muslim-dominated world that surrounds them. Regardless of the outcome of the present undecided state of affairs, Christians in Lebanon will continue to govern their own affairs and destiny.

The temporary breakdown of Muslim-Christian cooperation, complicated as it is by economic, social, and above all political factors extending beyond Lebanon's own frontiers, is in many respects the result of outside forces that have reason to resent, even fear Lebanon's historic example. To the conservative Muslim president of Libya, Mu'ammar Qaddâfî, a Christian-dominated state in the midst of the Arab World is an embarrassment as acute as that of Israel, and certainly one more vulnerable to the kind of threats and pressures he is able to wield. For Israel itself, a successful Christian-Muslim experiment makes Lebanon the most dangerous of all enemies to Zionist survival, for it is a living example of the kind of society the Palestinians have lately advocated in place of the narrowly nationalistic and ethnically based state that is Israel today. What is certain is that the Christians of Lebanon, more so than any of their brethren elsewhere in the Arab World, are determined to survive in the face of any challenge which Islam, whether in the guise of nationalism or not, might afford. "We have chosen to live and die," declared the then President Hélou in 1966, "on this narrow stretch of land, according to laws inspired by a pact of brotherhood. With the help of the one God in whom we all believe, we are achieveing a national community, a human synthesis, a universal society."[347]

The success or failure of the Lebanese Christian communities in perpetuating and restructuring their national society in the coming decades will irrevocably be shared by all Arabic-speaking Christians throughout the Middle East, and will in large part determine the outcome of their centuries-old striving to achieve a truly integrated and egalitarian Arab nation.

Appendix

Official population figures by religion of selected Christian centers in the Arab East, listed from West to East in an arc beginning with Aswan in Upper Egypt and ending with Baṣra on the Persian Gulf.

City/Town	Total Population	Christian	Muslim	Other
EGYPT (1960)				
Aswân	48,393	5,719	42,671	3
Armant	36,716	5,961	30,751	4
Al-Uqṣur (Luxor)	35,074	13,032	22,042	—
Naqâda	14,144	7,707	6,437	—
Qinâ (Kena)	57,417	8,172	49,243	2
Naj' Ḥammâdî	10,516	4,179	6,337	—
Al-Raḥmanîya	8,635	4,769	3,866	—
Bahjûra	17,028	7,166	9,862	—
Al-Balyâna	21,098	6,728	14,370	—
Al-Kashah	10,437	6,507	3,930	—
Jirja (Girga)	42,017	10,038	31,978	1
Al-Sûjâj (Sohag)	61,944	16,329	45,611	4
Ṭahṭâ	36,165	5,012	31,153	—
Timâ	27,810	9,595	18,215	—
Al-Badârî	23,937	5,520	18,417	—
Abû-Tîj	26,738	6,828	19,710	—
Al-Nakhîla	21,843	9,432	12,411	—
Asyûṭ	118,485	38,048	80,434	3
Al-Hammâm	7,330	5,554	1,776	—
Abnûb	27,751	8,778	18,973	—
Manfalûṭ	28,540	6,755	21,785	—
Al-'Izba	5,930	5,213	717	—
Balûṭ	6,277	4,167	2,110	—
Al-Qûṣîya	22,089	7,199	15,890	—
Dayrûṭ	41,009	8,753	32,236	—
Rizqat Dayr Al-Muḥarraq	3,864	3,729	'135	—
Mîr	11,407	4,074	7,333	—
Dayr Mawwâs	15,145	3,211	11,933	1
Mallawî	52,614	16,208	36,406	—
Dayr Abû-Ḥinnis	6,020	6,014	6	—
Dayr Al-Barshâ	4,270	4,238	32	—
Al-Bayâdîya	6,882	6,414	468	—
Abû-Qirqâs	8,629	6,068	2,611	—
Manharâ	4,647	4,428	219	—
Al-Minyâ (El-Minia)	94,507	25,183	69,317	7

City/Town	Total Population	Christian	Muslim	Other
EGYPT (1960 cont.)				
Samalûṭ	32,964	8,450	24,513	1
Al-Ṭayyiba	9,132	4,513	4,619	—
Banî Mazâr	30,583	7,471	23,112	—
Maghâgha	28,650	6,452	22,198	—
Al-Fashn	25,961	4,609	21,352	—
Bibâ	20,773	3,357	17,416	—
Banî Suwayf (Beni Sueif)	78,829	13,092	65,736	1
Al-Fayyûm	102,064	14,958	87,100	6
Al-Jîza (Gizeh)	250,434	16,525	233,813	96
Ambâbâ	136,429	5,283	131,146	—
Cairo	3,348,779	409,002	2,933,029	6,758
Shabra	100,607	4,906	87,100	6
Banha	52,686	2,282	50,402	2
Shabîn Al-Kawm	54,910	3,128	‘51,777	5
Zaqâzîq	124,417	10,386	114,030	1
Mît Ghamar	40,016	3,774	36,241	1
Al-Mansûra	141,192	10,829	130,331	32
Maḥallat Al-Kubrâ	178,288	9,400	168,879	9
Ṭanṭâ	184,299	18,460	165,804	35
Damanhûr	126,600	5,683	120,801	16
Kafar Al-Dawâr	43,317	3,579	39,638	—
Alexandria	1,516,224	153,474	1,359,468	3,292
Dumyât (Damietta)	71,780	850	70,921	9
Port Sa‘îd	245,318	18,775	226,499	44
Ismâ‘îlîya	284,114	13,741	270,342	32
Al-Suways (Suez)	203,610	16,370	187,206	34
LEBANON (1956)				
Beirut	220,849	119,517	93,178	8,154c
Beirut inclusive of suburban qadâs of B‘abdâ and Al-Matn	385,804	254,212	108,780	22,813d
No breakdown by other cities and towns available.				
SYRIA (1960)				
Suwaydâ	18,154	968	17,168	—e
Dir‘â	17,284	749	16,535	—
Izrâ‘	2,901	693	2,208	—
Al-Qunayṭira (Kuneitra)	17,080	1,822	15,249	9
Al-Qaṭanâ	10,578	1,877	8,701	—
Zabadânî	8,837	1,263	7,574	—
Damascus (inc. Al-Ghûta)	650,898	50,065	598,321	2,512f

City/Town	Total Population	Christian	Muslim	Other
SYRIA (1960 cont.)				
Al-Nabak	10,435	656	9,779	—
Homs (Ḥimṣ)	137,217	15,423	121,794	—
Ḥamâh	97,390	4,001	93,389	—
Sâfîtâ	6,234	4,324	1,910	—g
Tarṭûs	15,353	1,891	13,462	—
Bâniyâs	8,477	1,233	7,244	—
Latakia (Al-Lâdhiqîya)	67,604	10,456	57,145	3
Kasab	3,670	2,672	998	—
Al-Haffa	2,715	424	2,291	—
Jisr Al-Shughûr	10,366	635	9,739	—
Idlib	23,703	681	23,022	—
Aleppo (Ḥalab)	425,467	80,590	343,015	1,862f
‘Ayn Al‘Arab	4,394	791	3,603	—
Tall Abyaḍ	3,102	711	2,386	5
Dayr Al-Zawr (Deir ez-Zor)	42,036	1,249	40,787	—
Al-Ḥasaka	18,870	8,103	10,764	3
Qâmishlî	34,198	19,907	13,567	724f
Al-Malikîya	5,237	3,119	2,118	—
JORDAN (1964)				
Bethlehem	22,453	7,246	15,207	8
Bayt Jâlâ	7,966	4,530	3,436	—
Bayt Sâḥûr	5,316	3,458	1,858	—
Old Jerusalem	60,490	10,982	49,504	4
Al-Ṭûr	4,309	686	3,623	—
Jericho	10,166	935	9,231	—
Râm Allah	14,759	8,260	6,499	—
Bi ’r Zayt	3,253	1,424	1,829	—
Al-Ṭayyiba	1,677	1,176	501	—
‘Abûd	1,521	716	805	—
Nâbulus	45,768	627	44,929	212b
Al-Zabâbida	1,474	1,077	397	—
Al-Karak	7,422	1,622	5,800	—
Al-Simâkîya	674	567	107	—
Humûd	441	277	164	—
Mâdabâ	11,224	3,700	7,524	—
‘Ammân/Zarqâ	347,516	38,138	309,062	128
Al-Fuḥays (Fuheis)	2,946	2,391	555	—
Sâfût	421	344	77	—
Al-Rumaymîn	490	268	222	—
Al-Salṭ	16,176	2,157	14,019	—
‘Ajlûn	5,390	2,023	3,367	—
‘Anjâra	3,163	719	2,444	—

City/Town	Total Population	Christian	Muslim	Other
JORDAN (1964 Cont.)				
Al-Ḥuṣn	3,728	2,030	1,698	—
Shaṭanâ	383	306	77	—
Irbid	44,685	2,220	42,456	9
Al-Mafraq	9,499	1,297	8,202	—
ISRAEL (1972)				
Tel Aviv/Jaffa	6,351	2,402	3,904	45
New Jerusalem	2,109	973	1,074	62
Old Jerusalem	81,427	10,731	70,696	—
Ramla-Lydda	7,291	1,990	5,298	3
Haifa	12,397	8,152	4,178	67
'Isfîya	4,252	791	65	3,396a
Acre ('Akka) - Old City	8,202	1,310	6,852	40
Nazareth (Al-Nâṣira)	33,837	15,293	18,484	60
Yâfâ Al-Nâṣira	4,932	1,412	3,518	2
Al-Rayna	4,126	1,079	3,047	—
Kafar Kannâ	5,244	1,075	4,168	1
'Aylabûn	1,506	1,246	260	—
Al-Mughâr	6,477	1,884	847	3,746a
Al-Râma	3,922	2,421	420	1,081a
Shafâ 'Amru	11,616	4,558	5,012	2,046a
I'billîn	3,674	2,172	1,502	—
Kafar Yasîf	3,808	2,286	1,392	130a
Abû Sinân	3,586	942	1,482	1,162a
Tarshîḥa	1,823	1,162	661	—
Mi'ilyâ	1,565	1,565	—	—
Fasûṭa	1,596	1,596	—	—
Jish	1,736	1,415	320	1
IRAQ (1957)				
Zakhû	8,033	1,873	6,160	—
Mankaysh	1,374	1,276	98	—
Sirsank	851	709	142	—
Kânî Mâsî	544	516	28	—
Dahûk	7,680	1,839	5,841	—
'Ayn Sifni	2,250	290	863	1,097h
Al-Qûsh	4,396i	4,324	53	19
Tall Kayf	7,311	7,061	250	—
Tall Usquf	5,705j	5,705	—	—
Bâṭnayâ	3,104k	3,104	—	—
Barṭala	2,739l	2,614	125	—

City/Town	Total Population	Christian	Muslim	Other
IRAQ (1957 Cont.)				
Ba'shîqa	2,609	816	342	1,458m
Bahazânî	2,637n	450	n.a.	n.a.
Karamlays	2,100o	2,100	—	—
Qâra Qûsh	6,338p	6,310	26	2
Mosul (Al-Mawsil)	178,222	24,887	153,103	312
Sinjâr	4,987	599	3,685	703q
'Aqrâ	6,041	389	5,650	2
'Ayn Kâwa	2,858	2,670	188	—
Shaqlâwa	4,196	1,307	2,885	4
Bâṭâs	948	385	563	—
Al-Sulaymaniya	48,812	679	48,092	41
Kirkûk	120,402	12,691	107,390	312
Baghdâd	665,959	63,331	591,981	7,747r
Al-Kaẓimîya	127,224	1,056	126,036	132
Al-Baṣra	164,905	7,805	154,894	2,302s

a. Entirely Druze.
b. Composed of Samaritans.
c. Druze: 2,457; remainder Jew, Alawite, Bahai, etc.
d. Druze: 16,985
e. All but a few hundred of the population listed by the Census as Muslim are in fact Druze.
f. Nearly entirely Jewish: 2,392 in Damascus; 1,848 in Aleppo, and 723 in Qâmishlî.
g. Mostly Alawite.
h. All Yazidi.
i. Fiey, *op. cit.*, p. 387, vol. II, gives the total population as 5,500.
j. Figures from Fiey, *op. cit.*, p. 381, vol. II. The Census of 1957 gave the total population as 3,218, with no confessional breakdown.
k. Figures from Fiey, *op. cit.*, p. 376, vol. II.
l. Figures from the Census of 1947. The Census of 1957 gave the total population as 3,116, but with no confessional breakdown.

m. Fiey, *op. cit.*, p. 461, vol. II gives the population as consisting of 2,566 inhabitants, of which 791 were Christian, 258 Muslim, and 1,517 Yazidi.
n. Figures from Fiey, *op. cit.*, p. 468, vol. II. Only the total population and Christian figures are cited. The remainder of the population is largely Yazidi but with a small Muslim minority.
o. Figures from Fiey, *op. cit.*, p. 400, vol. II. The Census of 1957 gives the total population as 1,876, but with no confessional breakdown.
p. Fiey, *op. cit.*, gives the total populaton as 7,251, vol. II, p. 440.
q. All Yazidi.
r. Sabaean: 3,768; Jewish: 3,234.
s. Sabaean: 1,922.

Notes

Introduction

1 Charles Mâlik, "The Near East: The Search for Truth;" *Foreign Affairs* (January 1952), p. 214.

2 Fâtimid caliph of Egypt (996-1021), noted for his madness and ruthless persecution of Christians and Jews. During his reign a number of churches were destroyed including the Holy Sepulchre in Jerusalem (1009).

3 *The Holy Koran,* sura IX: verse 97.

4 As recorded in *The Acts of the Apostles,* 2:11, "Cretans and Arabians, we hear them telling in our tongues the mighty works of God."

5 Robert Browning, *Justinian and Theodora* (London: Weidenfeld and Nicholson, 1971), p. 241 ff.

6 Philip Khuri Hitti, *History of the Arabs* (New York: Saint Martin's Press, 1967), 9th edition, p. 84.

7 Beyond the northern frontiers of the Empire many of the Gothic tribes, converted in the 4th century by Arian missionaries, perpetuated Arianism into the 6th century, particularly in Italy where it survived under the Ostrogothic kingdom until the latter was overthrown by Justinian's general, Belisarius, in 552.

8 "Threatening to the vital truths of the Gospel as undoubtedly they were, heresies have rarely done more than provide battle flags for national and social quarrels. All the historic schisms which have endured have far more the work of the politician than the theologian." Canon J.A. Douglas, quoted in Donald Attwater, *The Dissident Eastern Churches* (London: Geoffrey Chapman, 1961), p. 12. "...Behind the varying standpoints taken up by different countries with regard to Christological dogma lay poli-

tical trends which were in fact nothing more than . . . the first signs of nationalism . . ." Jules Leroy, *Monks and Monasteries of the Near East,* translated from the French by Peter Collin (London: Harrap & Co., 1963), p. 23. W.B. Fisher, geographer at the University of Durham, asserts that the movements which separated the four provinces of the Church from one another were the result of a strong national sentiment in each which found in at least one of these heresies a vehicle for asserting their independence. W.N. Fisher, *The Middle East* (London: Methuen and Co., 1961), pp. 111-112.

9 The exact origins of the Maronite sect are extremely obscure. For a detailed study of this controversy, see Robert W. Crawford "William of Tyre and the Maronites," *Speculum* (April, 1955), pp. 225-228.

10 Hitti, *op. cit.,* p. 171.

11 Majid Khadduri, *War and Peace in the Law of Islam* (Baltimore: Johns Hopkins Press, 1955), p. 178.

12 Hitti, *op. cit.,* p. 195.

13 *Ibid.,* p. 222; from the narratives of Ibn Al-Jawzi.

14 Khadduri, *op. cit.,* p. 186.

15 *Ibid.,* p. 198.

16 The town has retained its Christian character to the present day. Known as " 'Arûs Filasṭîn" (The Bride of Palestine) from its favored location and lovely surroundings, it was a hub of early Western missionary activity (notably Quaker) and remains today one of the principle centers of Christian education in Palestine. For Tristram, "Christianity had here, as elsewhere, stamped the place and its substantial houses with a neatness and cleanliness to which the best of Moslem villages are strangers." H.B. Tristram, *The Land of Israel* (London: The Society for Promoting Christian Knowledge, 1865), p. 506.

17 Charles M. Doughty, *Arabia Deserta* (London: Jonathan Cape,

1926), p. 24. "It is strange," remarked the author, "to see here the Christian religion administered in the tents of Kedar!"

8 Gerald F. Peake, *The History of Jordan and its Tribes* (Coral Gables: The University of Miami Press, 1958), pp. 180-182.

9 Hitti, *op. cit.,* pp. 232-233. "Within the Moslem society these clients [Mawâlî] ... through their intermarriages with the conquering stock... served to dilute the Arabian blood and ultimately make that element inconspicuous amidst the mixture of varied racial strains."

0 'Izz Al-Dîn Ibn-Al-Athîr, *Kamîl Al-Tawârikh* ("The Perfect History"), *Recueil des Historiens des Croissades,* "Historiens Orientaux," ed. Barbier de Maynard, (Paris, 1972-1905), Vol. II, p. 5.

1 The leading Jacobite historian of the Crusading era, Michael the Syrian, observes that "although the Franks agreed with the Greeks on the duality of the two natures of Christ, they... never raised difficulties on the subject of the faith or attempted to arrive at a single form of worship for all Christian languages and peoples." *The Chronicle* of Michael, Jacobite Patriarch of Antioch 1166-1199, Vol. III, p. 228.

2 William (Guilelmus), Archbishop of Tyre, *Historia Rerum in Partibus Transmarinis Gestarum* ("A History of Deeds Done Beyond the Sea"), ca. 1185, translated from the Latin by E.A. Babcock and A.C. Krey (New York: Columbia University Press, 1943), pp. 458-459, and Kamal Salibi, *Maronite Historians of Medieval Lebanon* (Beirut: American University of Beirut Press, 1959), p. 16. "Beginning with Ibn Al-Qilâ'i, Maronite scholars rose to defend it [Maronite Orthodoxy] and went back to the history of their community for evidence." See also Salibi, "The Maronite Church in the Middle Ages and its Union with Rome," *Oriens Christianus* (1st Quarter, 1958), p. 104, and Joseph Debs, *La Perpétuelle Orthodoxie des Maronites* (Arras: Imprimerie Moderne, 1896).

23 John Meyendorff, *The Orthodox Church*, translated from the French by John Chapin (New York: Random House, 1962), p. 87.

24 Giuseppe Beltrami, "La Chiesa Caldea nel Secolo dell'Unione," *Orientalia Christiana* (1st Quarter, 1933), pp. 2-6.

25 Pierre Rondot, *Les Chrétiens d'Orient* (Paris: J. Peyronnet et Cie., 1955), p. 68; and Psalm 45:8, translation from the Book of Common Prayer.

26 William R. Polk, *The Opening of South Lebanon 1788-1840* (Cambridge: Harvard University Press, 1963), p. 137.

27 The greatest of the Ma'nid amîrs, Fakhr Al-Dîn II (1590-1635) openly favored ties with Christian Europe, and welcomed Catholic missionaries. Though heir to the religious traditions of the Druze faith, the amîr was favorably disposed towards Christians, having been raised in a Maronite household following the death of his father, Fakhr Al-Dîn, I, at the hands of Turkish assassins. (See Philip K. Hitti, *Lebanon in History,* [London: Macmillan, 1957] p. 374.) During the reign of Fakhr Al-Dîn II, Christian and Western influence grew rapidly in Lebanon, and many of the Druzes converted to Maronite Christianity. "Even the Amir himself [was] sufficiently alive to the advantages of ties with European powers to have considered conversion." Polk, *op. cit.,* p. 130.

28 Kamal Salibi, *A Modern History of Lebanon* (London: Weidenfeld and Nicholson, 1965), p. 114.

29 An official estimate of the religious distribution in the newly-established *mutasarrifîya* in 1861 counted 264,000 Christians (of whom 225,000 or 85% were Maronites), 25,000 Druzes, and 7,000 Muslims of both the Sunni and Shî'a sects. For these and other detailed demographic statistics, see Etienne de Vaumas, "La Répartition Confessionnelle au Liban et l'Equilibre de l'Etat Libanais," *Revue de Géographie Alpine* (July-September, 1955), p. 579.

30 Lady Duff-Gordon, *Letters from Egypt,* re-edited with additional

letters by Gordon Waterfield, (London: Routledge and Kegan Paul, 1969), p. 56.

1 "In 1913, the Chaldaean Patriarchate all-told counted approximately 102,000 faithful inhabiting 177 different localities, served by 296 priests, 153 churches, 81 chapels, and 130 schools." Raymond Jenin, *Les Eglises Orientales et Les Rites Orientaux* (Paris: Maison de la Bonne Presse, 1922), p. 580. For the effect of the War see the above, p. 580 ff., and Donald Attwater, *The Dissident Churches of the East* (London: Geoffrey Chapman, 1961), p. 191.

2 Hitti, *A Short History of Lebanon* (New York: Macmillan, 1965), pp. 216-217.

3 Sylvia Haim, *Arab Nationalism* (Berkeley: University of California Press, 1962), p. 91.

4 Hàrry N. Howard, *The King-Crane Commission* (Beirut: Khayats, 1963), p. 181.

5 Zeine N. Zeine, *The Struggle for Arab Independence* (Beirut: Khayats, 1960), p. 138.

6 Howard, *op. cit.,* p. 116.

7 *Ibid.,* pp. 130, 153.

8 Salibi, *A Modern History of Lebanon* (London: Weidenfeld and Nicholson, 1965), p. 161.

9 *Ibid.,* p. 166.

0 Howard., *op. cit.,* p. 117.

1 Manṣûr 'Awwâd, "Al-Baṭriyârk Al-Lubnânî: Ilyâs Buṭrus Al-Ḥuwayyik," *Al-Mashriq* (December, 1932), p. 932. Author's translation.

2 John Joseph, *The Nestorians and their Muslim Neighbors* (Princeton: Princeton University Press, 1961), pp. 151-152.

3 *The Constitution of Iraq (1924),* Article 13, and Article 4, Section 2. Also Stanley A. Morrison, "Religious Liberty in Iraq," *Moslem World* (April, 1935), pp. 125, 128.

44 Article 9 of the Constitution of Lebanon (1926) states: "Liberty of conscience is absolute. In rendering homage to the Most High, the State respects all confessions and guarantees and protects the free exercise of them... It also guarantees equally to populations belonging to every rite respect for their personal status and their religious interests." Author's translation.

45 Stephen Longrigg, *Iraq 1900-1950* (London: Oxford University Press, 1953), p. 236.

46 *Ibid.*, p. 271.

47 For a more complete view of the Assyrian question see Khaldun S. Hustry, "The Assyrian Affair of 1933," *International Journal of Middle East Studies* (April 1974), pp. 161-176; (June 1974), pp. 334-360.

48 Though Armenians had maintained a see of Jerusalem since the 4th century with their cathedral occupying the historic site of the martyrdom of the Apostle James the Younger the establishment of a patriarchate independent of Sis did not take place until 1311 when the Armenian bishop of Jerusalem broke with the Cilician patriarch over an issue of doctrine and was subsequently recognized by the Mamluk sultan of Cairo as "the independent patriarch and religious leader not only of the Armenian communities within the domains of the Egyptian sultanate but also of the other Eastern Christians who were in communion with the Armenian church." Avedis K. Sanjian, *The Armenian Communities in Syria under Ottoman Dominion* (Cambridge: Harvard University Press, 1965), p. 98. It should be noted that yet a fourth Patriarch of Jerusalem exists in the person of the Greek Catholic Patriarch of Antioch, who includes the Jerusalem patriarchate in his title. But in that there exists a Greek-Catholic Archbishop of Jerusalem (Hilarion Capucci), it would appear that this claim is made only as a ceremonial challenge to the Orthodox throne.

49 At the time of the elevation of a native Arab to the Anglican bishopric (following the Suez Crisis), the English mother Church,

apparently not sufficiently certain of this venture's success, established an Archbishopric "in" (not "of") Jerusalem. Two British incumbents occupied the throne of this artificial see in succession until 1974. Two years later the Church transferred archepiscopal authority to the synod of the newly established province of Jerusalem and the Near East (composed of four dioceses, the aforementioned Jordan, Lebanon, and Syria — which now includes the city of Jerusalem as well — whose bishop since 1974 has been the Rt. Rev. Fa'iq Ḥaddâd; Cyprus and the Persian Gulf; Iran; and Egypt and North Africa), which in turn elected the Bishop of Iran, the Rt. Rev. Hassan Dehqani-Tahti as first president on January 7, 1976.

0 In 1850 there were about 220 Jacobite villages in what is today Turkey: 150 in the Mârdîn-Midyat heartland, 50 in the districts of Urfa and Gawar (Edessa), 15 near Kharpût, and 6 in the vicinity of Diyârbâkîr. Speaking of the Jacobite clergy whom he met at this time during a visit to the Mârdin district, the Rev. G.P. Badger observed that "the bishops generally are illiterate men, but little versed in Scripture and thoroughly ignorant of ecclesiastical history . . . [and] as might naturally be expected, the lower orders of the Syrian clergy are generally more illiterate than the bishops." As for popular education, Badger noted that "notwithstanding the comparative affluence of this community, I believe that there do not exist among them more than twenty small schools in the whole of Turkey . . . " The Rev. George Percy Badger, *The Nestorians and Their Rituals* (London: George Masters, 1852), pp. 62-64.

1 Porter's reference was made specifically to the desert dwellers of Ṣadad, still Jacobite today. "Ninety years ago," he wrote "not a single Jacobite was found save in that village, but now they number 6,000 souls, and colonies of them occupy Zeidan, Meskineh, Feirouzy, Furtaka and Kuseib, and others have settled in Kusein and Hamah. The Jacobites are thus increasing while almost all other sects are diminishing; and this is all the more remarkable as their homes are, with one or two exceptions, on

the very outskirts of civilization and they are forced to contend singlehanded with the wild tribes of the desert." J.L. Porter, *Five Years in Damascus* (London: John Murray, 1870), pp. 327-328. This "bold and resolute conduct" to which Porter referred 125 years ago lives on among the Syrian Orthodox of Turkey, whose isolation since the emergence of Atatürk's republic half a century ago equals that of the villagers of Ṣadad in Porter's day. An American clergyman from Beirut who visited the town of Kilith (renamed Dereici by the Turks, see pp. 110 ff.) in the summer of 1975 tells how the modern inhabitants of this prosperous community near Mardîn dealt with a recent attempt by local Muslims to move in. A Muslim who bought property in the village from a Christian citizen departing for Istanbul was forced to leave in a time-honored way. On a Friday, while he was resting at home with his family and all the Christian men were at work in the fields, the Christian women of the hamlet banded together, attacked his house and beat him severely, so shaming him in front of his wife and children that he had no choice but to pick up his belongings and flee.

52 In contrast to the practical absence of schools among the Jacobites in 1920, the community by 1940 could boast of schools in nearly every one of its principal settlements. In the town of Qâmishlî in eastern Syria in 1952, the two Jacobite schools there accounted for 25% of the Christian educational institutions and the same percentage of the total enrollment. See Roupen Boghossian, *La Haute-Djézireh* (Aleppo: Imprimerie Chiras, 1952), p. 52. In 1939 a seminary for the training of clergy was opened at Zaḥlah and in 1945 transferred to Mosul. In 1966 the cornerstone was laid for a second seminary at Atshana in the Matn district of Lebanon. Much of this progress was achieved through the direct involvement of Patriarch Ifrâm Barṣawm (1932-1957), throughout his life a noted scholar and author. G. Troupeau, "Sa Béatitude Mar Ignace-Ephrem Ier Barsaum" (Notice Nécrologique). *Orient Syrien* (fourth quarter 1957), pp. 436-439. See also Joseph Mounayer, *Les Synodes Syriens Jacobites* (Beirut: Imprimerie Catholique, 1963), pp. 106-110, and P. Behnam, *Nafaḥât Al-Khizâm Aw Ḥayât Al-Baṭriyark Ifrâm* (Mosul: Syrian Orthodox Archdiocese Press, 1959).

3 Henri Lammens, "Fra Gryphon et le Liban au XVe Siècle," *Revue de l'Orient Chrétien* (4th quarter, 1899), p. 87.

4 Quoted in Joseph Debs, *La Perpétuelle Orthodoxie des Maronites* (Arras: Imprimerie Modern, 1896), p. 19.

5 Kamal Salibi, *Maronite Christians of Medieval Lebanon* (Beirut: American University of Beirut Press, 1959), p. 15.

6 The Maronite claim to the patriarchal title of Antioch was recognized in 1254 by Pope Alexander IV.

7 Hitti, *Syrians in America* (New York: George H. Doran, 1924), p. 22.

8 Salibi, *Middle-East Forum* (March 1959), p. 18.

9 Kamal Salibi, interview with author, 28 February 1966.

0 The Egyptian Census of 1947, the last to list the Christian population by sect, counted 72,674 Catholic Copts.

1 Harry Luke, *Mosul and its Minorities* (London: Martin Hopkinson, 1925), pp. 90-91. See also Edmund Hill, O.P. "The Church and the Mongols, 1245-1291," *Eastern Churches Quarterly* (Spring, 1957), p. 12.

2 Bayard Dodge, "The Settlement of the Assyrians on the Khabbur," *Journal of the Royal Central Asian Society* (July, 1940), p. 309.

3 Stephen Longrigg, *Iraq 1900-1955* (London: Oxford University Press, 1953), p. 198. In carrying out British policy in Kurdistan, however, the Levies frequently went to brutal extremes such as the incident in 1924 at Kirkûk where, "admittedly after having suffered a good deal of provocation, [they] ran amok killing fifty of the townspeople including a shaykh of much religious sanctity." Ronald S. Stafford, *The Tragedy of the Assyrians* (London: Allen & Unwin, 1953), p. 47.

4 Despite a visit to Baghdad in 1971, for the first time since his eviction in 1933, in order to reassert his jurisdiction there, the aging patriarch, though still officially recognized as head of his church, placed his authority once again in jeopardy by his marriage in 1973 to a woman some forty years his junior, prompting

the leading Christian journal of the Middle East, *Proche Orient Chrétien,* to conclude that "la crise assyrienne est loin d'être terminée" (First Quarter, 1975), vol. XXV, issue 1, p. 98 — a prophetic remark indeed. Less than one year later the patriarch, aged 66, was assassinated at his home in San José, California, on November 7, 1975 by a member of his own community in reprisal for this unprecedented abrogation of the centuries-old tradition of patriarchal celibacy. On October 14, 1976, Denkha IV, former Bishop of Iran, was elected Katholikos and became the first Nestorian patriarch resident in Baghdad since 1933.

65 The Rev. Justin Perkins, *Residence of Eight Years in Persia Among the Nestorian Christians* (New York: Allen, Morrill and Wardwell, 1843), p. 22.

66 The Rev. G.P. Badger in middle of the 19th century estimated that the Chaldaean Catholic membership consisted of 2,683 families, while that of the parent Nestorian Church consisted of 11,378 families. At an average of six individuals per family unit this would give 17,000 Chaldaeans and 68,000 Nestorians. Badger, *op. cit.,* vol. I, pp. 174-175, and vol. II, p. 400.

67 For a detailed demographic survey of Christians in Iran, see Hubert de Mauroy, "Chrétiens en Iran;" *Proche-Orient Chrétien,* Third Quarter 1974, vol. XXIV, issue 3, pp. 139-162.

68 See Avadis K. Sanjian, *The Armenian Communities in Syria Under Ottoman Dominion* (Cambridge: Harvard University Press, 1965), especially pp. 55-57 and 60-61.

69 Rondot, *Les Chrétiens d'Orient,* p. 20.

70 Tristram, *op. cit.,* p. 403.

71 Attwater, *The Uniate Churches of the East* (London: Geoffrey Chapman, 1961), p. 19.

72 Quoted in *Eastern Churches Quarterly* (Winter 1956-1957), p. 372.

73 Raphael Patai, *The Kingdom of Jordan* (Princeton: Princeton University Press, 1958), p. 18.

4 The Egyptian Census of 1947, the last to list Christians by sect, counted 86,918 Protestant Copts.

5 At present there are still seven active Coptic monasteries in Egypt: Dayr Al-Muḥarraq in Upper Egypt near Dayrûṭ, the four monasteries of the Wâdî Al-Naṭrûn in the desert depression to the west of the Cairo-Alexandria highway, and the two Red Sea desert monsteries of Saint Antony and Saint Paul, midway between Suez and Qusayr. According to figures recently released by Bishop Samwîl (Samuel), oecumenical and social services spokesman for the Coptic patriarchate of Alexandria, the number of monks has grown from 230 in 1960 to 350 in 1976. Many of them are young and well educated novices who have brought new life to the historic desert monasteries following the example set by the dynamic monk, Mattâ Al-Maskîn (*see* fn. 195).

5 In 1900 Egypt was reported by the Census of that year to have been composed of 8,977,702 Muslims (all but 5,941 of them Egyptian nationals) and 731,235 Christians, of whom 612,011 were Copts, 592,374 Monophysites, 12,507 Protestants, and 4,630 Uniate Catholics, and all but 34,351 resident in the predominantly rural areas outside Cairo, Alexandria, and the Canal Zone. The remaining 121,724 Christians were foreigners, chiefly Greeks, Armenians, Syrian-Lebanese, Palestinians, and Europeans. Karl Beth, *Die Orientalische Christenheit der Mittelmeerländer* (Berlin: E.K. Schwetechke und Sohn, 1902), pp. 129-130, and the Rev. Montague Fowler, *Christian Egypt, Past, Present, and Future* (London: Church Newspaper Company Ltd., 1901), p. 286.

7 Jay Walz, the *New York Times* correspondent for the Middle East, was cited by Edward Wakin as quoting the four million figure in 1962 (Edward Wakin, *The Lonely Minority* [New York: William Morrow and Co., 1963]), while the late Rev. Henry Habib Ayrout, formerly rector of the Jesuit College of the Holy Family in Cairo, quoted the same figure in his preface to Meinardus's *Christian Egypt* (p. xviii) in 1965. Monsignor Raymond Etteldorf, writing in the mid 1950's, had estimated the

Christian population of Egypt to be 3,700,000 out of a total population of 22,500,000 (Raymond Etteldorf, *Catholic Churches in the Middle East* [New York: Macmillan, 1955], p. 61), and Father Dalmais of Saint Joseph University, Beirut, concluded that the Copts constituted between 13-15% of the total population of Egypt in 1963, or about 3,800,000 souls ("Les Chrétiens en Pays d'Islam", *Croissance des Jeunes Nations* [June-July, 1963], p. 41).

78 Otto F.A. Meinardus, *Christian Egypt, Ancient and Modern* (Cairo: American University of Cairo Press, 1965), p. 8.

79 *Ibid.*, p. 11.

80 According to the Census of 1960 the Muslim population of these towns was, respectively, 6,437; 3,930; 486; 2,611, and 6.

81 It was in this region that a large percentage of the some 1,000 exclusively Muslim villages noted by the 1960 Census were located.

82 Figures from the *Statistical Bulletin of the United Nations Relief and Works Agency for Palestinian Refugees*, May, 1950 — June, 1951, pp. 24-33.

83 Figures from the British Mandate Census of Palestine, 1931, and the Israeli Population and Housing Census of 1961.

84 In a recent interview with noted American columnists Rowland Evans and Robert Novak, King Husayn of Jordan charged that "30,000 Christians have been pushed out of Jerusalem since Israel conquered the Arab section of the city in 1967, leaving only 10,000 there," with the intention of making East Jerusalem a Jewish city, "a fact of which the world's Christian religions seem to be surprisingly unaware." In that the total Christian population of Jerusalem by official Jordanian reckoning in 1964 was only 11,000, it would appear that Husayn's fears are exaggerated, unless of course he was referring to the 30,000 figure as encompassing all Arab Christians on the West Bank, which appears unlikely. There is no doubt, however, that many

Arab Christians have left Arab Jerusalem since 1967 and that the Israelis are unofficially encouraging this migration. See the *International Herald Tribune,* 26 July 1971, p. 4.

Tristram, *op. cit.,* pp. 65-73.

Statistics are from the Jordanian Ministry of Information Statistical Yearbooks (*Al-Nashra Al-Ihṣâ'îya Al-Sanawîya*) from 1951-1966.

Ibid.

Ministry of Social Affairs, *A Social Survey of Amman* (1960) p. 54.

Statistical Abstract of Israel, 1965, pp. 58-59.

Statistical Abstract of Israel 1974, Jerusalem: Central Bureau of Statistics, 1975, Table iii/10, p. 67.

Throughout the Middle East the Christian percentage of the total population over age 65 exceeds their share of the national total. In Israel, for instance, the Christian percentage of this age group was 20% higher than their share of the total Arab population.

Statistical Abstract of Israel 1974, op. cit., Table iii/23, p. 76. Christian live births in 1973 numbered 2,112 in contrast to 1,693 and 17,954 for the Druzes and Muslims respectively, or only 9.7% of the total non-Jewish live births in Israel for that year. (Table iii/29, p. 82).

Don Peretz, *The Middle East Today* (New York: Holt, Rinehart and Winston, 1964), p. 156.

Projection of the Population in Israel up to 1993, Jerusalem: Central Bureau of Statistics, 1975, special series no. 490.

Pierre Rondot, *Les Institutions Politiques du Liban* (Paris: Institut d'Etudes de l'Orient Contemporain, 1947), p. 26.

96 Hitti, *Lebanon in History* (London: Macmillan, 1957), p. 476.

97 Rondot, *op. cit.*, p. 26.

98 Leila M.T. Meo, *Lebanon: Improbable Nation* (Bloomington: University of Indiana Press, 1965), p. 60.

99 *Ibid.*, p. 162.

100 Stephen Longrigg, *The Middle East* (London: Duckworth, Ltd., 1968), p. 94.

101 In the villages of Lebanon, the general family pattern is the same for Christian, Druze, and Muslim. The household unit generally averages out at 6 individuals, a figure noted by John Gulick in his study of the Christian village of Al-Munṣif (Greek Orthodox) near Byblos. John Gulick, *Social Structure and Cultural Change in a Lebanese Village* (New York: Greek Foundation, 1955), pp. 48-49.

102 David Yaukey, *Fertility Differences in a Modernizing Country* (Princeton: Princeton University Press, 1961), p. 29.

103 *Ibid.*, p. 69.

104 The 1961 Census of Israel, for example, showed that 6.8% of the married Muslim women were under the age of 15, as opposed to only 2.4% of the Christian women.

105 Salim Khamis, *Report of Infant Mortality Survey of Rural Lebanon* (Beirut: American University of Beirut Press, 1955), p. 16.

106 Yaukey, *op. cit.*, p. 29.

107 Jamal Karam Harfouche, *Social Structure of Low-Income Families in Lebanon* (Beirut: Khayat's, 1965), p. 35. A total of 365 mothers were interviewed: 120 Maronite, 114 Sunni, and 131 Armenian.

108 *Area Handbook for Lebanon*, p. 176.

Etienne de Vaumas, "La Repartition Confessionelle au Liban et l'Equilibre de l'Etat Libanais," *Revue de Géographie Alpine,* Third Quarter, 1955, p. 589. See also Elie Safa, *L'Emigration Libanaise* (Beirut: Imprimerie de l'Université Saint Joseph, 1960).

Peretz, *The Middle East Today,* p. 330.

Daniel Lerner, *The Passing of Traditional Society,* (Glencoe, Illinois: The Free Press, 1958), p. 73.

Extracted by the annual report of the French Mandate Administration of Syria and Lebanon to the League of Nations, 1932, p. 139.

See Pierre Rondot, *Les Institutions Politiques du Liban,* pp. 28-29, Albert Hourani, *Minorities in the Arab World,* (London: Oxford University Press, 1947), p. 63, and Safa, *L'Emigration Libanaise,* p. 23.

Published in *Al-Nahâr* (Beirut daily newspaper), 28 April 1956.

Confessional figures for Aleppo in 1890 and 1925 show a Muslim increase of only 3,721 during that time, whereas during the same 35-year period refugee influx augmented the Christian population two and a half times from 21,755 to 58,965. Christians, who accounted for only 18% of the total in 1890 were, on the eve of independence, well over one third of the population (35%). Of the 136,583 Aleppine Christians in 1955, 64% were Armenians of the Gregorian (76,243) and Catholic (10,929) branches; also contributing to the Armenian population were an unknown number of Protestants, probably 2,000 out of a total Protestant community of 3,547. Hamidé, *La Ville d'Alep* (Paris: Imprimerie de l'Université de Paris, 1959), p. 15.

Leroy, *op. cit.,* p. 125.

Rondot, *Les Chrétiens d'Orient,* p. 23.

118 Leroy, *op. cit.*, p. 125.

119 Badger, *The Nestorians and Their Rituals* (London: George Masters, 1852), Vol. 1, p. 69.

120 *Ibid.*

121 Jacques Weulersse, *Pays des Alouites* (Tours: Arrault, 1940), Vol. 1, p. 54.

122 Of the 361,064 resident settled Christians, 344,467 or 95% were Syrian nationals, 9,660 Lebanese or other Arab, 2,357 Palestinian, 701 Egyptian, 186 Turk, and 3,693 of other, largely European, nationality. The Muslim population of 3,986,791 included a 4% minority of non-Syrians, chiefly Palestinians (110,202) and Lebanese and other Arabs (25,657). The Bedouin population of Syria in 1960 (not included in above figures) was 211,847, of which a tiny fraction (177) was Christian, the rest being nominally, at least, Sunni Muslim. The Muslim figures for the settled population is inclusive of the non-Sunni minorities (Druzes, Alawites, Ismailis, Shî'a, and Yazidis) which were not broken down by the Census.

123 *Dalîl Al-Hâtif li Madîna Ḥalab 1961:* of the 8,769 private listings the author identified 5,737 as being Muslim, 1,859 as Arab Christian, 914 as Armenian, 8 as Jewish, and 251 as indeterminate.

124 The population of Tall Tâmir was 1,250 in 1960 as opposed to 1,244 in 1936.

125 In recent years the Syrian government has attempted to secularize the area's name (which means "Valley of the Christians") by referring to it as Wâdî Al-Naḍâra, or "Valley of the Blossoms" (e.g. in the Census of 1960), a change easily accomplished in Arabic by simply adding a diacritical dot over the "ṣ" making it a "ḍ." To the inhabitants of this region, however, their home remains the Christian Valley, a fact confirmed by the author on his visit to the area in July of 1975 in conversations with young villagers of the Greek Orthodox settlements of Kafra and Marmarîtâ.

S. Reich, *Etudes sur Les Villages Araméens de l'Anti-Liban* (Beirut: Imprimerie Catholique, 1936), p. 13.

Colin Thubron, *Mirror To Damascus* (London: Heineman, 1967), p. 56.

Newsweek, June 17, 1974, p. 11.

Seminaria Ecclesiae Catholicae, 1963.

Stafford, *The Tragedy of the Assyrians*, p. 37.

Writing of Northern Iraq in the early years of the British Mandate, Sir Charles Luke wrote: 'There are few parts of the world so baffling to the ethnographic map-maker as the district which was once known as the Vilayet of Mosul. Not only do there dwell within its limits multitudinous sects, as little-known, in many cases, as they are ancient; it is rare to find, as one ranges the great Mosul plain, two consecutive villages peopled by the same tongue, worshipping the same God." Sir Henry Charles Luke, *Mosul and its Minorities* (London: Martin Hopkinson, 1925), p. 137. For a detailed and definitive description of the Christian and part-Christian villages of the Mosul plain, see J.M. Fiey, *Assyrie Chrétienne* (Beirut: Imprimerie Catholique, 1965), pp. 354-469.

Interview, H.E. Emmanuel Delly, Baghdad, 26 November 1965. At that time the Chaldaeans reported four new churches under construction to meet the spiritual needs of the immigrants.

The most recent Nestorian exodus occurred in late 1968 and early 1969, following the celebrated rash of hangings of alleged CIA/Israeli spies, several of whom were Assyrian Christians, and the contemporaneous, but probably unrelated, intervention of the Ba'thist government in the internal matters of the Nestorian community through support of illegally consecrated bishops and clergy in Baghdad and Basra favorable to the regime.

Table XXXII of the General Census of Iraq 1957 (Al-Jumhûrîya Al-'Irâqîya, Wizârat Al-Dâkhilîya, Mudîrîya Al-Nufûs Al-'Ama, *Al-Majmû'a Al-Iḥṣâ'îya Tasjîl 'Am 1957)* (Baghdad: 1962, ten volumes). 38.5% of the Christian men and 25.6% of the Christian women over the age of 15 had never been married, as opposed to only 31.3% of the Muslim men and 17.1% of the Muslim women.

135 General Census of Iraq 1957, Table XXIV. Iraqis under the age of one year included 7,498 Christians and 197,788 Muslims; between the ages of 20 and 25 the figures were 17,608 Christians and 374,809 Muslims.

136 The Census counted 38,110 Christian, and 1,155,241 Muslim, family units.

137 The Iraqi Census of 1965 counted 232,406 Christians out of a total population of 8,097,230, a numerical increase of nearly 14% over the 1957 figure, but representing only 2.9% of all Iraqis as opposed to 3.25% eight years earlier. Many knowledgeable Christians contest this figure, however, asserting that they are now well in excess of 300,000. Other minority groups included Yazîdîs (69,683), Sabaeans (14,262), and Jews (3,187).

138 Dr. Norman A. Horner, lately of the Near East School of Theology in Beirut, has estimated Syrian Christians in Turkey to number 60,000, based on figures of the Syrian Orthodox patriarchate, and his own observations. See Horner, *Rediscovering Christianity Where it Began* (Beirut: Heidelberg Press, 1974), p. 96.

139 Chaldaean villages are still found today in the vicinity of Siirt (e.g. Ekinduzu), Cizre (e.g. Harbol and Hasana), Uludere and Çolemerik (the former Nestorian Hakkâri heartland). Some 500 Chaldaeans, recent emigrants from such villages, make up the majority of the Catholic parish of Mersin (port city of Adana), while several dozen Chaldaean families cluster within the confines of their 19th-century churches in Mârdîn and Diyârbâkîr. A Chaldaean priest from Mârdîn serves both urban and rural congregations in Eastern Turkey, while another priest in Istanbul attends to a small flock of Anatolian emigrés there. Elsewhere they come under the jurisdiction of Roman Catholic priests (e.g. Mersin, Ankara, Antioch, and Alexandretta).

Freya Stark, *Riding to Tigris* (London: Harcourt Brace & Co., 1959), p. 101.

Badger, *op. cit.,* vol. I, pp. 53-54. What Badger would not recognize is the modern cooperative winery which today's villagers are building on their own initiative to provide local employment and thus stem the flow of young male Syrian Orthodox villagers to the cities.

Rev. W.A. Wigram, *The Cradle of Mankind* (London: A.& C. Black, Ltd., 1922), p. 46.

Edward Atiya, *An Arab Tells His Story: A Study in Loyalties* (London: John Murray, 1946), p. 12.

Doughty (p. 3) noted for example that in late 19th-century Damascus there were no Muslim practitioners of this craft, only Christian.

In areas of the Arab World where non-Muslim communities no longer flourished, such as in most of the Arabian Peninsula, these necessary trades were of course carried on by Muslims, though frequently of non-Arab, e.g. Persian, origin, so that in such places as Kuwait one finds many Muslim families with names such as Al-Ṣâ'igh and individuals with given names such as would in the Levant denote possible, even probable Christian faith on the part of the bearer.

Hitti, *History of the Arabs,* (New York: Saint Martin's Press, 1967), 9th edition, p. 246.

Manṣûr Ibn-Sarjûn, who, according to Muslim historians, connived with the Melkite bishop of Damascus in surrendering the city to the Muslim army of Khâlid Ibn-Walîd in 635. *Ibid.*

Ibid., p. 315.

Ibid., p. 639.

Atiya, *op. cit.,* pp. 3-4.

151 Rev. Bliss's opinion of the native Christian churches was notably biased. In his personal memoires, the founder of the A.U.B. notes that there had been no formal plan to create a native Protestant church. "The hope was," states Bliss, "that through the presentation of a pure Gospel and by the example of a nobler code of ethics, these churches might be led to reform themselves." The organization of a Syrian Protestant Church in 1848, concludes Bliss, "was forced upon the missionaries by the logic of circumstances. Though not in their program it might have been foreseen. The preaching of truth was inevitably followed by the exposure of error." (!) On another occasion, commenting on his impressions of one of the first Communion Services held by the infant Arab Protestant community in Beirut (some 30 members at that time), Bliss was moved to the following observation. "Although the service was in an unknown tongue [Arabic], it was deeply solemn and impressive, and when I looked upon these converts and realized from what depth of ignorance and superstition they had been raised [Greek Orthodoxy] and to what they had been raised [New England Calvinism], I could but feel this work a glorious, noble one." Howard Bliss, ed., *The Reminiscences of Daniel Bliss* (New York: Fleming H. Revell, 1920), pp. 102-103, 121.

152 Of the 138,500 students enrolled in Lebanese schools during the academic year 1941-1942, 97,000 were Christian, 34,000 Muslim, 5,000 Druze, 2,000 Jewish, and 500 other. Public school enrollment totalled only 21,000 (of which 13,000 was Muslim), the great majority of students being registered in foreign (44, 000) and private (74,000) institutions. Lebanese Ministry of of Information, *Recueil de Statistiques de la Syrie et du Liban 1942-43* (Beirut: Imprimerie Catholique, 1945), p. 31.

153 The Salim survey of literacy and bilingualism in rural Lebanon in 1962 showed the Christian rate of illiteracy to be 31.5% (ranging from 24.0% among Greek Catholics to 32.7% among Maronites) and that of Muslims to be 47.0% (ranging from 35.6% for Druzes to 68.9% for Shî'a).

54 Christians literate: 423,260 (258,555 male, and 154,594 female); illiterate: 598,379 (226,407 male, 371,972 female). Muslims literate: 3,046,582 (2,345,619 male, 700,963 female); illiterate: 9,715,903 (3,726,727 male, 5,989,176 female). Figures are for those Egyptian nationals over age 20 at time of the Census (1960).

55 Christians literate: 102,583 out of 193,285 over the legal marriageable age; Muslims literate: 555,974 out of a total of 1,907,200 of legal age.

56 Christians literate: 92,102 (57,913 male, 34,189 female); illiterate: 79,738 (32,882 male, 46,856 female). Muslims literate: 79,738 (32,882 male, 46,856 female). Muslims literate: 776, 742 (625,560 male, 149,182 female); illiterate: 4,095,807 (1,806,422 male, 2,289,385 female). Figures for Iraqi nationals over age five.

57 See Israel: *The Population and Housing Census of 1961,* publication number 17, table XXXIX.

58 Of the 421 Christian household heads interviewed, 79 had no education, 146 had completed primary schooling, 164 had a secondary diploma, 30 had been to university, and 2 had completed formal technical-vocational training. The respective figures for the 2,323 Muslim household heads surveyed were 1,076, 856, 317, 69, and 5.

59 In 1968 the enrollment of the Arab University was 15,350; that of the University of Lebanon stood at 8,019. Enrollment figures for the private institutions were as follows: American University of Beirut (3,692), Université Saint Joseph (2,792), Beirut College for Women (719), Hagazian College (455), Middle East College (154).

60 Christian secondary school graduates totalled 3,759, Muslim graduates 13,882. Of the little more than 2,000 University graduates in Iraq in 1957, 942 were Christian, 1,266 Muslim.

61 Of the Arab faculty staffing Arab schools in Israel in 1955, 347 were Christian, 293 Muslim, 40 Druze, and 5 Bahai. Muslim

male instructors outnumbered Christian men 242 to 204, but Christian predominance among women instructors (143 as opposed to 51 Muslim women teachers) gave Christians a definite edge.

162 Though Jibrân's works are replete with Christian mysticism, his ideas were sufficiently heterodox for the Maronite Church to prevent his burial in hallowed ground for some years, a case similar to that of Greek writer Nikos Kazantzakis whose burial was delayed by Orthodox Church authorities in Crete who objected to the author's writings, likewise imbued with Christian mysticism but critical of the established church. Unlike Kazantzakis, Jibrân left a legacy of more than literature to his town. A homesick emigré at the time of his death, Jibrân bequeathed all his belongings to Bisharrî. Ever since his works achieved world-wide popularity, their royalties, currently amounting to an estimated $1 million annually, have reverted to this picturesque town of 12,000 Maronite inhabitants, precipitating a violent struggle over the proceeds by the two rival tribal clans that govern the town — the Kayrûz and the Ṭawq. Among the wealthiest villages in the entire country from the income of Jibrân's and other emigrés' remittances, Bisharrî has been rent with dissention over the distribution of this lump of annual income. At one point in October 1972, open warfare broke out between the two armed family camps, punctuated by murders and attempted assassinations, bombings, and mortar fire, reminiscent of the perennial feud between Faranjîya and Duwayḥî in Zaghartâ at the bottom of the Wâdî Qadîsha gorge which Bisharrî crowns. Today the tribal hostilities have been pushed aside in the face of a greater threat from the Muslims of the coastal plain, but nothing is forgotten, except perhaps the words of peaceful counsel which underlined Jibrân's original bequest. For a summary of the events leading to the October 1972 outbreak, see *The International Herald Tribune*, December 15, 1972, p. 7.

163 For a detailed study of the Eastern Catholic liturgies, see Nikolaus Liesel, *The Eucharistic Liturgies of the Eastern Churches* (Saint John's Abbey, Collegeville, Minnesota: The Liturgical Press, 1963), p. 243 (for Chaldaean rite).

4 Leroy, *op. cit.*, pp. 169-170.

5 Desmond Stewart and John Haylock, *New Babylon: A Portrait of Iraq* (London: Collins, Ltd., 1956), pp. 64-66.

6 *Al-Ḥayât*, Beirut, 6 December 1965, p. 1.

7 See *Al-Nahâr* and *L'Orient*, Beirut, 7-9 April 1966. Also *The International Herald Tribune*, 9 April 1966, p. 12.

8 See *L'Orient* and the *Beirut Daily Star*, 5 May 1968, also *The Washington Post* of same date, p. A27.

9 See *L' Orient*, Beirut, 5 June 1968.

0 For an analysis of this and the earlier-mentioned apparitions of the Virgin, see Meinardus, "A Critical Examination of Collective Hallucinations after the Six Day War in the Middle East," *Ethnomedizin* 1, 2-3, (Hamburg, 1971).

1 Rondot, *Chrétiens d'Orient*, p. 29.

2 Hamidé, *La Ville d'Alep* (Paris: Imprimerie de l'Université de Paris, 1959), p. 17.

3 Charles Issawi, "Economic Development and Liberalism in Lebanon", *Middle East Journal* (Summer, 1964), p. 289.

4 Daḥdaḥ later rose briefly to political office as Minister of Finance in the short-lived military government of May 1975.

5 The effective manner in which a run on the British Bank of the Middle East in March, 1967, was handled by both Bank officials and the Central Bank of Lebanon indicated that the lesson of Intra's failure had been learned well in just five months' time.

6 Since independence the Minister of Finance has been a Christian, in considerably more than half the cabinets invariably a Maronite, though the incumbent appointed by incoming President Faranjîya in September of 1970 was a Greek Orthodox, Ilyâs Sâbâ.

177 *Dalîl Al-Hâtif li Madîna Ḥalab wa Surîya Al-Shamâlîya 1960-1961*; a survey made by the author on the basis of identifiable given and surnames.

178 Ministry of Social Affairs of the Kingdom of Jordan, *A Social Survey of Amman* (Amman: Government Press, 1960), p. 101.

179 A survey conducted among the Arabs of Nazareth, predominantly Christian, in 1966, "found that the annual income per Arab family was higher than that of the average Jewish Oriental family and was approaching that of the average Jewish family of any origin" (7,000 Israeli Pounds per annum, as opposed to 6,600 for the Oriental immigrant and 7,360 for the Jewish average). And since the Arab figure included a substantial minority of less-affluent Muslims, the actual Christian figure probably equalled, if not surpassed, the national Jewish average. *New York Times,* 24 December 1966, p.12.

180 In Egypt the 1960 Census revealed a total of 2,012 Christian and 216,402 Muslim divorcees. In Cairo and Alexandria the rate of Muslim divorce was five times that of the Christian rate, and in such rural districts as Asyûṭ, the Muslim rate was twenty times greater. The 1957 Census of Iraq counted 187 Christian and 34,531 Muslim divorcees. The Lebanese divorce figures for 1947 were 390 for Muslims and Druzes, 72 for Christians, and 3 for others. *Recueil de Statistiques Générales* (Beirut: Ministère de l'Economie Nationale du Liban, 1948), p. 12.

181 *Beirut Daily Star,* 5 March 1966, p. 4. In the same year, the Lebanese government, at Iraq's request, arrested and repatriated Iraqi Christian Joseph Ketto, an important figure in the Defense Ministry under Kassem, wanted by the Ba'thist regime on charges of having embezzled $1.5 million while in office. *L'Orient,* 27 August 1966, p. 2.

182 Robert Fedden, *Syria* (London: John Murray, 1964), p. 180.

183 Lerner, *The Passing of Traditional Society,* p. 302.

4 Emille Eid, *La Figure Juridique du Patriarche* (Rome: Scuola Grafica Silesiana Pio XI, 1962), p. 116.

5 *Ibid.*, p. 115.

6 In reply to a letter from the Iraqi Minister of the Interior dated 28 May 1933, in which it was made clear that "the government cannot agree to delegate to you any temporal authority," the patriarch replied in June of that year as follows: "This patriarchal authority is a great historical and traditional usage of the Assyrian people and Church... The temporal power has not been assumed by me, but it has descended to me from centuries past as a legalized delegation of the people to the patriarch... and it is only they who can take it away." Stanley Morrison, "Religious Liberty in Iraq," *The Moslem World* (April 1935), p. 120.

7 Quoted in *Proche-Orient Chrétien* (July-September, 1961), p. 285.

8 In his first address to the nation, Patriarch Khuraysh stressed the traditional Maronite attachment to an independent Lebanon, but also made a wider appeal for the restoration of Jerusalem to Arab rule, and aid to the victims of Israeli attacks in South Lebanon (for a complete text of Khuraysh's speech, see the Beirut daily, *Al-Anwâr*, February 4, 1975). The patriarch's references to Israeli aggression were aimed at lessening Muslim suspicions of secret Maronite (especially Phalangist)-Israeli connections and at indicating his personal interest in the South. He is a native of the Maronite village of 'Ayn Ibil which looks directly into Israel (and the ruins of Kafar Bir'im, the former Maronite village on the other side whose inhabitants were forcibly evicted in 1948, see p. 212). On July 24, 1975, less than six months after the patriarch's enthronement, the Israelis attacked 'Ayn Ibil on July 24, 1975, killing two villagers and wounding four members of the Khuraysh family.

89 Quoted in *Time* (5 July 1963), p. 34.

90 Quoted in *L'Orient*, 16 August 1966, p. 5.

91 Rondot, *Les Chrétiens d'Orient*, p. 215.

192 In the following year, 1964, the Metropolitan of Leningrad made a pilgrimage to Jerusalem and since that time numerous bishops have made the same "non-political" voyage for purposes of nourishing ties of the Arab patriarchates with the Russian Church. Patriarch Alexandros was quoted in 1951 as reaffirming "le constant attachement de l'Eglise d'Antioche à l'Eglise Russe et dénonce les intrigues anglo-américaines tramées en vue de briser ces liens..." Rondot, p. 216.

193 *Ibid.*, p. 516. Patriarch Alexandros stated publicly that he viewed Athenagoras as unable to support world peace, in that he had received his title through American influence.

194 Meinardus, *Christian Egypt: Ancient and Modern,* p. 9.

195 Bishop Shanûda was by no means the popular choice. The favorite of most Copts was the monk of Dayr Al-Makâryûs, Mattâ Al-Maskîn (Matthew the Beggar), at one time a prosperous pharmacist in Cairo. He received the call to monastic life at the age of 29, sold his considerable belongings to the benefit of the poor, and retired to the desert where, according to *Time* (December 29, 1975, p. 55), he receives up to 500 visitors daily. Though popular with the Coptic masses, he is viewed with suspicion by both the church authorities and middle- and upper-class churchmen who regard his political philosophy as Marxist and criticize him as a self-seeking demagogue.

196 Quoted in *Proche-Orient Chrétien* (Quarters I & II, 1964), p. 69.

197 *Ibid.*, extracted from *Al-Nûr,* journal of the Orthodox Youth League, 15 January 1964, pp. 1,3.

198 *Al-Safâ'*, 7 December 1963, p. 1.

199 *The Economist,* 18 January 1964, p. 8.

200 *Al-Ḥayât,* Beirut, 7 December 1965, and *L'Orient,* same date, pp. 1, 3. One month later on 1 January 1966, the Coptic observer at the Vatican Council, Mikẖâ'îl Tuwarrus, in an article in the Coptic weekly, *Al-Waṭanî,* urged his patriarch to lift the sentence of excommunication levelled against Pope Leo in 451 by Dioskorus, first Monophysite patriarch of Alexandria.

1 Quoted in *L'Orient,* 19 November 1966, p. 9.

2 Bouwen, Frans, "Vers le dialogue théologique entre l'Eglise catholique et l'Eglise orthodoxe," *Proche Orient Chrétien* (vol. I-II, 1976), pp. 105-131.

3 In an effort to remove the ambiguity with which many Western Catholics viewed the idea of rite, the late Pope Pius XII, in an encyclical published on the occasion of the 15th centenary of the death of Saint Cyril of Alexandria, urged uniate and non-uniate Christians in the East "to be persuaded and hold for certain that they will never be compelled to exchange their own legitimate rites and ancient institutions for Latin rites and institutions; both are to be regarded with equal esteem and veneration, for they surround our common mother the Church with, as it were a regal variety." Quoted in Dom Polycarp Sherwood, "The Sense of Rite," *Eastern Churches Quarterly* (Winter, 1957-1958), pp. 137-38. More recently, Pope Paul VI in his encyclical *Orientalium Ecclesiarum,* on 21 November 1964, only six weeks prior to his celebrated meeting with Athenagoras in Jerusalem, reiterated even more strongly the sentiments expressed by Pius XII and his predecessors in regard to the inviolability of the non-Latin Catholic rites. "Let all Oriental Christians know with absolute certainty that they may and ought always to retain their legitimate liturgical rites and their discipline... To those who, for reasons of ministry, are in frequent contact with the Eastern Churches and their faithful, rests the grave responsibility of acquiring an intimate knowledge of the rites, discipline, doctrine and characteristics of Oriental Christians and to hold them in highest esteem... And that their apostolic mission may enjoy the greatest efficacy, it is strongly recommended that the institutions and organizations of the Latin Rite which labor in Oriental fields subordinate themselves as much as possible to the institutions and ecclesiastical authority of the Oriental Rites." Quoted in Joseph Habbi, "L'Union de Mar Salaqa avec Rome," *L'Orient Syrien* (Second Quarter, 1966), p. 230.

4 Quoted in *Proche-Orient Chrétien* (Quarters I and II, 1964), pp. 59-60.

205 Maurice Villain, "Reflections on the Christian Communities of the Near East in Communion with Rome", *Eastern Churches Quarterly,* Autumn, 1961, p. 187.

206 Quoted in *Proche-Orient Chrétien* (Quarters I and II, 1966), pp. 71-72.

207 Cardinal Agaganian was succeeded by Ignatius Peter Batanian, who resigned in April 1976 because of age and was succeeded in turn by Hemaiagh Ghedighian, a native of Trebizond in the Pontus.

208 *Ibid.*, p. 74.

209 At the Vatican Council's concluding session, Melkite Metropolitan Ilyâs Zughbi accused the Western Church of "subtle casuistry" in its divorce practices. Referring to the not uncommon pattern in which a couple, well-connected and wealthy, "suddenly discovers an impediment that permits everything to be resolved as if by magic," Zughbi observed that "our faithful are sometimes stupefied and scandalized by it all," and concluded by urging the Church to allow divorce on certain grounds, such as abandonment, as the Orthodox Churches do. *L'Eglise Grecque Melkite au Concile,* Discours et Notes du Patriarche Maximos IV et des Prélats de son Eglise au Concile Oecuménique Vatican II (Beirut: Dar Al-Kalima, 1967), pp. 279-372. See also *Time* (18 March 1966), p. 67.

210 *The International Herald Tribune,* March 18, 1973.

211 *The Holy Qur'ân,* Sûra IV: 156-158.

212 *Al-Ḥayât,* Beirut, 17 October 1965, p. 2.

213 *The Economist,* 5 December 1963.

214 *L'Orient,* 16 October 1965, p. 1.

215 Quoted in *Al-Jundî,* Damascus, 28 December 1965, page "*mim.*"

216 *Beirut Daily Star,* 17 October 1965, p. 1.

17 *Al-Ḥayât,* 17 October 1965, p. 3.

18 *Al-Ahrâm,* Cairo, 16 October 1965, p. 1.

19 *L'Orient,* 16 October 1965, p. 1.

20 *Beirut Daily Star,* 17 October 1965, p. 1.

21 *L'Orient,* 24 October 1965, pp. 1,8.

22 *Al-Jundî,* Damscus, 28 December 1965, page "lâm."

23 *Beirut Daily Star,* 16 October 1965, p. 1.

24 *Ibid.*

25 *L'Orient,* 17 October 1965, p. 6.

26 *Ibid.*

27 Not only the Orthodox, whose patriarch's legitimacy is challenged by the presence of the Latin Patriarch, resent this situation. The Melkites themselves regard it as a primary obstacle in achieving union. Writing in 1962, Patriarch Cardinal Ṣâ'igh termed the Latin patriarchate "non seulement une inutilité, un non-sens, mais un obstacle authentique à l'unité de l'Eglise, à la nécessaire réconciliation orthodoxie-catholicisme." In an unprecedented appeal to the some 45,000 Latinized Palestinian Christians, "fruit de l'activité latine usurpante," the patriarch urged them to abandon the Latin Rite with the call: "Reviens à tes frères, à tes ancêtres, à toi-même, à ce que la Providence du Christ et son Esprit t'ont fait!" See M. Sayegh, *Catholicisme ou Latinisme* (Harisa, Lebanon:Melkite Patriarchal Press, 1962), pp. 88-90. Partly in response to the intensity with which the Melkites pursued their case Pope John in the following year (1963) abolished the titular Latin patriarchates of Antioch, Alexandria, and Constantinople; and while the Latin seat in Jerusalem is for the moment secure, its future is without doubt in jeopardy. George Every, editor of the *Eastern Churches Review,* in a letter fifteen years ago to Dom Bede Winslow, Catholic orientalist and late editor of the *Eastern Churches Quarterly,* predicted that in

"twenty years the Melkites and the local Orthodox will be sharing control of the Holy Places, and the Latins will be under Melkite protection rather than vice versa."

228 Don Peretz, *The Middle East Today,* (New York: Holt, Rinehart and Winston 1964), p. 140.

229 George Antonius, *The Arab Awakening* (Beirut: Khayat's 1939), p. 79.

230 Zeine N. Zeine, *Arab-Turkish Relations and the Emergence of Arab Nationalism* (Beirut: Khayat's, 1958), pp. 56-57.

231 *Al-Qaḥṭanîya* (1909) was indebted to Amîn Kaẓma of Homs, and the *Ḥizb Al-Lâmarkazîya Al-Idârîya Al-'Uthmânîya* (the Ottoman Decentralization Party, 1912) to Iskandar 'Ammûn of Lebanon. Antonius, *The Arab Awakening,* pp. 109-110.

232 Pierre Rondot, "The Minorities in the Arab Orient Today," *Middle East Affairs* (June-July, 1959), p. 218.

233 Hourani, *Syria and Lebanon* (London: Oxford University Press, 1946), p. 40.

234 Sâṭi' Al-Ḥuṣrî, *Muḥaḍarât fî Nushû' Al-Fikra Al-Qawmîya* (Lectures on the Evolution of Nationalist Thought), (Cairo: no publisher 1951), pp. 185-187.

235 One such leading Orthodox nationalist was Khalîl Sakâkînî who later was to serve as the first secretary of the executive committee of the Arab Congress of Palestine, which functioned in the 1920's, and as a high official in the Palestinian education ministry. In his diary, published shortly after his death in 1953, Sakâkînî recalled how in 1914 a delegation of Orthodox clergy and laity came from Jaffa to Jerusalem to propose a formation of a party to protect Christian interests. In opposing this move he told the delegation: "If your aim is political, then I do not approve it, because I am an Arab first of all, and I think it preferable that we should form a national party to unite all the sons of the Arab Nation, regardless of religion and sects, to awaken national feelings and become imbued with a new spirit." Hala Sakâkînî,

ed., The Diary of Khalîl Sakâkînî, *Kadha Anâ Yâ Dunyâ* (Such as I am, O World), (Jerusalem, Jordan: 1955), Entry 14, March, 1914, p. 71.

6 Sir Anton Bertram and Y.W.A. Young, *The Orthodox Patriarchate of Jerusalem* (London: Oxford University Press, 1926), p. 78.

7 Hourani, *Minorities in the Arab World* (London: Oxford University Press, 1947), p. 83.

8 Sa'âda "relegated Islam and Christianity to the background by reducing them to a common origin and by characterizing all belief as submission [Islam] to a metaphysical reality which is beyond the realm of rational discourse." Hisham Sharabi, "The Transformation of Ideology in the Arab World," *Middle East Journal* (Autumn, 1965), pp. 480-481. In 'Aflaq's own words, "when their national consciousness will awake completely and when they will regain their true uncorrupted characteristics, the Arab Christians will recognize that Islam constitutes for them a national culture in which they must immerse themselves so that they may understand and love it, and so that they may preserve Islam as they would preserve the most precious element in their Arabism." Quoted in Sylvia Haim, *Arab Nationalism,* p. 64.

9 *Ibid.,* p. 58.

0 Nabîh Fâris, *Al-'Arab Al-Aḥyâ'* (The Living Arabs), (Beirut: 1974), pp. 61-68, quoted in Haim, *op. cit.,* p. 62.

1 Quoted in Rondot, "Minorities in the Arab Orient Today," *Middle East Affairs* (June-July, 1959), p. 219.

2 Dr. Charles Mâlik, "The Near East: The Search for Truth," *Foreign Affairs* (30 January 1952), p. 214.

3 Haim, *op. cit.,* p. 62.

4 Hugh McLeave, *The Last Pharaoh* (London: Michael Joseph, 1969), p. 153.

245 Edward Wakin relates in *The Lonely Minority* (New York: William Morrow Co., 1963), (p. 18), how the late Salâma Mûsâ, a Copt and leading figure in contemporary Arabic literature, recalled the halcyon days of post-World War I nationalism. "Unity between Moslem and Copt was the symbol of the 1919 revolution and we used to cry out: "Long live the Crescent and the Cross." I heard learned men from Al-Azhar speaking in the churches and I saw and heard priests greeted by Al-Azhar. This unity should have been with us today, but the new developments deflected the tide of our history."

246 At the same time there were two Christian Deputy Ministers, of Housing (Najîb Ibrâhîm) and Communications ('Abd Al-Malik Sa'ad).

247 Otto F.A. Meinardus, *Christian Egypt: Faith and Life* (Cairo: The American University of Cairo Press, 1970), p. 37.

248 For a detailed analysis of the Khanka incident see *Middle-East Sketch,* December 22, 1972, pp. 17-23.

249 For a more complete view of the role of the Christian communities in the highly tribalized politics of this southern Jordanian town, see Peter Gubser, *Politics and Change in Al-Karak, Jordan,* (Oxford: Oxford University Press, 1975).

250 It should be noted that two of the four Muslim delegates from Amman were not Arabs but Circassians, descendants of that Muslim community from the Caucasus which had been settled by the Sultan in the 19th century on the East Bank of the Jordan (primarily in the towns of Amman, Jarash, and Na'ûr) to protect the annual caravan of pilgrims from Damascus to Mecca against Badu marauders.

251 Constitution of 1952 [part VI; 104 (ii), and 109(i)].

252 See The *New York Times,* 24 December 1966, p. 12.

253 Moshe M. Czudnowski and Jacob N. Landau, *The Israeli Communist Party and the Elections for the Fifth Knesset, 1961* (Palo Alto, California: The Hoover Institution on War, Revolution,

and Peace of Stanford University, 1965), p. 46.

4 Jacob M. Landau, *The Arabs in Israel* (London: Oxford University Press, 1969), pp. 141-148.

5 *The International Herald Tribune,* November 7, 1975, p. 1; December 11, 1975, p. 2.

6 *The Observer* (London), August 19, 1973, p. 6.

7 A recent example of this alliance was found in the Knesset elections of December 31, 1973. A Badu tribal leader of the Bi'r Sab'a (Beersheeba) desert region, running on the Labor alignment grouping of then Prime Minister Golda Meir, awarded his 1,500 surplus votes to Druze Shaykh Jâbir Mu'âdî, Deputy Minister of Communications and Knesset Representative from Northern Galilee, who was in danger of losing his seat by over 1,000 votes. *The International Herald Tribune,* January 4, 1974.

8 *Beirut Daily Star,* 4 November 1968, p. 1.

9 Walter Schwarz, *The Arabs in Israel* (London: Faber and Faber, 1959), p. 147.

0 For a more detailed examination of the controversy and personalities involved, see Gordon Torrey, *Syrian Politics and the Military* (Columbus, Ohio: Ohio State University Press, 1964), pp. 111-112.

1 Among the leading opponents of the move was Christian political leader and later Prime Minister, Fâris Al-Khûrî, who denounced attempts to give Islam official status as "an empty formula, ambiguous and in any case obsolete." Rondot, *Middle East Affairs* (June-July, 1959), p. 220. Repeating the principal thesis of Al-Khûrî's objection, Patriarch Ṣâ'igh in his Easter Sunday (April 9) sermon of 1950 charged that "Qui dit réligion d'Etat dit un certaine discrimination entre Musulmans et non-Musulmans... Ceux-ci seraient soumis à des obligation que chacun connaît et que nul n'a d'interêt à énumérer, étant donné les prescriptions auxquelles les dhimmi sont astreints." Rondot, *Les Chrétiens d'Orient* (Paris: J. Peyrounet et Cie., 1955), p. 229.

262 Raymond Etteldorf, *The Catholic Church in the Middle East* (New York: Macmillan, 1959), p. 74.

263 Hitti, *Lebanon in History* (London: Macmillan, 1957), p. 480.

264 Quoted in *Proche-Orient Chrétien* (July-September, 1961), p. 285.

265 A number of official sources identify Haṭûm as a Greek Orthodox Christian from the community of several thousand resident in the Jabal Al-Durûz district, but knowledgeable Druzes of the author's acquaintance claim him as one of their own.

266 See The *Beirut Daily Star,* 28 February 1966, p. 1.

267 Another U.N. Ambassador, Jamîl Bârûdî of Saudi Arabia is likewise of Arab Christian birth. A Greek Orthodox from the 'Alayh district of Mount Lebanon, Bârûdî emigrated to Saudi Arabia at the beginning of the oil boom some years before World War II, rising to political prominence only after his conversion to Islam.

268 Christians were allotted two seats from the *liwâ'* of Mosul, and one each from Baghdad and Basra.

269 Ḥannâ Khayâṭ, Minister of Health under the first provisional government of the Mandate era.

270 Phebe A. Marr, "The Political Elite in Iraq," in George Lenczowsky (ed.), *Political Elites in the Middle East,* American Enterprise Institute for Public Policy Research, Washington, D.C., 1975, p. 137.

271 Quoted in Bernard Venier, *L'Irak d'Aujourd'hui* (Paris: Librairie Armand Colin, 1963), p. 346.

272 Hilâl Najî, *Hattâ Lâ Nansâ* (Lest We Forget), (Cairo: Karnak Publishing House, 1962), pp. 60-82.

273 Interview, Father Joseph Connell, Society of Jesus (Jesuits) Al-Hikma University, Baghdad, 30 November 1965.

274 Dana Adams Schmidt, *Journey Among Brave Men* (Boston:

Little, Brown, and Company, 1964), p. 71.

75 Otto F.A. Meinardus, "Notes on Some Non-Byzantine Monasteries and Churches in the East," *Eastern Churches Review,* Volume III, No. 1, 1970, p. 55.

76 The *New York Times,* 17 August 1966, p. 8; and the *Washington Post,* same date, pp. A-1, and A-12.

77 The *New York Times,* 17 August 1966, p. 8. The defecting pilot remarked that he had been one of five or six Christians in the Air Force to have attained the rank of officer.

78 *L'Orient,* 30 January 1969, p. 6.

79 *The Daily Star,* 22 February 1969, p. 1.

80 *Al-Râ'î Al-'Am,* Kuwait, 30 January 1969, p. 1.

81 Ralph E. Crow, "Religious Sectarianism in the Lebanese Political System," *Journal of Politics* (August, 1962), pp. 494-495.

82 An effort to bring about a substantive change in the area of civil jurisdiction early in 1951 was frustrated by the passage of a new law on 2 April of that year which again left jurisdiction of all matters relating to personal status in the hands of the religious courts. A general strike of lawyers in Lebanon at the end of the year calling for repeal of the statute and the establishment of one civil legal system for all communities was successfully opposed by the heads of the religious sects, especially the Christian leaders, who managed to prevent a parliamentary attempt to reach a compromise by which the power of religious courts would have been limited. In 1953 a number of deputies proposed the abolition of communalism in the parliament, and of all ecclesiastical courts. Its passage, however, was prevented both by Muslims who insisted on attaching unacceptable demands for more Muslim representation and economic union with Syria, as well as by zealous Christians who maintained that if the present system were changed Lebanon would cease to be the haven for minorities it had always been. See Gabriel Baer, *Population and Society in the Arab East* (London: Routledge Press, 1959), p. 74; Rondot, *Les Institutions Politiques au Liban*

(des Communautés Traditionnelles à l'Etat Moderne), (Paris: Institut d'Etudes de l'Orient Coutemporain, 1947), pp. 74-75; and The *Area Handbook for Lebanon,* pp. 176-177.

283 The Constitution of Iraq, 1924, Article 13 ("provided such forms of worship do not conflict with the maintenance of order and discipline or public morality"); Syria, Constitution of 1950, Chapter I, Article 3 (iii) ("consistent with public order"); Jordan, Constitution of 1952, Part II, Article 14, quoted in text; even Lebanon included such a provision as a legal safeguard, although for different reasons.

284 Morrison, "Arab Nationalism and Islam," *Middle East Journal,* April, 1948, p. 152.

285 *Ibid.*

286 Rondot, "The Minorities in the Arab Orient Today," *Middle East Affairs* (June-July, 1959), p. 225.

287 This well-known conversion to Catholicism is said to have grown out of Fakhrî's having attended a philosophy class at the American University of Beirut, instructed by Dr. Charles Malik, a Greek Orthodox whose two brothers are Catholic priests.

288 Salibi, *A Modern History of Lebanon* (London: Weidenfeld and Nicholson, 1965), p. 173.

289 George Kirk, *Contemporary Arab Politics* (New York: Frederick A. Praeger, 1961), p. 119.

290 *Oriente Moderno* (1958), pp. 399-401. Most Christian men (save for Copts and some Armenians) in the Muslim World are not circumcized, while virtually all Muslims are circumcized.

291 Engineered by members of the Partie Populaire Syrienne, whose goals embody the Syrian nationalism of Antûn Sa'âda.

292 The Phalangist militia has not infrequently been called into service in times of crisis; it was very active during the 1958 Crisis, and during the June War of 1967 cordonned off the Jewish quarter of Beirut against possible Muslim attack.

3 Traditionally the Lebanese parliamentary districts have consisted of multi-seat constituencies, i.e. districts in which as many as six deputies are elected simultaneously. And though the seats in these districts are allotted on a proportional basis to the various sects resident there (e.g. Al-Shûf which in 1962 elected two Maronites, two Druzes, one Greek Catholic, and one Sunni Muslim deputy), all voters in the district regardless of their religion vote for every one of the sectarian seats. Frequently, therefore, slates consisting of one candidate for each of the seats would run, and, as a rule, the more moderate slate which was able to attract both Christian and Muslim (or Druze) support would win. Under Chamoun in 1952, however, the size of parliament was reduced and the districts re-organized on the basis of one-man constituencies and, where that was not possible, small-list constituencies. The latter system, while more modern and more democratic, tended to result in districts being drawn so as to include primarily one sect, and thus permit the election of a radical Christian or Muslim, whereas in the past the larger, multi-confessional districts tended to produce a more moderate representative who had successfully appealed to both Christian and Muslim voters. It was this system which was restored in 1958 and which is in force today.

4 Michael C. Hudson, "The Electoral Process and Political Development in Lebanon," *Middle East Journal* (Spring, 1966), p. 176.

5 *Ibid.*

6 *Ibid.*, p. 178. In 1943, landlords comprised 46.5% of the deputies, lawyers 33.9%, businessmen and professionals 10.4% and 10.2% respectively. In 1964 the percentages were, in the same order, 23.2%, 27.3%, 17.2%, and 32.3%, professionals now comprising the largest single bloc.

7 The Druzes, though only one third as numerous as the Shî'a Muslims, were given nearly twice as many cabinet posts. This imbalance, however, has not been reflected in recent governments.

298 Maronites held the portfolios of Defense, Agriculture, Transportation, and Health; the Orthodox controlled Education, Information, and Finance; Foreign Affairs was in the hands of a Melkite. On the Muslim side, Sunnis presided over ministries of the Interior, Economy, Tourism, Justice, and Communications; Shî'a ministers held portfolios of Labor and National Resources, while the single Druze member of the cabinet served as Minister of Planning. As may be seen from the above, several of the ministers presided over two ministries in that the latter numbered 16 and the former only 12.

299 Crow, *Journal of Politics* (August, 1962), p. 518. The Christian figure for the individual sects were Maronite (40.0%), Greek Orthodox (11.7%), Melkite (9.0%); other (2.2%). The neglect of the Shî'a in the past by the diplomatic service has generally been attributed to that community's greatly inferior level of education in comparison with all other religious sects.

300 Quoted in Crow, *op. cit.*, p. 518.

301 *Ibid.*, pp. 508-509.

302 *Ibid.*, p. 518.

303 Charles Issawi, *Middle East Journal* (Summer, 1964), p. 280.

304 *Ibid.*

305 Salibi, interview, 26 February 1966.

306 Albert Hourani, "The Christians of Lebanon," *Eastern Churches Quarterly* (Winter, 1957-58), pp. 139-40.

307 *Ibid.*

308 Quoted in an interview published in *La Revue du Liban*, 12 July 1969, p. 12.

309 Despite his successful career, Naṣrallah was generally considered to be a powerless pawn of the Christian establishment, with no authority of his own. The ambitious son of poor parents from the village of Al-Judayda in the Shûf district directly across the

Bârûk Valley from Al-Mukhtâra, home of Kamâl Junbalâṭ, traditional political leader of the Al-Shûf Druze, Naṣrallah abandoned Junbalâṭ in favor of the latter's enemy, Camille Chamoun of Dayr Al-Qamar, and it is through Chamoun's influence that he reached his present position.

10 Early in December 1975, a large truck laden with hundreds of Korans (stacked on top of a large quantity of weapons and ammunition) overturned at Kaḥḥâla, a Maronite-*Katâ'ib* stronghold commanding a precarious hairpin curve on the Damascus-Beirut highway, and scene of earlier clashes (see p. 202), whereupon the holy books were contemptuously thrown into a bonfire and burned by Jumayyil's forces. Muslims in retaliation, attacked and damaged three churches in Tripoli.

11 From an address by President Faranjîya to the Lebanese people, February 14, 1976, quoted in Kamal Salibi, *Crossroads to Civil War* (Delmar, N.Y.: Caravan Books, 1976), p. 163.

12 *Monday Morning* (a Beirut weekly), June 30 - July 6, 1975, pp. 30-31.

13 *Ibid.*, June 23-30, 1975, p. 26.

14 *L'Orient-Le Jour* (a Beirut daily), July 19, 1975, pp. 1, 14. For an earlier summary of Al-Ṣadr's views on Muslim-Christian cooperation given in an address from the high altar of the Latin (Capucin) church in the Al-Ḥamrâ' district of Beirut, see *Al-Nahâr*, February 20, 1975, p. 1.

15 *Monday Morning*, June 9-15, 1975, pp. 26-30.

16 Elie Kedourie, "Religion and Politics," *Saint Antony Papers* (Vol. IV, 1958), p. 85.

17 Peretz, *The Middle East Today* (New York: Holt, Rinehart and Winston, 1964), p. 259.

18 Hourani, *Minorities in the Arab World*, p. 57. Nor were the nationalist activities of Palestinian Christians restricted to peaceful methods alone. In one of the earliest Arab attempts to deal forcefully with Zionist expansion, an Orthodox Christian, Khalîl 'Isâ Al-Ṣabbâgh, from the heavily Muslim town of

Ṭulkaram (Christian population 208 out of a total Arab population of 3,327 in 1922), led a large-scale raid in 1923 on the nearby Jewish settlement of Hadera (Khuḍayra) for which he was sentenced to one year in prison by the British authorities.

319 See Rondot, *Les Chrétiens d'Orient,* pp. 233-234.

320 The Rt. Rev. Najîb Cubain, Interview, 26 January 1966.

321 *Statistical Bulletin of the UNRWA*, May, 1950-June, 1951, p. 28.

322 Etteldorf, *op. cit.,* p. 170, and Thomas Hussey, S.J., Director of the Pontifical Mission for Palestine, in conversation with the author, December, 1966.

323 *Ibid.*

324 Najîb Cubain, Interview, 26 January 1966.

325 Quoted by Maj. Gen. Moshe Dayan, "Israel's Border and Security Problems," *Foreign Affairs* (January, 1955), p. 7.

326 *The Times* of London, 24 March 1970, p. 19.

327 *The International Herald Tribune,* November 4, 1975, p. 2.

328 *The Washington Post,* December 23, 1975, p. B9.

329 Ḥasan Sa'ab, "Communication between Christianity and Islam," *Middle East Journal* (Winter, 1964), p. 54.

330 Hourani, *Eastern Churches Quarterly* (Winter, 1956-1957), p. 144. "The Arabic language," states Hourani, "is not only the language of the Qur'ân, it is also the language of Christian liturgy and thought; implicit in this fact lie the special problems of the Eastern Catholics, and also their unique opportunities."

331 Fayez Sayegh, "An Arab Looks at His World," *Moslem World* (October 1952), p. 256.

332 Quoted in Dalmais, *Croissance des Jeunes Nations* (June-July, 1963), p. 40.

3 Joseph Hajjar, *Les Chrétiens Uniates du Proche Orient* (Paris: Editions du Seuil, 1962), p. 341.

4 Kamal Salibi, Interview, Beirut, 26 February 1966.

5 Even 'Aflaq, however, for all his contempt for his fellow Christians who relied on the old *millet* system as the basis for their political survival, agreed that Muslims must make concessions as well by accepting Arab Christians as their equals. "Devons-nous ménager le Liban," he remarked before a conference of Algerian students in 1955, "et dire qu'il n'est pas arabe pour la seule raison que des Chrétiens-nourris de fausse idées grâce à l'impérialisme y vivent?" Michel 'Aflaq, "Notre Nationalisme Libéral Face à la Discrimination Raciale," *Orient* (Fourth Quarter, 1963), p. 189.

36 For a detailed study of one aspect of the resurgence of Coptic arts and handicrafts see the *New York Times,* 16 March 1964.

37 Quoted in Dalmais, *op. cit.,* p. 40.

38 *Al-Ḥayât,* Beirut, 29 January 1966, pp. 1,9.

39 *Ibid.,* p. 9.

40 Elie Salim, "Nationalism and Islam," *The Moslem World* (October, 1962), p. 285.

41 Quoted in *Newsweek,* 16 August 1965, p. 53.

42 Al-Ḥuṣrî, *op. cit.,* p. 185. Contrast his views (that a Christian need not give up his faith to be fully Arab) with a publication which appeared in Cairo in 1931 (apparently encouraged by the government) entitled *"Da' wa Naṣâra Al-'Arab lîl' Dukhûl fî'l-Islâm"* (A Call to Christian Arabs to Embrace Islam) by one Khalîl Iskandar Qubruṣî, a Palestinian (though his name indicates family ties with Cyprus) of Orthodox Christian origin, who urged his fellow Christians to adopt Islam because it was "the religion of the Arabs;" otherwise they would continue to give rise to suspicions in Muslim quarters that they were in league with European Christian imperialists. Quoted in Haim, *Arab*

Nationalism, (Berkeley: The University of California Press, 1962), pp. 59-61.

343 Hourani, *Minorities in the Arab World,* p. 124.

344 Hazim Nuseibeh, *The Ideas of Arab Nationalism* (Ithaca: Cornell University Press, 1956), p. 91.

345 *L'Orient,* 17 October 1965, p. 8.

346 Sa'ab, *Middle East Journal* (Winter, 1964), p. 54.

347 *L'Orient,* 1 January 1966, p. 1.

BIBLIOGRAPHY

Public Documents

Iraq, *Al-Majmû'a Al-Iḥṣâ'îya Tasjîl ' Amm, 1957* (The General Census of 1957), Wizâra Al-Dâkhilîya (Ministry of the Interior), Baghdad, 1962. Ten volumes.

Iraq, *The Statistical Yearbook of Iraq* (1962-69), Ministry of the Interior, Baghdad.

Iraq, *Al-Iḥṣâ' Al-Tarbîyi: Taqrîr Al-Sanawî 1961/62* (Educational Statistics, Annual Report 1961/62), Wizâra Al-Tarbîya wa Al-Ta'lîm (Ministry of Education and Guidance), Baghdad, 1963.

Israel, *Census of Population and Housing 1972,* Bureau of Statistics, Jerusalem, 1976.

Israel, *The General Census of Housing, 1961,* Ministry of the Interior, 1963, Jerusalem.

Israel, *The Statistical Abstract of Israel* (1965), Central Bureau of Statistics, Tel Aviv, 1966.

Jordan, *Awwal Ta'dâd 'Amm li Al-Sukân wa Al-Musâkin 1964* (The First Census of Population and Housing, 1964), Dâ'ira Al-Iḥṣâ'ât Al-'Amma (General Bureau of Statistics), Amman, 1961-65. Ten Volumes.

Jordan, *Al-Taqrîr Al-Sanawî li Al-'Amm Al-Dirâsîyi 1960-61* (Annual Report of the Academic Year 1960-61), Wizâra Al-Tarbîya wa al-Ta'lîm (Ministry of Education and Guidance), Amman, 1961.

Jordan, *Quarterly Bulletin of Statistics,* Ministry of the Interior, Amman (1st, 2nd, 3rd, and 4th quarters of 1965).

Jordan, *A Social Survey of Amman,* Ministry of Social Affairs, Amman, 1960.

Jordan, *The Statistical Yearbook of Jordan* (1958-1970), Ministry of the Interior, Amman.

Lebanon, *Recueil de Statistiques de la Syrie et du Liban 1942-43*, Ministry of Information, Beirut, 1945.

Palestine, *The General Census of 1922*, The British Mandate Administration, Jerusalem.
Palestine, *The General Census of 1931*, The British Mandate Administration, Jerusalem.
Palestine, *The Statistical Abstract of Palestine 1944-45*, Central Bureau of Statistics, Jerusalem, 1946.

Syria, *The 1960 Census of Population and Housing*, Ministry of the Interior, Damascus, 1962.
Syria, *The Statistical Abstract of Syria* (1950-1966), Ministry of the Interior, Damascus.

The United Arab Republic, *Al-Taʿdâd Al-ʿAmm li Al-Sukân 1960* (General Census of Population, 1960) Maṣlaḥa Al-Iḥṣâ' wa Al-Ta'dâd (Bureau of Statistics and the Census), Cairo, 1962.

Books

Abou, Selim. Le Bilinguisme Arabe-Français au Liban. Paris: Presses Universitaires de France, 1962.
Abou, Selim. *Enquêtes sur les Langues en Usage au Liban*. Beirut: Imprimerie Catholique, 1961.
Addison, James Thayer. *The Christian Approach to the Moslem*. New York: Columbia University Press, 1942.
Adeny, Walter F. *The Greek and Eastern Churches*. New York: Charles Scribner's Sons, 1908.
Agwani, M.S., ed. *The Lebanese Crisis of 1958*. London: Asia Publishing House, 1965.
Akrawi, Metti, and Matthews, R.D. *Education in the Arab Countries of the Near East*. Washington, D.C.: American Council on Education, 1949.
Antonius, George. *The Arab Awakening*. Beirut: Khayat's, 1939.

Arberry, A.J., ed. *Religion in the Middle East,* London: Cambridge University Press, 1969, 2 vols.

Armstrong, A.H., and Fry, E.L.B. *Rediscovering Eastern Christendom* (Essays in Memory of Dom Bede Winslow). London: Darton, Longman and Todd, 1963.

Atamian, Sarkis. *The Armenian Community.* New York: The Philosophical Library, 1955.

Al-Athîr, 'Izz Al-Dîn, Ibn. *Kâmil Al-Tawârikh* (The Perfect History). A Twelfth Century Chronicle of the Crusades. Portions translated from Arabic into French by Barbier de Reynard in "Historiens Orientaux," *Recueil des Historiens des Croissades,* Paris: 1872-1905; and into English by E.J. Costello in Francesco Gabrielli, ed., *Arab Historians of the Crusades,* London: Routledge and Kegan Paul, 1969.

Atiya, Aziz S. *A History of Eastern Christianity.* Notre Dame, Ind.: University of Notre Dame Press, 1968.

Atiyeh, Edward. *An Arab Tells His Story: A Study in Loyalties.* London: John Murray, 1946.

Attwater, Donald. *The Uniate Churches of the East.* London: Geoffrey Chapman, 1961.

Attwater, Donald. *The Dissident Churches of the East.* London: Geoffrey Chapman, 1961.

Ayrout, Henry Habib, S.J. *The Egyptian Peasant.* Boston: Beacon Press, 1963.

Badger, Rev. George Percy. *The Nestorians and Their Rituals.* London: Joseph Masters, 1852. Two Volumes.

Baer, Gabriel. *Population and Society in the Arab East.* London: Routledge Press, 1959.

Bannister, J.T. *A Survey of The Holy Land.* Bath: Binns & Goodwin, 1844.

Barenton, Père Hilaire, F.M.C. *La France Catholique en Orient.* Paris: Poussielgue, 1920.

Bartlett, W.H. *Jerusalem Revisited.* London: Arthur Hall, Virtue & Co., 1855.

Batal, James. *Assignment: Near East* (A Survey of Past and Present Christian Missions in the Near East). New York: Friendship Press, 1950.

Bell, Richard. *The Origin of Islam in its Christian Environment.* London: Macmillan, 1926.

Benham, P. *Nafaḥât Al-Khizâm aw Ḥayât Al-Baṭriyârk Ifrâm* (Biography of the late Ephraim Barṣawm, Jacobite Patriarch of Antioch). Mosul: Archdiocese Press, 1959.

Benz, Ernst. *The Eastern Orthodox Church.* Garden City, New York: Doubleday and Company, 1963.

Bertram, Sir Anton, and Young, Y.W.A. *The Orthodox Patriarchate of Jerusalem* (Report of the Commission appointed by the Government of Palestine to inquire and report upon certain controversies between the Orthodox Patriarchate of Jerusalem and the Arab Orthodox Community). London: Oxford University Press, 1926.

Beth, Karl. *Die Orientalische Christenheit der Mittelmeerländer.* Berlin: E.K. Schwatoschke und Sohn, 1902.

Binder, Leonard. *The Ideological Revolution in the Middle East.* New York: Wiley and Sons, 1964.

Binder, Leonard, ed. *Politics in Lebanon.* New York: Wiley and Sons, 1966.

Bliss, Frederick Jones. *The Religions of Modern Syria and Palestine.* New York: Charles Scribner's Sons, 1912.

Bliss, Howard S., ed. *The Reminiscences of Daniel Bliss.* New York: Fleming H. Revell Co., 1920.

Boghossian, Roupen. *La Haute-Djézireh.* Aleppo: Imprimerie Chiras, 1952.

Bréhier, Louis. *Le Schisme Oriental du XIe Siècle.* Paris: Ernest Leroux, 1899.

Bridgeman, Charles T. *Jerusalem at Worship.* Jerusalem: Syrian Orthodox Orphanage Press, 1932.

Browne, W.H. *The Catholicos of the East and His People,* Being the Impressions of Five Years' Work in the Archbishop of Canterbury's Assyrian Mission. London: Faith Press, 1892.

Browing, Robert. *Justinian and Theodora.* London: Weidenfeld and Nicholson, 1971.

Burckhardt, John L. *Travels in Syria and the Holy Land.* London: John Murray, 1822.

Butcher, Edith L. *The Story of the Church in Egypt.* London: Smith, Elder and Company, 1897. Two Volumes.

Carne, John. *Syria, The Holy Land and Asia Minor, Etc.* London: Fisher, Son & Co., 1836.

Cattan, Basile. *L'Hellénisme dans la Première Constitution de l'Eglise Gréco-Melkite.* Rome: Institut Pie IX, 1920.

Chamoun, Camille. *Crise au Moyen-Orient.* Paris: Editions Gallimard, 1963.

Charles, H., S.J. *Jésuites Missionaires dans la Syrie et le Proche-Orient.* Paris: Gabriel Beauchesne, 1929.

Charles-Roux, François. *France et Chrétiens d'Orient.* Paris: no publisher, 1939.

Chauleur, Sylvestre, *Histoire des Coptes d'Egypte.* Paris: Edititions de Vieux Colomber, 1960.

Cheiko, L. *Al-Adâb Al-'Arabîya fî Al-Qarn Al-Tâsi' 'Ashar* (Arab Culture in the XIXth Century). Beirut: Imprimerie Catholique, 1924-1926. Second Edition. Two Volumes.

Churchill, Col. Charles Henry. *The Druzes and the Maronites under Turkish Rule 1840-1860.* London: Quaritch, 1862.

Churchill, Charles W. *The City of Beirut.* Beirut: Dâr Al-Kitâb, 1954.

de Ciercq, Abbé Charles. *Les Eglises Unies d'Orient.* Paris: Bloud et Gay, 1934.

Cohen, Abner. *Arab Border Villages in Israel.* Manchester: Manchester University Press, 1965.

Cramer, Maria. *Das Christlich-Koptische Ägypten Einst und Heute.* Wiesbaden: Otto Harrassowitz, 1959.

Cromer, The Earl of. *Modern Egypt.* London: Macmillan & Co., Ltd., 1908, 2 vols.

Curzon, Robert Jr. *Visits to Monasteries in the Levant.* London: John Murray, 1849.

Czudnowski, Moshe M., and Landau, Jacob M. *The Israeli Communist Party and the Elections for the Fifth Knesset 1961.* Palo Alto, California: The Hoover Institution on War, Revolution and Peace of Stanford University, 1965.

Davis, Helen Clarkson. *Some Aspects of Religious Liberty of Nationals in the Near East.* New York: n.p. 1938.

Davis, Helen Miller. *Constitutions, Electoral Laws and Treaties of the States of the Near and Middle East.* Durham, North Carolina: Duke University Press, 1953.

Devresse, Robert. *Le Patriarcat d'Antioche depuis la Paix de l' Eglise jusqu'à la Conquête Arabe.* Paris: J. Gabalda et Cie., 1945.

Dib, Pierre. *L'Eglise Maronite.* Paris: Librairie Letouzey et Ané, 1930. Two Volumes.

Al-Dibs, Joseph. *Ta'rîkh Sûriyâ* (A History of Syria). Beirut: Imprimerie Catholique, 1893-1905, Volume XV.

Al-Dibs, Joseph. *La Perpétuelle Orthodoxie des Maronites.* Arras: Imprimerie Moderne, 1896.

Dick, Ignace. *Qu'est-ce que l'Orient Chrétien?* Paris: Casterman, 1965.

ed-Dine, Chehab. *La Géographie Humaine de Beyrouth.* Paris: Imprimerie de l'Université de Paris, 1953.

Dodd, Stuart Carter. *A Controlled Experiment on Rural Hygiene in Syria.* Beirut: The American University of Beirut Press, 1934.

Dodd, Stuart Carter. *Social Relations in the Middle East.* Beirut: The American University of Beirut Press, 1946.

Doughty, Charles. *Arabia Deserta.* London: Jonathan Cape, Ltd., 1926.

Duff-Gordon, Lady Lucie. *Letters from Egypt* (reedited, with additional letters,by Gordon Waterfield). London: Routledge and Kegan Paul, 1969.

Al-Duwayhî, Istafân. *Ṭa' rîkh Al-Ṭâ' ifa Al-Mârûnîya* (A History of the Maronite Sect). Beirut: Imprimerie Catholique, 1870.

Eddé, Jacques. *La Géographie Humaine du Liban et de la Syrie.* Beirut: Imprimerie Catholique, 1941.

Eid, Emile. *La Figure Juridique du Patriarche.* Rome: Scuola Grafica Salesiana Pio XI, 1962.

Einhardt, W.C., and Lamsa, George N. *The Oldest Christian People.* New York: Macmillan, 1926.

Ellis, Harry B. *Israel and the Middle East.* New York: Ronald Press, 1957.

Etteldorf, Raymond. *The Catholic Church in the Middle East.* New York: Macmillan, 1959.

Famin, César. *L'Histoire de la Rivalité et du Protectorat des Eglises Chrétiennes en Orient.* Paris: Fiemin-Didot, 1853.
Faris, Nabih Amin, and Hussein, Muhammad Tewfik. *The Crescent in Crisis.* Lawrence: The University of Kansas Press, 1955.
Fattal, Antoine. *Le Statut Légal des non-Musulmans en Pays d'Islam.* Beirut: Imprimerie Catholique, 1958.
Fedden, Robin. *Syria.* London: Robert Hale, Ltd., 1946.
Festugière, A.J. *Les Moines d'Orient.* Paris: Cerf, 1964.
Fiey, J.M., O.P. *Assyrie Chrétienne* (Contribution à l'Etude de l'Histoire et de la Géographie Ecclésiastiques et Monastiques du Nord de l'Iraq). Beirut: Imprimerie Catholique, 1967, Two Volumes.
Fiey, J.M., O.P. *Mossoul Chrétienne.* Beirut: Imprimerie Catholique, 196?
Fisher, Sidney, ed. *Social Forces in the Middle East.* Ithaca, New York: Cornell University Press, 1955.
Fisher , W.S. *The Middle East.* London: Methuen, 1961.
Foley, Rolla. *The Song of the Arab* (The Religious Ceremonies, Shrines, and Folk Music of the Holy Land Christian Arabs). New York: Macmillan, 1953.
Foreign Area Studies Division of the American University. *Area Handbook for Syria.* Washington, D.C.: 1965.
Fortescue, Adrian. *The Eastern Uniate Churches.* New York: Frederick Ungar, 1923.
Fortescue, Adrian. *The Orthodox Eastern Church.* London: The Catholic Truth Society Press, 1916.
Fowler, Rev. Montague. *Christian Egypt, Past, Present and Future.* London: Church Newspaper Company, Ltd., 1901.
Fuller, Anne H. *Buarij: Portrait of a Lebanese Muslim Village.* Cambridge: Harvard University Press, 1961.

Gallman, Waldemar J. *Iraq under General Nuri.* Baltimore: Johns Hopkins Press, 1963.

Geary, Grattan. *Through Asiatic Turkey* (Narrative of a Journey from Bombay to Bosporus). London: Sampson Low, Marston, Searle & Rivington, 1878, 2 vols.

Al-Ghazâlî, Muḥammad. *Al-Ta'sûb wa Al-Tasâmûḥ bayn Al-Masîḥîya wa Al-Islâm* (Fanaticism and Tolerance between Christianity and Islam). Cairo: Dâr Al-Kitâb Al-'Arabîyi, no date.

Ghibrâ'îl, Mîkhâ'îl 'Abd-Allah. *Ta'rîkh Al-Kanîsa Al-Anṭakîya Al-Siryânîya Al-Mârûnîya* (The History of the Syrian Antiochaean Maronite Church). Ba'bda: Maṭb'a Lubnânîya, 1904. Two Volumes.

Giannini, Amadeo. *L'Ultimo Fase della Questionne Orientale 1913-1932*. Rome: Instituto per l'Oriente, 1933.

Gibb, H.A.R., and Bowen, Harold. *Islamic Society and the West*. London: Oxford University Press, 1957. Volume I.

Gillen, J.F.J., ed. *Area Handbook for Lebanon*. Washington, D.C. Human Relations Area Files, 1957.

Glubb, Sir John Bagot Pasha. *A Soldier with the Arabs*. London: Hobber and Stoughton, 1957.

Gordon, Helen Cameron. *Syria As It Is*. London: Methuen, 1939.

Gubser, Peter, *Politics and Change in Al-Karak, Jordan*. Oxford: Oxford University Press, 1973.

Gulick, John. *Social Structure and Cultural Change in a Lebanese Village*. New York: Wenner-Green Foundation for Anthropological Research, 1955.

Gulick, John. *Tripoli, A Modern Arab City*. Cambridge: Harvard University Press, 1967.

Haddad, George. *Fifty Years of Modern Syria and Lebanon*. Beirut: Dâr Al-Ḥayât, 1950.

Haim, Sylvia G., ed. *Arab Nationalism*. Berkeley: The University of California Press, 1962.

Hajjar, Joseph. *Les Chrétiens Uniates du Proche Orient*. Paris: Editions du Seuil, 1962.

Hamidé, Abdul Rahman. *La Région d'Alep*. Paris: Imprimerie de l'Université de Paris, 1959.

Hamidé, Abdul Rahman, *La Ville d'Alep*. Damascus: Imprimerie de l'Université de Damas, 1959.

Hardy, Edward Rochie. *Christian Egypt* (Christianity and Nationalism in the Patriarchate of Alexandria). New York: Oxford University Press, 1952.

Harfouche, Jamal Karam. *Social Structure of Low-Income Families in Lebanon*. Beirut: Khayat's, 1965.

Harris, George C., ed. *Area Handbook for Iraq*. Washington, D.C.: Human Relations Area Files, 1958.

Harris, George C., ed. *Area Handbook for Jordan*. Washington, D.C.: Human Relations Area Files, 1957.

Hayek, Michel. *Al-Masîḥ fî Al-Islâm* (The Christ in Islam). Beirut: Imprimerie Catholique, 1962.

Hayek, Michel. *Liturgie Maronite*. Paris: Maison Mame, 1964.

Hernandez, A.S. *Iglesias de Oriente*. Santander: Sal Terrae, 1963.

Hid, Evangelos. *Etude sur l'Origine des Grecs-Melkites*. Rome: Imprimerie de la Propagande, 1901.

Hitti, Philip Khuri. *History of the Arabs*, 9th edition. New York: Saint Martin's Press, 1967.

Hitti, Philip Khuri. *The Impact of the West on Syria and Lebanon in the XIXth Century*. Paris: Librarie des Méridiens, 1955.

Hitti, Philip Khuri. *Lebanon in History*. London: Macmillan, 1957.

Hitti, Philip Khuri. *The Near East in History*. New York: Macmillan, 1961.

Hitti, Philip Khuri. *A Short History of Lebanon*. New York: Macmillan, 1965.

Hitti, Philip Khuri. *Syrians in America*. New York: George H. Doran Company, 1924.

Hopwood, Derek. *The Russian Presence in Syria and Palestine 1843-1914* (Church and Politics in the Near East). Oxford: Clarendon Press, 1969.

Horner, Norman A. *Rediscovering Christianity Where it Began*. Beirut: Heidelberg Press, 1974.

Hosmy, Basile. *Capitulations et Protections des Chrétiens au Proche-Orient*. No publisher, no date.

Hourani, Albert H. *Arabic Thought in the Liberal Age*. London: Oxford University Press, 1962.

Hourani, Albert H. *Minorities in the Arab World*. London: Oxford University Press, 1947.

Hourani, Albert H. *Syria and Lebanon*. London: Oxford University Press, 1946.

Howard, Harry N. *The King-Crane Commission*. Beirut: Khayat's 1963.

Hudson, Ellis H. *Non-Venereal Syphilis* (A Sociological and Medical Study of *Bejel* in Deir-ez-Zor). London: E.& S. Livingstone, 1958.

Hudson, Michael C. *The Precarious Republic* (Political Modernization in Lebanon), New York: Random House, 1968.

Hughes, Philip. *The Church in Crisis*. London: Oxford University Press, 1961.

Hurewitz, J.C. *Diplomacy in the Near and Middle East* (A Documentary Record: 1535-1914). New York: D. Van Nostrand Co., 1956.

Al-Ḥusaynî, Isḥâq Mûsâ. *The Moslem Brethren*. Beirut: Khayat's 1956.

Al-Ḥuṣrî, Sâṭî'. *Muḥâḍarât fî Nushû' Al-Fikra Al-Qawmîya* (Lectures on the Evolution of Nationalist Thought). Cairo: 1951. no publisher.

Al-Ḥuṣrî, Sâṭî'. *Arabism First*. Beirut: Dâr Al-'Ilm, 1958.

Al-Ḥuṣrî, Sâṭî'. *Reports on the Condition of Education in Syria During the Year 1945*. Damascus: Government Press, 1945.

Inchbold, A.C. *Under the Syrian Sun*. London: Hutchinson & Co., 1906, 2 vols.

Izzeddin, Halim Sa'id Abu, ed. *Lebanon and its Provinces*. Beirut: Khayat's 1963.

Jenin, Raymond. *Les Eglises Orientales et Les Rites Orientaux*. Paris: Maison de la Bonne Presse, 1922.

Jessup, Henry Harris. *Fifty-Three Years in Syria*. New York: Revell & Company, 1910. Two Volumes.

Joseph, John. *The Nestorians and Their Muslim Neighbors*. Princeton: Princeton University Press, 1961.

Jugie, Martin. *Le Schisme Byzantin* (Aperçu Historique et Doctrinal). Pairs: P. Lethielleux, 1941.

Jurji, Edward Jabra. *The Middle East: Its Religion and Culture.* Philadelphia: Westminster Press, 1956.

Kawerau, Peter. *Amerika und die Orientalischen Kirchen* (Ursprung und Anfang der Amerikanischen Mission unter den Nationalkirchen Westäsiens). Berlin: Walter de Gruyter, 1958.

Kawerau, Peter. *Die Jakobitische Kirche im Zeitalter der Syrichen Renaissance.* Berlin: Walter de Gruyter, 1960.

Kerr, Walter, ed. *Lebanon in the Last Years of Feudalism 1840-1868.* Beirut: Imprimerie Catholique, 1959.

Keramé, Oreste. *Notre Vocation et Notre Ame de Chrétiens d'Orient.* (no publisher, no date).

Khadduri, Majid. *War and Peace in the Law of Islam.* Baltimore: Johns Hopkins Press, 1955.

Al-Khalidi, Mustafa, and Al-Farrukh, Omar. *Missions and Imperialism.* Beirut: No publisher, no date.

Khamis, Salim H. *Report on Infant Mortality Survey of Rural Lebanon.* Beirut: American University of Beirut Press, 1955.

Khuri, Fred J. *The Arab Israeli Dilemma.* Syracuse, New York: Syracuse University Press, 1968.

King, Archdale A. *The Rites of Eastern Christendom.* Rome: The Catholic Book Agency, 1947-48. Two Volumes.

Kirk, George. *Contemporary Arab Politics.* New York: Frederick A. Praeger, 1961.

Konikoff, A. *Transjordan — An Economic Survey.* Jerusalem: Economic Research Institute of the Jewish Agency for Palestine, 1946.

Kyriakos, Mikha'il. *Copts and Moslems under British Control.* London: Smith, Elder and Company, 1911.

Lammens, Henri. *La Syrie.* Beirut: Imprimerie Catholique, 1921.

Landau, Jacob M. *The Arabs in Israel.* London: Oxford University Press, 1969.

Lerner, Daniel. *The Passing of Traditional Society.* Glencoe, Illinois: The Free Press, 1958.

Leroy, Jules. *Monks and Monasteries of the Near East*. London: G. Harrap, Ltd., 1963. Translated from the French edition of 1958 by Peter Collins.

Lewis, Bernard. *The Emergence of Modern Turkey*. London: Oxford University Press, 1961.

Liesel, Rev. Nikolaus. *The Eucharistic Liturgies of the Eastern Churches*. Collegeville, Minnesota: Saint John's Abbey Press: 1963.

Longrigg, Stephen. *Iraq: 1900-1950*. London: Oxford University Press, 1953.

Longrigg, Stephen. *The Middle East*. London: Duckworth, 1963.

Longrigg, Stephen. *Syria and Lebanon under French Mandate*. London: Oxford University Press, 1958.

Luke, Harry Charles. *The Handbook of Palestine and Transjordan*. London: Macmillan, 1930.

Luke, Harry Charles. *Mosul and its Minorities*. London: Martin Hopkinson, 1925.

Malek, Yusuf. *The British Betrayal of the Assyrians*. Chicago: The National Assyrian League of America Press, 1935.

Mansour, Atallah. *Waiting for the Dawn*. London: Secker & Warburg, 1975.

Meinardus, Otto F.A. *Christian Egypt: Ancient and Modern*. Cairo: Cahiers d'Histoire Egyptienne, 1965.

Meinardus, Otto F.A. *Christian Egypt: Faith and Life*. Cairo: The American University in Cairo Press, 1970.

Meinardus, Otto F.A. *Monks and Monastereis of the Egyptian* Deserts. Cairo: American University in Cairo Press, 1961.

Melia, Jean. *Chez les Chrétiens d'Orient*. Paris: Fasquelle, 1929.

Meo, Leila M.T. *Lebanon: Improbable Nation*. Bloomington, Indiana: University of Indiana Press, 1965.

Meyendorff, John. *The Orthodox Church*. New York: Random House, 1962. Translated from the French edition of 1960 by John Chapin.

Meyendorff, John. *Orthodoxie et Catholicité*. Paris: Editions du Seuil, 1965.

Morrison, Stanley, A. *Middle East Survey* (The Political, Social and Religious Problems). London: The SCM Press, 1954.

Mounayer, Joseph. *Les Synodes Syriens Jacobites*. Beirut: Imprimerie Catholique, 1963.

Najî, Hilâl. *Ḥattâ Lâ Nansâ* (Lest We Forget). Cairo: Karnak Publishing House, 1962.

Nau, François. *Les Arabes Chrétiens de Mesopotamie et de la Syrie*. Paris: Imprimerie Nationale, 1933.

Nouss, Izzet. *La Population de la Syrie* (Etude Démographique et Géographique. Paris: no publisher, 1951.

Nuseibeh, Hazim Zaki. *The Ideas of Arab Nationalism*. Ithaca, New York: Cornell University Press, 1956.

Patai, Raphael. *The Kingdom of Jordan*. Princeton: Princeton University Press, 1958.

Patriarcat Grec-Melkite Catholique. *L'Eglise Grecque Melkite au Concile* (Discours et Notes du Patriarche Maximos IV et des Prélats de son Eglise au Concile Œcuménique Vatican II). Beirut: Dâr Al-Kalima, 1967.

Peake, Frederick Gerald. *The History of Jordan and its Tribes*. Coral Gables, Florida: University of Miami Press, 1958.

Peretz, Don. *Israel and the Palestine Arabs*. Washington, D.C.: Middle-East Institute, 1958.

Peretz, Don. *The Middle East Today*. New York: Holt, Rinehart and Winston, 1964.

Perkins, Justin. *Residence of Eight Years in Persia Among the Nestorian Christans, with Notices of the Muhammedans*. New York: Allen, Morrill and Wardwell, 1843.

Polk, William Rowe. *The Opening of South Lebanon 1788-1840* (A Study of the Impact of the West on the Middle East). Cambridge, Massachusetts: Harvard University Press, 1963.

Porter, J.L. *Five Years in Damascus*. London: John Murray, 1870.

Qub'ayn, Fâhin 'Isâ. *Crisis in Lebanon*. Washington, D.C.: Middle-East Institute, 1961.

Rabbânî, Thomas J. *La Cathedrale du Saint-Esprit et les Œuvres Missionaires du Diocèse de Homs et Hama*. Beirut: Imprimerie Catholique, 1935.

Rabbath, Antoine. *Documents Inédits pour Servir à l'Histoire du Christianisme en Orient*. Beirut: Imprimerie Catholique, 1907-1921. Two Volumes.

Rabbath, Edmond. *L'Evolution Politique de la Syrie sous Mandat*. Paris: Librairie Marcel Rivière, 1928.

Rabbath, Edmond. *L'Unité Syrienne et Devenir Arabe*. Paris: Librairie Marcel Rivière, 1937.

Riech, S. *Etudes sur les Villages Araméens de l'Anti-Liban*. Beirut: Imprimerie Catholique, 1936.

Ristelheuber, René. *Traditions Françaises au Liban*. Paris: Felix Alcan, 1918.

Rondot, Pierre. *Les Chrétiens d'Orient*. Paris: J. Peyronnet et Cie., 1955.

Rondot, Pierre. *Les Institutions Politiques du Liban* (des Communautés Traditionnelles à l'Etat Moderne). Paris: Institut d'Etudes de l'Orient Contemporain, 1947.

Runciman, Steven. *The Eastern Schism*. Oxford: Clarendon Press, 1955.

Runciman, Steven. *The Great Church in Captivity*. Cambridge University Press. London, 1968.

Rustow, Dankwart. *Politics and Westernization in the Near East*. Princeton: Princeton Center of International Studies, 1958.

Sa'ab, Ḥasan. *The Arab Federalists of the Ottoman Empire*. Amsterdam: Djambatan Press, 1958.

Safa, Elie. *L'Emigration Libanaise*. Beirut: Imprimerie de l'Université Saint-Joseph, 1960.

Salibi, Kamal. *Crossroads to Civil War — Lebanon 1958-76*. Delmar, New York: Caravan Books, 1976.

Salibi, Kamal. *Maronite Historians of Medieval Lebanon*. Beirut: American University of Beirut Press, 1959.

Salibi, Kamal. *A Modern History of Lebanon*. London: Weidenfeld and Nicholson, 1965.

Sanjian, Avedis K. *The Armenian Communities in Syria under Ottoman Dominion*. Cambridge, Massachusetts: Harvard University Press, 1965.

Sayegh, Anîs. *Lubnân Al-Ṭâ'ifî* (Sectarian Lebanon). Beirut: Dâr Al-Sirâ' Al-Fikrî, 1955.
Sayegh, Patriarch Maximos IV. *Catholicisme ou Latinisme?* Harisa, Lebanon: Patriarchal Press, 1961.
Sayegh, Patriarch Maximos IV. *The Eastern Churches and Catholic Unity*. Freiburg: Herder, 1963.
Sayegh, Patriarch Maximos IV. *Voix de l'Eglise Melkite*. Basel: Herder, 1962.
Schmemann, Alexander. *The Historical Road of Eastern Orthodoxy*. London: Harvill Press, 1963.
Schmidt, Dana Adams. *Journey among Brave Men*. Boston: Little, Brown, and Company, 1964.
Schumacher, Gottlieb. *Northern 'Ajlûn*. London: Alexander P. Watt, 1890.
Schwartz, Walter. *The Arabs in Israel*. London: Faber and Faber, 1959.
Seale, Patrick. *The Struggle for Syria* (A Study in Post-War Arab Politics 1945-1958). London: Oxford University Press, 1965.
Sellers Robert Victor. *The Council of Chalcedon*. London: SPC Press, 1953.
Sharabi, Hisham, *Arab Intellectuals and the West* (The Formative Years, 1875-1914). Baltimore: Johns Hopkins Press, 1970.
Smith, Margaret. *Studies of Early Mysticism in the Near and Middle East*. London: Macmillan, 1931.
Sparrow, Gerald. *Modern Jordan*. London: Allen and Unwin, 1961.
Stafford, Ronald S. *The Tragedy of the Assyrians*. London: Allen and Unwin, 1935.
Stebbing, Henry. *The Christian in Palestine*. London: George Virtue, ca. 1850.
Stewart, Desmond. *Turmoil in Beirut*. London: Allen and Wingate, 1958.
Stewart, Desmond, and Haylock, John. *New Babylon: A Portrait of Iraq*. London: Collins, 1956.
Sweetman, J. Windrow. *Islam and Christian Theology*. London: Lutterworth Press, 1955. Volume II.

Thoumin, Richard. *La Géographie de la Syrie Centrale*. Paris: no publisher, 1936.

Tibawi, A.L. *American Interests in Syria 1800-1901* (A Study of Educational, Literary and Religious Work). Oxford: Clarendon Press, 1966.

Thubron, Colin. *Mirror to Damascus*. London: Heinemann, 1967.

Torrey, Gordon. *Syrian Politics and the Military 1945-1958*. Columbus, Ohio: Ohio State University Press, 1964.

Touma, Toufic. *Un Village de Montagne au Liban*. Paris: Paris-La Haye, 1958.

Tristram, H.B. *The Land of Israel: A Journal of Travels in Palestine*. London: Society for Promoting Christian Knowledge, 1865.

Tütsch, Hans E. *Facets of Arab Nationalism*. Detroit: Wayne State University Press, 1965.

Venier, Bernard. *L'Irak d'Aujourd'hui*. Paris: Librairie Armand Colin, 1963.

de Vries, Guglielmo, S.J. *Oriente Cristiano Ieri e Oggi*. Rome: Societa Grafica Romana, 1949.

Wakin, Edward. *The Lonely Minority*. New York: William Morrow and Company, 1963.

Weulersse, Jacques. *Paysans de Syrie et du Proche-Orient*. Paris: Librairie Gailimard, 1946.

Weulersse, Jacques. *Pays des Alouites*. Tours: Arrault, 1940. Two volumes.

Wigram, Rev. W.A. *The Assyrians and Their Neighbors*. London: G. Bell and Sons, 1929.

Wigram, Rev. W.A. *The Cradle of Mankind*. London: A & C. Black, Ltd., 1922.

William (Guilelmus), Archbishop of Tyre. *Historia Rerum in Partibus Transmarinia Gestarum* (A History of Deeds Done Beyond the Sea). Translated from the Latin by Emily A. Babcock and A.C. Krey. New York: Columbia University Press, 1943. Original ca. 1185.

Winder, Bayly, and Kirtzek, James, eds. *The World of Islam*. London: Macmillan, 1959.
Worrell, William H. *A Short Account of the Copts*. Ann Arbor, Michigan: University of Michigan Press, 1945.
Wortabet, Gregory M. *Syria and the Syrians*. London: James Madden, 1856. Two Volumes.
Wortabet, Rev. John. *Researches in the Religions of Syria*. London: Nisbet and Company, 1860.

Ya'qûb, Ignatius III. *Dufqât Al-Ṭayyib fî Ta'rîkh Dayr Al-Qadîs Mâr Mattâ Al-'Ajîb* (A History of Mar Mattai Monastery). Beirut: Imprimerie Catholique, 1961.
Yaukey, David. *Fertility Differences in a Modernizing Country*. Princeton: Princeton University Press, 1961.
Young, T. Cuyler, ed. *Near-Eastern Culture and Society*. Princeton: Princeton University Press, 1951.

Zander, Walter. *Israel and the Holy Places of Christendom*. London: Weidenfeld & Nicolson, 1971.
Zankov, S. *The Eastern Orthodox Church*. London: The SCM Press, 1929.
Al-Zayla, Na'îm. *Sham'ûn Yatakalam* (Chamoun Speaks). Beirut: Maṭba'a Al-Jihâd, 1959.
Zeine, Zeine N. *Arab-Turkish Relations and the Emergence of Arab Nationalism*. Beirut: Khayat's 1958.
Zeine, Zeine N. *The Struggle for Arab Independence* (Western Diplomacy and the Rise and Fall of Faisal's Kingdom in Syria). Beirut: Khayat's, 1960.
Zeltzer, Moshe. *Aspects of Near East Society*. New York: Bookman Associates, 1962.
Zernov, Nicholas. *Eastern Christendom*. London: Putnam and Sons, 1961.
Ziadeh, Nicola. *Syria and Lebanon*. London: Ernst Benn, 1957.

Unpublished Material

Al 'Aqrâwî, Matta. *Curriculum Construction in the Public Primary Schools of Iraq* (In the light of a study of the political, economic, social, hygienic, and educational conditions and problems of the country, with some reference to the education of teachers). Unpublished Ph.D. dissertation, Columbia University, New York, 1942.

Al 'Aqrâwî, Matta. *The Role of University Education In Arab Life*. Report prepared for the Committee on the University and World Affairs, 196?. Mimeographed.

Crow, Ralph Earl. *The Civil Service of Independent Syria 1945-1958*. Unpublished Ph.D. dissertation, University of Michigan, 1964.

Gulick, John. *The Maronites*. Unpublished A.B. Honors thesis, Harvard University, 1949.

Ibbish, Yûsuf Jamâl Ḥusayn, *The Problems of Minorities in Syria*. Unpublished M.A. thesis, American University of Beirut, 1951.

Rizq, Ḥannâ. *Fertility Patterns in Selected Areas in Egypt*. Unpublished Ph.D. Dissertation, Princeton University, 1959.

Periodicals

Aflak, Michel. "Notre Nationalisme Libéral Face à la Discrimination Raciale," *Orient,* Fourth Quarter, 1963, pp. 185-195.

Alem, Jean-Pierre, "Troubles Insurrectionnels au Liban," *Orient,* Second Quarter, 1958, pp. 37-47.

Anderson, Rufus. "Objects of the Missions to the Oriental Churches and the Means of Prosecuting Them." *Missionary Herald,* January 1839, pp. 39-44.

Armala, Isḥâq. "Al-Malkiyûn: Baṭriyârkatuhum Al-Anṭâkîya, wa Lughatuhum Al-Waṭanîya, wa Al-Ṭaqsîya" (The Melkites: Their Patriarchate of Antioch, Their National and Religious Language). *Al-Mashriq,* January-March, April-June, July-September, and October-December 1936, pp. 37-66, 211-234, 361-394, and 497-526.

'Awwad, Manṣûr. "Al-Baṭriyârk Al-Lubnânî — Ilyâs Buṭrus Al-Huwayyik" (The Lebanese Patriarch — Ilyâs Buṭrus Al-Huwayyik). *Al-Mashriq,* February, March, April, July, September, November, and December 1932, pp. 81-92, 188-192, 272-281, 503-511, 640-652, 856-865, and 924-932.

Badeau, John Stothoff. "The Role of the Missionary in the Near East." *International Review of Missions,* October 1954, p. 397-403.

Bates, M. Seale. "Religious Liberty in Moslem Lands." *Moslem World,* January 1946, pp. 54-64.

Beltrami, Giuseppe. "La Chiesa Caldea nel Secolo dell'Unione." *Orientalia Christiana,* January-March 1933, pp. 1-280.

Beynon, E.D. "The Near East in Flint, Michigan: Assyrians and Druzes and their Antecedents." *Geographical Review,* April 1944, pp. 259-274.

Bianchi, E.C. "Catholic-Orthodox Dialogue." *America,* 28 November 1964, pp. 688-691.

Bishai, Wilson. "The Transition from Coptic to Arabic." *Moslem World,* April 1963, pp. 145-150.

Bogardus, Emory S. "Social Change in Lebanon." *Sociology and Social Research,* April 1955, pp. 254-260.

Bouwen, Frans. "Vers le dialogue théologique entre l'Eglise catholique et l'Eglise orthodoxe." *Proche-Orient Chrétien,* (vol. I-II) 1976, pp. 105-131.

Bridgeman, Charles T. "Jerusalem Then and Now." *Bulletin of the Near East Society,* April, 1954, pp. 3-6, 13-17.

Burnier, Roger, "Christianisme Occidental et Oriental Face à l'Islam de 1963." *Le Monde Non-Chrétien,* October-December 1963, pp. 232-241.

Chejne, Anwar G. "Arabic: Its Significance and Place in Arab Muslim Society." *Middle-East Journal,* Autumn 1965, pp. 447-470.

Cleland, W. Wendell. "Social Conditions and Social Change." *Journal of International Affairs,* January 1952, pp 7-20 (Special Issue on "The Middle-East at Mid-Century").

Codrington, H.W. "The Chaldaean Liturgy." *Eastern Churches Quarterly,* 1st, 2nd, and 3rd Quarters, 1937, pp. 79-83, 138-152, and 207-209.

Crawford, Robert W. "William of Tyre and the Maronites." *Speculum,* April 1955, pp. 222-228.

Crist, R.E. "The Mountain Village of Dahr, Lebanon." *General Appendix to the Smithsonian Report for 1953,* 1954, pp. 407-418.

Crow, Ralph E. "Religious Sectarianism in the Lebanese Political System." *Journal of Politics,* August 1962, pp. 489-520.

Crowfoot, John Winter. "Syria and Lebanon: The Prospect." *Geographical Journal,* March 1952, pp. 130-141.

Dahane, Dominique. "Réorganisation des diocèses chaldéens." *L'Orient Syrien,* 4th Quarter, 1958, pp. 433-435.

Dalmais, R.P. "Chrétiens en Pays d'Islam." *Croissance des Jeunes Nations* (Numéro Spécial sur le Moyen-Orient), June-July, 1963, pp. 38-42.

Dawn, C. Ernest. "Arab Islam in the Modern Age." *Middle-East Journal,* Autumn 1965, pp. 435-446.

Dodge, Bayard, "The Settlement of the Assyrians on the Khabbur." *Journal of the Royal Central Asian Society,* July 1940, pp. 301-320.

Duprey, Pierre. "Les Résultats de la Conférence Inter-Orthodoxe de Rhodes." *Proche-Orient Chrétien,* October-December, 1961, pp. 351-378.

Epstein, Eliahu. "Demographic Problems of the Lebanon." *Journal of the Royal Central Asian Society,* April 1946, pp. 150-154.

Epstein, Eliahu. "Le Hauren et ses Habitants." *L'Asie Française,* July 1936, pp. 244-254.

Every, Edward Canon. "The Ancient Churches of the East."

News Bulletin of the Near-East Christian Council, August 1955, pp. 27-31.

Every, George, "Reflexions of an Anglican in Syria." *Eastern Churches Quarterly,* Winter, 1956-1957, pp. 368-373.

Fernau, Frederick William. "L'Orthodoxie à l'Heure de la Rencontre de Jérusalem." *Orient,* 4th Quarter, 1963, pp. 55-72.

Févret, Maurice. "Un Village du Liban: El-Mtaîne." *Revue de Géographie de Lyon,* Fall, 1950, pp. 267-287.

Fish, W.B. "The Lebanon." *Geographical Review,* April, 1944, pp. 235-258.

Georgiadis, Helle. "Orthodoxy, Rome, and Oecumenism." *Eastern Churches Quarterly,* Winter, 1956-1957, pp. 345-361.

Goodsell, F. Field. "Religious Liberty in Moslem Lands." *Moslem World,* July 1940, pp. 262-268.

Habbi, Joseph. "L'Union de Mar Sulaqa avec Rome." *L'Orient Syrien,* 2nd Quarter, 1966, pp. 199-230.

Hakim, Archbishop Georges. "Chrétiens en Israël: L'Eparchie de Galilée." *Proche-Orient Chrétien,* July-September, 1951, pp. 239-245.

Hambye, E.R., S.J. "The 'Syrian Quadrilateral' Today." *Eastern Churches Quarterly,* Summer-Autumn, 1962, pp. 336-359.

Al-Ḥaṣṣ, Salîm. "Al-Hijra min Lubnân: Ta'rîkhuha wa Asbâbuha (Emigration from Lebanon: Its History and Its Causes). *Al-Abḥâth,* 1st Quarter, 1959, pp. 59-72.

Hess, Claude G., and Bodman, Herbert L. "Confessionalism and Feudality in Lebanese Politics." *Middle-East Journal,* Winter, 1954, pp. 11-26.

Hill, Edmund, O.P. "The Church and the Mongols 1245-1291." *Eastern Churches Quarterly,* Spring, 1957, pp. 1-13.

Hornus, Jean-Michel. "Le Protestantisme au Proche-Orient." *Proche-Orient Chrétien,* October-December, 1961, pp. 321-339.

Hourani, Albert. "The Christians of Lebanon." *Eastern Churches Quarterly,* Winter, 1957-1958, pp. 135-144.
Hudson, Michael C. "The Electoral Process and Political Development in Lebanon." *Middle-East Journal,* Spring, 1966, pp. 173-186.
Husry, Khaldun S. "The Assyrian Affair of 1933." *International Journal of Middle East Studies,* April, 1974, pp. 161-176; June, 1974, pp. 344-360.

Issawi, Charles P. "Economic Development and Liberalism in Lebanon," *Middle-East Journal,* Summer, 1964, pp. 279-292.
Issawi, Charles P. "Population Movements and Population Pressures in Jordan, Lebanon and Syria." *Millbank Memorial Fund Quarterly,* 4th Quarter, 1951, pp. 385-403.

Jargy, Simon. "Le Patriarcat de Moscou et les Eglises d'Orient." *Orient,* 1st Quarter, 1961, pp. 23-35.

Kawerau, Peter. "Die Nestorianischen Patriarchate in der Neuen Zeit." *Zeitschrift für Kirchengeschichte,* 1956, pp. 119-131.
Kedouri, Elie. "Religion and Politics." *Saint Antony Papers,* No. IV, 1958, pp. 77-94.
Khadduri, Majid. "The Franco-Lebanese Dispute and the Crisis of November, 1943." *American Journal of International Law,* October 1944, pp. 601-620.

Lammens, Henri, S.J. "Al-Rûm Al-Malkiyûn: Nabdah fî Asâlihim was Jinsiyâtihim" (The Melkites: A Study of their Origin and Community). *Al-Mashriq,* April 1900, pp. 267-279.
Levenq, P.G., S.J. "Akhîr Maẓhar Al-Siyâsa Rûsîyâ Al-Dînîya fî Al-Sharq Al-Adnâ" (The Last Display of Russian Religious Policy in the Middle East: 1895-1914). *Al-Mashriq,* October-December, 1935, pp. 574-585.
Levonian, Lootfy. "The Millet System in the Middle East." *Moslem World,* April, 1952, pp. 90-96.

Mâlik, Charles. "The Near East: The Search for Truth." *Foreign Affairs,* January, 1952, pp. 214-219.

de Mauroy, Hubert. "Chrétiens en Iran." *Proche-Orient Chrétion,* 3rd & 4th quarter, (vol. XXIV, issue 2) 1974, pp. 139-62; 1st quarter (vol. XXV, issue 1) 1975, pp. 296-313, (vol. XXV, issue 2) 1975, pp. 174-191), and (vol. XXVI, issue 1-2) 1976, pp. 66-85.

Meinardus, Otto F.A. "A Critical Examination of Collective Hallucinations after the Six Days' War in the Middle East." *Ethnomedicine I* 2, (1971), pp. 191-208.

Meinardus, Otto F.A. "Notes on some Non-Byzantine Monasteries and Churches in the East." *Eastern Churches Review,* Spring, 1970, pp. 50-58.

Mongin, Louis, S.J. "Al-Ṭuqûs wa Al-Ṭawâ'if fî Al-Kanâ'is Al-Sharqîya" (The Rites and Communities in the Eastern Churches). *Al-Mashriq,* October, December, 1932, pp. 721-728, and 894-903.

Morrison, Stanley A. "Arab Nationalism and Islam." *Middle East Journal,* April 1948, pp. 147-159.

Morrison, Stanley A. "Religious Liberty in Iraq." *The Moslem World,* April 1935, pp. 115-128.

Naṣrallah, Mgr. J.H. "Mgr. Grégoire 'Ata et le Concile du Vatican." *Proche-Orient Chrétien,* October-December, 1961, pp. 297-320.

Naṣrî, Buṭrus, "Tâ'ifa Al-Kaldân Al-Kâthûlîk" (The Chaldaean Catholic Community). *Al-Mashriq,* 15 September and 1 October 1900, pp. 818-828, and 878-890.

Nour, Francis. "Particularisme Libanais et Nationalisme Arabe." *Orient,* 3rd Quarter, 1958, pp. 29-42.

Peeters, P., S.J. "Arâ' wa Mulâḥaẓât fî 'Amal Al-Ḥayât Al-Rahbânîya Al-Qadîma 'alâ Al-Taqrib bayna Al-Kanâ'is wa Al-Shu'ûb Al-Sharqîya" (Views and Remarks on the Ancient Monastic Life as a Liaison Force between the Churches and Nationalities of the East). *Al-Mashriq,* July-September, 1936, pp. 321-344.

Reid, Donald M. "The Syrian Christians and Early Socialism in the Arab World." *International Journal of Middle East Studies,* April, 1974, pp. 177-193.

Rondot, Pierre. "Islam, Christianity and the Modern State." *Middle-East Affairs,* November, 1954, pp. 341-345.

Rondot, Pierre. "Quelques Réflexions sur les Structures du Liban." *Orient,* 2nd Quarter, 1958, pp. 23-36.

Rûfâ'îl, Buṭrus. "Dawr Al-Mawârna fî Irtidâd Al-Kanâ'is Al-Sharqîya" (The Rôle of the Maronites in the Return of the Eastern Churches). *Al-Mashriq,* July-December, 1949, pp. 399-462.

Sa'ab, Ḥasan. "Communication between Christianity and Islam." *Middle-East Journal,* Winter, 1964, pp. 41-62.

Salibi, Kamal. "Lebanon in Historical Perspective." *Middle-East Forum,* March, 1959, pp. 16-21.

Salibi, Kamal. "The Maronite Church in the Middle Ages and its Union with Rome." *Oriens Christianus,* 1958, pp. 92-104.

Sarafian, Vahé A. "Armenian Population Statistics." *Armenian Review,* Spring, 1958, pp. 78-84.

Sarkîs, Mîkhâ'îl Ilyâs. "Dhikra Al-Dhahabîya Al-Awwal Quddâs fî Kanîsa Bayrût Al-Siryânîya" (The Fiftieth Anniversary of the Syrian Orthodox Church of Beirut). *Al-Mashriq,* October 1933, pp. 779-788.

Sayegh, Fayez. "An Arab Looks at his World." *Moslem World,* October, 1952, pp. 249-256.

Sayegh, Maximos IV. "Déclarations." *Proche-Orient Chrétien,* January-June, 1964, pp. 59-61.

Sayegh, Maximos IV. "Discours de Sa Béatitude le Patriarche Maximos IV à la Clôture du Synode de l'Eglise Grecque Melkite Catholique Tenu à Jérusalem de 10 au 17 Juillet, 1960." *Proche-Orient Chrétien,* July, September, 1961, pp. 254-258.

Selim, Elie. "Nationalism and Islam." *Moslem World,* October 1962, pp. 277-287.

Sharabi, Hisham. "The Transformation of Ideology in the Arab World." *Middle-East Journal,* Autumn, 1965, pp. 471-486.

Shaykhû, Louis, S.J. "Ṭâ'ifa Al-Armân Kâthûlîk" (The Armenian Catholic Community). *Al-Mashriq,* 15 February 1900, pp. 150-157.

Sherwood, Dom Polycarp. "The Sense of Rite." *Eastern Churches Quarterly,* Winter, 1957-1958, pp. 112-125.

Spuler, Bertold. "L'Orthodoxie et les Autres Confessions Chrétiennes d'Aujourd'hui." *Le Monde Non-Chrétien,* January-March, 1965, pp. 3-14.

Strothmann, Rudolph. "Ein Orientalischer Patriarch der Gegenwart — Mar Ignatius Aphrem I Barsaum." *Zeitschrift für Kirchengeschichte* 1952/3, pp. 292-298.

Tannous, Afif. "The Arab Village Community in the Middle-East." *The Smithsonian Report,* 1943, pp. 527-544.

Tannous, Afif. "Emigration, a Force of Social Change in an Arab Village." *Rural Sociology,* March, 1942, pp. 62-74.

Tannous, Afif. "The Village in the National Life of Leanon." *The Middle-East Journal,* April, 1949, pp. 151-163.

Thurston, Burton. "The Eastern Churches." *Middle-East Forum,* January 1964, pp. 13-17.

Troppeau, G. "Sa Béatitude Mar Ignace-Ephrem 1er Barsaum — Notice Nécrologique." *L'Orient Syrien,* Fourth Quarter, 1958, pp. 436-439.

de Vaumas, Etienne. "La Répartition Confessionnelle au Liban et l'Equilibre de l'Etat Libanais." *Revue de Géographie Alpine,* 3rd Quarter, 1955, pp. 511-603.

de Vaumas, Etienne. "Le Djebel Ansarieh: Etudes de Géographie Humaine." *Revue de Géographie Alpine,* 2nd Quarter, 1960, pp. 267-311.

Villain, Maurice, S.M. "Reflexions on the Christian Communities of the Near East in Communion with Rome." *Eastern Churches Quarterly,* Summer, 1961, pp. 119-125, and Autumn, 1961, pp. 177-188.

Wakin, Edward. "The Copts in Egypt." *Middle Eastern Affairs,* (vol. XII, no. 7) Aug. - Sept., 1961, pp. 198-208.

Wardi, Chaim. "The Latin Patriarchate of Jerusalem." *Journal of the Middle-East Society,* Autumn, 1947, pp. 5-12.

Zarour, Miriam. "Ramallah: My Home Town." *The Middle East Journal,* Fall, 1953, pp. 430-439.

Zayât, Ḥabîb. "Adyâr Dimashq wa Barruhâ" (The Convents and Monasteries of Damascus and its Environs). *Al-Mashriq,* July-December, 1949, pp. 399-462.

Zayât, Ḥabîb. "Al-Malkyûn Al-Mashâriqa" (The Eastern Melkites). *Al-Mashriq,* April-June, 1934, pp. 273-281.

Newspapers and Newsmagazines

Al-Ahrâm, Cairo, U.A.R. Semi-official.

Al-Haraka, Damascus, Syria. Greek-Orthodox.

Al-Hayât, Beirut, Lebanon. Independent.

Al-Jundî, Damascus, Syria. Official military.

Al-Nahâr, Beirut, Lebanon. Independent, conservative, Christian ownership.

Al-Ra'îya, Beirut, Lebanon. Maronite.

Al-Râbita, Haifa, Israel. Greek Catholic.

Al-Râ'id, Israel. Anglican.

Al-Safâ', Beirut, Lebanon. Independent, Christian ownership.

The Daily Star, Beirut, Lebanon. Owned by *Al-Hayât.*

Eastern Churches Quarterly.

Eastern Churches Review.

The Economist, London.

Le Jour, Beirut, Lebanon. Independent, Christian ownership.

Le Monde, Paris.

L'Orient, Beirut, Lebanon. Independent, Christian ownership, merged with *Le Jour.*

Newsweek, Dayton, Ohio.

Orient Syrien.
Proche-Orient Chrétien.
The New York Times. New York.
The International Herald Tribune, Paris.
Time, New York.
The Washington Post, Washington, D.C.

Other Sources

'Ali, A. Yûsuf. *The Qur'ân with Commentary.* Washington, D.C.: The American International Printing Company, 1946.
Bliss, Edwin Munsell, ed. *The Encyclopaedia of Missions,* New York: Funk and Wagnalls, 1891.
Houtsman, M. Thomas et al., ed. *The Encyclopaedia of Islam.* London: Luzac and Company, 1913.
Mallory, Walter H., ed. *Political Handbook and Atlas of the World 1966.* New York: Harper & Row, 1966.
Massignon, Louise, ed. *L'Annuaire du Monde Musulman, 1954.* Paris: Presses Universitaires de France, 1955.
Annuario Pontifico 1966. Rome: Vatican Press, 1966.
Seminaria Ecclesiae Catholicae 1963. Rome: The Vatican Press, 1964.

Index

'Abd Al-Malik (Caliph 685-701), 9
'Abd Allah (King of Jordan 1920-1951), 39, 159
Abdulhamid (Sultan 1876-1908), 163
Abdullah (*see* 'Abd Allah)
Abdulmecid (Sultan 1839-1861), 22
Abnûb (Egypt), 229
Abu Dhabi, 110
Abû Qirqâs (Egypt), ix, 64, 229
Abû Sinân (Israel), 72, 232
Abû Tîj (Egypt), ix, 229
Abû Ẓabî (*see* Abu Dhabi)
'Abûd (Jordan), 72, 231
Acre ('Akkâ, Israel), 45, 73, 232
Adana (Turkey), 111
Ibn-'Adî, Abû 'Alî 'Isâ, 119
Adventists (Seventh Day), 58
'Aflaq, Michel, 165, 166, 181, 221, 275
Afqâ (Lebanon), xi
Agaganian, Gregory Cardinal (Armenian Catholic Patriarch 1937-1962)
Ahl Al-Kitâb, 8
Aḥmadî (Kuwayt), 110
Al-Ahrâm (Cairo daily newspaper), 126, 158
Ajlûn (Jordan), ix, 44, 67, 71, 231
Al-Akhbâr (Cairo daily newspaper), 126
'Akkâ (*see* Acre)
'Akkâr (district, North Lebanon), xi, 32, 49, 82, 88-94, 147
'Akkâr Al-'Atîqa (Lebanon), 82
'Alawî (Alawite), 36, 77, 95, 98, 101, 175, 180, 181, 182, 208
Alayh (Aley, Lebanon), xi, 81, 82, 83, 90-91, 193, 202, 268
Aleppo (Ḥalab, Syria), ix, 41, 45-47, 49, 54, 55, 58, 95, 97, 100, 103, 111, 128, 131, 134, 147, 157, 217, 231, 249, 250
Alexandretta (Iskanderun, Turkey), 36, 96, 110, 111
Alexandria (Egypt), ix, 43, 50, 58, 61, 62, 64, 230
Alexandria, Patriarchate of, 41-43, 50, 150, 154, 222
Alexandros III, Tahhân (Greek Orthodox Patriarch of Antioch 1932-1958), 145, 146
Almâ Al-Sha'b (Lebanon), xi, 83
Al-'Amâra (Iraq), ix, 109
'Amâṭûr (Lebanon), 81
Ambâbâ (Egypt), 230
Amerian, Surân Khân, 197
American Dutch Reformed Mission, 109
American University of Beirut, 26, 124, 125, 163, 215, 223
American University of Cairo, 26
Amida (*see* Diyârbâkîr)
'Amîq (Lebanon), 82
'Ammân (Jordan), ix, 44, 58, 68, 70, 74, 77, 123, 134-35, 158, 170, 231, 266
'Ammûn, Fu'âd, 159
'Amûda (Syria), 37, 98
Amyûn (Lebanon), 92
'Anâ (Lebanon), 82
'Anâyâ (Lebanon), 129
Anglican Church, 42, 52, 57, 58, 173, 214, 217, 240-41
Anglo-Egyptian Treaty of 1936, 39
'Anjar (Lebanon), xi, 82
Ankara (Turkey), 111
Anṭilyâs (Lebanon), xi, 56
Antioch (Anṭâkiya, Turkey), ix, 42, 96
Antioch, Partiarchate of, 42-45, 48, 144, 145, 154, 158, 224
Anṭûnyus, George (Antonius), 211
'Aqaba (Jordan), 8
'Aql, Bâṣil, 216
'Aqrâ (Iraq), ix, 105, 186
'Aqrâwî, Mattâ, 125
'Aqûra (Lebanon), xi
Arab Congress of Palestine, 211
Arab Society of Arts and Sciences, 162
Aramaic (language), 97, 101, 106, 113, 127
Archbishop of Canterbury's Mission to the Assyrians, 26, 52
Arianism, 2, 3, 4, 51
'Arîḍa, Anṭûn (Maronite Patriarch of Antioch 1932-1955), 143, 144,

Khaddûrî, Majîd, 126, 184
Khaddûrî, Rose, 141
Khâlid Ibn Al-Walîd, 9
Khâlid, Layla, 217
Khâmis, Salîm, 85
Khanka (Egypt), 170
Kharput (Elâziğ, Turkey), 241
Khatîb, Ḥasan, 160, 209
Khuraysh, Anṭûn (Maronite Patriarch, 1975-), 144, 209, 259
Al-Khûrî, Bishâra (President of Lebanon, 1946-1952), 37, 68, 78, 193, 213
Al-Khûrî, Fâris (Prime Minister of Syria 1955-1956), 179, 180, 214-215, 247, 267
Al-Khûrî, Rev. Ilyâs, 217
King-Crane Commission, 31, 33
Kirkûk (Iraq), ix, 104, 105, 107, 231, 243
Al-Kisrawân (district of Lebanon), xi, 48, 90-91, 138
Knesset (*see* Israel, parliament)
Krak des Chevaliers (Syria), 96
Küçük Kainarca, Treaty of 1774, 27
Al-Kûra (district of Lebanon), xi, 44, 90-92, 206
Kurdistan, 52, 53, 95, 186
Kurds, 34, 36, 52, 53, 98, 105, 106, 112, 184-188
Al-Kuwayt, ix, 69, 87, 109-110, 133, 160, 210-211
Kyrillos VI (Coptic Patriarch of Alexandria 1959-1971), 129, 149-150, 223

Al-Lâdhiqîya (*see* Latakia)
Lakhmids, 3
Lammens, Fr. Henri, 48
Laqlûq (Lebanon), xi, 92
Latakia (Syria), ix, 36, 95, 100-101, 103, 147, 151, 181, 208, 231
Latins (Roman Catholics in the Middle East), 14, 16, 18, 42, 56-58, 66, 76, 93, 103, 152, 159, 211, 224, 263
Lausanne, Treaty of (1923), 78
Lebanese Army, 203-204
Lebanese National Pact (Al-Mîthâq Al-Waṭanî), 37, 189, 191, 194, 197-98, 200, 205, 209, 210
Lebanese Parliament (Chamber of Deputies), 189, 190, 194-97, 198
Lebanese University, 124
Lebanon, ix, 21, 24, 25, 30-37, 40, 43, 45, 47-49, 53, 54, 55, 56, 58, 68, 77-94, 96, 103, 104, 107, 110, 111, 122-126, 129, 131-133, 140, 143, 144, 147, 156, 158, 160, 162, 173, 177, 184, 188-210, 213, 225-227, 230
Lebanon (education and literacy), 122-124, 254
Lebanon, Mount (province of Lebanon), 90-91, 93, 147, 197, 268
Lebanon, North (province of Lebanon), 90-91, 93
Lebanon, South (province of Lebanon), 90-91, 93
Leo X, Pope (1513-1522), 48
Leo the Isaurian (Emperor of Byzantium, 717-741), 119
Lerner, Daniel, 87, 140
Leroy, Jules, 127
Lîṭânî River (Lebanon), 202
Literacy in the Arab East, 122-125, 254-256
Longrigg, Stephen, 80
Luwayza, Synod of (1736), 48
Luxor (Al-Uqṣur, Egypt), ix, 61, 229
Lydda (Israel), 68, 232

Ma'an (Jordan), 172
McInnes, Rt. Rev. Campbell, 173
McMahon, Sir Henry, 30
Mâdabâ (Jordan), ix, 67, 71, 172, 231
Al-Madîna, 2
Al-Mafraq (Jordan), 231
Maghâgha (Egypt), 61, 230
Maḥallat Al-Kubrâ (Egypt), 64, 230
Maḥfûẓ, Gen. Ra'ûf, 169
Al-Makr (Israel), 72
Mâlik, Charles, i, 50, 166-167, 192, 221, 224
Al-Mâlikîya (Syria), 101, 231
Mallawî (Egypt), ix, 229
Ma'lûf (family), 152
Ma'lûf, Fâris, 184
Ma'lûla (Syria), ix, 97, 101
Mamlûks, 13, 24, 48, 120, 121, 240
Al-Ma'n (family), 21, 25
Manfalûṭ (Egypt), 229
Manharâ (Egypt), 229
Mankaysh (Iraq), 105, 232
Manṣûr, 'Aṭallah, 176
Manṣûr, Warda, 129